Course Slides

Data Science, Data Analytics, and Decision Modeling with AI

A complete curriculum for modern analytics, from exploratory analysis to causal inference and generative AI strategy

Powered By

Julius AI

Ch

Presented By

Dr. Johnathan Mun
Professor & Chair (Business Division)
San Francisco Bay University (California)

Course Outline and Agenda

1. Generative AI, Architecture, Prompting, and Agentic Systems
2. Probabilistic Analytics, Power, and Theoretical Constructs
3. Multivariate Statistical Significance
4. Nonparametric Analysis & Data Reliability, Validity, and Efficacy
5. Exploratory Data Analysis and the AI Analytics, Sampling and Experimental Design
6. Multivariate Regression to Advanced Regression Methods
7. AI-Powered Prediction, Classification and Clustering
8. Forecasting, Predictive Modeling, and Time Series Analytics
9. Risk-Based Simulation and Prescriptive Analytics Optimization
10. Text Analytics, NLP, Unstructured Data, Ethics, and Governance

Course Overview & Learning Outcomes

CLO 1 Analytical Problem Framing and Data Preparation

Define and structure complex business problems in ways amenable to data-driven analysis, prepare, clean, and explore datasets — both structured and unstructured — using exploratory data analysis and statistical summary techniques to surface patterns, anomalies, and relationships among variables before modeling.

CLO 2 Statistical Modeling and Regression Analysis

Build, evaluate, and interpret a broad range of regression and statistical models — including multivariate, logistic, ridge, lasso, quantile, and other advanced regression approaches — selecting the correct method based on data characteristics, business objectives, and the interpretability-complexity tradeoff.

CLO 3 ML for Prediction, Classification, and Segmentation

Apply supervised and unsupervised machine learning methods — including decision trees, ensemble models, clustering, and forecasting — to generate predictions, discover hidden structure, optimize decisions, and evaluate model performance using appropriate metrics, communicating uncertainty and confidence to non-technical stakeholders.

CLO 4 Generative AI and Intelligent Analytics Tools

Leverage generative AI platforms, including ChatGPT and Julius AI, to accelerate analytical workflows — from data exploration and visualization through code generation, model interpretation, and executive communication — and critically evaluate model outputs, understanding the architecture of large language models, and deploying AI tools responsibly within organizational contexts.

CLO 5 Causal Inference, Experimentation, and Prescriptive Decision-Making

Design rigorous experiments and causal analyses to isolate the true impact of business interventions, apply optimization and simulation frameworks to prescribe the best course of action under uncertainty, and interpret analytical results in ways that drive evidence-based strategic and operational decisions.

CLO 6 Communication of Data-Driven Insights and Analytical Strategy

Synthesize complex analytical findings into coherent written reports and oral presentations tailored to executive and non-technical audiences, translating model outputs into actionable strategic recommendations while clearly articulating assumptions, limitations, governance considerations, and the conditions under which conclusions may not hold.

AI Tools Used

Anthropic Claude, Google Gemini, Julius AI, Notebook LM, OpenAI ChatGPT

Software Used

BizStats, Minitab, Power BI, Python, R, R-Studio, Risk Simulator

Toolkit & Platforms We'll Use

Core Analytical Platforms

Julius AI

Natural language-driven EDA, statistical modeling, and interactive dashboard creation.

ChatGPT (Advanced Data Analysis)

Code generation (Python, R, R-Studio), automated data cleaning, and narrative interpretation of results.

Excel with AI Integration

Advanced pivot analysis combined with Copilot features for rapid business reporting and Risk Simulator for advanced analytics.

Statistical Libraries (Python/R)

BizStats and Scikit-learn for rigorous modeling and forecasting.

Analytical Capabilities

Visualization & Diagnostics

Histograms, heatmaps, Partial Dependence Plots (PDP), and ROC/AUC values for model explainability.

Collaboration & Communication

Structured prompt templates, automated report drafting, and stakeholder presentation design.

Governance & Documentation

Model cards, data lineage tracking, and ethical compliance documentation.

Experimentation Frameworks

A/B testing protocols, causal inference design, hypothesis validation, DOE, and multivariate factor analysis.

1. Generative AI, Architecture, Prompting, and Agentic Systems

Core Theme

This opening section explains how large language models work — from tokenization and embeddings to transformer attention mechanisms, training, and alignment. It compares discriminative and generative AI, surveys major models (ChatGPT, Claude, Julius, Gemini). It teaches structured prompting techniques (zero-shot, chain-of-thought, and persona-based frameworks such as PICO and RTF). The module concludes with agentic AI architecture, multi-agent orchestration, and practical workflows that use ChatGPT and Julius AI for analytics tasks.

Module Objectives

Generative AI — Architecture, Prompting, and Agentic Systems

Transformer Fundamentals

Explain LLM architecture, including tokens, embeddings, vector spaces, and the self-attention mechanism.

Master Prompt Engineering

Apply zero-shot, few-shot, and chain-of-thought prompting to improve the quality of analytical output.

ChatGPT for Analytics

Utilize Advanced Data Analysis for code generation, data cleaning, modeling, and visualization workflows.

RAG & Tool Use

Understand Retrieval-Augmented Generation to ground AI in enterprise data and reduce hallucination.

Navigate Model Limits

Understand the model's constraints (e.g., hallucinations, context windows) and select the right model (e.g., GPT-4 vs. Claude).

Structured Prompting

Design robust prompt templates that enforce schemas, roles, and constraints for business reporting.

Julius AI Automation

Execute end-to-end data science tasks from EDA to forecasting using natural language commands.

Agentic AI Systems

Understand multi-agent architectures where AI planners orchestrate tools to solve complex, multi-step problems.

From Discriminative to Generative AI

The Shift from Classification to Creation

Discriminative vs. Generative Models

Discriminative: Learns the boundary between classes (P(Y|X)). Used for classification, regression, and ranking (e.g., "Is this email spam?"). This is the older generation of guesswork.

Generative: Learns the distribution of the data itself (P(X) or P(X,Y)). Capable of creating new data instances similar to the training set (e.g., "Write a new spam email").

Business Implications: Automation & Creativity

Generative AI moves beyond decision support to content creation. It enables **automated report drafting**, code generation, personalized marketing at scale, and conversational interfaces that understand context, reducing manual effort across creative and analytical tasks.

Constraints & Trade-offs

Generative models are **computationally expensive** (due to inference costs) and can suffer from **higher latency** than simple discriminative models. Control is harder; output may vary or hallucinate, requiring robust validation frameworks and human-in-the-loop (**HITL**) systems.

Paradigm Shift in Analytics

Instead of just predicting "This customer will churn" (Discriminative), we can now ask the model to "Generate a personalized retention email for this customer based on their purchase history" (Generative).

LLM Building Blocks

Tokens, Embeddings, and Vector Space Mathematics

1. Tokenization

$$T = \{t_1, t_2, \ldots t_n\},\ \ t_i \in \{0,1,\ldots,V-1\}$$

Text is converted into a sequence of integers (tokens) from a fixed vocabulary.

2. Embeddings

$$E: t_i \rightarrow v_i \in R^d$$

Each integer token is mapped to a high-dimensional dense vector.

3. Vector Space

$$dist\left(v_{king}, v_{queen}\right) \approx dist\left(v_{man}, v_{woman}\right)$$

Semantic meaning is encoded geometrically. Similar concepts are positioned closer together.

4. Cosine Similarity

$$\cos(\theta) = \frac{\mathbf{A} \cdot \mathbf{B}}{\| \mathbf{A} \| \| \mathbf{B} \|} = \frac{\sum A_i B_i}{\sqrt{\sum A_i^2}\sqrt{\sum B_i^2}}$$

The primary metric for measuring semantic similarity between two embedding vectors.

</> Tokenization Process

Data | Science | is | powerful

↓

2391 | 5821 | 318 | 9842

Semantic Vector Space (Simplified)

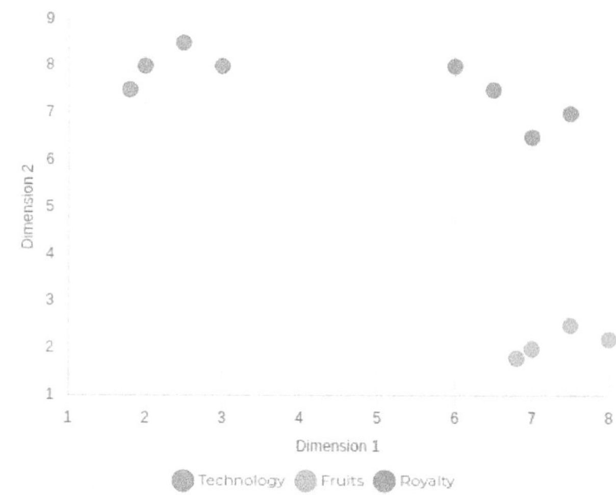

Transformers & Attention

Architecture of Generative AI: From Vectors to Meaning

$$\text{Attention}(Q, K, V) = \text{softmax}\left(\frac{QK^T}{\sqrt{d_k}}\right)V$$

Computes relevance scores between Query (Q) and Key (K), scaled by dimension d_k to stabilize gradients, then aggregates Values (V).

Multi-Head Attention

$$\text{MultiHead}(Q, K, V) = \text{Concat}(\text{head}_1, \dots, \text{head}_h)W^O$$

Allows the model to attend to information from different joint representation subspaces at different positions.

Positional Encoding

$$PE_{(pos,2i)} = \sin\left(pos/10000^{2i/d_{model}}\right)$$

Injects information about the relative or absolute position of tokens in the sequence, as transformers process data in parallel.

Scaled Dot-Product Attention Flow

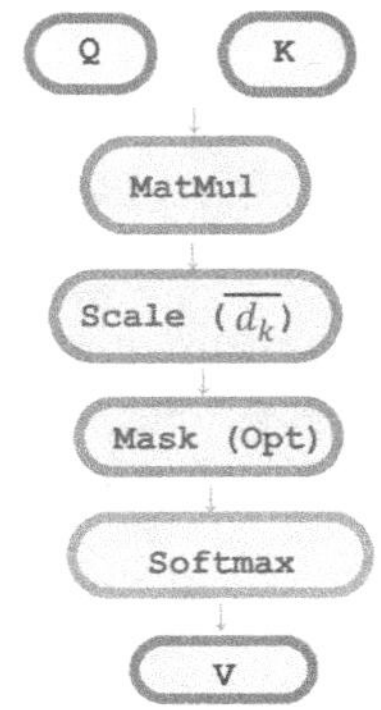

Transformer Architecture (High Level)

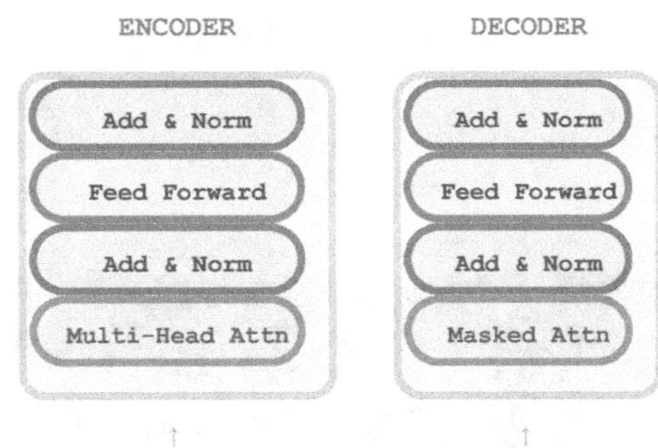

Training & Alignment

From Raw Intelligence to Helpful Assistant

Pretraining Objectives (The Foundation)

Models learn the statistical structure of language by **predicting the next token** on massive datasets. This unsupervised stage builds world knowledge and reasoning capabilities but lacks direction.

Supervised Fine-Tuning (SFT)

The base model is adapted to specific tasks (e.g., Q&A, summarization, coding) using smaller, high-quality datasets of human-curated instruction-response pairs.

Reinforcement Learning from Human Feedback (RLHF)

To align with human intent (Helpful, Honest, Harmless), a Reward Model is trained on human preferences, and the policy is optimized via algorithms to maximize reward scores.

The Alignment Tax: While RLHF makes models safer and more usable for business applications, rigorous alignment can sometimes **reduce the model's raw creativity** or ability to answer unrestricted queries.

Limitations & Model Choices

Navigating the LLM Landscape and Key Constraints (Constant Updates Are Always Available, Making Some Comparisons Moot)

GPT-4 / 4o

Strengths

- Highest reasoning capability
- Best code generation
- Robust ecosystem (Plugins)

Best For:
Complex **coding**, advanced **reasoning**, data analysis **workflows**.

Claude 3.5 Sonnet

Strengths

- Huge context window (200k+)
- More natural writing style
- Less refusal/safety triggers

Best For:
Large document **summaries**, **creative writing**, and nuanced **text tasks**.

Gemini Pro/Ultra

Strengths

- Native multimodal (Video/Img)
- Integration with Google Workspace
- Large context (1M+)

Best For:
Video analysis, multimodal tasks, and **Google ecosystem** users.

Llama 3 (Open)

Strengths

- Open weights (Self-hostable)
- Cost-effective & customizable
- Data privacy control

Best For:
Private deployments, fine-tuning, **cost-sensitive** scaling.

Hallucinations
Confidently generating false info

Knowledge Cutoffs
Limited recent world knowledge

Math Gaps
Struggles with precise calculation

Sycophancy
Agreeing with user bias

Prompting Techniques

Strategies for Effective LLM Interaction

Zero-shot vs. Few-shot Prompting

Zero-shot relies on the model's pre-trained knowledge for **immediate answers**. Few-shot significantly improves performance on complex tasks by providing specific input-output examples to guide style, format, and logic.

Chain-of-Thought (CoT)

Explicitly instructing the model to "**think step-by-step**" or break down the problem. This technique drastically reduces hallucination and improves accuracy on mathematical and logical reasoning tasks.

Structured Prompt Schema

Standardizing inputs **reduces ambiguity**. A robust schema includes **Role** (Persona), **Context** (Background info), **Task** (Specific instruction), **Constraints** (Limitations), and **Output Format**.

Schema Example: "[Role] Act as a Data Scientist. [Context] We have messy sales logs. [Task] Write Python code to parse dates. [Constraints] Use pandas only, no loops. [Output] Python code block."

Advanced Prompting & Safety

Strategies for Complex Reasoning & Security

Tree-of-Thought & Self-Consistency

Enhance reasoning by prompting models to explore multiple solution paths (Tree-of-Thought) or generating multiple answers to find the consensus result (Self-Consistency), significantly improving accuracy on complex logic tasks.

Prompt Chaining

Break monolithic tasks into sequential sub-tasks where the output of one step becomes the context for the next. This reduces cognitive load on the model, minimizes hallucinations, and enables complex workflows.

Prompt Injection & Adversarial Risks

Identify vulnerabilities in which malicious user input overrides system instructions (e.g., "Ignore previous rules"). Implement input sanitization and adversarial testing to prevent jailbreaking and data leakage.

Mitigation Strategy: Use clear delimiters (e.g., ###) to separate data from instructions and implement the "sandwich defense" by placing critical instructions both before and after user input.

ChatGPT for Analytics Workflows

Advanced Data Analysis (ADA): Upload, EDA, Modeling & Code Gen

Step 1: Data Upload & EDA

Advanced Data Analysis

```
User:
Upload 'marketing_campaign.csv'.
1. Check data types and identify missing values.
2. Visualize the distribution of the target
   variable 'Response'.
3. Perform a correlation analysis on numerical
   features.
```

Step 2: Modeling & Code Gen

Python Generation

```
User:
Fit a Logistic Regression model to predict
'Response'.
- Split data 80/20.
- Handle categorical variables using OneHotEncoder.
- Evaluate model using ROC Curve and AUC score.
- Provide the complete Python code.
```

Execution Results

Status: Analysis Complete.
EDA: Dataset loaded (2240 rows, 29 cols). 'Income' imputed with median.
Model Performance: Logistic Regression trained. Accuracy: 86.4%. AUC: 0.88.

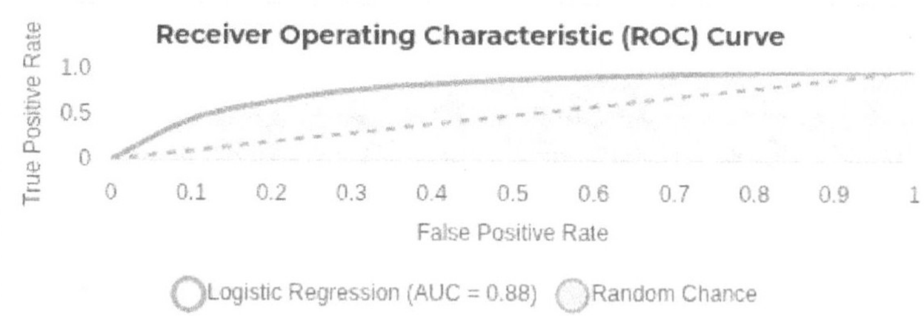

Generated Insight:

The model demonstrates strong predictive power with an AUC of 0.88. The ROC curve shows a high True Positive Rate with a low False Positive Rate. Key features driving predictions include 'Recency', 'NumWebVisitsMonth', and 'Teenhome'.

Julius AI for Data Science Workflows

From Raw Data to Advanced Models via Natural Language

Regression & Statistics

Julius AI Prompt

```
User:
Run a multivariate linear regression to predict
'Sales'. Use 'AdSpend', 'Price', and 'Season' as
predictors.
1. Show the regression table with coefficients
   and p-values.
2. Check for multicollinearity using VIF.
3. Plot Actual vs. Predicted values.
```

Clustering Request

Unsupervised Learning

```
User:
Perform K-Means clustering on the customer dataset.
1. Determine the optimal K using the Elbow method.
2. Create 3 clusters based on 'Annual_Income' and
   'Spending_Score'.
3. Visualize the clusters with centroids.
```

Generated Regression Output

Model Summary: $R^2 = 0.85$. 'AdSpend' ($p<0.001$) and 'Price' ($p=0.02$) are significant predictors. 'Season' is not statistically significant.
Diagnostics: All VIF values are below 5.0, indicating no severe multicollinearity.

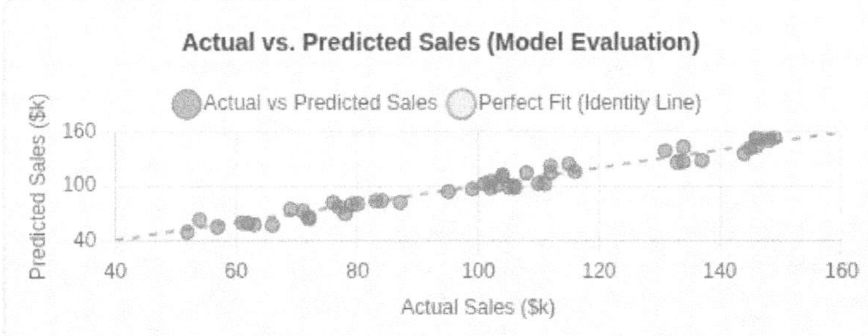

Automated Insight:

The model fits the data well with strong predictive power ($R^2=0.85$). The positive coefficient for 'AdSpend' suggests a $1000 increase in spend leads to a ~150 unit increase in sales, holding price constant. The scatter plot shows a tight alignment along the 45-degree line, confirming homoscedasticity.

Julius AI vs. ChatGPT in Practice

Selecting the Right Tool for the Analytical Workflow

Analytical Task	Best Tool	Rationale	Integration & Handoffs
Data Cleaning	Julius AI	Superior visual interface for spreadsheets; handles larger CSV files more reliably; offers persistent storage and direct cell editing like Excel.	**Handoff:** Export the cleaned, structured dataset from Julius as CSV, then upload to ChatGPT for narrative analysis.
EDA & Visualization	Julius AI	Auto-generates publication-ready visualizations; allows interactive refinement of charts; specialized native Python environment for plotting.	**Handoff:** Copy specific visualization images from Julius into ChatGPT to request a business interpretation or summary.
Logic & Code	ChatGPT	Stronger general reasoning capabilities for complex algorithm design, debugging obscure errors, and writing reusable Python scripts.	**Handoff:** Ask ChatGPT to write a complex Python function or model class, then paste the code into Julius to run on data.
Reporting	ChatGPT	Best-in-class natural language generation; excellent at translating statistical outputs (p-values, coefficients) into executive business narratives.	**Handoff:** Paste statistical summary tables from Julius into ChatGPT with the prompt: "Draft an executive summary based on these results."
Adv. Modeling	Julius AI	Managed environment better suited for iterative model training (Regression, Clustering) where state persistence is key.	**Handoff:** Train the model in Julius, extract the list of feature importances, and ask ChatGPT to explain the business logic behind the top features.

Agentic AI & Multi-Agent Systems

Architecture for Autonomous Decision Making & Execution

Orchestrator

Planning & Control

Task Decomposition: Breaks complex goals into manageable steps.

Chain-of-Thought: Plans execution path and logic.

Delegation: Assigns sub-tasks to specialized worker agents.

Planner Router Critic

Worker Agents

Specialized Execution

Role-Based: Agents with specific personas (Coder, Analyst).

Parallel Processing: Simultaneous task execution.

Collaboration: Inter-agent communication protocols.

Coder Researcher Reviewer

Memory & Tools

Capabilities & Context

RAG / Vector DB: Long-term semantic memory and retrieval.

Tool Use: API calls, calculators, web search, code interpreters.

State Mgmt: Tracking conversation history.

Vector DB APIs Functions

Human-in-the-Loop

Oversight & Validation

Approval Gates: Reviewing critical actions before execution.

Feedback Injection: Correcting agent logic mid-flight.

Safety Alignment: Ensuring outputs meet ethical standards.

Review UI Feedback Audit

Data Science, Machine Learning & AI Foundations

Understanding the nested relationships between these three concepts

Data Science
Broad Discipline

Data science is the broad discipline of extracting insights from data using statistical methods, programming, and technical expertise. It focuses on transforming raw data into practical understanding that informs decisions.

Machine Learning
Subset of Data Science

Machine learning (ML) is a powerful subset of data science. Instead of writing explicit rules for every decision, ML algorithms learn patterns from data and improve through experience.

Artificial Intelligence
Systems with Human-like Intelligence

AI refers to systems that can perform tasks requiring human-like intelligence—reasoning, learning, and adapting. Much of today's AI is built using ML techniques.

The Nested Relationship

Data science provides the foundation. **Machine learning** operates within it as the core engine that learns from data. **AI** builds on these elements to produce the outcome—a set of capabilities increasingly integrated into everyday tools, services, and decisions.

- **Foundation** — Data Science provides the base
- **Engine** — ML learns patterns from data
- **Outcome** — AI delivers capabilities

SF Inc. Case Study & Machine Learning Lifecycle

Working through a complete ML lifecycle with a fictional fresh-food delivery company

SF Inc. (SFI)

A fictional fresh-food delivery company facing challenges with serving a growing customer base

Traditional approaches to categorizing customers no longer provide needed insights

1 Define Business Problem

What question are we trying to answer?

Identify the core business challenge and formulate the right question to solve

2 Explore the Data

What patterns or issues emerge?

Analyze raw data to understand patterns, outliers, and data quality issues

3 Prepare Data for Modeling

How do we clean and structure?

Clean, structure, and transform data for modeling readiness

4 Build the Model

How can ML address the challenge?

Develop machine learning models to solve the business problem

5 Evaluate Performance

Are results accurate and reliable?

Assess model accuracy, reliability, and actionable insights

6 Deploy and Monitor

What do insights mean for business?

Implement insights and monitor business impact

SF Inc. Case Study & Machine Learning Lifecycle

Why This Matters For You

You may not write code or build models yourself, but teams at an organization will work with these technologies, products will be shaped by them, and strategic decisions will depend on understanding what questions to ask, what's possible, and what's practical.

It's important to understand these fundamentals so you can:

Ask Right Questions
Evaluate proposals from tech teams

Identify Opportunities
Where AI can create real value

Assess Risks
Trade-offs with deploying systems

Bridge Gap
Between tech and strategy

You don't need to become a data scientist. You need to know the language well enough to evaluate proposals, guide teams, and recognize when AI is the right tool—and when it's not.

Prompting Tactics

Task, Persona, Background & Iterative Improvements

Tactic	Tips	Examples
TASK Clearly specify your goals	• Breakdown workflows into simple tasks • Use action verbs • Have the bot think step-by-step ("chain of thought" prompting) • Be nice! Research shows this is effective	• Action Verbs: generate, evaluate, improve • Stepped Logic: "Think step by step: Step 1: Examine market, Step 2: Analyze" • Politeness: Say please, ask it to "take a deep breath"
PERSONA Embody a persona	• An expert for accuracy • A character for creativity	• Experts: SEO specialist, pro copywriter, professor • Characters: Elon Musk, Bill Gates, Eminem
BACKGROUND & EXAMPLES Provide ample context	• The more context, the better • Provide one example (one shot) or multiple ("multi shot") • Examples can be in the prompt or attached files	• Situation: "3 days to travel", "Cooking for 5 people", "Graduate students" • Background: Age, Gender, Preferences • "Follow the job posting." "Use this writing style."
CRITERIA & FORMAT Control output	• Set desired response structure or guardrails • Ask the bot to check its own work	• Tone: Casual, formal, witty • Format: Tables, bullets, code • Output: Email, cover letter, checklist

Tactics for Iterative Improvements

The conversational UI lets you chat back to the bot — take advantage of this by being iterative.

Tactic	Tips & Examples
Interviewer Bot	Ask the bot to ask you questions. "Ask me a list of questions about everything you need to know to give me the best response."
Meta-Prompting	• "Improve my prompt" • "Critique your response" • "Review and improve your response" • "Recursively improve this. Do it 5×."

Also explore: PICO · RTF · RISEN · RODES · PAIN · CREATE frameworks for structured prompt design.

Control for Your Desired Output

Criteria & Format

Control for your desired output
Controlling the output can balance accuracy with creativity. It can also open the door to producing more advanced outputs such as data analysis and even coding your own applications.

Tactic	Tips	Examples
CRITERIA Set output preferences	Set desired response structure or guardrails	• Verbosity: "Terse", "Detailed", "Comprehensive" • Tone: Casual, formal, witty • Temperature: "Temperature: 0.7" (ranges from 0 to 1 — lower = more accurate, higher = more creative) • Parameters: "List 15 examples"
FORMAT Determine how you want it structured	Ask the bot to check its own work and provide suggestions	• Visuals: Tables, bullets, code, paragraphs, markdown • Data analysis: "Generate Excel file with tabs" • Output: Email, cover letter, Instagram post

Prompt Frameworks

Prompt engineering is both an art and a science—there is no one right way. Choose one framework to start or make it your own based on what you're looking to accomplish.

Framework	Components
PICO	Persona, Instructions, Context, Output
RTF	Role, Task, Format
RISEN	Role, Instructions, Steps, End Goal, Narrowing
RODES	Role, Objective, Details, Examples, Sense Check
PAIN	Problem, Action, Information, Next Steps
CREATE	Context, Request, Examples, Analysis, Takeaway, Enhancement

Example of a Well-Written Prompt

Below is an example of a well-written prompt using multiple tactics. Feel free to copy and paste it into ChatGPT, iterate on parameters, and see how outputs change.

Assume you are a personal trainer with expertise in diet and fitness.

Please help me reach my health and fitness goals. First, ask me a list of questions about everything you need to know about me in order to create a tailor-made fitness plan. Suggest improvements to my prompt.

My preferences include:

- Context: Male, 31, weighing 160lbs, moderate physical activity
- Goal: Gain muscle while maintaining overall health
- Constraints: 45 min/session, 3 days/week, rotating upper/lower/core
- Sample Facilities: Matrix EFX, Precor AMT, Treadmills, Spin Bikes, free weights (squat racks, bumper plates, kettlebells)

Output: Markdown table format (Date, Body Part, Exercise, Recommended Weight, Reps, Importance out of 3). Then, for each exercise, provide 2 advanced tips to enhance the routine.

⚠ Note on Personal Data

- Don't share personal identifiers (name, address, account numbers)
- Use anonymized or rounded data instead of real documents
- This is for learning only — not financial, health, or medical advice
- Only upload information you're comfortable sharing publicly

Zero-Shot Chain-of-Thought

A Quick Alternative

What Is Zero-Shot CoT?

Zero-shot CoT is a simpler variant of traditional CoT. Unlike standard CoT, which requires providing multi-step examples to guide reasoning, or few-shot prompting, where task examples are given to help the model learn patterns, zero-shot CoT is accomplished in a single step.

The Key: Simply append

"Let's think step by step" to any prompt.

- ✗ **Standard CoT** — Requires multi-step examples to guide reasoning
- ✗ **Few-Shot Prompting** — Needs examples of tasks for the model to learn patterns
- ✓ **Zero-Shot CoT** — One step — just append the phrase. No examples needed

When to use Zero-Shot CoT

- Novel marketing scenarios where specific examples might bias the model
- When you want efficient reasoning without complex setup

Example Prompt — All in One Step

Key phrase: "Let's think step by step"

"My objective is to buy a home in the next couple of months. Please help me, and let's think step by step.

Step 1 — Budget

First, based on the attached document with my financial details, determine my total home-buying budget, including down payment, monthly mortgage, and a range of HOA fees.

Step 2 — Neighborhoods

Then, considering current housing prices in my city, recommend neighborhoods suitable for families, taking into account school districts and local amenities. For each neighborhood, explain your reasoning, the data used to assess each area, and any potential drawbacks.

Step 3 — Specific Homes

Finally, identify three specific homes in each recommended neighborhood within my budget, each with at least three bedrooms and two bathrooms. Include details on the age of the home, renovations (if any), square footage, outdoor space, parking, and your reasoning for these selections, citing any web sources you reviewed."

Key Takeaways

Key Takeaways from AI & LLMs

1. **Dual Purpose of GenAI**
GenAI focuses on content creation & innovation; ML is used for predictions & decisions—a dynamic combo for business.

2. **Prompt Engineering Matters**
Clear, concise prompts significantly enhance effectiveness, controlling outputs and improving accuracy and creativity.

3. **Iterate for Better Outcomes**
Iterating prompts and using feedback mechanisms can dramatically improve AI output over time.

4. **Customizable AI Tools**
RAG and custom GPTs allow for highly tailored, creative, and efficient applications across business processes.

5. **Advanced Multimodality**
Voice and image inputs are broadening AI's horizons—from customer service to creative industries.

GenAI Can Enhance Creativity

1. **Promote Divergent Thinking**
Making associations among remote concepts to produce novel ideas beyond linear reasoning.

2. **Challenge Expertise Bias**
Inspiring designers to think beyond preconceptions of what is possible or desirable.

3. **Assist Idea Evaluation**
Increasing specificity of ideas and analyzing their pros and cons to find the strongest.

4. **Support Idea Refinement**
Combining or merging a large number of ideas to produce stronger, more coherent concepts.

5. **Facilitate Co-Creation**
Supporting collaboration between designers and users in the co-creation of new offerings.

AI vs. Human Judgment

AI excels at objective decisions

AI is good at standardizing decisions using objective criteria—quantifiable, measurable facts—where consistency and speed matter most.

Humans defer to AI for subjective calls

Domain experts and non-experts alike are more likely to defer to AI for subjective decisions, especially when AI provides narrative justifications.

Human judgment remains critical

AI should assist, not replace, human expertise—especially in creative, high-stakes decision-making. Human judgment is irreplaceable for subjective evaluations.

Key Takeaways

Generative AI presents both significant opportunities and challenges. Its ability to enhance productivity, creativity, and empathy can transform how organizations innovate and manage teams. Thoughtful implementation—recognizing limitations, carefully aligning tasks, and understanding how to mitigate unintended consequences—will be key to successful adoption. AI's role as a tool for augmenting human potential, rather than replacing it, will become more evident as it continues to evolve.

Key Takeaways from This Pathway

1. **GenAI Boosts Productivity**
   AI enhances worker efficiency—increasing speed by 25% and performance by over 40% in studies with consultants, especially for lower-performing employees.
2. **Complex AI-Human Collaboration**
   Different approaches—such as "cyborg" vs. "centaur" methods—result in varied outcomes. Understanding these methods is crucial for success.
3. **Enhanced Creativity & Innovation**
   AI augments creativity by promoting divergent thinking and supporting idea refinement, helping merge multiple ideas into stronger ones.
4. **Empathy & AI**
   GenAI challenges the notion of empathy as uniquely human, providing effective empathetic responses—opening new possibilities for customer service and team management.
5. **Market Research Value**
   AI demonstrates potential as a tool for understanding consumer behavior, with responses consistent with economic theory.

Building a Business with Generative AI

- Prompt engineering basics — how to frame effective prompts for better AI responses.
- Using GenAI tools for product ideation, market research, and targeting a customer base.
- Leveraging GenAI for packaging design and marketing strategies, including using tools like DALL-E for visual mockups.
- Automating customer research and creating synthetic personas to simulate interviews and focus groups.
- Chain-of-thought prompting to break down complex tasks like manufacturing logistics and go-to-market strategies.
- Using generative AI to structure a business model and create monetization strategies.

Key Takeaways

Prompting Basics

1. **Clear Communication**
   Treat GenAI like a junior colleague — provide clear instructions and specific feedback to guide outputs.
2. **Use Personas**
   Use personas in prompts to assign the AI a role, improving the relevance and quality of responses.
3. **Leverage Frameworks**
   Apply frameworks like PICO to structure prompts and enhance task completion systematically.

5. **Upload Files**
   Use the upload feature to integrate documents into your GenAI tool for efficient data analysis.
6. **Guide with Prompts**
   Use prompts to guide AI in analyzing documents and data step by step.
7. **Verify Outputs**
   Always verify AI-generated outputs — large language models can hallucinate inaccurate results.
8. **Use Formatting Options**
   Request specific formats such as charts, tables, or bullet points to customize outputs.

The PICO Framework

Apply PICO to structure any prompt and enhance task completion:

P Persona
Define the LLM's role and expertise.
e.g., "You are a senior financial analyst."

I Instructions
Clearly articulate your requirements — what the model should do, step by step.

C Context
Supply relevant background information — the situation, data, or files needed.

O Output
Specify the desired format and structure of results — table, bullets, report, etc.

Customer Research with AI

1. **Outline Customer Journeys**
   Use GenAI to outline customer journeys and identify pain points for target personas.
2. **Automate Question Development**
   Automate customer interview question development and reduce bias by framing the type of questions AI should ask.
3. **Synthetic Personas**
   Create synthetic personas for scalable and cost-effective customer insights without recruiting real participants.
4. **Automated Focus Groups**
   Conduct autonomous focus groups to explore how different personas interact and respond to offerings.

Generative AI for Business

Key Takeaways and Business Architecture

Key Takeaways — GenAI for Business

1. **GenAI for Business Ideation**

   AI can brainstorm product ideas, perform market research, and develop customer personas — enhancing creativity and decision-making.

2. **AI as a Strategic Partner**

   GenAI assists in building business models, optimizing manufacturing logistics, and refining go-to-market strategies, use frameworks like business model canvas.

3. **Enhanced Market Research & Packaging**

   AI enables automated analysis of consumer trends and helps design packaging through tools like DALL-E for visual mockups.

4. **Improved Decision Making**

   Chain-of-thought prompting breaks down complex tasks, enabling AI to assist in strategic decisions such as sourcing ingredients and selecting suppliers.

5. **Marketing Innovation with AI**

   GenAI supports the creation of marketing content, from podcast commercials to visual packaging mockups, in multi-modality capabilities.

Business Architecture

The business architecture of a firm is shaped by its business and operating models.

Business Model

The way a firm promises to create and capture value for customers.

Value Creation

Reasons customers choose the company's products — solutions to problems customers are trying to solve.

Value Capture

The firm's ways of turning the value it creates for customers into revenue.

×

Operating Model

The way a firm delivers its promised value to customers.

Scale

The ability to deliver as much value to as many customers as possible at the lowest cost.

Scope

The range of products and services a firm offers to its customers.

Learning

A firm's ability to continuously improve and develop new products and services.

Generative AI: Training & Deployment Strategies

1 Pre-Training

Training the baseline/foundation model on massive datasets. Creates general language understanding. Example: training ChatGPT or BloombergGPT from scratch (note: most organizations now use existing open-source models rather than pre-training from scratch).

Alignment: Think of alignment as the destination, and all of these methods as different paths to get there—each aiming to make GenAI safer, smarter, and more useful.

2 Post-Training (Fine-Tuning)

Adapting the pre-trained model for specific behaviors or domains:
- Supervised Fine-Tuning (SFT): Teaching the model to mimic good examples via high-quality question-answer pairs.
- Domain-Specific Fine-Tuning (DSFT): Uses industry-specific data (healthcare, finance) to specialize behavior.
- Reinforcement Learning from Human Feedback (RLHF): Model learns from human rankings—not just what to say, but how to say it well.

3 Deployment & Usage Strategies

Strategies for using the model effectively in production:
- Human-in-the-Loop (HITL): Adding human oversight for high-stakes decisions. A reviewer approves, corrects, or intervenes in model outputs.
- Retrieval-Augmented Generation (RAG): Gives the model access to reliable external information at runtime—like letting it "look something up" instead of guessing.

Five Key Use Cases for Generative AI

1 Information Compression

The foundational ability to learn and store vast amounts of information in a highly efficient, compressed internal model. This learned knowledge is the basis for all other capabilities.

2 Content Creation & Synthesis

The most well-known capability—generating new, original content like text (emails, code), photorealistic images, music, and voice.

3 Information Transformation & Restructuring

Taking existing information and altering its format while preserving meaning: summarizing documents, translating languages, or rewriting text in a different style.

4 Data Analysis, Simulation & Prediction

Using learned patterns to model complex systems and predict future outcomes—used in scientific modeling (protein folding) and forecasting trends.

5 Complex Reasoning & Problem Solving

Applying logic and multi-step deduction to solve problems—from mathematical word problems and debugging code to creating a step-by-step business plan.

How the Five GenAI Use Cases Connect & Build on Each Other

The five use cases for GenAI don't operate in isolation. They often build on one another, with one capability enabling or amplifying another. Understanding this progression can help you diagnose why a task might succeed or fail, and how to prompt more precisely based on what you're asking the model to do.

1 **Information Compression — FOUNDATIONAL** FOUNDATION

Before a model can generate, translate, or solve anything, it must first learn patterns and relationships across vast amounts of data. This compressed knowledge is the basis for all other capabilities.

2 **Content Creation & Synthesis + Information Transformation & Restructuring** RELIES ON ①

Both rely on compression. The model must "understand" what makes a sentence formal vs. casual—or what a poem vs. an email looks like—before it can generate or rewrite them.

3 **Data Analysis, Simulation & Prediction** BUILDS ON ① ②

Draws on compressed knowledge but adds modeling power. Reflects the model's ability to apply what it has learned to new inputs or scenarios.

4 **Complex Reasoning & Problem Solving — MOST DEMANDING** BUILT ON ALL LAYERS

Depends on the model's ability to synthesize knowledge, track logic, and make step-by-step deductions—built on all the other layers. Requires the deepest integration of all capabilities.

One-Shot & Schema-Based Prompting

Why Prompting Is Still Critical
As LLMs evolve, it might seem like prompting is becoming less important. But prompting is still critically important—especially in today's complex GenAI systems. Many tools (e.g., ChatGPT, Microsoft Copilot) now integrate multiple models behind the scenes. A well-structured prompt doesn't just guide the model's output—it can help route the input to the appropriate model or capability within the system. Prompting is still part of unlocking the full power of GenAI.

ONE-SHOT PROMPTING

The Simplest Structured Prompting

What it is: Give the model one example of the task you want it to perform alongside your request. That example teaches the model what you're aiming for.

Key distinction: Does NOT retrain the model—it sets the context for generating an answer.

Works best for: Tasks needing a clear example of tone, structure, or format—e.g., writing an email, generating social media copy, or rephrasing a paragraph.

Less effective for: Multi-step problem-solving or data-driven predictions—one example isn't enough. The model needs more context and a wider variety of patterns to reason effectively. Also, cannot help with foundational tasks like knowledge compression—that's built during training.

If it feels inconsistent: That's not a failure—it's a signal that the task may call for more examples (→ few-shot prompting).

\+ COMBINE

SCHEMA-BASED PROMPTING

Structured Output for Consistency & Evaluation

What it is: Ask AI to respond in a specific format (template, JSON object, etc). Then ask the AI to validate the schema—creating a rubric for self-evaluation. Easier to spot mistakes and tell whether the response meets your needs.

Strength: Produces clear, consistent, structured output that's easier to scan, compare, and reuse.

Best for: Information transformation & restructuring (summarizing into bullets, translating tone, reformatting input); Content creation & synthesis (consistent formatting across briefs, reports, checklists); Some data analysis tasks (explaining trends or returning predictions in a structured format).

Limitations: Not designed to improve analytical accuracy—just how results are presented. Less effective on its own for open-ended reasoning or complex problem-solving.

Power move: Combine one- and few-shot prompting with schema-based prompting—provide examples within a schema-based approach for maximum effect.

The 3 Ps of AI — and Generative AI's 4th P

These three Ps have formed the foundation of AI for the past half century, known as machine learning. Machines learn by taking information you already have (training data) and developing insights on information you don't have—solving for ambiguity with predictions to help make better data-driven decisions.

P

Process Automation

AI enables you to automate key business processes, especially dull, dirty, and dangerous tasks. Any repetitive task involving lots of data is particularly prime for AI automation.

P

Pattern Recognition

Automation creates big data. From that data, AI excels at recognizing patterns—like finding similarities (grouping customer segments) or differences (detecting anomalies like fraud).

P

Prediction

AI does prediction by identifying patterns. Predictions unlock the ability to make better decisions. If you know the weather forecast, it's easier to decide what to wear.

P

Production (Generative AI)

Generative AI creates entirely new content: text, images, video, audio, code, and more. It does this by learning the underlying patterns in existing content and generating novel examples that replicate them. While ML is like a diligent data analyst—learning from data to make predictions—Generative AI is akin to a creative thought partner: drafting emails, designing graphics, and brainstorming ideas, adding a layer of innovation to your business operations.

Horizontal, Vertical & Multi-Agent Systems

Agents, Chatbots & LLM APIs

HORIZONTAL AGENTS

Also known as: Declarative Agents

Broad capabilities to execute tasks by leveraging models, tools, and vertical agents. Frequently chatbots that have ingested custom instructions and data.

Lower agency within a broad range of tasks.

Example prompt:
"Given a set of articles, write a short summary of each and give the output in a specific output format."

VERTICAL AGENTS

Also known as: Trigger-Based Agents

Defined trigger, input, and expected output. Greater agency within narrow, defined tasks. Activate upon a specific trigger condition being met.

Greater agency within narrow, defined tasks.

Example trigger:
"Every day at 8am, search to see if the company has been in the news and compile a report of all such articles."

MULTI-AGENT SYSTEMS

What They Are

Most AI tools today focus on single-agent tasks: one agent receives a prompt, does a task, and responds. But real-world problems often involve multiple steps, roles, and decisions—too much for one agent. In a multi-agent setup, agents delegate tasks to other agents, each with a specific role (researcher, writer, planner) or stage (input → analysis → output). When coordinated well, they act like a small autonomous team.

Benefits & Challenges

Benefits: Handle broader, more complex workflows than any single model—scalability, speed, and the ability to simulate entire business processes end-to-end. Challenges: Can suffer from miscommunication between agents, conflicting outputs, and higher system complexity. Raises questions about accountability—who is responsible when agents make poor decisions or act on outdated information?

Keys to Success

Careful design and orchestration are essential. Each agent needs a clearly defined role and task boundary, with strong logic governing how information flows between them. In advanced setups, organizations use a meta-agent to monitor and manage others—supervising the process, resolving conflicts, and maintaining alignment with the overall goal. Balancing opportunity with oversight is the central challenge.

Chain of Thought Prompting – PRACTICE

Step-by-Step Reasoning

1 Set the Scene — Establish Context

Open the conversation by giving the LLM all relevant background before asking anything. This lets the model prepare rather than guess.

Example prompt:
"You are in the market for a new home. I have attached a document with your financial information, including income, expenses, credit score, dependents, location, and savings. You are in the market to buy a home and would like to understand your options. Please take a moment to look at the attached document; let me know when you are ready for my first question."

2 Break It Down — One Aspect at a Time

Break a complex task down into logical steps. The LLM is prompted to focus on only one aspect of a larger problem at a time.

Example prompt:

"Please look at the attached document with the financial information. What is your total budget to buy a house? Please include down payment, monthly mortgage, and calculate it with a range of HOA fees."

3 Show the Work — Explain Reasoning & Sources

Ask the LLM to explain its reasoning and include its web sources. Transparency in outputs makes results more trustworthy and auditable.

Example prompt:

"Next, look at housing prices in the desired city and recommend neighborhoods. Please consider the school district and local amenities for families in your analysis. Explain your reasoning for each neighborhood, what data you are using to rate neighborhoods, and any potential drawbacks for each neighborhood."

4 Synthesize — Actionable Recommendations

Conclude with a synthesis of findings and specific recommendations. The LLM transparently combines all prior steps into concrete, justified options.

Example prompt:
"In each of the recommended neighborhoods, in your price range, please give three examples of homes you could afford. You want at least three bedrooms and two bathrooms. Please include the age of the home/any renovations, bedrooms/bathrooms, outdoor space, parking, and square footage. Please explain your reasoning and tell me what web sources you analyzed to recommend these homes."

Using Personas in Customer Research - PRACTICE

AI Prompts & Applications

Customer Research Prompts — Using Personas

1. Outline a Gen Z health-conscious buyer's customer journey in table format — key phases, touchpoints, jobs-to-be-done, and pains/gains where AI can reduce friction.
2. Generate a 10-question problem exploration interview guide for Gen Z snack buyers. Avoid leading questions to prevent unintended bias.
3. Create one-liner persona prompts for three users: a Gen Z multitasker, a Gen X sustainability-focused consumer, and a Baby Boomer avoiding bold flavors — all exploring snack foods.
4. [Auto-Generated Persona] Tell me about your snack food preferences, including the types of products you'd like to purchase.
5. Use words, slang, and phrases each persona would realistically use — reflecting their age, background, profession, and location.
6. Address [Jamie] = Gen Z persona, [Alex] = Gen X persona, [Pat] = Baby Boomer. Each responds in character when addressed by their name.
7. [Pat]: From now on, your snack food choices are constrained by a peanut allergy.

Brainstorming & Ideation

1. Use GenAI to brainstorm product ideas and iterate as you would with a colleague.
2. Adjust temperature settings to control the creativity level of AI outputs.
3. AI can suggest product variations — always fact-check and apply personal judgment.

Logistics & Manufacturing

1. Use GenAI to identify local suppliers and optimize ingredient sourcing.
2. Prompt GenAI to evaluate multiple factors when selecting a factory location.
3. Use chain-of-thought prompting for solving complex supply chain problems.

Business Planning & GTM

1. Use frameworks like the business model canvas to structure planning with GenAI.
2. Employ the "flipped interaction pattern" — have GenAI interview you to refine strategy.
3. Use ChatGPT to guide go-to-market strategies and acquire your first customers.

2. Probabilistic Analytics, Power, and Theoretical Constructs

Core Theme

This section builds the statistical foundation—hypothesis testing (z, t, and F tests), probability distributions (normal and standard normal), Type I–IV errors and power analysis with non-centrality corrections. It includes worked examples on batteries, IQ scores, and water heaters. The module concludes with the philosophy of scientific theory: constructs, propositions, boundary conditions, and both inductive (grounded theory) and deductive approaches to theory building.

The Concept of Theory: Constructs, Propositions, Logic, and Boundary Conditions (I)

- Knowledge that is obtained through a rigorous scientific method typically includes a collection of theories and laws. A theory is a system that incorporates a series of constructs or concepts as well as a series of propositions or the relationships between those constructs, where, collectively, these constructs and propositions present a logical, coherent, and systematic explanation of the researched phenomenon, within some assumptions, constraints, and boundary conditions.

- **Constructs** can be seen as the conceptual or theoretical level. They must be operationalized and measurable at the empirical and observational level in order to be tested. Operationalized constructs are known as variables. These operationalized variables are typically defined as independent (the input variable that may cause or impact a change in the dependent variable, which itself is not caused by any other variable, within the context of the research) or dependent (the output variable to be measured, whose output possibly depends on the independent variable). However, in most research problems, certain variables can also be considered as endogenous, mediating, interacting, or moderating. These variables will be modeled later in the book.

The Concept of Theory: Constructs, Propositions, Logic, and Boundary Conditions (II)

- **Propositions** are the relationships or associations among constructs that are hypothesized to exist, based on deductive logic. Propositions within the concepts of a theory are typically declarative in nature and may indicate an association (e.g., a high level of A is associated with a high level of B) or even a direct cause and effect (e.g., A causes B). Propositions in a theory are usually conjectures but must be operationalizable and testable. Propositions can be rejected if not supported by empirical analysis. Constructs and propositions are stated at the theory level, and they can only be tested if operationalized as variables and made measurable. Therefore, hypotheses are simply empirical formulations of constructs and propositions, stated as relationships between operationalized variables.

- **Logic** is the justification of the propositions of the constructs. It connects the theoretical constructs and explains the relationships among them. Without incorporating logic, constructs and propositions are simply a collection of random thoughts devoid of meaning and would not constitute the cohesive system necessary to form a theory.

Theories are constrained and restricted by certain assumptions of space, time, and other **Boundary Conditions**. These constraints identify when and where the theory can or cannot be applied.

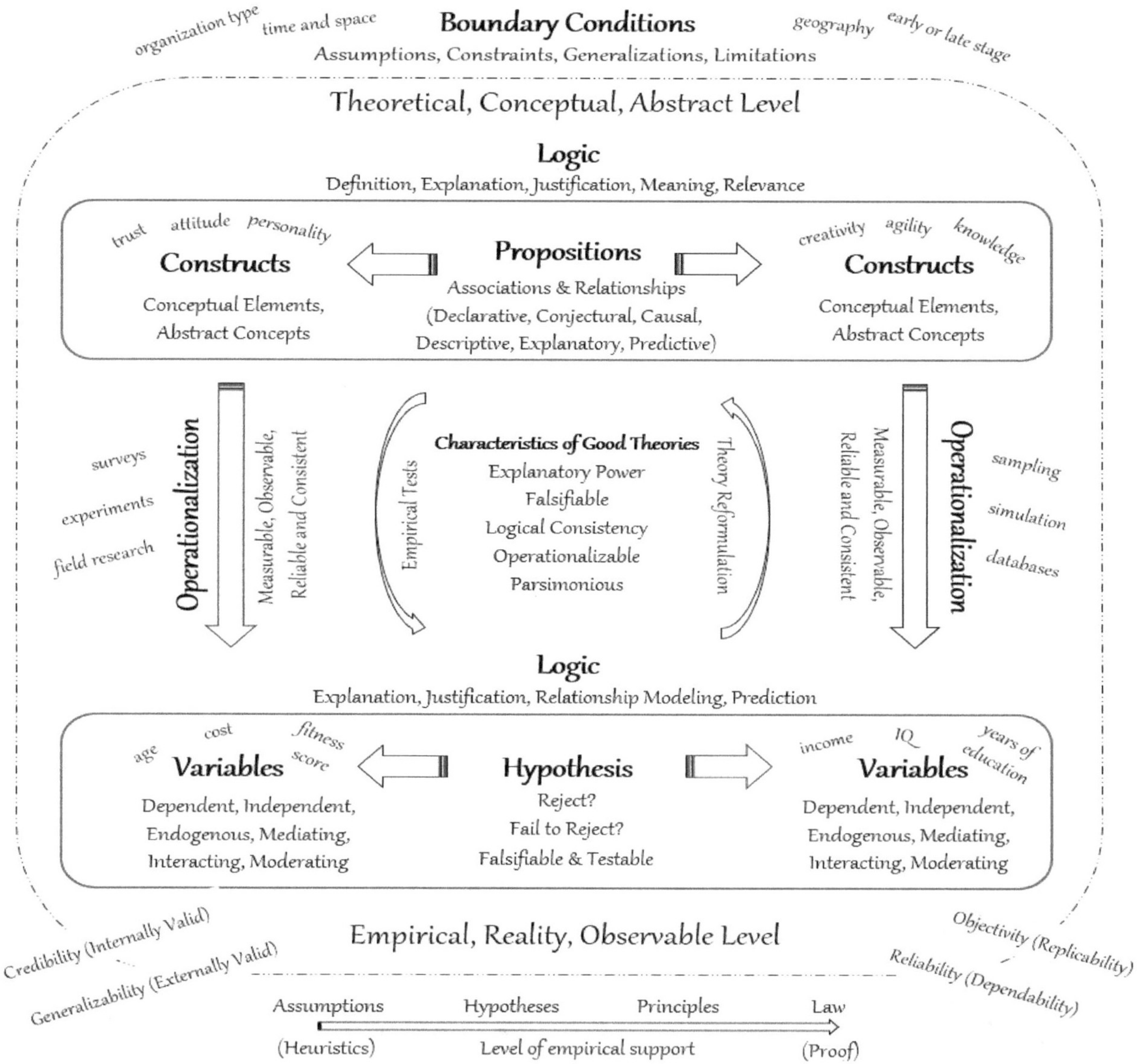

A theory can be heuristic and used to describe and explain a phenomenon.

Components of a Scientific Theory

- Constructs (What or Who)
- Propositions (How)
- Logic (Why)
- Boundary (When and Where)

Theory Building Approaches

- Inductive
  - Explanation of Observables
  - Grounded Theory
- Conceptual
  - Bottom Up
  - Cause-Effect
  - Input-Output
  - Interpretive
  - Process-Output
- Deductive
  - Extension to Existing Theory
  - Modify, Add, Fit to Context
- New Context
  - Deductive Approach to New Boundaries
  - Reasoning by Analogy

Attributes of a Good Theory

Explanatory Power: Akaike Information Criterion or adjusted R-square can be used to measure a model's predictive and explanatory power, which in turn allows the researcher to validate or invalidate the theory.

Principal of Parsimony: Ockham's Razor states that among competing explanations that sufficiently explain the observed evidence, the simplest theory with the smallest number of independent variables having the least amount of assumptions and restrictions is typically the best.

Testability and Falsifiability: For theories to be valid, they must be testable and falsifiable. Falsifiability means the theory can be potentially disprovable or rejected when empirical data is collected and modeled. A theory is not a valid theory unless it can be empirically tested.

Operationalizability: In order to be tested, a theory needs its constructs and propositions to be operationalizable. That is, variables can be constructed from the constructs and propositions, data can be obtained on these variables, and the data can be empirically tested.

Logical Consistency: The theoretical constructs, theoretical propositions, theoretical logic, and theoretical boundary conditions must all be consistent with each other.

Approaches to Theory Building (I)

Grounded Theory (Inductive Reasoning)

Theories can be built inductively using empirically observed events, behaviors, outcomes, and patterns. This approach is grounded on empirical observations and hence, aptly named grounded theory. It relies on the observations and interpretations of the researcher, and the theory may be subjective and difficult to test. The main difficulties involved in this approach include the need to go beyond a researcher's subjective interpretations and the large set of observations sufficient to generate consistent explanations for the observed patterns and events.

Select & Regularize Variables Conceptual Analysis (Bottom up)

A conceptual or bottom-up analysis identifies different sets of explanatory variables and predictors relevant to explaining the event or pattern within certain predefined frameworks. Frameworks can take on various forms, such as interpretive, input-output, cause-effect, and process-output. This is similar to the grounded theory approach in that it relies heavily on the researcher's subjective interpretations.

Approaches to Theory Building (II)

Extension and Modification of Existing (Deductive Reasoning)

Another approach is to extend or modify existing theories to describe the phenomenon under a new context. Concepts, propositions, logic, and boundary conditions of the existing theory are retained, added, or modified to fit the new context. This approach is considered deductive, as it can effectively incorporate a large body of existing theories and is the most efficient way to build new theories by taking advantage of existing ones. An example might be to develop a momentum investment theory by leveraging the inverse rationality of contrarian theory through empirical modeling of economic agents' perceptions during market downturns.

New Context

The new context approach to theory building utilizes existing theories in entirely new contexts by applying their structural similarities. The difficulty with this approach is using reasoning by analogy and creatively applying a deductive approach to a completely new set of boundaries. An example might be applying quantum theory from physics to financial markets (a new context and new boundaries) to develop new theories of stochastic movements in equity prices.

Hypothesis Testing

The hypotheses tested are typically:

H_0: $\mu_1 = \mu_2$, or $\mu_1 - \mu_2 = 0$, that is, the two samples' means are statistically similar

H_a: $\mu_1 \neq \mu_2$, or $\mu_1 - \mu_2 \neq 0$, where the two samples' means are statistically significantly different

The null hypothesis (H_0) generally has the equivalence sign (i.e., =, ≥, ≤), whereas the alternative hypothesis (H_a) has its complement (i.e., ≠, <, >). The sign of the alternate hypothesis points to whether the test is a two-tailed test (≠) or a one-tailed test (right tail is denoted with >, whereas a left tail test uses <). As an example, to get started in a two-sample hypothesis test, a dataset with some number of data points for two variables (with μ_1 and μ_2 sample sizes) are put side by side. Then, their respective sample averages ($\bar{x}_1$ and $\bar{x}_2$) and sample standard deviations (s_1 and s_2) are computed. The t-statistic is then calculated using the relevant formula (depending on the specific test) and compared against the critical t-values. In most situations, the p-values of this calculated t-statistic are calculated and compared against some predefined level of significance (i.e., the standard α significance levels of 0.10, 0.05, and 0.01 will be assumed throughout these examples) using the t-distribution with a certain degree of freedom (df). If the p-value is below these α significance levels, we reject the null hypothesis and accept the alternate hypothesis.

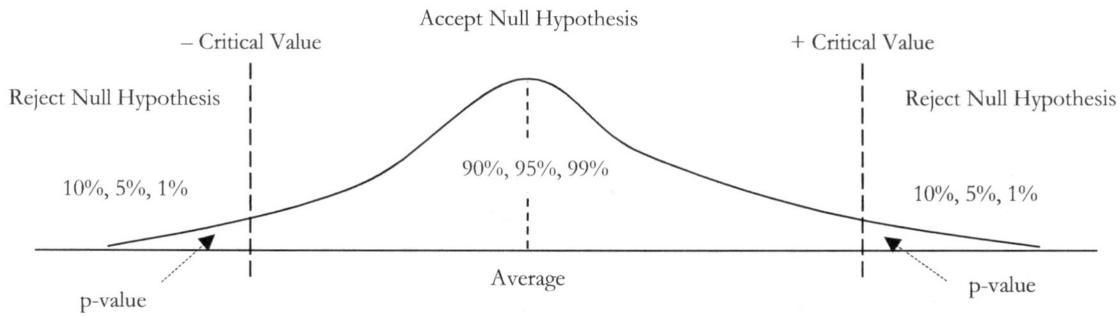

Statistical Methods for One Variable

- 1 Variable Tests
  - Testing Population Mean μ
    - Known σ
      - Normality Assumed → Z-Test $Z = \frac{\bar{x} - \mu_{\bar{X}}}{\sigma_{\bar{X}}} = \frac{\bar{x} - \mu_{\bar{X}}}{\frac{\sigma}{\sqrt{n}}}$ $\sigma_{\bar{X}} = \frac{\sigma}{\sqrt{n}}\left(\sqrt{\frac{N-n}{N-1}}\right)$
      - Data is Not Normal
        - $n \geq 30$ → Z-Test
        - $n < 30$ → Wilcoxon Signed-Rank Test for 1 Variable $W = \Sigma (R+)$
    - Unknown σ
      - Normality Assumed or $n \geq 30$ → T-Test $t = \frac{\bar{x} - \mu}{s_{\bar{X}}} = \frac{\bar{x} - \mu}{\frac{s}{\sqrt{n}}}$
      - Data is Not Normal or $n < 30$ → Wilcoxon Signed-Rank Test for 1 Variable $W = \Sigma (R+)$ Testing Medians
  - Testing Population Proportion π
    - $n\pi \geq 5$ or $n(1 - \pi) \geq 5$ → Z-Test for Proportions $Z = \frac{p - \pi}{\sigma_p}$ $\sigma_p = \sqrt{\frac{\pi(1-\pi)}{n}}$
  - Testing Normality $\Phi(N)$
    - $n \geq 30$ → Kolmogorov-Smirnov, Anderson-Darling, Akaike, Bayes' Criterion $KS = \max_{1 \leq i \leq N}\left|F(Y_i) - \frac{i}{N}\right|$ $\chi^2 = \sum_{i=1}^{k}(O_i - E_i)^2 / E_i$
    - $n < 30$ → Lilliefors Test $D = max\,|O_i - CDF_i|$
  - Testing Randomness → Runs Test $z = \frac{T - \left(\frac{2n_1n_2}{n_1+n_2} + 1\right)}{\sqrt{\frac{2n_1n_2(2n_1n_2 - n_1 - n_2)}{(n_1+n_2)^2(n_1+n_2-1)}}}$

Statistical Methods for Two Variables

2 Variable Tests

- **Normality Assumed & Testing Population Means ($\mu_1 = \mu_2$)$_{Ho}$**
  - $\sigma_1 = \sigma_2$ ► Equal Variance T-Test with Pooled Variance: $t = \frac{(\bar{x}_1 - \bar{x}_2) - (\mu_1 - \mu_2)}{\sqrt{s_p^2\left(\frac{1}{n_1} + \frac{1}{n_2}\right)}}$, $s_p^2 = \frac{(n_1 - 1)s_1^2 + (n_2 - 1)s_2^2}{n_1 + n_2 - 2}$, $df = n_1 + n_2 - 2$
  - $\sigma_1 \neq \sigma_2$ ► Unequal Variance T-Test: $t = \frac{(\bar{x}_1 - \bar{x}_2) - (\mu_1 - \mu_2)}{\sqrt{\left(\frac{s_1^2}{n_1} + \frac{s_2^2}{n_2}\right)}}$, $df = \frac{\left[s_1^2/n_1 + s_2^2/n_2\right]^2}{\frac{\left(s_1^2/n_1\right)^2}{n_1 - 1} + \frac{\left(s_2^2/n_2\right)^2}{n_2 - 1}}$
  - Variables are Dependent ► Dependent Variables T-Test: $t = \frac{\bar{d}}{s_d/\sqrt{n}}$, $df = n - 1$
- **Normality Assumed & Testing Population Variances ($\sigma_1 = \sigma_2$)$_{Ho}$** ► F-Test: $F = \max\left(s_1^2/s_2^2, s_2^2/s_1^2\right)$ $F(\alpha/2, n_L - 1, n_S - 1)$
- **Normality Assumed & Testing Population Proportions $\mu(p_1 = p_2)_{Ho}$**: n_1p_1, $n_1(1 - p_1)$, n_2p_2, $n_2(1 - p_2) \geq 5$ and each $n \geq 30$; $z = \frac{(p_1 - p_2)}{\sqrt{\bar{p}(1 - \bar{p})\left(\frac{1}{n_1} + \frac{1}{n_2}\right)}}$, $\bar{p} = \frac{n_1p_1 + n_2p_2}{n_1 + n_2}$
- **Normality Assumed & Testing Population Means ($\mu_1 = \mu_2$)$_{Ho}$**: n_1 and $n_2 \geq 30$; $z = \frac{(\bar{x}_1 - \bar{x}_2) - (\mu_1 - \mu_2)}{\sqrt{\left(\frac{s_1^2}{n_1} + \frac{s_2^2}{n_2}\right)}}$
- **Assumed Not Normal & Testing Population Medians ($m_1 = m_2$)$_{Ho}$** ► Wilcoxon Signed-Rank Test for 2 Variables: $W = \Sigma(R+)$
- **Relationship Tests**
  - Measuring Co-movements ► Linear and Nonlinear Correlations: $r_{x,y} = \frac{n\sum x_iy_i - \sum x_i \sum y_i}{\sqrt{n\sum x_i^2 - \left(\sum x_i\right)^2}\sqrt{n\sum y_i^2 - \left(\sum y_i\right)^2}}$
  - Measuring Explanatory Effects ► Linear and Nonlinear Bivariate Regression: $\beta_1 = \frac{\sum_{i=1}^{n}(X_i - \bar{X})(Y_i - \bar{Y})}{\sum_{i=1}^{n}(X_i - \bar{X})^2} = \frac{\sum_{i=1}^{n} X_iY_i - \frac{\sum_{i=1}^{n} X_i \sum_{i=1}^{n} Y_i}{n}}{\sum_{i=1}^{n} X_i^2 - \frac{\left(\sum_{i=1}^{n} X_i\right)^2}{n}}$, $\beta_0 = \bar{Y} - \beta_1\bar{X}$

Statistical Methods for Two or More Variables

- ≥ 2 Variable Tests
  - Normality Assumed & Testing Population Means ($\mu_1 = \mu_2 = \ldots = \mu_n)_{Ho}$
    - Straightforward Treatments → Single ANOVA Multiple Treatments

      $$\tilde{x} = \frac{\sum_{j=1}^{t}\sum_{i=1}^{t} x_{ij}}{N} \qquad SSTR = \sum_{j=1}^{t} n_j(\bar{x}_j - \tilde{x})^2 \qquad SST = \sum_{j=1}^{t}\sum_{i=1}^{n_j}(x_{ij} - \tilde{x})^2 \qquad SSE = \sum_{j=1}^{t}\sum_{i=1}^{n_j}(x_{ij} - \bar{x}_j)^2$$

    - Blocking Effects Exist → ANOVA with Blocking Variables

      $$\tilde{x} = \frac{\sum_{j=1}^{t}\sum_{i=1}^{t} x_{ij}}{N} \qquad SSTR = n\sum_{j=1}^{t}(\bar{x}_j - \tilde{x})^2 \qquad SSB = t\sum_{j=1}^{t}(\bar{x}_i - \tilde{x})^2 \qquad SST = \sum_{j=1}^{t}\sum_{i=1}^{n_j}(x_{ij} - \tilde{x})^2$$

    - Multiple Factors and Multiple Levels
      - Two Factors → Two-Way ANOVA

        $$SSA = rb\sum_{i=1}^{a}(\bar{x}_i - \tilde{x})^2 \qquad SSB = ra\sum_{j=1}^{b}(\bar{x}_j - \tilde{x})^2 \qquad SST = \sum_{i=1}^{a}\sum_{j=1}^{b}\sum_{k=1}^{r}(\bar{x}_{ijk} - \tilde{x})^2$$

      - > Two Factors → MANOVA
  - Assumed Not Normal & Testing Population Medians $(m_1 = m_2 = \ldots = m_n)_{Ho}$
    - Straightforward Treatments → Nonparametric Kruskal-Wallis

      $$H = \frac{12}{N(N+1)}\left[\frac{(\Sigma R_1)^2}{n_1} + \frac{(\Sigma R_2)^2}{n_2} + \ldots + \frac{(\Sigma R_K)^2}{n_K}\right] - 3(N+1)$$

    - Blocking Effects Exist → Nonparametric Friedman's Test

      $$F_r = \frac{12}{bt(t+1)}\sum_{j=1}^{t} R_j^2 - 3b(t+1)$$

  - Relationship Tests
    - Measuring Co-movements → Linear and Nonlinear Correlation Matrix

      $$r_{x,y} = \frac{n\sum x_i y_i - \sum x_i \sum y_i}{\sqrt{n\sum x_i^2 - \left(\sum x_i\right)^2}\sqrt{n\sum y_i^2 - \left(\sum y_i\right)^2}}$$

    - Measuring Explanatory Effects
      - → Linear and Nonlinear Multivariate Regression
      - → Linear and Nonlinear Nonparametric Limited Dependent Variables

      $$Y = \beta_0 + \beta_1 X_1 + \beta_2 X_2 + \beta_3 X_3 \ldots + \beta_k X_k + \varepsilon$$

      $$\beta_1 = \frac{\sum_{i=1}^{n}(X_i - \bar{X})(Y_i - \bar{Y})}{\sum_{i=1}^{n}(X_i - \bar{X})^2} = \frac{\sum_{i=1}^{n} X_i Y_i - \frac{\sum_{i=1}^{n} X_i \sum_{i=1}^{n} Y_i}{n}}{\sum_{i=1}^{n} X_i^2 - \frac{\left(\sum_{i=1}^{n} X_i\right)^2}{n}}$$

      $$\beta_0 = \bar{Y} - \beta_1 \bar{X}$$

Examples: Standard Normal Distribution

Example 1: The batteries from a particular watch battery manufacturer last, on average, for 15 months with a standard deviation of 1.5 months. Assume that the battery life is normally distributed. If a battery is randomly selected from the manufacturer's production line, find the probability that it has a life of:

(i) P(x = 15 months) = 0 since for a point, the probability is 0.

(ii) P($x \geq$ 15 months) = 0.50 as half of the curve or Z = (15 – 15)/1.5 yields the value Z = 0 or an area of 0.0, hence, 0.5 – 0.0 = 0.5.

(iii) P($x \geq$ 16.5 months) $\Rightarrow$ Z = (16.5 – 15)/1.5 = 1 or A = 0.3413. Hence, we have 0.5 – 0.3413 = 0.1587 = 15.87%. See the chart below.

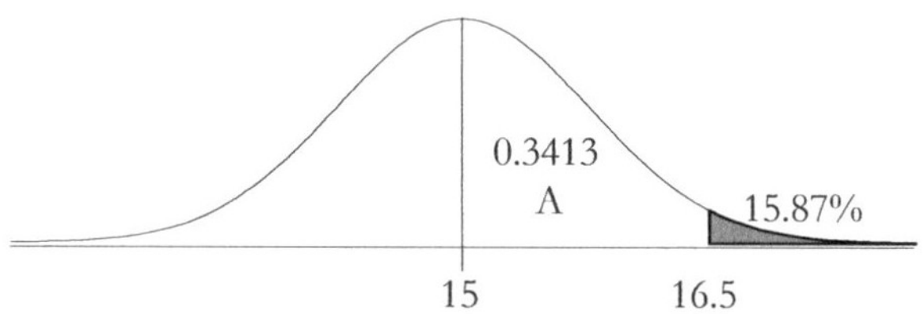

A Z-value of 1 on a Normal (0,1) can be obtained using Risk Simulator's Distributional Analysis Tool, as shown on the left in the accompanying figure. The CDF is the left tail, and the 1 – CDF value is the right tail. For the problem above, the right tail is required, which yields 15.87%.

Alternatively, use Excel and enter the function "=NORMSDIST(1)" which will return the CDF of 84.13% for the left tail, or "=1-NORMSDIST(1)" which will return 15.87% for the right tail.

An even simpler approach may be to use Risk Simulator's Distributional Analysis Tool to enter a mean of 15 and a standard deviation of 1.5 for a normal distribution and compute the CDF for 16.5 months (see the figure on the right). The tool returns the 1 – CDF or right tail of 15.87%. The tool performs the computations directly, without needing to obtain Z-scores and convert them to probabilities.

PDF, CDF, ICDF

Probability Density Function, Cumulative Distribution Function, Inverse Cumulative Distribution Function

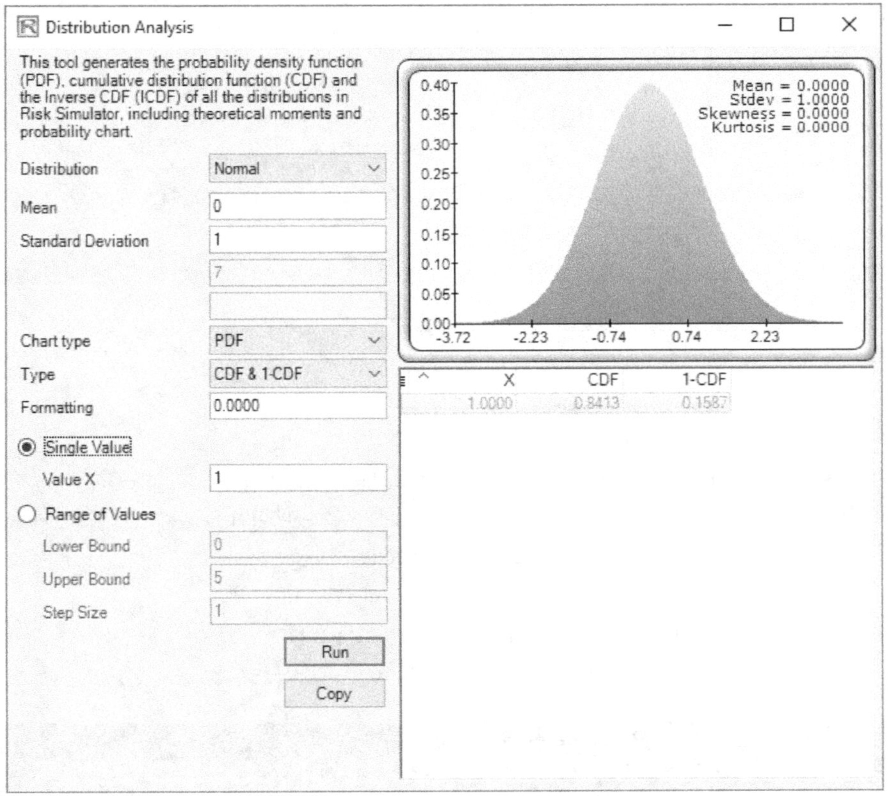

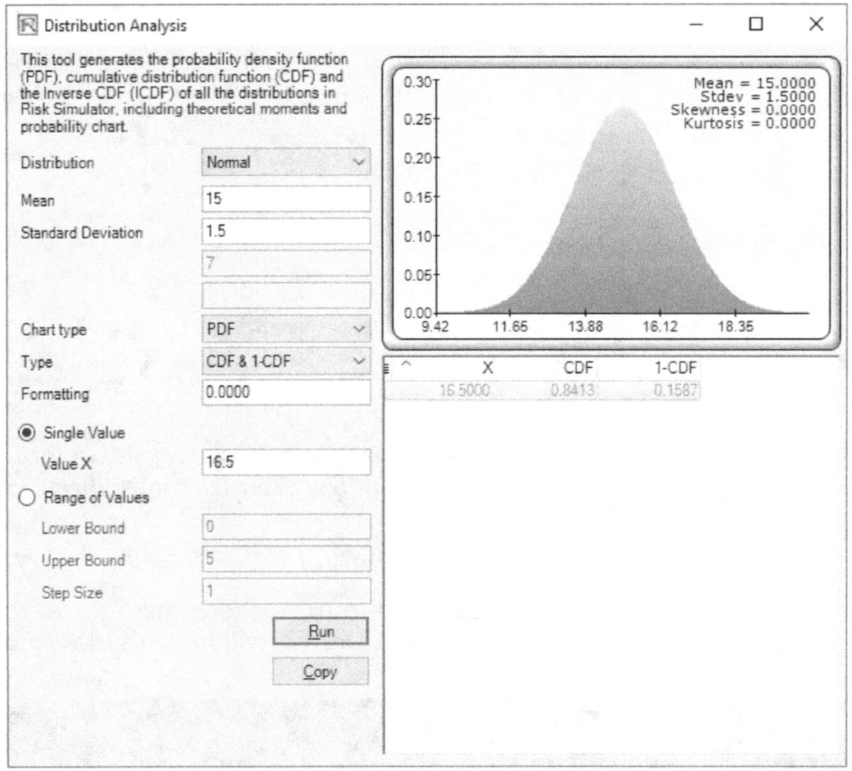

Standard Normal Z

Example 2: The battery manufacturer from example 1 wants to offer a 12-month warranty on her batteries: a full refund if the battery dies before 12 months. What are the chances that this refund will have to be provided?

So, we get $P(x \leq 12) \Rightarrow Z = (12 - 15)/1.5 = -2.0$ or A = 0.4772 to the left since a negative Z. Hence, 0.5 – 0.4772 = 0.0228 or 2.28% probability.

Using a Z-score of –2.0, we get 2.28% in Risk Simulator (below, left) and in Excel, "=NORMSDIST(-2)" yields 2.28%. Alternatively, direct calculations using a normal distribution's CDF also yields 2.28% (below, right).

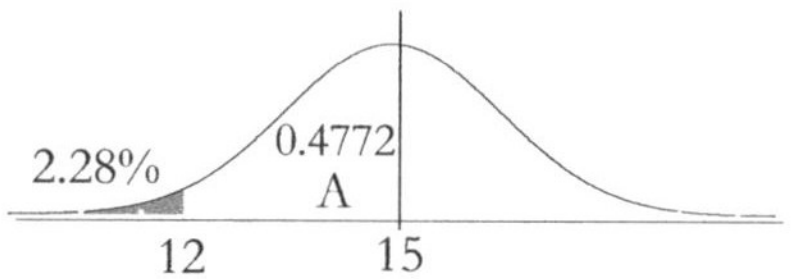

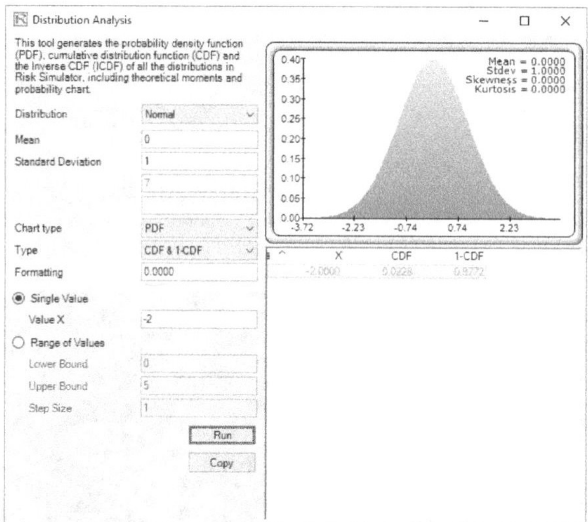

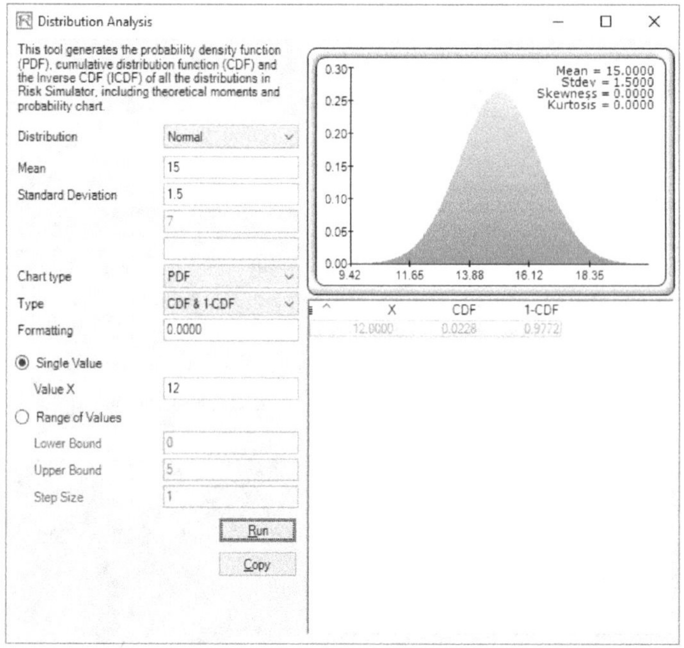

ICDF with Z

Example 3: Suppose the probability calculated in example 2 is too high and, hence, too costly for the manufacturer. To minimize the cost and lower the probability of having to make a refund to a 1% probability, what would be a suitable warranty date (in months)?

Working backward, to obtain a $P(x \le X) = 0.01$, first look at the graph and then find the Z value for A = 0.49, which yields Z = 2.33. Hence, $Z = -2.33 = (x - 15)/1.5$. Solving, $x = (-2.33 \times 1.5) + 15 = 11.5$ months. Watch out! If you use 2.33 without the negative sign, you get 18 months, which does not make any sense!

Similarly, you can easily solve the problem by using Risk Simulator to compute the Inverse CDF (ICDF) on a 1% CDF left-tail probability, which yields 11.5 months (see the figure below).

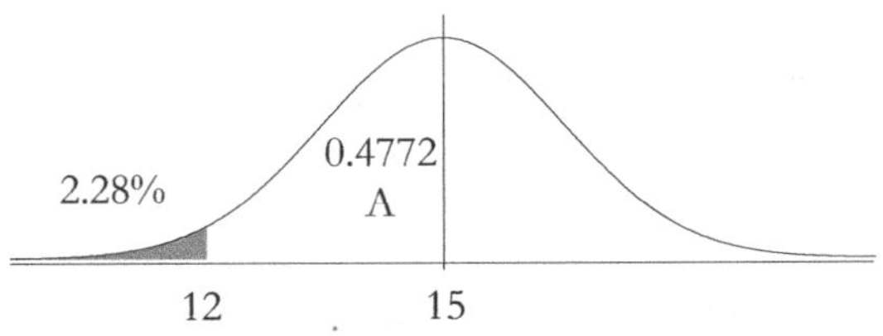

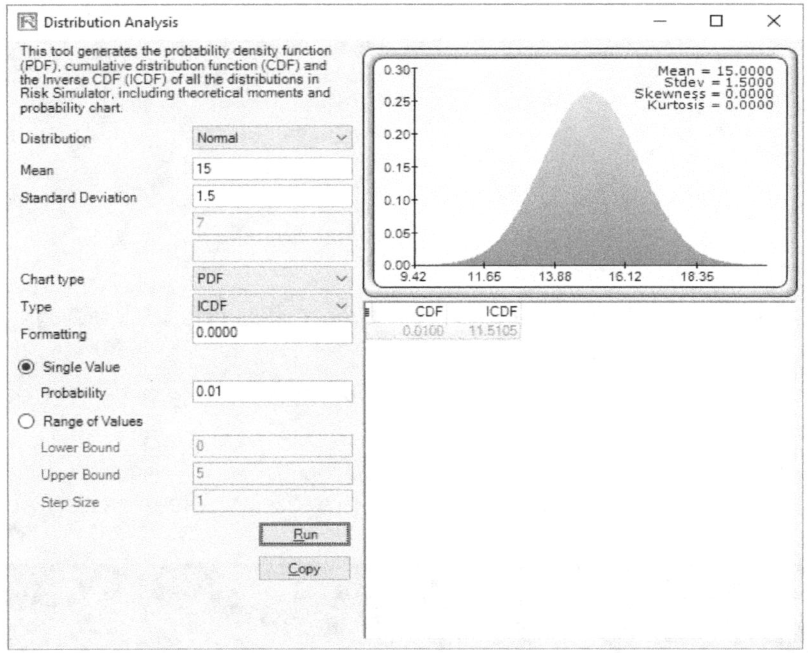

Normal CDF

Example 4: The population mean of an IQ test based on the Cattell scale is 100, and its standard deviation is 15; the *genius threshold* is 140 points, while the *not-so-genius threshold* is 50. What is the probability that an individual is a genius? What is the probability that an individual is considered not-so-genius?

(i) For $P(x \geq 140) \Rightarrow Z = (140 - 100)/15 = 2.67$, $A = 0.4962$. Hence, $0.5 - 0.4962 = 0.0038$ or 0.38% or about 4 people in 1,000 would be considered a genius.

(ii) For $P(x \leq 50) \Rightarrow Z = (50 - 100)/15 = -3.33$, yielding $A = 0.4996$, the probability of being not so genius is $0.5 - 0.4996 = 0.0004$ or

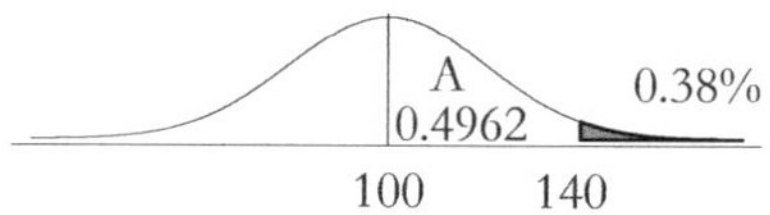

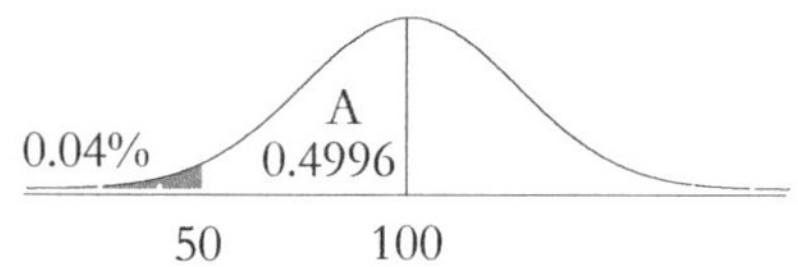

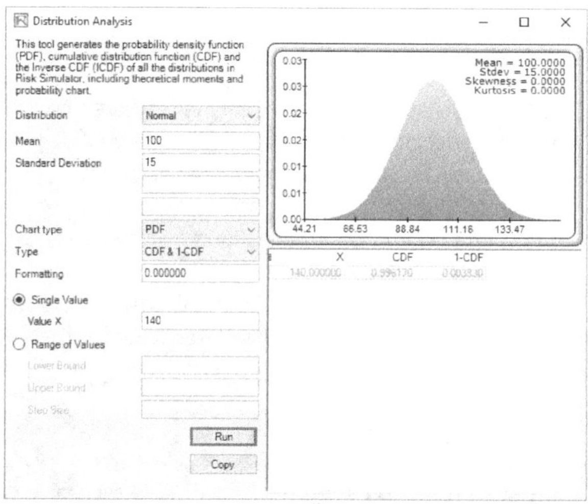

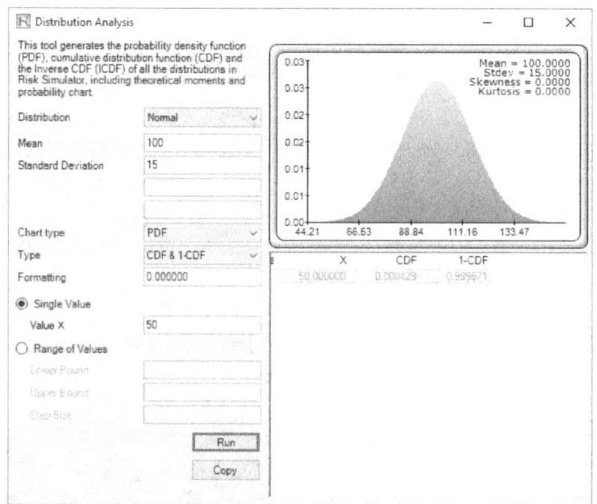

CDF and 1-CDF with Z

Example 5: Use the table of standard normal probability distribution at the end of the book or ROV BizStats to determine the following. To facilitate answering the question, draw a standard normal curve and shade in the area you are attempting to calculate.

a. $P(0.00 < z < 1.96) = 47.5\%$

$A = 0.4750$

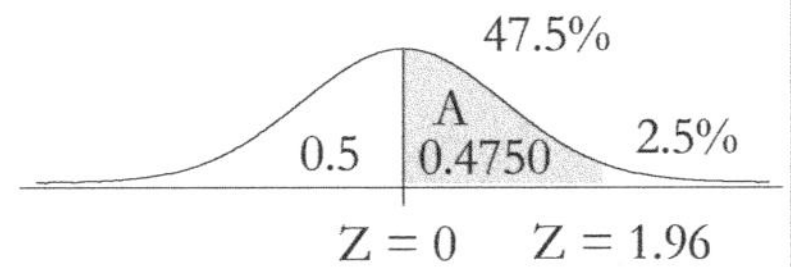

b. $P(z > 1.64) = 1 - (0.5 + 0.4495) = 5\%$

$A = 0.4495$

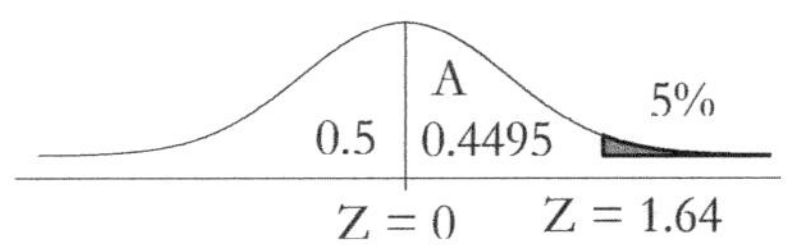

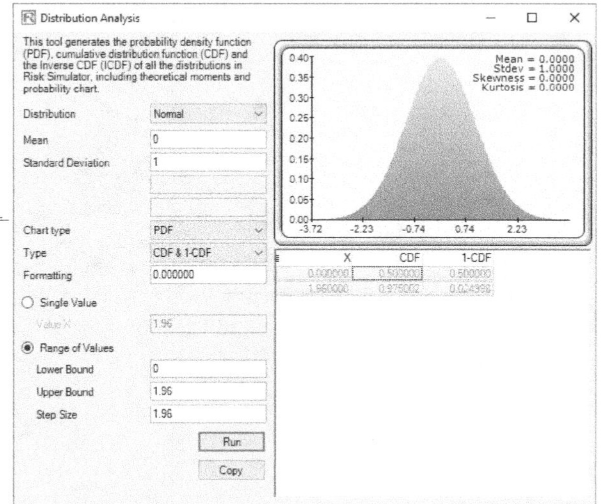

c. $P(z < 1.28) = 0.5 + 0.3997 = 89.97\%$

$A = 0.3997$

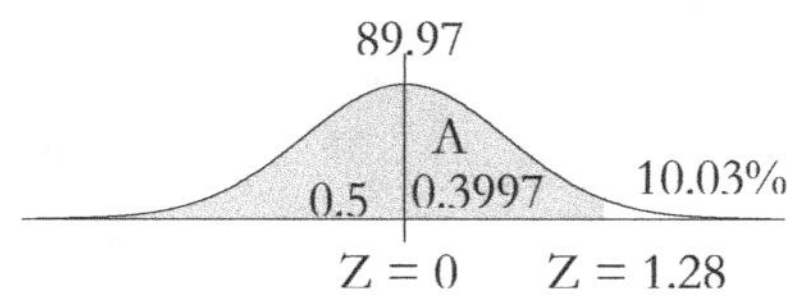

d. $P(-2.00 < z < 2.00) = 0.4772 + 0.4772 = 95.44\%$

$A1 = A2 = 0.4772$

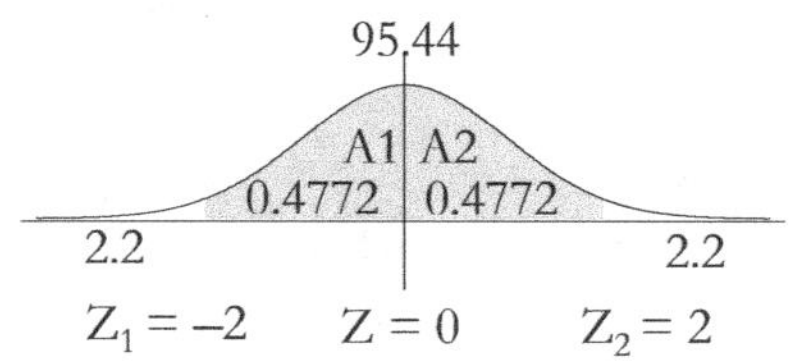

e. $P(z < 1.50) = 0.4332 + 0.5 = 93.32\%$

$A = 0.4332$

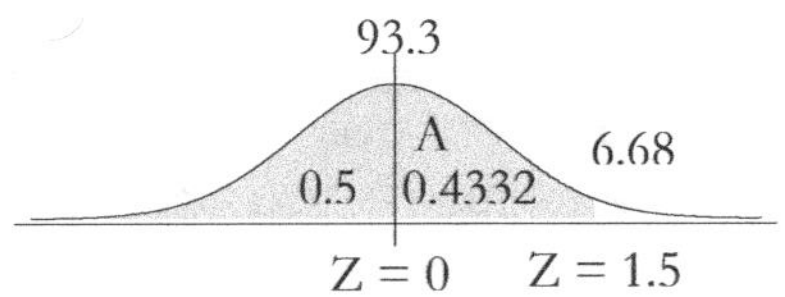

Example 6: The operating life of 50-gallon hot water heaters is known to be normally distributed with a mean of 12 years and a standard deviation of 3 years. The heaters are all sold with an 8-year guarantee. Sketch a normal distribution and shade the appropriate areas.

a. What proportion of customers will get double the guaranteed life, that is, an operating life of 16 years?

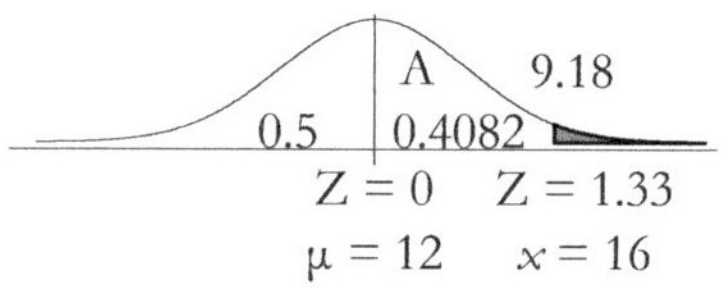

$$Z_{16} = \frac{16 - 12}{3} = 1.33 \text{ which yields an } A$$
$$= 0.4082 \text{ while } P(x \geq 16) = 1 - (0.5 + 0.4082) = 9.18\%$$

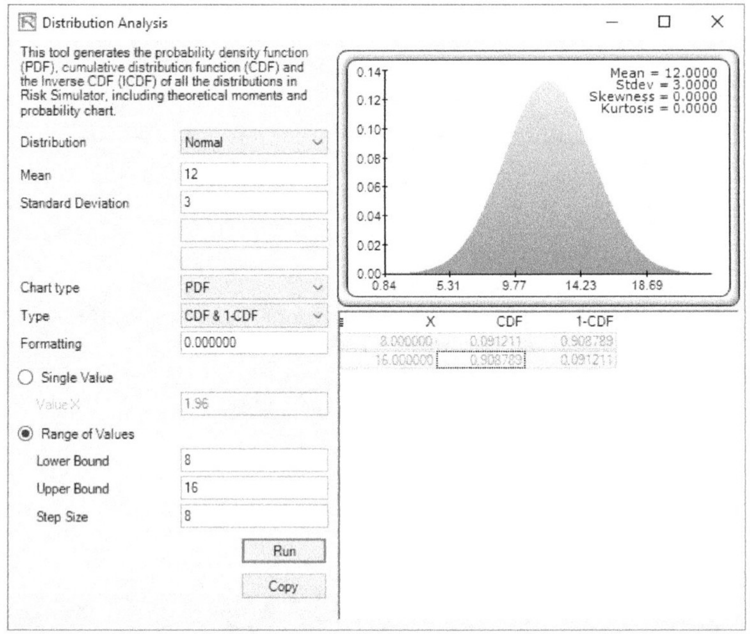

b. What proportion of heaters will be eligible to be returned for failing to satisfy the guarantee?

$$Z_8 = \frac{8 - 12}{3} = -1.33 \text{ which yields an } A$$
$$= 0.4082 \text{ while } P(x \leq 8) = 0.5 - 0.4082 = 9.18\%$$

Example 7: Calculate the 95% confidence interval for the population mean for each condition:

a. $\bar{x} = 680$ $\sigma = 20$ $n = 70$

$$680 \pm 1.96\frac{20}{\sqrt{70}} \text{ means a confidence range of } 675.315 \text{ to } 684.685$$

b. $\bar{x} = 31$ $\sigma = 9$ $n = 50$

$$31 \pm 1.96\frac{9}{\sqrt{50}} \text{ means a confidence range of } 28.505 \text{ to } 33.495$$

c. $\bar{x} = 26{,}000$ $\sigma = 48{,}000$ $n = 500$

$$26000 \pm 1.96\frac{48000}{\sqrt{500}} \text{ means a confidence range of } 21792 \text{ to } 30207$$

Example 8: The following amounts from telephone bills for 10 residential homes in a particular town have historically been found to follow a normal distribution: \$20.95, \$123.50, \$55.00, \$38.95, \$75.00, \$155.00, \$23.50, \$79.90, \$50.50, \$100.50

a. Estimate the monthly telephone bill for the town using a point estimate and calculate the 95% confidence interval.

Calculated $\bar{x} = 72.28$ and $s = 43.7493$

b. How large a sample of' telephone bills would have to be taken to make the error of estimate no more than \$5.00?

$$72.28 \pm 1.96\frac{43.7493}{\sqrt{10}} \text{ implies a range of } 45.1639 \text{ to } 99.3961$$

$$5 = 1.96\frac{43.7493}{\sqrt{n}} \text{ means } \quad n = \frac{1.96^2(43.7493)^2}{5^2} = 294$$

Although we have not yet started using the BizStats software, there is a function called "Parametric: Percentiles and Confidence Intervals (Z & T)" where, after entering the data above, the following table is generated in BizStats, and we can read the confidence interval directly from the table (see results table on the right).

The 95% confidence interval (95% in the center of the distribution's body, with 2.5% on the left and 2.5% on the right) means a CDF of 2.50% and 97.50% or a confidence interval between 45.164 and 99.396. Similarly, a 90% confidence interval is between 49.524 and 95.036 (CDF of 5.00% and 95.00%, with a body of 90% and 5% in each of the two tails).

Another approach is to use Excel's function for the 95% confidence
=72.28-CONFIDENCE.NORM(0.05,43.7493,10) which yields 45.164 and
=72.28+CONFIDENCE.NORM(0.05,43.7493,10) which yields 99.396

And the following for the 90% confidence interval:
=72.28-CONFIDENCE.NORM(0.10,43.7493,10) for 49.524 and
=72.28+CONFIDENCE.NORM(0.10,43.7493,10) for 95.036

Note that the Confidence.Norm(alpha, stdev, size) function in Excel computes $1.96\frac{43.7493}{\sqrt{10}}$ and assumes a two-tailed distribution, and alpha is simply 1 – Confidence Interval. For a one-tailed distribution, simply double the value of alpha. Any slight discrepancies from the manual computations and Excel or BizStats are due to rounding.

CDF (Z)	ICDF (Z)	CDF (Z)	ICDF (Z)
0.50%	36.644	**95.00%**	**95.036**
1.00%	40.095	95.50%	95.735
1.50%	42.257	96.00%	96.500
2.00%	43.866	97.00%	98.300
2.50%	**45.164**	**97.50%**	**99.396**
3.00%	46.259	98.00%	100.693
3.50%	47.212	98.50%	102.302
4.00%	48.059	99.00%	104.464
4.50%	48.824	99.50%	107.915
5.00%	**49.524**	99.90%	115.032

Basic Hypothesis Testing Example

Example 1: A light bulb manufacturing company wants to test the hypothesis that its bulbs can last, on average, 1,000 burning hours. It employs a student who is currently taking statistics and has bribed the instructor to allow the student to complete this project in lieu of a final exam. So, for an A– in the class (since it's an easy problem): If the manager randomly selects 100 sample bulbs, and finds that the sample's mean is 980 hours and standard deviation is 80 hours, at a 5% significance level, what is the conclusion?

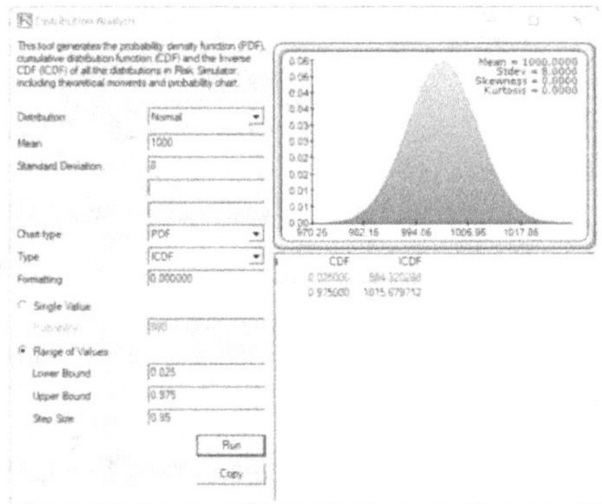

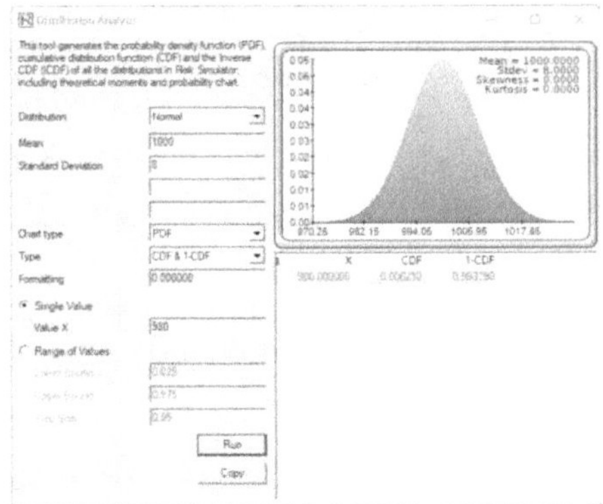

H_0: $\mu = 1000$ and H_a: $\mu \neq 1000$

Since $n > 30$, we can assume normality, and we can estimate σ

For $\alpha = 0.05$ level, the $Z = \pm 1.96$ for a two-tail test or $\alpha/2 = 0.025$

If the calculated values lie in the tails beyond the critical, reject H_0

Classical—Critical limits:

$$X_{critical} = \mu \pm Z\left(\frac{s}{\sqrt{n}}\right) = 1{,}000 \pm 1.96\left(\frac{80}{\sqrt{100}}\right)$$

$X_{upper} = 1015.68$ and $X_{lower} = 984.32$; so,

$980 < X_{lower}$ and we reject H_0

Standardized—Z-scores:

$$Z = \frac{\bar{x} - \mu}{\sigma_{\bar{x}}} = \frac{\bar{x} - \mu}{\frac{\sigma}{\sqrt{n}}} = \frac{\bar{x} - \mu}{\frac{s}{\sqrt{n}}} = \frac{980 - 1{,}000}{\frac{80}{\sqrt{100}}} = -2.5$$

$-2.5 < -1.96$ means it lies in the tail and we reject H_0

P-Value: For the calculated Z value of –2.5, we have p-value = 0.5 – 0.4938 yielding p-value 0.0062, which is less than α of 0.05, and so we reject H_0.

Confidence Interval: The confidence interval has already been calculated above using the classical method. Hence, C.I. ranges from 984.32 to 1015.68, and since the measured sample $\bar{x} = 980$ does not fall within this region, we reject H_0. In all cases, the approaches might be slightly different but yield similar conclusions, that is, reject H_0. Hence, we accept H_a stating that the population mean is significantly different from 1000.

Basic Hypothesis Testing Example

Example 2: A firm wants to know with a 95% level of confidence if it can claim that the boxes of detergent it sells contain more than 500 g of detergent. From past experience, the firm knows that the amount of detergent in the boxes is normally distributed. Taking a random sample of n = 25, the average was found to be 520 g and the standard deviation was 75 g. Perform a hypothesis test.

Note: "Fail to Reject" is the correct term as opposed to "Accept H_0"

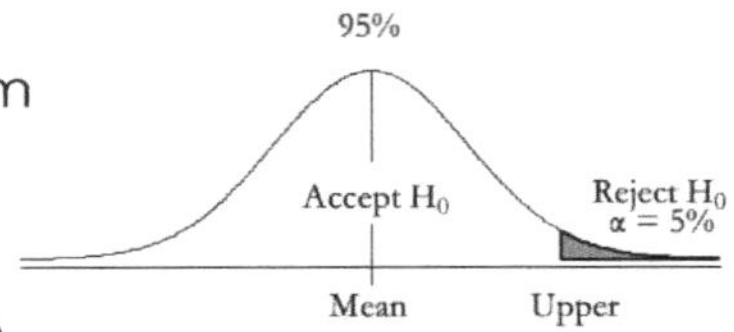

H_0: μ = 500 and Ha: $\mu \neq 500$

Since n = 25, we use a t-distribution

Critical t for $df = n - 1 = 25 - 1 = 24$ is 1.711 at α = 0.05 for a one-tail test

Classical Approach: Since 520 < critical level 525.66, we accept H_0

$$X_{critical}^{upper} = \mu \pm t\left(\frac{s}{\sqrt{n}}\right) = 500 + 1.711\left(\frac{75}{\sqrt{25}}\right) = 525.66$$

Standardized Approach: It falls within the acceptance region; so, accept H_0

$$t = \frac{\bar{x} - \mu}{\sigma_{\bar{X}}} = \frac{\bar{x} - \mu}{\frac{\sigma}{\sqrt{n}}} = \frac{\bar{x} - \mu}{\frac{s}{\sqrt{n}}} = \frac{520 - 500}{\frac{75}{\sqrt{25}}} = 1.33$$

P-value Approach: With the calculated t-value as 1.33, for df = 24, the p-value is between 0.05 and 0.10. We accept the H_0 since it is above α of 0.05.

Confidence Interval: Using the results from the classical method, C.I. ranges from 0.00 to 525.66, and since 520 falls within this C.I. region, we accept H_0.

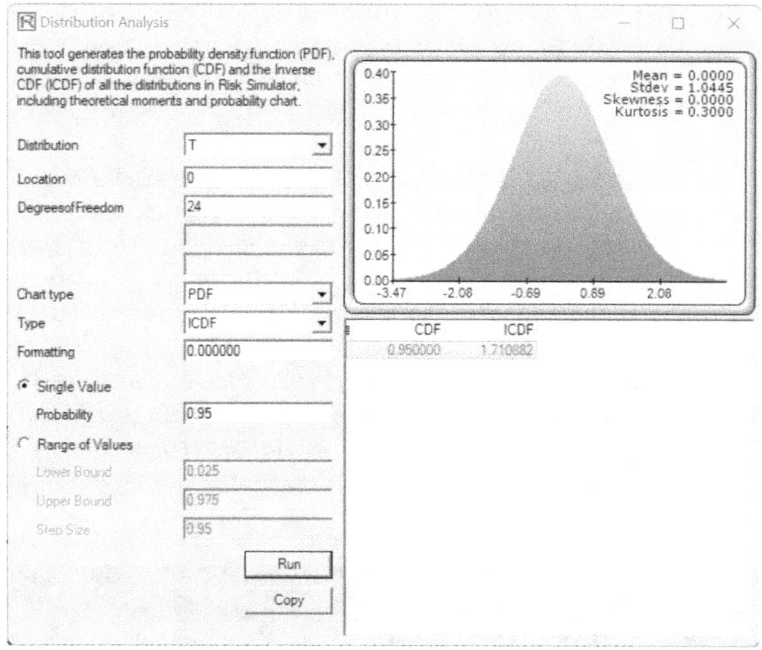

Type I – Type IV Errors

A related issue to consider is that of Types I–IV errors. The significance level α is actually a control for the Type I error. A Type I error is the probability that you will *reject the null hypothesis when it is true*. Another name for a Type I error is *an alpha error, or a false positive*. We want this to be set low, of course. This error occurs when we reject the null even though it is actually true and should not be rejected. Stated another way, we say that there is an effect when, in fact, no effect exists at all. A simple analogy might better explain this concept. We can all agree that for a civilized society, it is better to let a guilty man go free rather than incarcerate an innocent man. Hence, if we assume innocence is true, the null hypothesis is innocence, i.e., that there is zero guilt. So, if we reject this null hypothesis, we reject innocence and zero guilt, which means you throw an innocent person in jail. This creates a false positive (*false* because he is innocent, but we say he is guilty; and *positive* because we found him guilty). Therefore, in this situation, you would want the false-positive error rate to be small, i.e., a low alpha, which is traditionally set at 1%, 5%, or 10%.

Type II errors occur when we *accept a null hypothesis that is false*. We use the term "accept" here interchangeably with "failure to reject," as discussed above. This error is also known as a *beta error* or *false negative*. Accepting or failing to reject the null hypothesis when it is false means that we miss or ignore an effect when that effect actually exists. A simple analogy is a fire alarm in your home. Let us assume a binary condition in which the alarm either goes off or does not. Further, this binary state also includes whether there is a house fire or not. The null hypothesis is that there is zero instances of a fire. In this case, a Type I error means that you reject when the null hypothesis is true (i.e., alarm goes off when there is no fire, no big deal, it just wakes you up, and you get annoyed). However, a Type II error is a much bigger deal because it means that you accept the null hypothesis when it is false (i.e., the alarm does not go off when there really is a fire). In this example, we would want to minimize beta error, or maximize $1 - \beta$, its complement. Another name for this complement is the *power of the test* (Power = $1 - \beta$). The following matrix summarizes the first two types of errors.

Type I – Type IV Errors

There are also less commonly known Type III and Type IV errors. A Type III error occurs when the correct conclusion is made but for the wrong reason. For instance, you incorrectly used a one-tailed hypothesis instead of a two-tailed hypothesis, or vice versa, a wrong question was posed, if the hypothesis is incorrectly formulated. A Type IV error occurs when there is data aggregation bias, errors in interpreting the results, or when you correctly reject the null hypothesis but the dataset has multicollinearity or data collection bias.

Type IV errors are more difficult to quantitatively measure. The chapter on regression modeling and data diagnostics covers how to test for some of these biases, whereas the chapter on hypothesis testing covers some examples of using the Shannon Diversity Index model, the Grubbs Outlier test, the Runs model for randomness, and others.

Null Hypothesis	True	False
Accept	True Negative (1-α)	TYPE II (β) False Negative
Reject	Type I (α) False Positive	Power (1-β) True Positive

One-Tailed Power Analysis: Sample Calculations (Without Non-centrality Corrections)

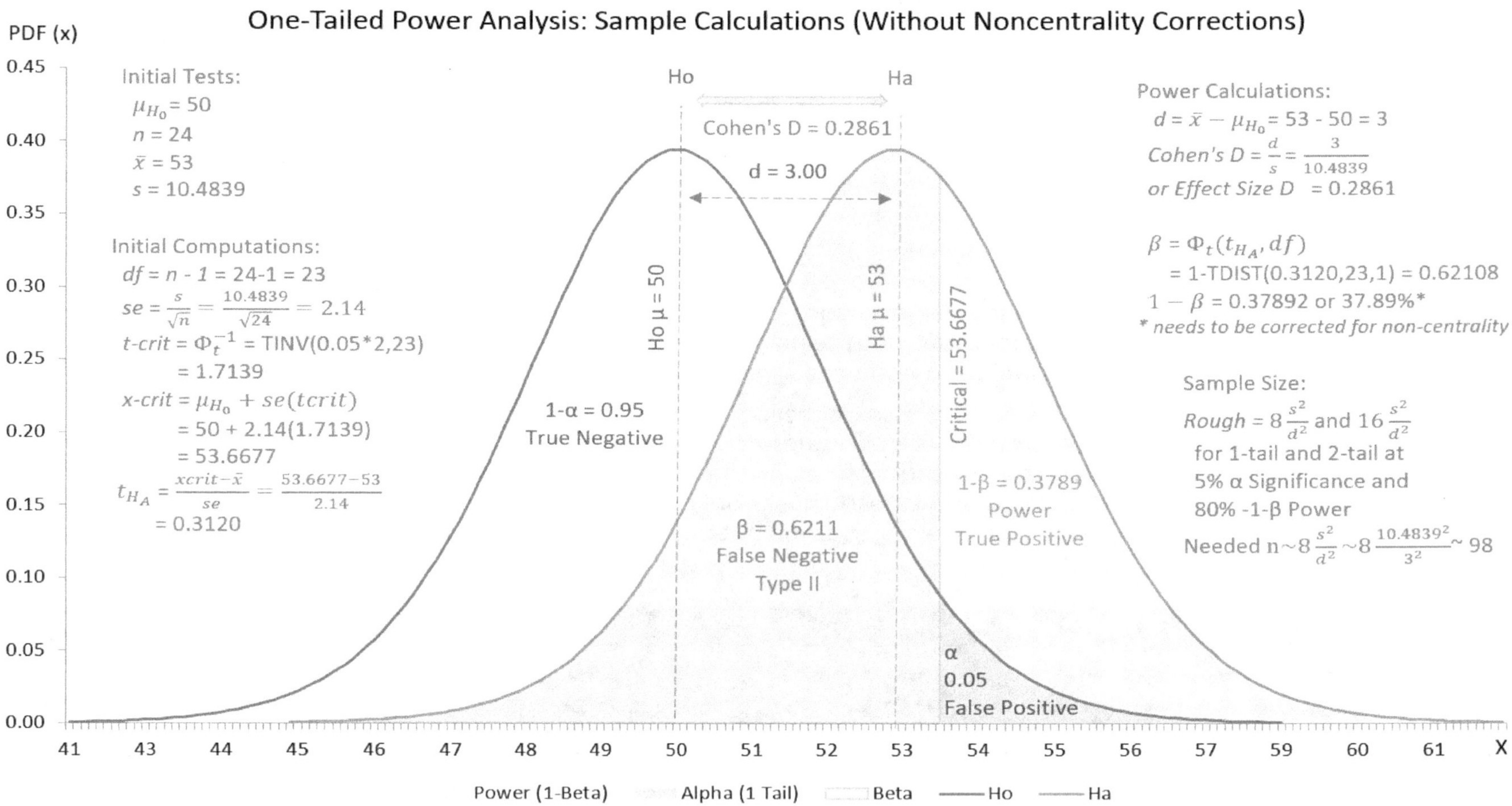

Power Curves and Cohen's Delta

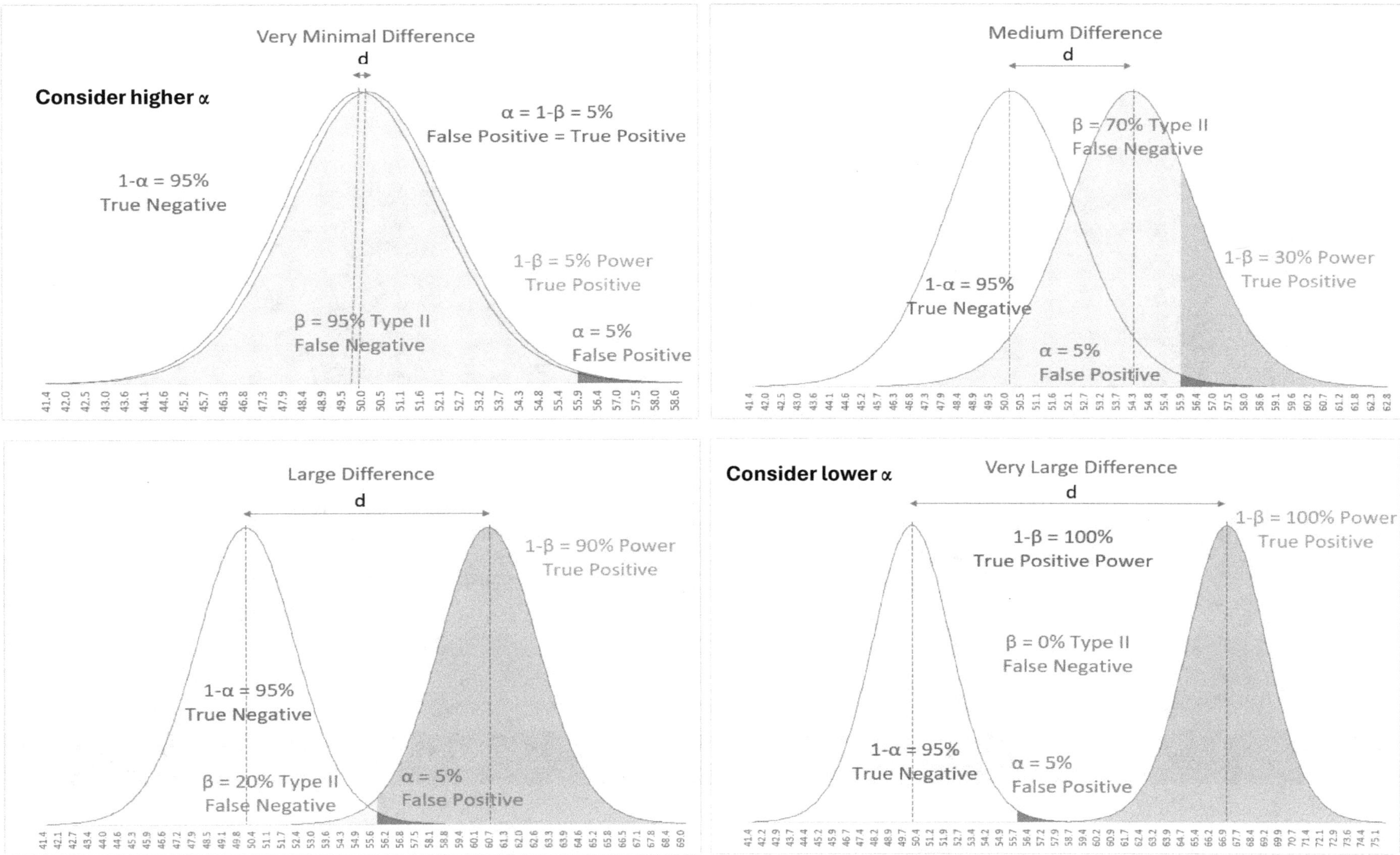

The Symmetry of Power Curves

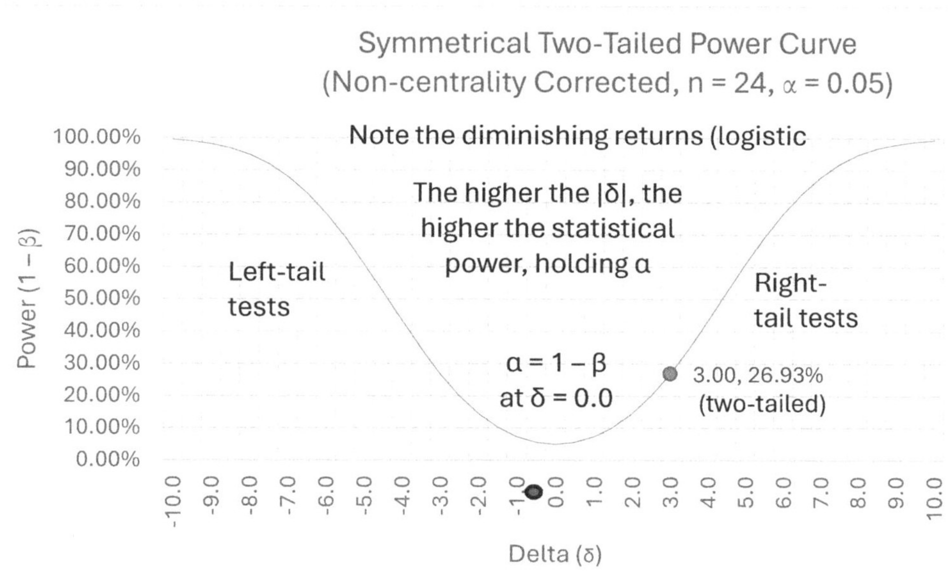

The higher the |δ|, the higher the statistical power, holding α constant

BZSTATS: Power for a Single Variable Test (corrected for noncentral t-distribution)

Delta	Hypothesis	Effect δ	Beta	Power (=)	Power (>)	Power (<)
-10.00	43.00	-0.9538	0.0060	99.40%	0.00%	99.80%
-9.50	43.50	-0.9061	0.0111	98.89%	0.00%	99.61%
-9.00	44.00	-0.8585	0.0195	98.05%	0.00%	99.25%
-8.50	44.50	-0.8108	0.0328	96.72%	0.00%	98.63%
-8.00	45.00	-0.7631	0.0528	94.72%	0.00%	97.62%
-7.50	45.50	-0.7154	0.0815	91.85%	0.00%	96.03%
-7.00	46.00	-0.6677	0.1207	87.93%	0.00%	93.67%
-6.50	46.50	-0.6200	0.1715	82.85%	0.00%	90.34%
-6.00	47.00	-0.5723	0.2342	76.58%	0.00%	85.88%
-5.50	47.50	-0.5246	0.3079	69.21%	0.00%	80.19%
-5.00	48.00	-0.4769	0.3904	60.96%	0.00%	73.30%
-4.50	48.50	-0.4292	0.4782	52.18%	0.01%	65.37%
-4.00	49.00	-0.3815	0.5670	43.30%	0.03%	56.71%
-3.50	49.50	-0.3338	0.6525	34.75%	0.06%	47.70%
-3.00	50.00	-0.2862	0.7307	26.93%	0.13%	38.81%
-2.50	50.50	-0.2385	0.7985	20.15%	0.27%	30.47%
-2.00	51.00	-0.1908	0.8542	14.58%	0.53%	23.04%
-1.50	51.50	-0.1431	0.8969	10.31%	1.00%	16.74%
-1.00	52.00	-0.0954	0.9267	7.33%	1.79%	11.68%
-0.50	52.50	-0.0477	0.9442	5.58%	3.06%	7.81%
0.00	53.00	0.0000	0.9500	**5.00%**	**5.00%**	**5.00%**
0.50	53.50	0.0477	0.9442	5.58%	7.81%	3.06%
1.00	54.00	0.0954	0.9267	7.33%	11.68%	1.79%
1.50	54.50	0.1431	0.8969	10.31%	16.74%	1.00%
2.00	55.00	0.1908	0.8542	14.58%	23.04%	0.53%
2.50	55.50	0.2385	0.7985	20.15%	30.47%	0.27%
3.00	56.00	0.2862	0.7307	26.93%	38.81%	0.13%
3.50	56.50	0.3338	0.6525	34.75%	47.70%	0.06%
4.00	57.00	0.3815	0.5670	43.30%	56.71%	0.03%
4.50	57.50	0.4292	0.4782	52.18%	65.37%	0.01%
5.00	58.00	0.4769	0.3904	60.96%	73.30%	0.00%
5.50	58.50	0.5246	0.3079	69.21%	80.19%	0.00%
6.00	59.00	0.5723	0.2342	76.58%	85.88%	0.00%
6.50	59.50	0.6200	0.1715	82.85%	90.34%	0.00%
7.00	60.00	0.6677	0.1207	87.93%	93.67%	0.00%

3. Multivariate Statistical Significance

Core Theme

Expanding from two-variable tests, this section covers equal/unequal variance t-tests, dependent means t-tests, F-tests for variances, Box's M test, and z-tests for proportions. It then scales to ANOVA (single-factor, randomized-block, two-way), factorial/DOE designs, the General Linear Model taxonomy, MANOVA, and the ANOVA-vs.-regression distinction. A/B testing design — including sample size, power analysis, heterogeneous treatment effects, and the CAUSE framework — is also introduced here.

A/B Testing: Anatomy & Design

Anatomy of an A/B Test

In a simple experiment, we want to understand the effectiveness of a new version (the treatment) relative to t standard version (the control) on an outcome.

In an effective experiment, people or units are randomly assigned to either group, ensuring that no systematic differences exist. The only difference is the change being tested, which reveals the causal relationship.

- Control (A): Experiences the standard version
- Treatment (B): Exposed to the change being tested

Users must remain in the same group throughout, so any differences in outcomes can be attributed solely to the treatment. If users switch, carryover effects contaminate both groups, violating the assumption that each user's outcome depends only on their assigned condition. Most A/B tests enforce persistent assignment unless explicitly designed as crossover studies.

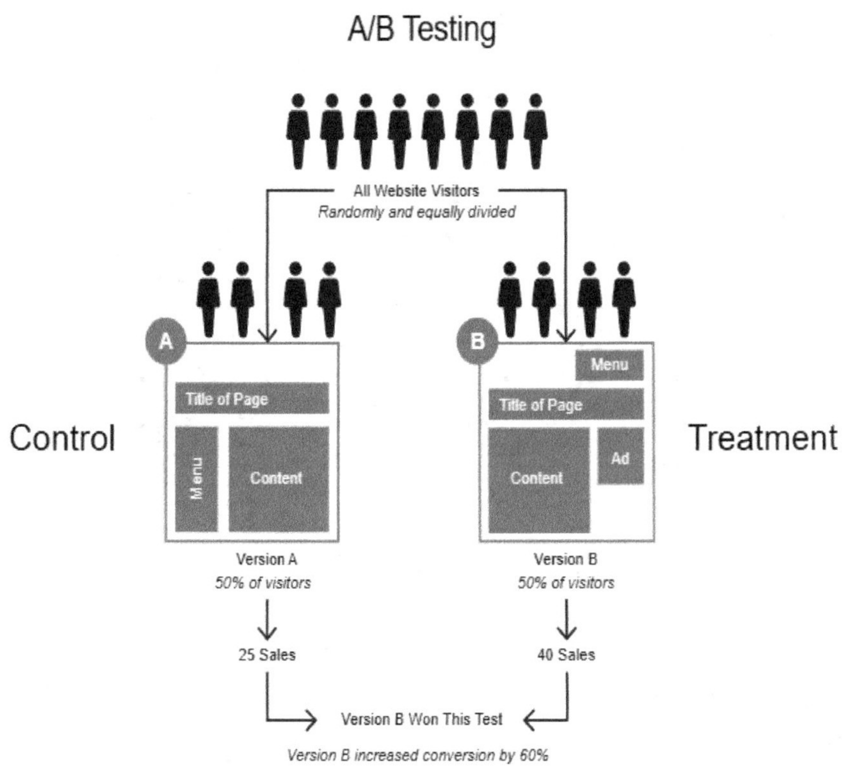

A/B Testing: Sample Size, Power Analysis, Duration & Persistent Assignment

Sample Size

An important step in designing an A/B test is determining the sample size and the split between the control and treatment groups.

- ↓ Small expected effects → larger sample sizes needed to tease out signal from noise.
- ↑ Large expected effects → smaller sample sizes sufficient for more significant changes.

Power Analysis

Used to determine how much data you need to confidently detect a meaningful effect.

Calculates the minimum sample size required to ensure that, if a real difference exists between treatment and control, the test has a high enough probability ("power") to detect it—balancing statistical rigor with practical limits on time and cost.

Power can be defined as the probability of detecting a true effect when it exists.

Experiment Duration

Duration depends on the required sample size—directly tied to how quickly you can collect enough data to reach statistical confidence.

e.g., Seeing a few hundred users/day → much longer to reach the required sample than millions/day.

⚠ Stopping Too Soon

Drawing conclusions before reaching the required sample size → increased risk of false positives or false negatives.

Persistent Assignment — Why Users Must Stay in the Same Group

KEY PRINCIPLE

In A/B testing, users must remain in the same group throughout the experiment so that any differences in outcomes can be attributed solely to the treatment rather than to users switching conditions. If users move between the control and treatment groups, their behavior can contaminate both groups through carryover effects, making results unreliable and potentially masking or falsely amplifying the true effect of the change.

Exception: Crossover studies explicitly model carryover effects—allowing users to experience both conditions while statistically accounting for order effects. Most standard A/B tests are not designed this way.

Restaurant Example

If a customer first dines under Menu A and later returns to Menu B, their prior experience may shape expectations or satisfaction. The outcome under Menu B is no longer independent of Menu A—the groups are no longer cleanly separated, violating the assumption that each user's outcome depends only on their assigned condition.

→ This is why most A/B tests enforce persistent assignment.

Heterogeneous Treatment Effects, Cohort Analysis

COHORT ANALYSIS

Heterogeneous Treatment Effects

Not all users behave the same way—and that's why cohort analysis matters. After running an experiment, it's important to look beyond the overall average and analyze how different user groups responded.

What is cohort analysis?
A form of post-experiment segmentation that breaks users into meaningful groups—such as by signup month, geography, device type, or engagement level—to reveal patterns that averages often hide.

Why it matters — Example:

One version of a product might improve retention for new users but decrease satisfaction among longtime users. If we focus only on the overall average, those effects could cancel each other out, leading us to the wrong conclusion.

✓ **New Users**

Retention improves → positive effect

X **Longtime Users**

Satisfaction decreases → negative effect

Cohort analysis helps us understand these heterogeneous treatment effects—how the same change can help one group but hurt another. Looking only at the aggregate masks this insight entirely.

A/B Testing: CAUSE Framework & Addressing Pitfalls

CAUSE Framework

C — Correlation (does not imply causation)

A — Alternatives Matter (other interacting variables)

U — Understand Your Statistical Power (experiment duration, randomization)

S — Specific Metrics: clear metrics and hypotheses

E — Experiment Design (external validity, constraints awareness, differences)

Pitfall 1: Not Looking Beyond the Average

→ Design tests that reflect the diversity of users and markets. Use metrics that capture value across different customer segments. Advanced techniques like interleaving A/B testing—mixing results from control and treatment into a single ranked list and inferring preferences from where users click—can detect subtle behavioral differences.

Pitfall 2: Forgetting That Customers Are Connected

→ Account for interactions among users using network A/B testing—placing all users who might influence each other in the same experimental group. Alternatively, run switchback experiments by alternating the entire market between control and treatment conditions, preventing market-wide equilibrium shifts from biasing the results.

Pitfall 3: Focusing Predominantly on the Short Term

→ Ensure experiment length is adequate—run experiments long enough to capture stabilized behavior rather than short-term effects. Conduct holdout experiments: exclude a small subset of users from treatment for an extended period (often a month or more) to detect slow-to-materialize effects that short-term tests would miss.

Two Variable Equal Variance T-Test

The two-sample equal variance t-test, as its name suggests, compares two sample datasets against each other to determine if there is a statistically significant difference between their population means (μ). In other words, the test can identify if a certain event or experiment has an effect. This t-test assumes that the unknown population standard deviations (σ) of both samples are roughly equal, and the populations are roughly normal. The t-distribution is appropriate here as the true standard deviations of the populations are unknown, and when smaller sample sizes are available (typically < 30). This test is also known as the pooled-variances t-test because it takes the standard deviations of both samples and pools them into a single parameter in the model. The hypotheses tested are typically:

H_0: $\mu_1 = \mu_2$, that is, the two samples' means are statistically similar

H_a: $\mu_1 \neq \mu_2$, that is, the two samples' means are statistically significantly different

$$t = \frac{(\bar{x}_1 - \bar{x}_2) - (\mu_1 - \mu_2)}{\sqrt{s_p^2\left(\frac{1}{n_1} - \frac{1}{n_2}\right)}} \qquad s_p^2 = \frac{(n_1 - 1)s_1^2 + (n_2 - 1)s_2^2}{n_1 + n_2 - 2}$$

$$df = n_1 + n_2 - 2$$

Note: When we test $H_0: \mu_1 = \mu_2$, this means we set $\mu_1 - \mu_2 = 0$ in the equation above and we set 0 as the hypothesized mean in BizStats.

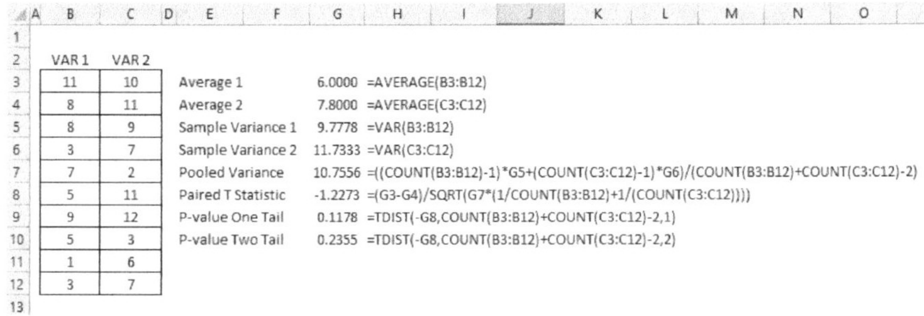

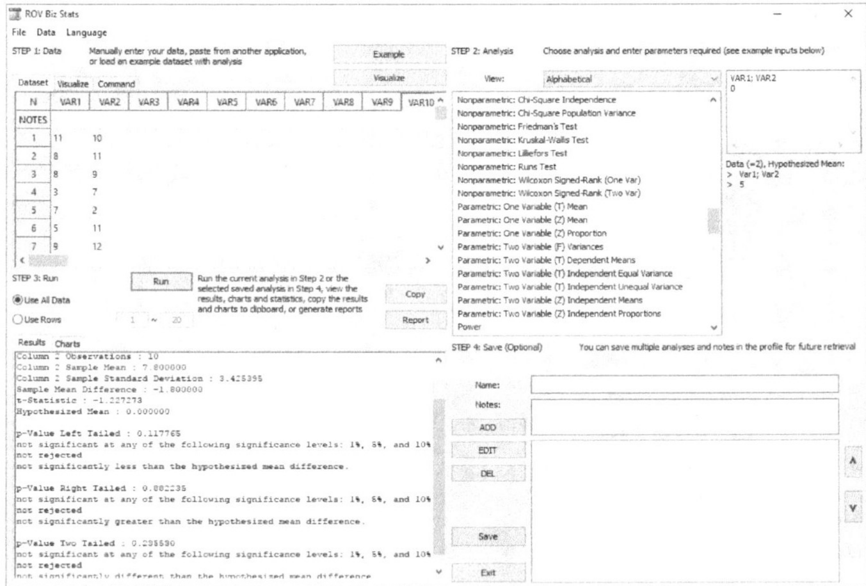

Two Variable Unequal Variance T-Test

If the standard deviations of the two sample datasets are still unknown but assumed to be different, combining them into a single pooled estimate, as done previously, would be inappropriate. Therefore, the sample standard deviations (s) will be used independently to estimate the population standard deviations (σ).

Nonetheless, normality of the underlying dataset is assumed, although this assumption becomes less important with larger datasets. The two-sample unequal variance t-test would be needed. The hypotheses tested are typically:

H_0: $\mu_1 = \mu_2$, that is, the two samples' means are statistically similar

H_a: $\mu_1 \neq \mu_2$, that is, the two samples' means are statistically significantly different

As a reminder, the null hypothesis (H_0) generally has the equivalence sign (i.e., =, ≥, ≤), whereas the alternate hypothesis (H_a) has its complement (i.e., ≠, <, >). The sign of the alternate hypothesis points to whether the test is a two-tailed test (≠) or a one-tailed test (right tail is denoted with >, whereas a left-tailed test uses <).

$$t = \frac{(\bar{x}_1 - \bar{x}_2) - (\mu_1 - \mu_2)}{\sqrt{\left(\frac{s_1^2}{n_1} + \frac{s_2^2}{n_2}\right)}} \qquad df = \frac{[s_1^2/n_1 + s_2^2/n_2]^2}{\frac{(s_1^2/n_1)^2}{n_1 - 1} + \frac{(s_2^2/n_2)^2}{n_2 - 1}}$$

Note: When we test $H_0: \mu_1 = \mu_2$, this means we set $\mu_1 - \mu_2 = 0$ in the equation above and we set 0 as the hypothesized mean in BizStats.

	B	C	D	E
3	Mean 1	18.2229		
4	Stdev 1	2.6319		
5	Count 1	35		
6	Mean 2	20.1000		
7	Stdev 2	3.8865		
8	Count 2	35		
10	Calculated T	-2.3659	=((C3-C6)-0)/SQRT((C4^2/C5)+(C7^2/C8))	
11	Calculated DF	60	=ROUND((((C4^2/C5)+(C7^2/C8))^2/(((C4^2/C5)^2/(C5-1))+((C7^2/C8)^2/(C8-1)))),0)	
12	P-Value	0.0212	2 Tails	=TDIST(C10,C11,2)
13	Critical T @ 0.10	1.6706	2 Tails	=TINV(0.1,C11)
14	Critical T @ 0.05	2.0003	2 Tails	=TINV(0.05,C11)
15	Critical T @ 0.01	2.6603	2 Tails	=TINV(0.01,C11)
16	P-Value	0.0106	1 Tail	=TDIST(C10,C11,1)
17	Critical T @ 0.10	1.2958	1 Tail	=TINV(0.1*2,C11)
18	Critical T @ 0.05	1.6706	1 Tail	=TINV(0.05*2,C11)
19	Critical T @ 0.01	2.3901	1 Tail	=TINV(0.01*2,C11)

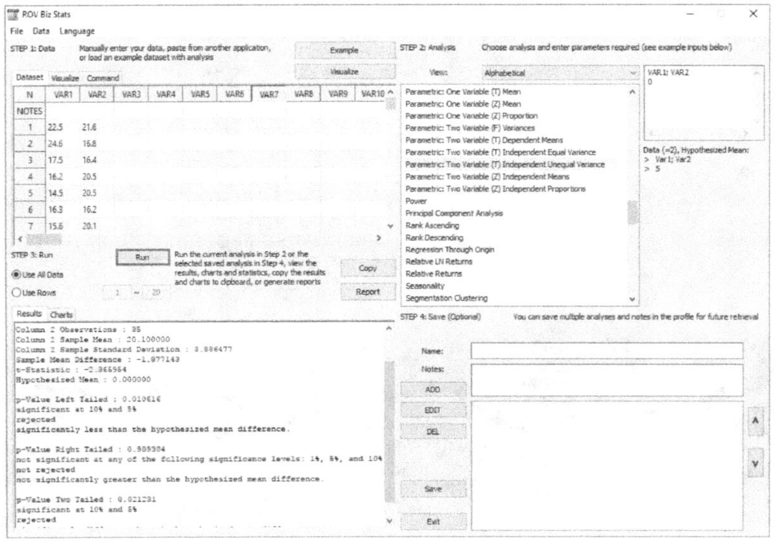

Two Variable Dependent Means T-Test

When the two datasets are dependent, the two-sample t-test with dependent means is used. This test is also known as the paired observations test, which means that the number of observations in each of the two datasets has to be the same ($n = n_1 = n_2$). For example, if the researcher is interested in testing the before-and-after effects of a change in work hours on productivity in the same sample of employees, the data are obtained from the same dataset (i.e., the same employees are tested).

The hypotheses tested are the typical two-tailed or one-tailed test. Example of a one-tailed left-tailed test:

H_0: $\mu_1 \geq \mu_2$, that is, the two samples' means are statistically similar
H_a: $\mu_1 < \mu_2$, that is, the two samples' means are statistically significantly different

In the book, Figure 9.7 provides an example of a productivity study in which X1 was measured after the change in work hours, compared with the pre-change measurement X_2. The numbers indicate the total hours required to complete a given activity, and each row of the dataset represents an individual.

$$t = \frac{\bar{d}}{s_d/\sqrt{n}} \qquad d = x_1 - x_2 \qquad df = n - 1$$

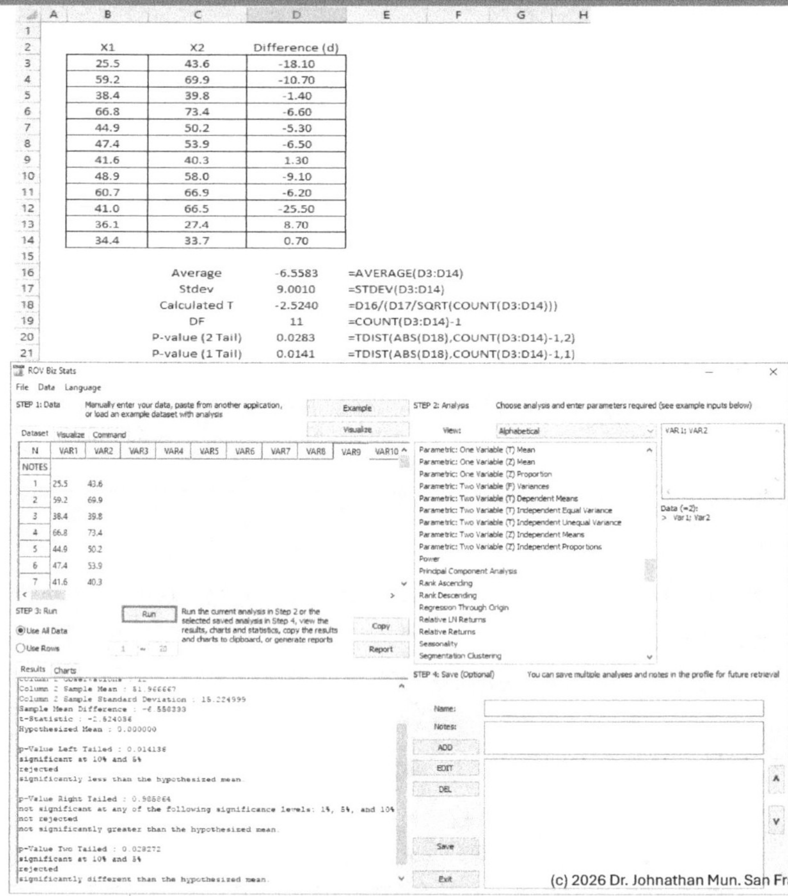

X1	X2	Difference (d)
25.5	43.6	-18.10
59.2	69.9	-10.70
38.4	39.8	-1.40
66.8	73.4	-6.60
44.9	50.2	-5.30
47.4	53.9	-6.50
41.6	40.3	1.30
48.9	58.0	-9.10
60.7	66.9	-6.20
41.0	66.5	-25.50
36.1	27.4	8.70
34.4	33.7	0.70

Average	-6.5583	=AVERAGE(D3:D14)
Stdev	9.0010	=STDEV(D3:D14)
Calculated T	-2.5240	=D16/(D17/SQRT(COUNT(D3:D14)))
DF	11	=COUNT(D3:D14)-1
P-value (2 Tail)	0.0283	=TDIST(ABS(D18),COUNT(D3:D14)-1,2)
P-value (1 Tail)	0.0141	=TDIST(ABS(D18),COUNT(D3:D14)-1,1)

Two Variable F-Test of Variances from Independent Variables

On occasion, we may need to compare the variances of two independent sample sets. For instance, when comparing the mean time between failures (MTBF) of two different equipment setups and measuring the variation in MTBF, we can determine whether the variation in MTBF of the old or new equipment is greater. The F-test is used in this instance, where we test the following hypotheses:

H_0: $\sigma_1^2 = \sigma_2^2$ there is no difference in variation between the two samples

H_a: $\sigma_1^2 \neq \sigma_2^2$ there is a difference in variation between the two samples

In the book, see the example provided in Figure 9.9. Suppose two equipment sets were each implemented in seven different locations, and their respective MTBF in months were collected. The sample standard deviations were calculated as 0.7091 and 0.5350 for these two equipment sets. The F statistic is computed as 1.7571 with a corresponding one-tailed p-value of 0.2552, which means we do not reject the null hypothesis and conclude that there is no statistically significant difference in variation of the MTBF.

$$F = \max(s_1^2/s_2^2\,, s_2^2/s_1^2) \qquad F(\alpha/2, n_L - 1, n_S - 1)$$

	A	B	C	D
1				
2		X1	X2	
3		2.5	5.2	
4		2.6	5.6	
5		3.4	5.4	
6		2.9	5.9	
7		4.3	5.9	
8		4.1	6.2	
9		3.6	6.8	
10				
11	Mean	3.3429	5.8571	=AVERAGE(B3:B9) and =AVERAGE(C3:C9)
12	Stdev	0.7091	0.5350	=STDEV(B3:B9) and =STDEV(C3:C9)
13	Count	7	7	=COUNT(B3:B9) and =COUNT(C3:C9)
14	F Statistic	1.7571	One Tail	=MAX(B12^2/C12^2,C12^2/B12^2)
15	P-value	0.2552	One Tail	=FDIST(B14,B13-1,C13-1)

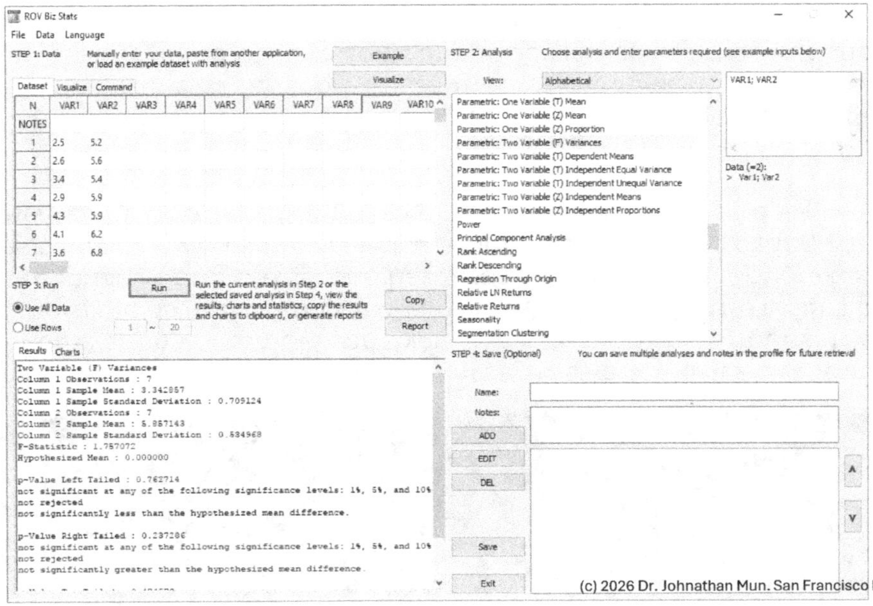

Box Test of Covariance & CV Test for Homogeneity

A related test is the Box Test of Covariance Homogeneity, which extends the F-test for variances. The latter tests two variables simultaneously for similarities in their variances, whereas the former examines multiple variables across two distinct groups. The null hypothesis is such that the covariance matrix of the first group is the same as that of the second group. For example, the results below are based on running the Box test, in which the first group has three variables and the second has three as well. The Chi-Square test and F-test can be applied in this example. Both p-values for these tests indicate we cannot reject the null hypothesis, indicating that the covariances are similar between the two groups of variables. This test is also useful for assessing the consistency of data variation between two groups.

Another related test is the Coefficient of Variation Homogeneity (CV Homogeneity) test, where, instead of looking at variances (F-test) or covariance matrices (Box Test), we can test the similarities among coefficients of variation. Recall that CV is a relative measure of risk, spread, and uncertainty of a distribution. It is dimensionless (no units) and can be used to compare dispersion across distributions with different units (e.g., we can compare kilograms with meters, millions of dollars with multibillion-dollar investment risks). Hence, testing the homogeneity of CV is sometimes important. The following is an example set of results from BizStats, in which the CV Homogeneity test tests the null hypothesis that the CVs are equal across multiple variables. A low p-value indicates we can reject the null hypothesis and conclude that the CVs are not similar among the test variables.

```
Box Test of Covariance Homogeneity
Group 1 Covariance
          1.25674      -9.94263       3.26632
         -9.94263     169.31316     -38.30000
          3.26632     -38.30000      31.80000
Group 2 Covariance
          1.49673     -10.43072       0.64771
        -10.43072     175.15359     -28.56209
          0.64771     -28.56209      24.45752
Pooled Covariance
          1.37007     -10.17312       2.02975
        -10.17312     172.07114     -33.70154
          2.02975     -33.70154      28.33272
```

```
Box's Test with Chi-Square
Chi-Square    2.85467
P-Value       0.82685

Box's Test with F-Test
F-Stat        0.47543
P-Value       0.82709

Homogeneity of Coefficients of Variation
   Average CV: 0.128503
   Pooled CV: 0.129837
   Chi-Square: 7.324772
   P-Value: 0.025671
Null hypothesis tested is that all CVs are equal or homogeneous
```

Two Variable Z-Test for Proportions and Means

In certain situations, proportions (p) are used instead of raw values. In such situations, when there are two sets of data, the two proportions can be tested using the following hypotheses:

H_0: $\mu(p_1 - p_2) = 0$, there is no difference between the two datasets
H_a: $\mu(p_1 - p_2) \neq 0$, there is a difference between the two datasets

This approach assumes that n_1p_1, $n_1(1 - p_1)$, n_2p_2, and $n_2(1 - p_2) \geq 5$ and each $n \geq 30$ so that the underlying binomial distribution (a proportion is equivalent to a binomial probability distribution with two outcomes) approaches the normal distribution, hence the ability to use the z-test.

For the independent means test, the two samples' means are tested using:

H_0: $\mu(\bar{x}_1 - \bar{x}_2) = 0$, there is no difference between the two datasets
H_a: $\mu(\bar{x}_1 - \bar{x}_2) \neq 0$, there is a difference between the two datasets

$$z = \frac{(p_1 - p_2)}{\sqrt{\bar{p}(1-\bar{p})\left(\frac{1}{n_1} + \frac{1}{n_2}\right)}} \qquad z = \frac{(\bar{x}_1 - \bar{x}_2) - (\mu_1 - \mu_2)}{\sqrt{\frac{s_1^2}{n_1} + \frac{s_2^2}{n_2}}} \qquad \bar{p} = \frac{n_1p_1 + n_2p_2}{n_1 + n_2}$$

	A	B	C	D	E
1					
2		Proportion 1	0.0815		
3		Proportion 2	0.0983		
4		Count 1	1903		
5		Count 2	1903		
6					
7		Pooled P	0.0899		=(C4*C2+C5*C3)/(C4+C5)
8		Z-Score	-1.8117		=(C2-C3)/SQRT(C7*(1-C7)*(1/C4+1/C5))
9		P-Value	0.0350	1 Tail	=NORMSDIST(C8)
10		P-Value	0.0700	2 Tail	=NORMSDIST(C8)*2
11		Z Critical @ 0.10	-1.2816	Left 1 Tail	=NORMSINV(0.1)
12		Z Critical @ 0.05	-1.6449	Left 1 Tail	=NORMSINV(0.05)
13		Z Critical @ 0.01	-2.3263	Left 1 Tail	=NORMSINV(0.01)

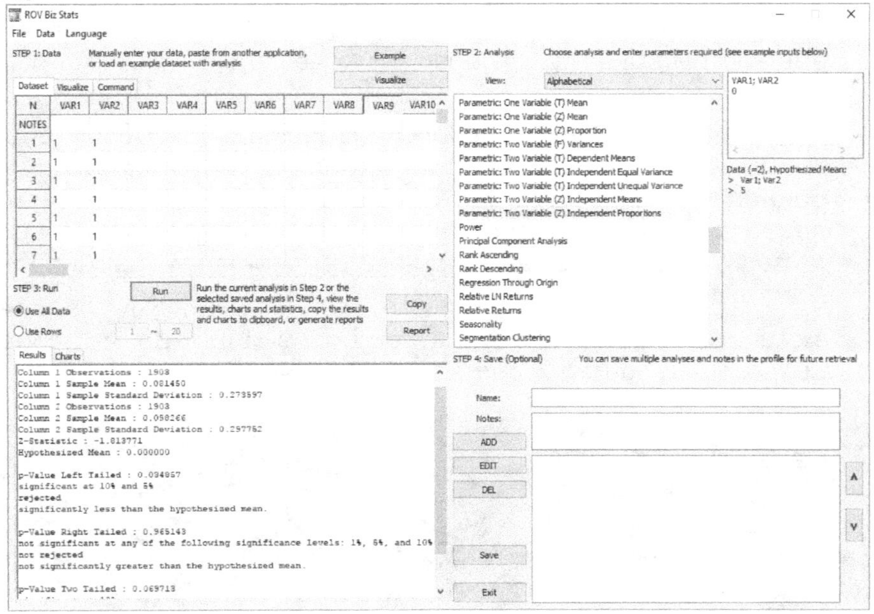

Single ANOVA with Multiple Treatment Variables

The previously described t-tests, z-tests, and F-tests are applied to two variables at a time to determine whether their means, proportions, or variances differ significantly, or whether small differences are attributable to random chance. When two or more sample means need to be tested simultaneously, we use Analysis of Variance (ANOVA).

The single ANOVA with multiple treatments tests *one* categorical independent variable (with multiple treatment levels, types, or categories) and *one* numerical dependent variable (randomly allocated into the multiple treatment categories) to determine if their population means are equal. Each data column will have a different treatment (e.g., a new manufacturing method, a new training regimen or a new technology). This test assumes that the treatments are completely and randomly assigned to all the persons in the experiment, and the underlying data is normally distributed with equal variance. Note that the nonparametric equivalent is the Kruskal–Wallis test, which is presented later in the chapter.

Example: Nine staff members in an organization were randomly divided into three teams, each consisting of three individuals, and each team was provided a different type of training. There are three distinct training courses or treatments in this case. Upon completing the training course, each individual was assigned a task, and the time it took to complete the task was recorded and displayed in the data grid. Because the selection is random, we use the randomized single ANOVA with multiple treatments to test the following hypotheses:

H_0: $\mu_1 = \mu_2 = \ldots = \mu_t$ for treatments 1 to t (there is no effect in the treatments)
H_a: Population means are not equal (there is an effect in at least one of the treatments)

$$Global\ Average\ \tilde{x} = \frac{\sum_{j=1}^{t} \sum_{i=1}^{t} x_{ij}}{N} \qquad SS\ Treatment = \sum_{j=1}^{t} n_j(\bar{x}_j - \tilde{x})^2 \qquad SS\ Error = \sum_{j=1}^{t} \sum_{i=1}^{n_j} (x_{ij} - \bar{x}_j)^2 \qquad SS\ Total = \sum_{j=1}^{t} \sum_{i=1}^{n_j} (x_{ij} - \tilde{x})^2$$

Mean Squares of Between Treatment (MS Treatment) = (SS Treatment)/(Number of Treatments – 1)

Mean Squares of Errors or Mean Squares Within Treatments (MS Error) = (SS Error)/(Total Observations – Number of Treatments)

F Statistic is computed as MS Treatment / MS Error

Results of Single ANOVA with Multiple Treatment Variables

	Method 1	Method 2	Method 3
Person 1	15	10	18
Person 2	20	15	19
Person 3	19	11	23

EXCEL ANALYSIS TOOL PAK
Anova: Single Factor

SUMMARY

Groups	*Count*	*Sum*	*Average*	*Variance*
Column 1	3	54	18	7
Column 2	3	36	12	7
Column 3	3	60	20	7

ANOVA

Source of Variation	*SS*	*df*	*MS*	*F*	*P-value*	*F crit*
Between Groups	104	2	52	7.4286	0.0238	5.1433
Within Groups	42	6	7			
Total	146	8				

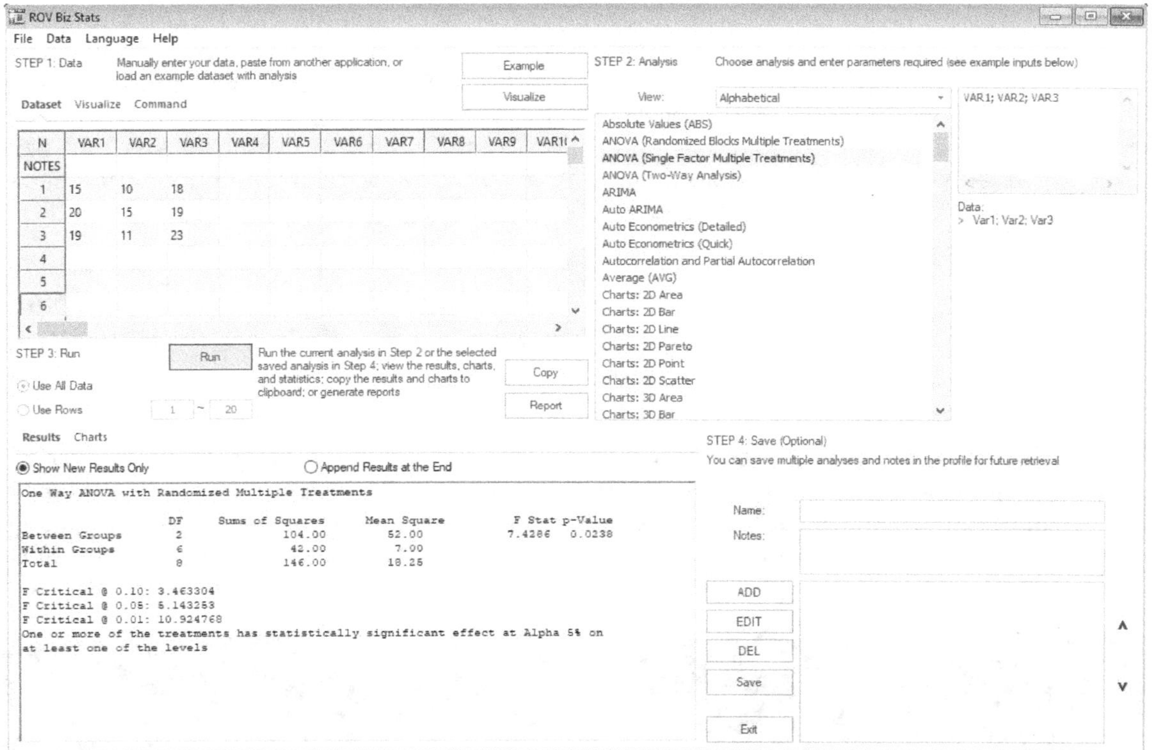

ANOVA with Randomized Block Test

In the previous single ANOVA test, the assumption was that the treatments were completely randomized and assigned to all participants in the experiment. This approach may result in overrepresentation and underrepresentation in some treatment groups simply by chance. If the properties or characteristics of the individuals participating in the experiment strongly influence the measurements and data obtained, a single ANOVA may end up measuring differences within this experimental group rather than the effects of the treatments. To resolve this issue, ANOVA with Randomized Block can be used. Note that the nonparametric equivalent is Friedman's test.

The specification tested in this ANOVA is $x_{i,j} = \mu + \tau_j + \beta_i + \varepsilon_{ij}$
H_0: $\tau_j = 0$ for treatments j = 1 to t (there is no effect in the treatments)
H_a: $\tau_j \neq 0$ for at least one treatment j = 1 to *t* (one or more treatments have an effect)
where τ is the treatments and β is the blocking variable.

Example: Suppose that there are four auto headlamps under development. The manufacturer wishes to test the visibility of each lamp design by measuring how far someone can see with each headlamp. Now, suppose 12 individuals were randomly selected to participate in this experiment, and we categorize them as young (Y), middle-aged (M), or old (O). If we completely randomize the selection of these individuals, each method may be over- or underrepresented across age groups, as seen in the first data grid on the left below. Now, further suppose that participants' properties (e.g., age) influence their vision (e.g., older participants cannot see as far as younger participants). Consequently, completely randomizing the participants into these groups will yield biased results. The better approach is to "block" this intervening age variable. The second data grid below on the right shows how to set up an ANOVA dataset with blocks. In this example, there are three blocks, and they are stratified into rows.

ANOVA One-Way Randomized Design

	Method 1	Method 2	Method 3	Method 4
Person 1	Y	M	O	Y
Person 2	Y	O	Y	M
Person 3	O	O	M	Y

ANOVA with Blocking Variable

	Method 1	Method 2	Method 3	Method 4
Block 1	Y	Y	Y	Y
Block 2	M	M	M	M
Block 3	O	O	O	O

ANOVA with Randomized Block Test

$$Global\ Average\ \tilde{x} = \frac{\sum_{j=1}^{t} \quad \sum_{i=1}^{t} x_{ij}}{N}$$

$$SS\ Treatment = n \sum_{j=1}^{t} (\bar{x}_j - \tilde{x})^2$$

$$SS\ Block = t \sum_{j=1}^{t} (\bar{x}_i - \tilde{x})^2$$

$$SS\ Error = \sum_{j=1}^{t} \quad \sum_{i=1}^{n_j} (x_{ij} - \tilde{x})^2$$

$$SS\ Error = SS\ Total - SS\ Treatment - SS\ Block$$

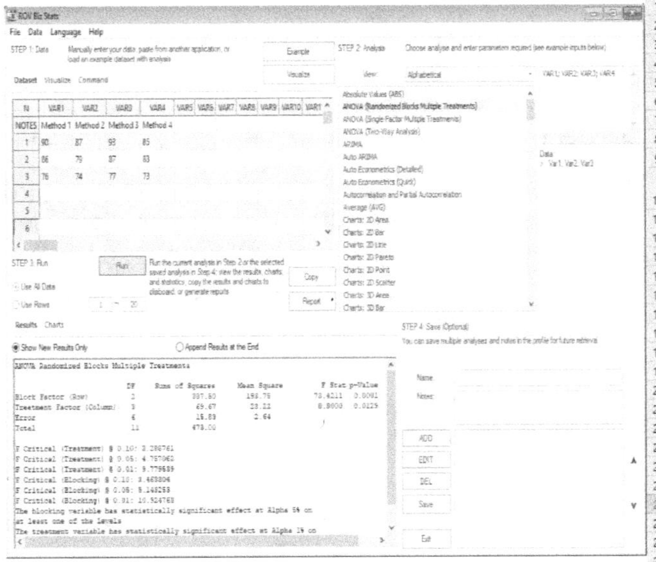

	A	B	C	D	E	F
1		**Method 1**	**Method 2**	**Method 3**	**Method 4**	**Average**
2	**Block 1**	90	87	93	85	88.7500
3	**Block 2**	86	79	87	83	83.7500
4	**Block 3**	76	74	77	73	75.0000
5	**Average**	84.0000	80.0000	85.6667	80.3333	
6						
7	**Global Average**	82.5000	=AVERAGE(B2:E4)			
8	**Number of Rows (Blocks)**	3	=COUNT(B2:B4)			
9	**Number of Columns (Treatments)**	4	=COUNT(B2:E2)			
10	**SS Total**	473.0000	=(B2-B7)^2+(B3-B7)^2+(B4-B7)^2+(C2-B7)^2+(C3-B7)^2+(C4-B7)^2+(D2-B7)^2+(D3-B7)^2+(D4-B7)^2+(E2-B7)^2+(E3-B7)^2+(E4-B7)^2			
11	**SS Blocking (Rows)**	387.5000	=B9*((F2-B7)^2+(F3-B7)^2+(F4-B7)^2)			
12	**SS Treatment (Columns)**	69.6667	=B8*((B5-B7)^2+(C5-B7)^2+(D5-B7)^2+(E5-B7)^2)			
13	**SS Errors**	15.8333	=B10-B12-B11			
14	**MS Block**	193.7500	=B11/B17			
15	**MS Treatment**	23.2222	=B12/B18			
16	**MS Error**	2.6389	=B13/B19			
17	**DF Block**	2	=B8-1			
18	**DF Treatment**	3	=B9-1			
19	**DF Error**	6	=B17*B18			
20	**F Statistic (Treatment)**	8.8000	=B15/B16			
21	**P-Value (Treatment)**	0.0129	=FDIST(B20,B18,B19)			
22	**F Statistic (Blocking)**	73.4211	=B14/B16			
23	**P-Value (Blocking)**	0.0001	=FDIST(B22,B17,B19)			
24	**F Critical (Treatment) @ 0.10**	3.2888	=FINV(0.1,B18,B19)			
25	**F Critical (Treatment) @ 0.05**	4.7571	=FINV(0.05,B18,B19)			
26	**F Critical (Treatment) @ 0.01**	9.7795	=FINV(0.01,B18,B19)			
27	**F Critical (Blocking) @ 0.10**	3.4633	=FINV(0.1,B17,B19)			
28	**F Critical (Blocking) @ 0.05**	5.1433	=FINV(0.05,B17,B19)			
29	**F Critical (Blocking) @ 0.01**	10.9248	=FINV(0.01,B17,B19)			
30	**The blocking variable has statistically significant effect at Alpha 5% on at least one of the levels**					
31	**The treatment variable has statistically significant effect at Alpha 1% on at least one of the levels**					

Mean Squares of Between Treatment (MS Treatment) = (SS Treatment)/(Number of Treatments – 1)
Mean Squares of Blocks (MS Block) = (SS Block)/(Total Observations – 1)
Mean Squares of Errors or Mean Squares Within Treatments (MS Error) = (SS Error)/((Total Observations – 1)(Number of Treatments – 1)
F Statistic is computed as MS Treatment / MS Error
F statistic *df* = (Number of Treatments – 1) in the numerator and (Total Observations – 1)(Number of Treatments – 1) in the denominator

Two-Way ANOVA

The one-way ANOVA models presented above examine a single factor affecting the dependent variable. In this section, we introduce the two-way ANOVA, a method that simultaneously examines the effects of two factors (*two* categorical independent variables) on *a numerical dependent variable, as well as the interactions between their levels.* That is, random assignments are made so that two or more participants are assigned to each possible combination of factor levels. The number of persons or participants in each of these combinations is called the number of replications (r), and r must be ≥ 2.

The specification tested in this ANOVA is $x_{ij} = \mu + \alpha_i + \beta_j + (\alpha\beta)_{ij} + \varepsilon_{ijk}$

Testing the main effect, factor A:
H_0: $\alpha_i = 0$ for each level of factor A, for $i = 1$ to a (no level of factor A has an effect)
H_a: $\alpha_i \neq 0$ for at least one value of i, where $i = 1$ to a (at least one level has an effect)

Testing the main effect, factor B:
H_0: $\beta_j = 0$ for each level of factor B, for $j = 1$ to b (no level of factor B has an effect)
H_a: $\beta_j \neq 0$ for at least one value of j, where $j = 1$ to b (at least one level has an effect)

Testing the interaction effects between levels of factors A and B:
H_0: $\alpha\beta_{ij} = 0$ for each combination of i and j (there are no interaction effects)
H_a: $\alpha\beta_{ij} \neq 0$ for at least one combination of i and j (at least one combination has effect)

$$SSA = rb\sum_{i=1}^{a}(\bar{x}_i - \tilde{x})^2 \qquad SSB = ra\sum_{j=1}^{b}(\bar{x}_j - \tilde{x})^2$$

$$SSE = \sum_{i=1}^{a}\sum_{j=1}^{b}\sum_{k=1}^{r}(x_{ijk} - \bar{x}_{ij})^2 \qquad SST = \sum_{i=1}^{a}\sum_{j=1}^{b}\sum_{k=1}^{r}(x_{ijk} - \tilde{x})^2$$

Example: Suppose an aircraft manufacturer is testing three different alloys (B1, B2, and B3) for the wing construction of a new plane, and each alloy type can be produced in four different thicknesses (A1 to A4). The number of twists and flexes is recorded until stress failure is detected.

	Factor B1	Factor B2	Factor B3
Factor A1	804	836	804
Factor A1	816	828	808
Factor A2	819	844	807
Factor A2	813	836	819
Factor A3	820	814	819
Factor A3	821	811	829
Factor A4	806	811	827
Factor A4	805	806	835

Degrees of freedom (*df*) for factor A is *(a – 1)*, factor B is *(b – 1)*,
Interaction AB is *(a – 1)(b – 1)*, Error is *ab(r – 1)*, and Total is *(abr – 1)*.
Mean Squares (MS) for factor A is *SSA/df(A)*, factor B is *SSB/df(B)*,
factor AB is *SSAB/df(AB)*, Error is *SSE/df(E)*.
The calculated F Statistic for factor A is MS(A)/MS(E), factor B is MS(B)/MS(E),
and AB interaction is MS(AB)/MS(E).

Two-Way ANOVA

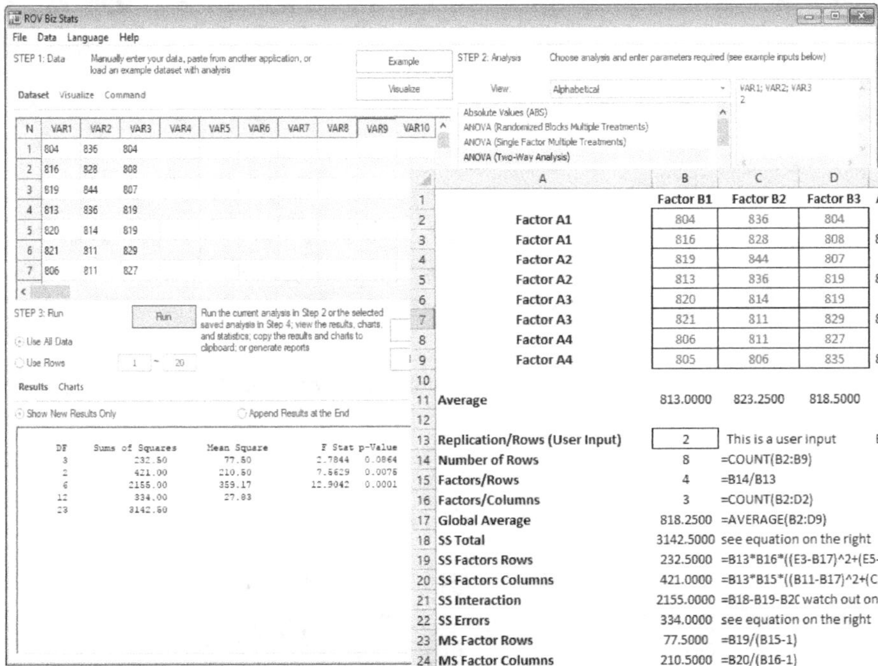

	A	B	C	D	E
1		Factor B1	Factor B2	Factor B3	Average
2	Factor A1	804	836	804	
3	Factor A1	816	828	808	816.0000
4	Factor A2	819	844	807	
5	Factor A2	813	836	819	823.0000
6	Factor A3	820	814	819	
7	Factor A3	821	811	829	819.0000
8	Factor A4	806	811	827	
9	Factor A4	805	806	835	815.0000
10					
11	Average	813.0000	823.2500	818.5000	

Two Way ANOVA

Careful with column E. We average the number of rows based on user input of number of Replication/Rows there are

	A	B	C
13	Replication/Rows (User Input)	2	This is a user input
14	Number of Rows	8	=COUNT(B2:B9)
15	Factors/Rows	4	=B14/B13
16	Factors/Columns	3	=COUNT(B2:D2)
17	Global Average	818.2500	=AVERAGE(B2:D9)
18	SS Total	3142.5000	see equation on the right
19	SS Factors Rows	232.5000	=B13*B16*((E3-B17)^2+(E5-B17)^2+(E7-B17)^2+(E9-B17)^2)
20	SS Factors Columns	421.0000	=B13*B15*((B11-B17)^2+(C11-B17)^2+(D11-B17)^2)
21	SS Interaction	2155.0000	=B18-B19-B2(watch out on this one... example has 2 Replication so we average two rows only, if replication 5 then average of all 5 rows and do the difference and square for all five items...
22	SS Errors	334.0000	see equation on the right
23	MS Factor Rows	77.5000	=B19/(B15-1)
24	MS Factor Columns	210.5000	=B20/(B16-1)
25	MS Interaction	359.1667	=B21/((B15-1)*(B16-1))
26	MS Errors	27.8333	=B22/(B15*B16*(B13-1))
27	F Statistic for Row Factors	2.7844	=B23/B26
28	F Statistic for Column Factors	7.5629	=B24/B26
29	F Statistic for Interaction	12.9042	=B25/B26
30	DF Row Factors	3	=B15-1
31	DF Column Factors	2	=B16-1
32	DF Interaction	6	=(B15-1)*(B16-1)
33	DF Both Factors	12	=B15*B16*(B13-1)
34	P-Value for Row Factors	0.0864	=FDIST(B27,B30,B33)
35	P-Value for Column Factors	0.0075	=FDIST(B28,B31,B33)
36	P-Value for Interaction	0.0001	=FDIST(B29,B32,B33)

```
B18=(B2-$B$17)^2+(B3-$B$17)^2+(B4-$B$17)^2+(B5-$B$17)^2+(B6-$B$17)^2+(B7-$B$17)^2+(B8-$B$17)^2+(B9-$B$17)^2+(C2-
$B$17)^2+(C3-$B$17)^2+(C4-$B$17)^2+(C5-$B$17)^2+(C6-$B$17)^2+(C7-$B$17)^2+(C8-$B$17)^2+(C9-$B$17)^2+(D2-
$B$17)^2+(D3-$B$17)^2+(D4-$B$17)^2+(D5-$B$17)^2+(D6-$B$17)^2+(D7-$B$17)^2+(D8-$B$17)^2+(D9-$B$17)^2
```

```
'B22=(B2-AVERAGE(B2:B3))^2+(B3-AVERAGE(B2:B3))^2 + (B4-AVERAGE(B4:B5))^2+(B5-AVERAGE(B4:B5))^2 + (B6-
AVERAGE(B6:B7))^2+(B7-AVERAGE(B6:B7))^2 + (B8-AVERAGE(B8:B9))^2+(B9-AVERAGE(B8:B9))^2 + (C2-
AVERAGE(C2:C3))^2+(C3-AVERAGE(C2:C3))^2 + (C4-AVERAGE(C4:C5))^2+(C5-AVERAGE(C4:C5))^2 + (C6-
AVERAGE(C6:C7))^2+(C7-AVERAGE(C6:C7))^2 + (C8-AVERAGE(C8:C9))^2+(C9-AVERAGE(C8:C9))^2 + (D2-
AVERAGE(D2:D3))^2+(D3-AVERAGE(D2:D3))^2 + (D4-AVERAGE(D4:D5))^2+(D5-AVERAGE(D4:D5))^2 + (D6-
AVERAGE(D6:D7))^2+(D7-AVERAGE(D6:D7))^2 + (D8-AVERAGE(D8:D9))^2+(D9-AVERAGE(D8:D9))^2
```

Two Way ANOVA Results

	DF	SS	MS	F	P
Row Factor	3	232.5000	77.5000	2.7844	0.0864
Column Factor	2	421.0000	210.5000	7.5629	0.0075
Interaction	6	2155.0000	359.1667	12.9042	0.0001
Error	12	334.0000	27.8333		

General Linear Models

GENERAL LINEAR MODEL	Dependent Variable(s)	Independent Variable(s)	Notes
ANOVA Single Factor Multiple Treatments	One	One	One factor with multiple treatment types.
ANOVA Single Factor with Repeated Measures	One	One	Repeating similar tests for reliability.
ANOVA with Blocking Variables	One	One	Controls and tests for exogenous impacts.
Two-Way ANOVA	One	Two	Two factors with multiple treatment types each and testing for their interactions. M x N factorial design.
Three-Way ANOVA	One	Three	Three factors with multiple treatment types each and testing for their interactions. P x Q x R factorial design.
ANCOVA	One	One	Controls for baselines using covariates.
MANOVA	Multiple	One	Simultaneous ANOVA by testing multiple dependent variables at once.
Two-Way MANOVA	Multiple	Two	Two factors with multiple treatment types each and testing for their interactions on multiple dependent variables at once. M x N factorial design.

Design of Experiments (DOE)

Design of Experiment DOE

N	Block	A	B	C
1	1	A1	B1	C1
2	1	A1	B1	C2
3	1	A1	B1	C3
4	1	A1	B1	C4
5	1	A1	B2	C1
6	1	A1	B2	C2
7	1	A1	B2	C3
8	1	A1	B2	C4
9	1	A2	B1	C1
10	1	A2	B1	C2
11	1	A2	B1	C3
12	1	A2	B1	C4
13	1	A2	B2	C1
14	1	A2	B2	C2
15	1	A2	B2	C3
16	1	A2	B2	C4

Factorial Design (DOE) Combinatorics

2×2 or 2^2

2 IV with 2 levels on IV(1) and 2 levels on IV(2)
2 Main Effects + 1 Interaction Effect +
4 Experimental Conditions

Two IV

3×3 or 3^2

2 IV with 3 levels on IV(1) and 3 levels on IV(2)
2 Main + 1 Interaction + 9 Conditions

Three IV

$2 \times 2 \times 4$ or 2^24

3 IV with 2 levels on IV(1), 2 levels on IV(2), and 4 levels on IV(3)
3 Main + 4 Interaction + 16 Conditions
Hint: AB, AC, BC, ABC

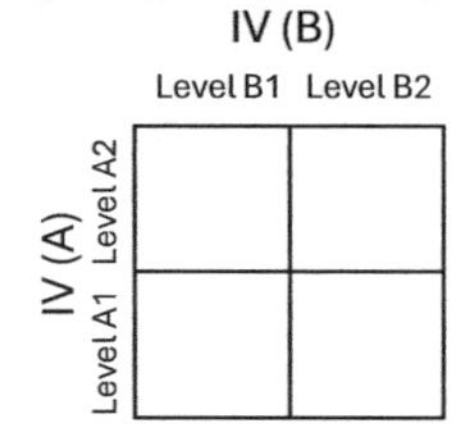

2 & 2 Treatment Levels
4 Exp. Conditions

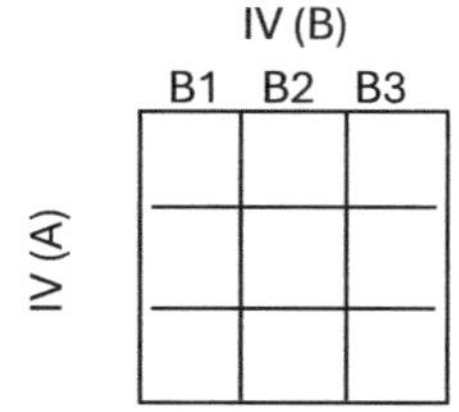

3 & 3 Treatment Levels
9 Exp. Conditions

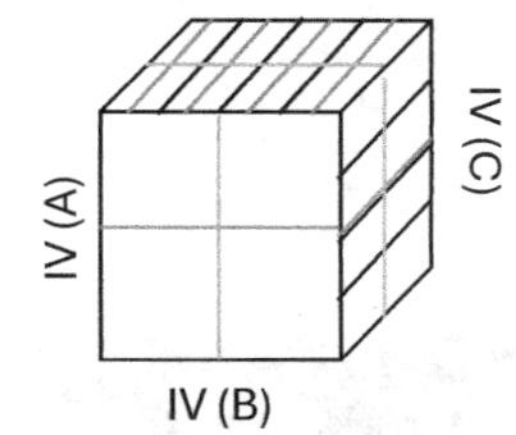

2, 2 & 4 Treatment Levels
16 Exp. Conditions

ANOVA vs. Regression

ANOVA	
Dep. Var.	Continuous
Indep. Var.	Categorical [1]
Requirements	Normality of data [2]

[1] If the dependent variable is categorical, use Discriminant Analysis, clustering, segmentation, and other AI/ML grouping methods; if the dependent variable is binary, bivariate, or truncated, use GLM methods
[2] Use nonparametric equivalence if nonlinear (Kruskal-Wallis, Friedman, Mood's Median)

REGRESSION	
Dep. Var.	Continuous [3]
Indep. Var.	Continuous [4]
Requirements	Multivariate normality and sphericity of errors, homoskedasticity, expected error is zero, no autocorrelation, no micronumerosity (k > n), non-stochastic, no multicollinearity, and so forth...

[3] Use Generalized Linear Models (Logit, Probit, Tobit) for Binary, Bivariate, and Truncated Data
[4] Dummy Variables (binary), Index Variables (1, 2, 3) can be used in multiple regression

SIMPLE RULES
Do not exceed ANOVA Three-Way or MANOVA Two-Way. Use regression instead.
Only differences is needed: ANOVA. Marginal impacts and predictions: regression.
MANOVA has difficulty in identifying the source of the difference, only that there is one.
Regression provides additional validity indicators: R-Sq, Akaike, Hannan-Quinn, Bayes...
Careful as categorical and dummy variables can sometimes cause multicollinearity issues. Select the right regression (Autoeconometrics, Correlated, Cox, Deming, Functional Forms, Instrumental Variables, Origin, Stepwise, Weighted, etc.).

Conclusion: Collect interval data if possible and run both! Each provides a different set of insights...

ANOVA, ANCOVA, MANOVA (One, Two, Three Way)

ANOVA for Single Factor Multiple Treatments

1 Dependent Variable vs. 1 Independent Variable (One Factor Multiple Treatments)

Participants	Method 1 Treatment	Method 2 Treatment	Method 3 Treatment
Person 1	58	80	96
Person 2	68	82	92
Person 3	70	88	90
...	...	...	...
...	...	...	...
Person 30	72	86	88

* Method 1: Russian Math; Method 2: Singapore Math; Method 3: U.S. Math
* The Single Factor Tested: Different Teaching Techniques
* Dependent Variable = Math Scores (continuous numerical values in the table)
* Independent Variable = Teaching Techniques (column groups)

ANOVA for Single Factor Repeated Measures

1 Dependent Variable vs. 1 Independent Variable (Repeated Tests)

Participants	Test 1	Test 2	Test 3
Person 1	50	52	50
Person 2	88	90	92
Person 3	60	62	58
...	...	...	...
...	...	...	...
Person 30	78	80	80

* The same treatment is used but the participants are tested multiple times
* Dependent Variable = Math Scores (continuous numerical values in the table)
* The same students are subjected to multiple tests

ANOVA with Blocking Variable

1 Dependent Variable vs. 1 Independent Variable with Blocking Variable

Blocks	Method 1 Treatment	Method 2 Treatment	Method 3 Treatment
Private School	66	82	94
Public School	68	84	90
Home School	70	88	90

* Method 1: Russian Math; Method 2: Singapore Math; Method 3: U.S. Math
* The Single Factor Tested: Different Teaching Techniques
* Dependent Variable = Math Scores (continuous numerical values in the table)
* Independent Variable = Teaching Techniques (column groups)
* Blocking Variable = Type of school (variable to control)

TWO-WAY ANOVA

1 Dependent Variable vs. 2 Independent Variable (One Factor Multiple Treatments)

Factor B	Method 1 Factor A1	Method 2 Factor A2	Method 3 Factor A3
Factor B1: 1 Month	68	82	96
Factor B2: 3 Months	72	84	86
Factor B3: 6 Months	66	90	92

* The Two Factors Tested: Different Teaching Techniques vs. Length of Time Taught
* Factor A:: Method 1: Russian Math; Method 2: Singapore Math; Method 3: U.S. Math
* Factor B:: 1 Month, 3 Month, 6 Months
* Dependent Variable = Math Scores (continuous numerical values in the table)
* This example is a 3 x 3 Factorial Model

MANOVA

Multiple Dependent Variables vs. 1 Independent Variable

Independent Var Schools	Dependent Var 1 Math Scores	Dependent Var 2 Satisfaction	Dependent Var 3 Teacher Ratings
Public	76.7	29.5	7.5
Public	60.5	32.1	6.3
Public	96.1	40.7	4.2
Private	76.9	20.4	3.0
Private	66.9	23.9	1.1
Private	55.4	29.1	5.0
Charter	62.8	25.9	2.9
Charter	45.0	15.9	1.2
Charter	47.8	36.1	4.1
Home School	52.5	39.0	3.1
Home School	80.0	54.2	4.0
Home School	54.7	32.1	5.7

* Multiple Dependent Variables = The numerical values in the table include test scores, student satisfaction survey scores, and teacher ratings
* One Independent Variable = Type of school

TWO WAY MANOVA

Multiple Dependent Variables vs. 2 Independent Variables

Independent Var 1 Schools	Independent Var 2 Economic	Dependent Var 1 Math Scores	Dependent Var 2 Satisfaction	Dependent Var 3 Teacher Ratings
Public	Wealthy	29.50	29.50	7.50
Public	Wealthy	32.10	32.10	6.30
Public	Middle	40.70	40.70	4.20
Public	Middle	29.50	29.50	7.50
Public	Poor	32.10	32.10	6.30
Public	Poor	40.70	40.70	4.20
Private	Wealthy	20.40	20.40	3.00
Private	Wealthy	23.90	23.90	1.10
Private	Middle	29.10	29.10	5.00
Private	Middle	25.90	25.90	2.90
Private	Poor	15.90	15.90	1.20
Private	Poor	36.10	36.10	4.10
Home School	Wealthy	39.00	39.00	3.10
Home School	Wealthy	54.20	54.20	4.00
Home School	Middle	32.10	32.10	5.70
Home School	Middle	39.00	39.00	3.10
Home School	Poor	54.20	54.20	4.00
Home School	Poor	32.10	32.10	5.70

* Multiple Dependent Variables = The numerical values in the table include test scores, student satisfaction survey scores, and teacher ratings
* Two Independent Variable = Type of school vs. Economic status of the school district

MANOVA

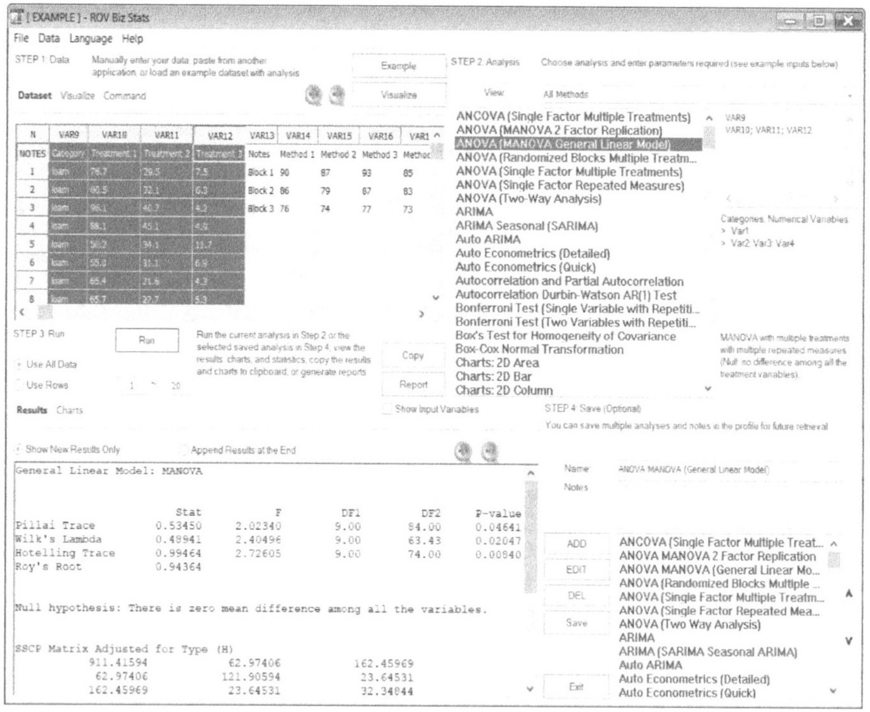

Between Subjects Effects Test

	Sum of Squares	DF	Mean Square	F Stat	P-Value
Variable A on Treatment 1	0.8313	2	0.4157	8.0235	0.0032
Variable A on Treatment 2	1.6406	2	0.8203	7.6865	0.0039
Variable A on Treatment 3	0.6323	2	0.3162	0.2977	0.7461
Variable B on Treatment 1	1.4715	2	0.7357	14.2013	0.0002
Variable B on Treatment 2	0.0287	2	0.0144	0.1346	0.8749
Variable B on Treatment 3	0.6737	2	0.3368	0.3172	0.7322
Interactions AB on Treatment 1	2.6117	4	0.6529	12.6030	0.0000
Interactions AB on Treatment 2	0.6232	4	0.1558	1.4599	0.2556
Interactions AB on Treatment 3	1.8303	4	0.4576	0.4308	0.7845
Errors on Treatment 1	0.9325	18	0.0518		
Errors on Treatment 2	1.9209	18	0.1067		
Errors on Treatment 3	19.1167	18	1.0620		

Multivariate Tests

VAR A	Stat	DF1	DF2	F Stat	P-Value
Pillai's Trace	0.6935	6.0000	34.0000	3.0082	0.0182
Wilk's Lambda	0.3302	6.0000	32.0000	3.9486	0.0046
Hotelling's Trace	1.9571	6.0000	30.0000	4.8926	0.0014
Roy's Largest Root	1.9197				

VAR B	Stat	DF1	DF2	F Stat	P-Value
Pillai's Trace	0.6541	6.0000	34.0000	2.7542	0.0273
Wilk's Lambda	0.3594	6.0000	32.0000	3.5631	0.0081
Hotelling's Trace	1.7448	6.0000	30.0000	4.3621	0.0028
Roy's Largest Root	1.7230				

VAR AB	Stat	DF1	DF2	F Stat	P-Value
Pillai's Trace	0.7855	12.0000	54.0000	1.5962	0.1205
Wilk's Lambda	0.2233	12.0000	42.6235	2.7076	0.0083
Hotelling's Trace	3.4382	12.0000	44.0000	4.2022	0.0002
Roy's Largest Root	3.4266				

4. Nonparametric Analysis & Data Reliability, Validity, and Efficacy

Core Theme

This module covers distribution-free tests: chi-square (goodness-of-fit, independence, homogeneity), runs tests, Wilcoxon signed-rank (one- and two-variable), Kruskal–Wallis, and Friedman's test. Normality testing (Lilliefors, Shapiro–Wilk, D'Agostino–Pearson, Q-Q plots) and Box–Cox transformations are included. The second half addresses data quality rigorously — inter-rater reliability (Cohen's Kappa, ICC, Kendall's W), internal consistency (Cronbach's Alpha, Guttman's Lambda), diversity indices (Shannon, Simpson), internal/external validity, predictive accuracy metrics (AIC, BIC), outlier detection (Grubbs, Mahalanobis), discriminant analysis, and PCA.

Nonparametric Tests

Some methods and tests are considered nonparametric. Compared to parametric tests (e.g., t-test, z-test, F-test, ANOVA), nonparametric tests have the following advantages and a single disadvantage:

- Fewer assumptions are required for the underlying data's population. Specifically, a nonparametric test does not require that the population be normally distributed. In fact, it does not require any specific distributional assumption and is therefore sometimes called distribution-free or nonparametric (i.e., tests without specific population parameters).
- Smaller sample sizes can be used.
- Data with nominal and ordinal scales can be tested.
- Nonparametric methods have lower power and use the data less efficiently. Therefore, if assumptions have been met, it is better to use parametric tests whenever possible.

Some of the most common nonparametric tests are the Runs test for randomness, the Wilcoxon test, the Lilliefors test, the Kruskal–Wallis test, and Friedman's test.

Nonparametric Chi-Square Test

The chi-square distribution is used to model three different types of tests:

1. Goodness-of-Fit Test

    H_0: The sample is from the specified distribution.

    H_a: The sample is not from the specified distribution.

2. Test of Independence

    H_0: The variables are independent of each other.

    H_a: The variables are not independent of each other.

3. Comparing Proportions of Multiple Independent Samples

    H_0: $\pi_1 = \pi_2 = ... = \pi_k$ for the $j = 1$ to k populations.

    H_a: At least one of the π_j values differs from the others.

Nonparametric Runs Test for Data Randomness

The Runs test evaluates the randomness of a series of observations by analyzing the number of runs it contains. A run is a consecutive appearance of one or more observations that are similar. The null hypothesis is that the data sequence is random, versus the alternative that it is not.

H_0: The sequence is random
H_a: The sequence is not random

For nominal data with two outcomes (e.g., heads and tails in a coin toss, arrival of male and female customers in a bank), the series of events is captured, and the number of runs is computed. For instance, in the series F M M M F F M, there would be a total of 4 runs, or in the series H H T T T T H H, there would be 3 runs. For ordinal, interval, and ratio data, the median is first calculated, and the runs are converted into + and – signs above and below the median. Then, a z-statistic is computed based on the number of runs (*T*) observed, and the total number of observations in each of the types (n_1 and n_2):

$$z = \frac{T - \left(\frac{2n_1n_2}{n_1 + n_2} + 1\right)}{\sqrt{\frac{2n_1n_2(2n_1n_2 - n_1 - n_2)}{(n_1 + n_2)^2(n_1 + n_2 - 1)}}}$$

The standard normal p-value is then calculated, if sample sizes $n_1 \geq 10$ and $n_2 \geq 10$.

Nonparametric Runs Test for Data Randomness

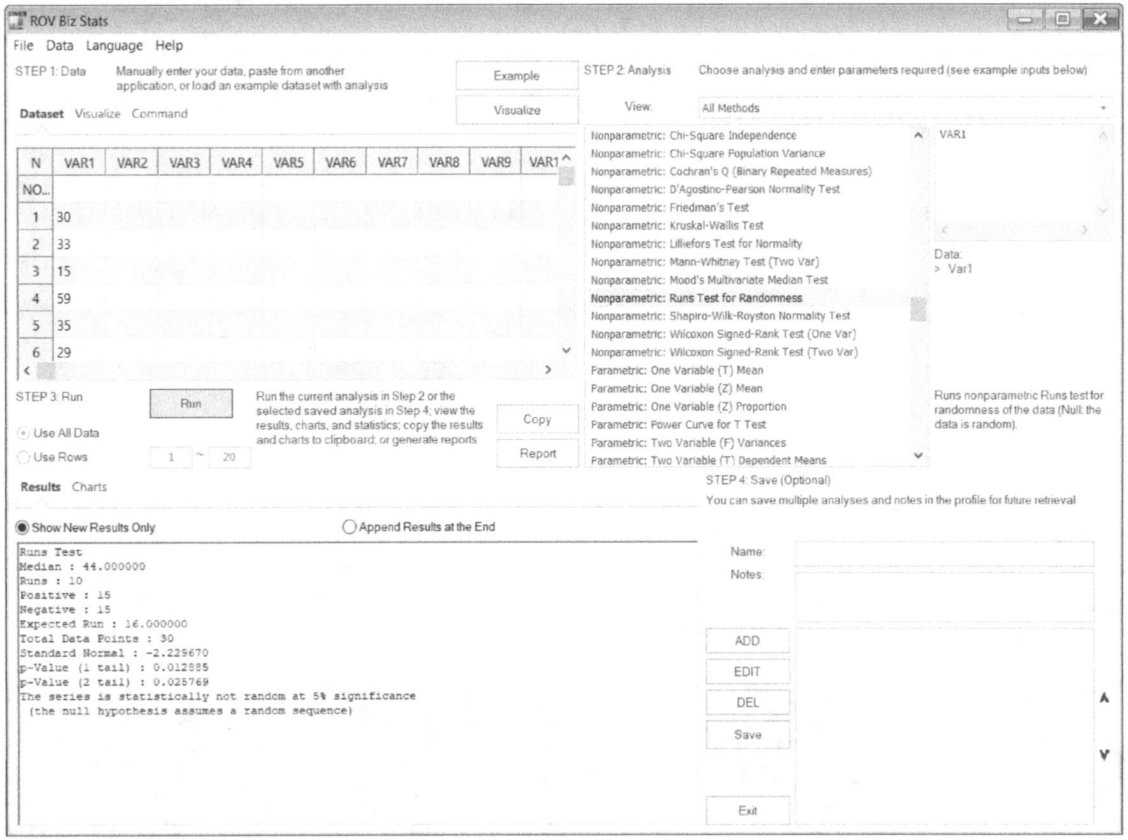

Nonparametric Wilcoxon Signed-Rank Test (One Variable)

Nonparametric techniques make no assumptions about the specific shape or distribution of the population from which the sample is drawn. This lack of assumptions is different from the other hypothesis tests, such as ANOVA or t-tests (parametric tests), where the sample is assumed to be drawn from a population that is normally or approximately normally distributed. If normality is assumed, the test's power is higher due to this assumption. However, if flexibility on distributional requirements is needed, then nonparametric techniques are superior.

The nonparametric Wilcoxon Signed-Rank Test (WSRT) for a single variable assesses whether a sample dataset could have been randomly drawn from a population whose median is hypothesized. The corresponding parametric test is the one-sample t-test, which should be used if the underlying population is assumed to be normal, providing higher power. In this single variable test, the following hypotheses are tested:

H_0: Population Median = m

H_a: Population Median ≠ m

Of course, the null hypothesis can take the standard equality signs of =, ≥, or ≤, and m can be any hypothesized value to test. The alternate hypothesis will have the appropriate complementary sign of ≠, <, or >.

The WSRT uses a W-statistic, and its corresponding critical values are usually provided in a statistics table (these will be automatically calculated in a statistics software package such as ROV BizStats). The first step in calculating W is to take the difference $d_i = x_i - m$. All $d = 0$ values are ignored. Then, these $|d_i|$ values are ranked from smallest (rank of 1) to largest. All tied ranks are assigned their average values. For all ranks that have a positive value or where $x_i > m$, we sum all these positive ranks to obtain the W, that is, $W = \Sigma (R+)$.

The next slide shows an example of the WSRT for a single variable. The calculated W statistic is 13, and the two-tailed critical limits at a 0.05 significance are 9 and 46. The W falls within these critical limits, which means we fail to reject the null hypothesis and conclude that the population median is statistically not different than the hypothesized median (in this example, it is set as 40 in ROV BizStats, as seen in the next slide).

Nonparametric Wilcoxon Signed-Rank Test (One Variable)

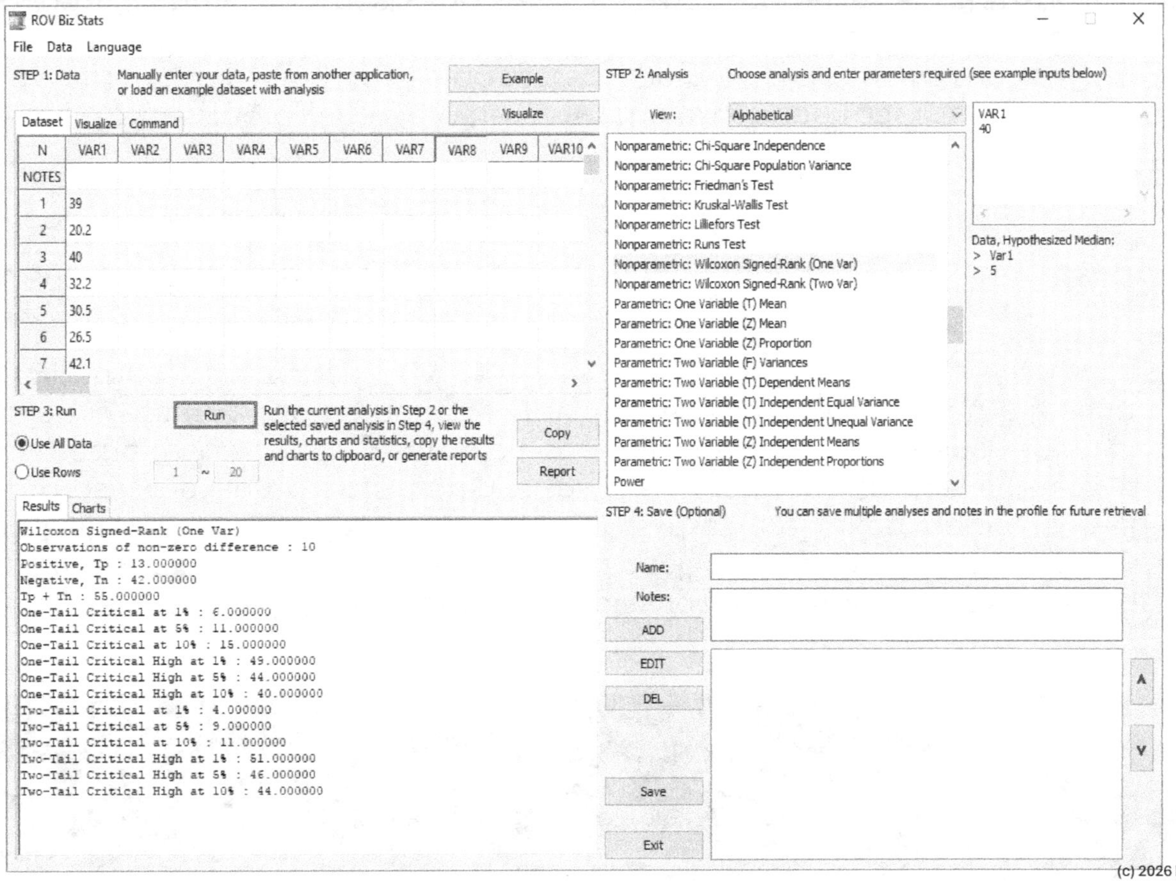

Nonparametric Wilcoxon Signed-Rank Test (Two Variable)

In contrast, the Nonparametric WSRT for Paired Variables looks at whether the *medians* of the differences between the two paired variables are equal. This test is specifically formulated for testing the same or similar samples before and after an event (e.g., measurements that are taken before a medical treatment are compared against those measurements taken after the treatment to see if there is a difference). The corresponding parametric test is the two-sample t-test with dependent means, which should be used if the underlying population is assumed to be normal, providing a higher power on the test. In this paired variable test, the following hypotheses are tested:

H_0: Population Median of Differences $m_d = 0$

H_a: Population Median of Differences $m_d \neq 0$

The approach is similar to the single variable WSRT with the exception that the difference d is computed as $d_i = x_i - y_i$ where x and y are the two variables being tested. The next slide shows the WSRT for two variables. The calculated W is 44.5 with a hypothesized difference of 0, and the 0.05 significance. The conclusion is we cannot reject the two-tailed null hypothesis and state that the differences are statistically close enough to 0.

Nonparametric Wilcoxon Signed-Rank Test (Two Variable)

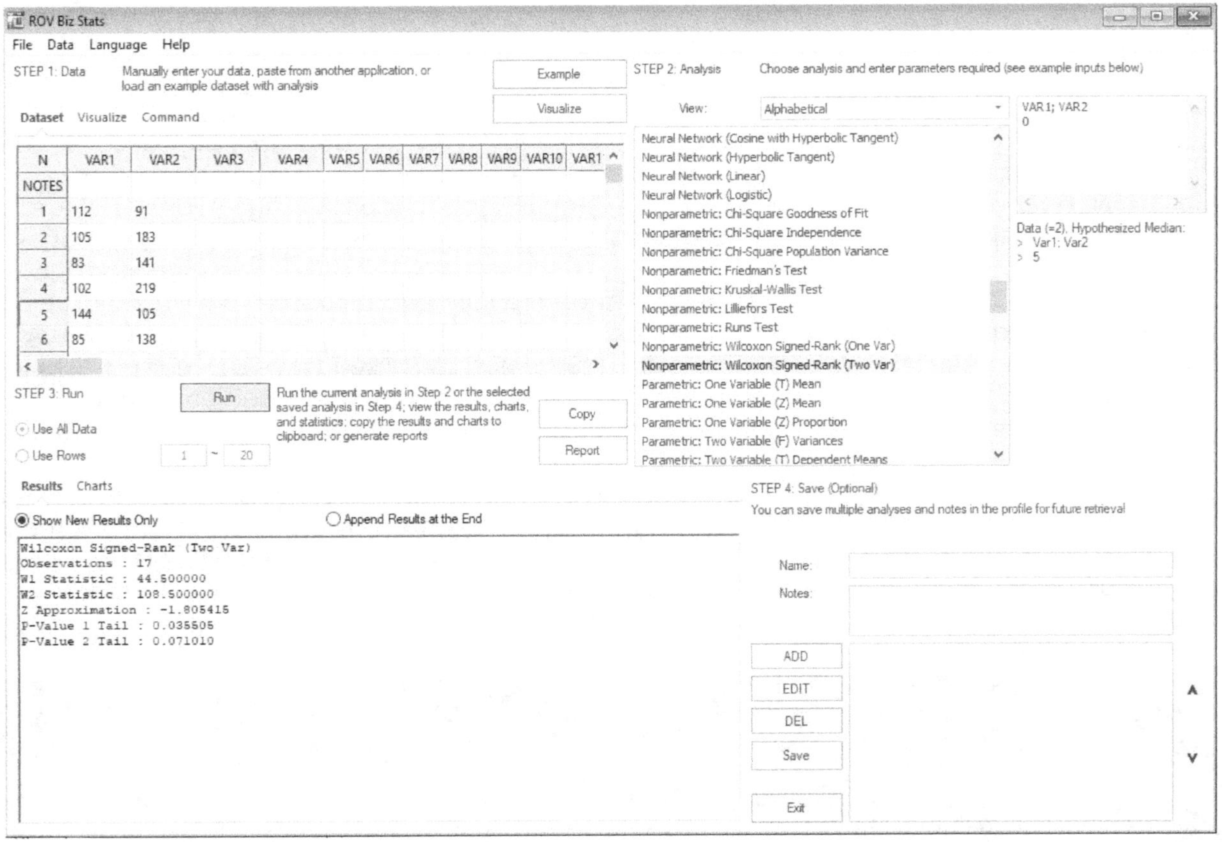

Parametric and Nonparametric Normality Tests

- **Distributional Fitting.** Which distribution does an analyst or engineer use for an input variable in a model? What are the relevant distributional parameters? The null hypothesis tested is that the fitted distribution is the same as the distribution of the population from which the sample data are drawn.
    - **Akaike Information Criterion (AIC).** Rewards goodness-of-fit but also includes a penalty that is an increasing function of the number of estimated parameters (although AIC penalizes the number of parameters less strongly than other methods).
    - **Anderson–Darling (AD).** When applied to testing whether a normal distribution adequately describes a dataset, it is one of the most powerful statistical tools for detecting departures from normality and testing the normality of the tails. However, in non-normal distributions, this test has lower power than others.
    - **Kolmogorov–Smirnov (KS).** A nonparametric test for the equality of continuous probability distributions that can be used to compare a sample with a reference probability distribution, making it useful for testing abnormally shaped distributions and non-normal distributions.
    - **Kuiper's Statistic (K).** Related to the KS test, Kuiper's Statistic is as sensitive in the tails as at the median and is invariant under cyclic transformations of the independent variable. This test is invaluable for detecting cyclic variations over time. In comparison, the AD provides equal sensitivity at the tails as the median, but it does not provide the cyclic invariance.
    - **Schwarz/Bayes Information Criterion (SC/BIC).** The SC/BIC introduces a penalty term for the number of parameters in the model, with a larger penalty than AIC.
    - **Discrete (Chi-Square).** The Chi-Square test is used to assess the fit of a distribution to discrete data.

- **Box–Cox Normal Transformation.** Although this is not strictly a test of normality, it takes your existing dataset and transforms it into a normally distributed dataset. The original dataset is tested for normality using the Shapiro–Wilk test (H0: the data is normal), then transformed using the Box–Cox method, either with your custom Lambda parameter or with an internally optimized Lambda. The transformed data is tested again for normality using the Shapiro–Wilk.

- **Grubbs Test for Outliers.** The Grubbs test is used to identify potential outliers and to test the null hypothesis that all the values are from the same normal population with no outliers.

Parametric and Nonparametric Normality Tests

- **Nonparametric Chi-Square Goodness-of-Fit for Normality (Grouped Data).** The chi-square test for goodness of fit is used to examine whether a sample dataset could have been drawn from a population with a specified probability distribution. The probability distribution tested here is the normal distribution. The null hypothesis tested is such that the sample is randomly drawn from the normal distribution.

- **Nonparametric Lilliefors Test for Normality.** The Lilliefors test evaluates the null hypothesis that the data sample was drawn from a normally distributed population, versus the alternative that it is not normally distributed. If the calculated p-value is less than or equal to the alpha significance value, then reject the null hypothesis and accept the alternative hypothesis. Otherwise, if the p-value is higher than the alpha significance value, do not reject the null hypothesis. This test relies on two cumulative frequencies: one derived from the sample dataset and one from a theoretical distribution based on the sample mean and standard deviation. An alternative to this test is the chi-square normality test. The chi-square test requires more data points than the Lilliefors test.

- **Nonparametric: D'Agostino–Pearson Normality Test.** The D'Agostino–Pearson test is used to assess, nonparametrically, whether a dataset is approximately normal. This tests the null hypothesis that the data is normally distributed.

- **Nonparametric: Shapiro–Wilk–Royston Normality Test.** The Shapiro–Wilk test for normality uses the Royston algorithm to test the null hypothesis that the data is normally distributed.

- **Q-Q Normal Chart.** The Quantile-Quantile chart is a normal probability plot, a graphical method for comparing a probability distribution with the normal distribution by plotting its quantiles against those of the normal distribution. It only provides a visual inspection of the dataset's near-normality.

- **Skew and Kurtosis: Shapiro–Wilk and D'Agostino–Pearson.** You can run the Skewness and Kurtosis tests to see whether the data have both statistics equal to zero. A normal distribution has skew and kurtosis equal to zero. The D'Agostino–Pearson test assesses whether the skewness and kurtosis of the data are simultaneously statistically equal to zero. The null hypothesis is that the data have zero skewness and zero kurtosis, thereby approximating normality.

Nonparametric Lilliefors, Q-Q Chart, D'Agostino–Pearson, and Shapiro–Wilk–Royston Tests

The Lilliefors test evaluates the null hypothesis that the data sample was drawn from a normally distributed population, versus the alternative that it is not normally distributed. This test relies on two cumulative frequencies: one derived from the sample dataset and one from a theoretical distribution based on the sample mean and standard deviation. An alternative to this test is the chi-square normality test. The chi-square test requires more data points than the Lilliefors test.

H_0: The sample is from a Normal Distribution

H_a: The sample is not from a Normal Distribution

In this test, the sample dataset is first sorted from smallest to largest. Its observed (*O*) cumulative frequency is calculated, and a corresponding cumulative distribution function (*CDF*) of the normal distribution is computed based on the observed dataset's mean and standard deviation. The differences *D* between *O* and *CDF* are calculated, and the *D* statistic is computed as $D = max\,|O_i - CDF_i|$. An example Lilliefors test administered shows a computed *D* of 0.2782, which is less than the α α = 5% significance level threshold of 0.3370, so we are unable to reject the null hypothesis and conclude that the small sample size is normally distributed. Note that nonparametric methods have less power but are applicable in smaller sample sizes, as illustrated in this example. However, if a larger dataset is available, it is always better to perform parametric distributional fitting such as those described previously (Kolmogorov–Smirnov, Akaike, Bayes Criterion, Kuiper, and so forth). There are other nonparametric approaches in BizStats used for normality tests, which are slightly more powerful than the Lilliefors test:

- **Nonparametric D'Agostino–Pearson Normality Test**. The D'Agostino–Pearson test is used to nonparametrically assess whether a dataset is approximately normal. This tests the null hypothesis that the data is normally distributed.
- **Nonparametric Shapiro–Wilk–Royston Normality Test**. The Shapiro–Wilk test for normality uses the Royston algorithm to test the null hypothesis that the data is normally distributed. This test does require more data points to compute than the Lilliefors and D'Agostino–Pearson tests. For example, the small dataset in Figure 9.35 will be insufficient to run this test.
- **Q-Q Normal Chart**. This Quantile-Quantile chart is a normal probability plot, a graphical method for comparing a probability distribution with the normal distribution by plotting its quantiles against those of the normal distribution. It only provides a visual inspection of the dataset's near-normality. However, if a larger dataset is available, it is always better to perform parametric distributional fitting such as those described previously (Kolmogorov–Smirnov, Akaike, Bayes Criterion, Kuiper, and so forth).

Nonparametric Lilliefors, Q-Q Chart, D'Agostino–Pearson, and Shapiro–Wilk–Royston Tests

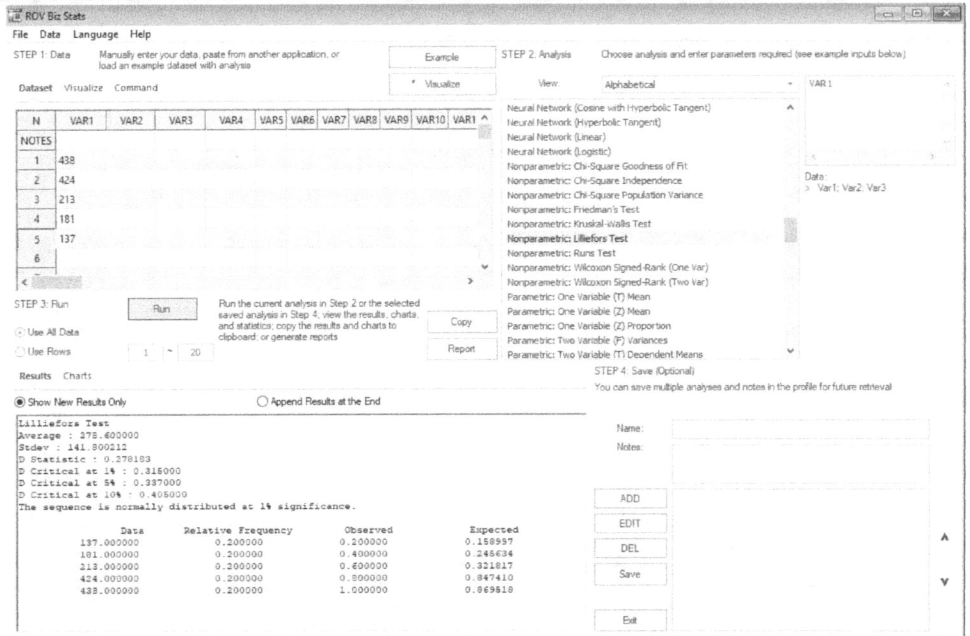

Model Inputs:
VAR1

Nonparametric d'Agostino-Pearson Test for Normality

DAP Stat: 2.554537
DAP P-Value: 0.278798

Null hypothesis: The data is normally distributed

Model Inputs:
VAR1

Lilliefors Test

Average: 278.600000
Stdev: 141.800212
D Statistic: 0.278183
D Critical at 1%: 0.315000
D Critical at 5%: 0.337000
D Critical at 10%: 0.405000

The data is statistically normal at the 1%, 5% and 10% significance level (null hypothesis tested is that the data is normally distributed).

Data	Relative Frequency	Observed	Expected
137.000000	0.200000	0.200000	0.158997
181.000000	0.200000	0.400000	0.245634
213.000000	0.200000	0.600000	0.321817
424.000000	0.200000	0.800000	0.847410
438.000000	0.200000	1.000000	0.869518

Box–Cox Transformation

In our focus on testing data normality so that most parametric tests can be run, we sometimes get ahead of ourselves and modify the data to normalize it. For instance, the dataset 4.5, 1.8, 9.3, 6.1, 8.2, 13.9, 23.5, 3.2, 56.8, 80.7 is subjected to BizStats' Box–Cox Transformation, yielding 0.55492, 1.03910, 1.30106, 1.52037, 1.72135, 1.80337, 2.05196, 2.34839, 2.78224, 2.93490. In fact, the before- and after-transformation results look rather astounding. The original data reject normality (p-value = 0.0017), whereas the post-transformation data show a p-value of 0.9691 and a very high normality fit. However, the data completely loses its efficacy and meaning with such a drastic change. Nonetheless, there are applications in Six Sigma, such as computing process capability, that require this transformation to obtain valid estimates.

```
Original Data
Shapiro-Wilk: 0.723918
P-value: 0.001719
Null Hypothesis: Normality
R-Squared to Normal Fit: 0.613784

Box-Cox Transformed Data
Shapiro-Wilk: 0.980764
P-value: 0.969126
Null Hypothesis: Normality
R-Squared to Normal Fit: 0.987518
```

Nonparametric Kruskal–Wallis Test

The Kruskal–Wallis test is the extension of the Wilcoxon Signed-Rank test by comparing more than two independent samples. The corresponding parametric test is the One-Way ANOVA, but unlike the ANOVA, the Kruskal–Wallis does not require that the dataset be randomly sampled from normally distributed populations with equal variances. The Kruskal–Wallis test is a two-tailed hypothesis test for treatment groups. Similar to the ANOVA method, the Kruskal–Wallis test tests the following hypotheses:

H_0: $m_1 = m_2 = \ldots = m_K$ for $i = 1$ to k (population medians are identical)

H_a: At least one of the medians m differs from the others

The method starts off with k variables to be tested. For each variable, the data are ranked from smallest to largest, with the smallest value receiving rank 1, and all tied ranks are assigned the average rank. Then, sum all the ranks for each variable, yielding a list of summed ranks $\Sigma(R_1)$, $\Sigma(R_2)$, ..., $\Sigma(R_K)$.

$$H = \frac{12}{N(N+1)}\left[\frac{(\Sigma R_1)^2}{n_1} + \frac{(\Sigma R_2)^2}{n_2} + \ldots + \frac{(\Sigma R_K)^2}{n_K}\right] - 3(N+1)$$

Nonparametric Kruskal–Wallis Test

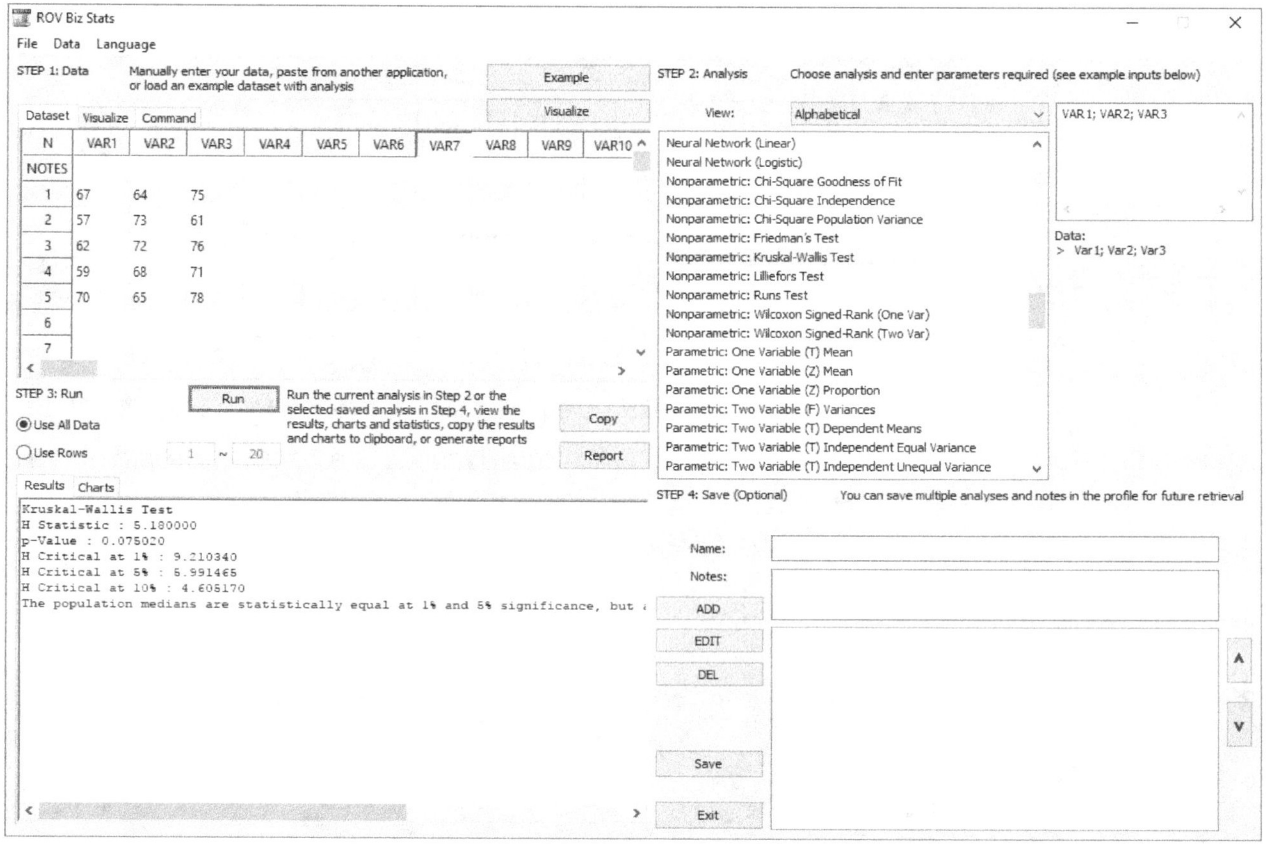

Nonparametric Friedman's Test

The Friedman test is the extension of the Wilcoxon Signed-Rank test for paired samples. The corresponding parametric test is the Randomized Block Multiple Treatment ANOVA, but unlike the ANOVA, the Friedman test does not require that the dataset be randomly sampled from normally distributed populations with equal variances. The Friedman test is a two-tailed hypothesis test in which the null hypothesis states that the population medians of the treatments are statistically identical; that is, there is no effect among the treatment groups. Similar to the ANOVA method, the Friedman test evaluates the following hypotheses:

H_0: $m_1 = m_2 = \ldots = m_K$ for $i = 1$ to k (population medians are identical)

H_a: At least one of the medians m differs from the others

Similar to the ANOVA with Blocking Variable, the data needs to be set up in a $B \times T$ fashion, where the blocking variables (B) are listed in rows, and the treatments (T) are in columns as different variables. The next slide illustrates an example with the correct data setup. For example, assume a company is testing a new liquid stain remover and has developed four distinct formulations. These formulations are listed as the treatments, T, as different variables (columns). For each formulation or treatment, the stain remover was applied to various stain types (the blocking variable, B). In the example, six types of stains were tested (e.g., chocolate, red wine, coffee, ink, paint, crayon), and they are listed in the rows. Each row represents one specific type of stain (e.g., row 1 may represent red wine). The numerical data in the grid range from 1 to 10, with higher values indicating that the stain was completely removed. The computed F_r statistic is 8.45, which is statistically significant at the 5% alpha level, so we can reject the null hypothesis and conclude that at least one of the formulations is different than the rest.

Nonparametric Friedman's Test

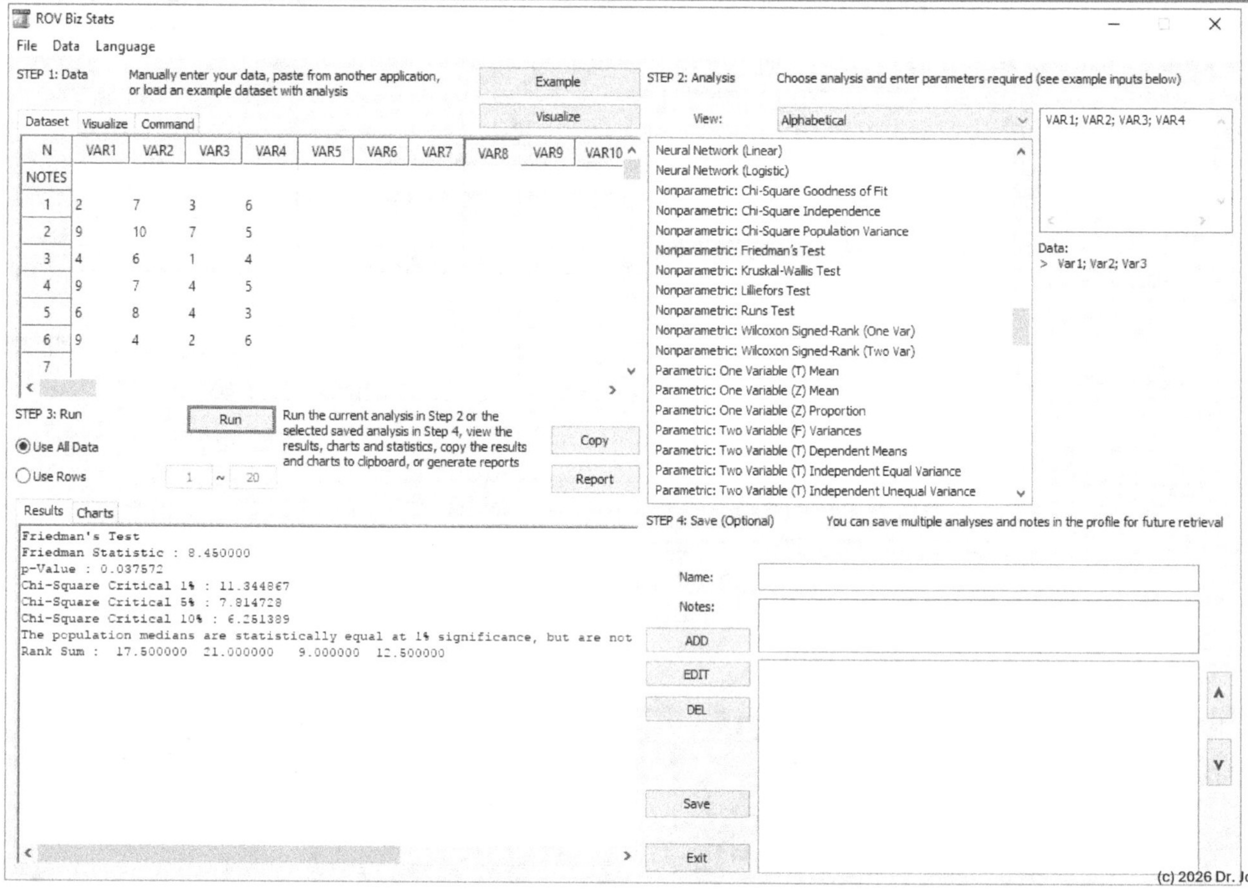

Consistency, Reliability, Validity

Accuracy

In Data: Accuracy refers to how close your measurements or predictions are to the true values. In Baking: Accuracy is like making sure you measure your ingredients exactly so your cake turns out as intended.

Bias

In Data: Bias is a systematic error that skews your results in a particular direction. In Baking: Bias is like always using the same brand of flour that might be a bit heavier, so your cake always comes out denser.

Consistency

In Data: Consistency means that results or data agree with each other over time, across sources, or across different parts of the dataset because the same rules and procedures are applied in the same way. In Baking: Consistency is like always following the same recipe and steps—same oven temperature, same mixing order, same baking time—so everything in the process is done the same way each time, helping your cakes turn out uniform from one batch to the next. Layers have the same level of softness and consistency.

Precision

In Data: Precision refers to how consistent your measurements are when repeated under the same conditions. In Baking: Precision is like always measuring the exact same amount of sugar every time you bake, so your cake is consistently sweet.

Reliability

In Data: Reliability means you get the same results consistently when you repeat the measurement. In Baking: It's like baking the same cake multiple times and having it turn out just as delicious each time.

Replicability

In Data: Replicability is when other researchers can use your methods and data and get the same results. In Baking: It's like giving your recipe to a friend and having them bake the same cake successfully in their own kitchen.

Validity

In Data: Validity is about how well your method measures what it's supposed to measure. In Baking: Validity is like making sure your recipe actually produces the type of cake you promised—like a fluffy sponge if that's what you claimed.

Threats to Validity

Internal Validity asks if the treatments in an experiment make a difference in the specific boundary conditions of the research. For example, if a new teaching method helps improve students' test scores.

External Validity, in contrast, looks to inductively identify how the results and conclusions can be generalized and under what boundary conditions, assumptions, settings, and treatments.

Examples:

Attrition Bias	Confirmation Bias	Confounding Variables Bias
Cultural Bias	Exclusion Bias	Friendliness Bias
Habituation Bias	Historical Bias	Inclusion Bias
Instrumentation Bias	Maturation Bias	Measurement Bias
Mortality Bias	Nonresponse Bias	Observer Bias
Outlier Bias	Over- and Underfitting Bias	Question Order Bias
Prejudice Bias	Recall Bias	Reporting Bias
Researcher Bias	Respondent Bias	Response Bias
Sampling Bias	Selection-Maturation Bias	Self-Selection Bias
Social Desirability Bias	Sponsor Bias	Survivorship Bias
Testing Bias		

Inter-rater Reliability, Intra-rater Reliability, Consistency, Credibility, Diversity, Internal Validity, External Validity, and Predictability

The concept of data reliability can be complicated and can take many forms. In general, reliability can be defined as the accuracy of the data and the consistency of the collected data. In other words, the extent to which an experiment, test, or measuring procedure yields the same results on repeated trials is the measure of its reliability. For example, if one were to take a tape measure to find the length of a specific table, measuring it repeatedly should yield the same result. If this is the case, then the data obtained are reliable.

Reliability can also be characterized as inter-rater (different people using the same measuring tape to measure the same table multiple times) vs. intra-rater (the same person measuring the same table several times using the same measuring tape). There are statistical tests that can be run to identify the data's reliability and consistency.

Inter-Rater Reliability with Pairwise Cohen's Kappa

Cohen's Kappa test can be used to assess the reliability of two raters. The null hypothesis tested is that both sets of judgments agree and are consistent. In the following table, we see 4 example cases. In each situation, there are two judges or raters.

CASE A	Judge 2 Psychotic (16)	Judge 2 Borderline (23)	Judge 2 Neither (11)
Judge 1 Psychotic (15)	10	4	1
Judge 1 Borderline (24)	6	16	2
Judge 1 Neither (11)	0	3	8

CASE B	Judge 2 Psychotic (600)	Judge 2 Borderline (600)	Judge 2 Neither (600)
Judge 1 Psychotic (600)	200	200	200
Judge 1 Borderline (600)	200	200	200
Judge 1 Neither (600)	200	200	200

CASE C	Judge 2 Psychotic (100)	Judge 2 Borderline (100)	Judge 2 Neither (100)
Judge 1 Psychotic (100)	100	0	0
Judge 1 Borderline (100)	0	100	0
Judge 1 Neither (100)	0	0	100

CASE D	Judge 2 Psychotic (135)	Judge 2 Borderline (99)	Judge 2 Neither (114)
Judge 1 Psychotic (124)	0	55	69
Judge 1 Borderline (95)	50	0	45
Judge 1 Neither (129)	85	44	0

In Case A, there are 50 patients, and the first rater (physician or healthcare worker) judges 15 of them as being psychotic, 24 borderline, and 11 neither. In comparison, the second rater or judge identifies 16, 23, and 11 patients in these categories. Patients who fall into the same judgment categories are shown in the grid. Both judges agree that 10 are psychotic, 16 are borderline, and 8 are neither, with a total of 34 findings in agreement out of 50 cases (this can be read off the diagonal in the data grid). The results from BizStats indicate that Cohen's Kappa = 0.4959 or 49% agreement. In Case B, we see that the data grid is evenly distributed, with 200 patients in each block, and the computed Cohen's Kappa = 0.0000, indicating absolutely no consistency or reliability between these two raters. Case C, as you would imagine, returns Cohen's Kappa = 1.0000. Finally, in Case D, where reliability is actually not just zero, but there is no value between the corresponding pairs, we obtain a Cohen's Kappa = –0.50902. Clearly, a high positive Cohen's Kappa measure is desirable for inter-rater reliability.

Internal Consistency and Reliability with Cronbach's Alpha for Binary Data

When there are more than two raters or judges, we can use Cronbach's alpha to assess internal consistency and reliability. The null hypothesis for Cronbach's Alpha is that there is zero alpha reliability, and, therefore, there is no internal consistency among the different raters. We see in Case E that there are 12 respondents to a survey comprising 11 different questions. Note that to run Cronbach's Alpha test, the data obtained must be binary. If you look at the data carefully by *row*, we see that respondents such as Albert and Bob tend to respond with 1 regardless of the question, whereas Kim and Larry might do the opposite, with a 0 response. One might even think that some respondents are too lazy to actually answer the questions and will simply fill in the blanks with similar responses throughout. In fact, the calculated Cronbach's Alpha p-value = 0.6659 in BizStats, which means we cannot reject the null hypothesis and conclude that in Case E, there is no internal consistency among the different respondents. The survey data is therefore inconsistent and unreliable.

Conversely, in Case F, if you look down each column, there appears to be consistency among all respondents. For instance, in Questions 6 and 7 (Q6 and Q7), almost all respondents agreed it would be 0, whereas in Q5, all 1s were in the column. Q2 and Q3 show that the respondents are equally spread between 0s and 1s. In this case, F, the computed Cronbach's Alpha p-value = 0.002723 in BizStats, indicating that the null hypothesis can be rejected, and we conclude that there is indeed statistically significant alpha-level reliability among the respondents.

CASE E	Q1	Q2	Q3	Q4	Q5	Q6	Q7	Q8	Q9	Q10	Q11
Albert	1	1	1	1	1	1	1	1	1	1	1
Bob	1	1	1	1	1	1	1	1	0	1	0
Cathy	1	0	1	1	1	1	1	1	1	0	0
Derek	1	1	1	0	1	1	0	1	1	0	0
Eric	1	1	1	1	1	0	0	0	1	0	0
Flo	0	1	1	0	1	1	1	1	0	0	0
Gale	1	1	1	1	0	0	1	0	0	0	0
Henry	1	1	1	1	1	0	0	0	0	0	0
Indi	0	1	0	1	1	0	0	0	0	1	0
Jack	1	0	0	1	0	1	0	0	0	0	0
Kim	1	1	1	0	0	0	0	0	0	0	0
Larry	1	0	0	1	0	0	0	0	0	0	0

CASE F	Q1	Q2	Q3	Q4	Q5	Q6	Q7
Andy	1	1	0	1	1	0	1
Becky	0	1	0	1	1	0	0
Colin	1	1	0	0	1	0	0
Dave	0	1	0	0	1	0	0
Even	1	1	0	1	1	0	0
Flynn	0	1	0	1	1	0	0
George	1	0	1	0	1	0	0
Hope	0	0	1	0	1	0	0
Isaac	1	0	1	1	1	0	0
John	0	0	1	1	1	0	0
Kern	1	0	1	0	1	0	0
Lisa	0	0	1	0	1	0	0

Internal Consistency and Reliability with Guttman's Lambda

When the responses are not binary but categorical, we can use the Guttman's Lambda test for inter-rater consistency and reliability. A quick scan of Case G indicates a familiar problem, where the vertical entries are almost identical in each column, but the columns themselves are not consistent across the different raters. For instance, Alex might always select a low score regardless of the question or issue posed, whereas Cory is an optimist and consistently provides a high score. The raters themselves might be consistent with themselves, but they are certainly not consistent with other raters. The computed Guttman's Lambda = 0.07563, with a corresponding Spearman–Brown Correlation Correction Factor = 0.07782 using BizStats (note that if multiple correlation correction factors are presented, we usually look at the more conservative measure). Low correlation corrections and low lambda scores mean there is low reliability and low consistency among the raters. Note that the data matrix is inverted in this test, as opposed to the Cronback's test, where we show the questions as rows and respondents or judges/raters as columns. In comparison, for Case H, Guttman's Lambda = 0.99004 and the conservative Spearman-Brown Correlation Correction Factor = 0.9909. This indicates a very high consistency and reliability of the responses. For instance, Question A received a very low score regardless of the rater, whereas Question C scores high consistently. Looking across the rows shows consistency and reliability in the data.

Case G	Alex	Ben	Cory	Dick	Emma	Flo	Ginny	Hale	Izzy	John
Question A	1	4	8	2	7	5	6	2	5	3
Question B	1	4	8	2	7	1	6	3	5	3
Question C	1	4	8	2	7	2	6	2	5	3
Question D	1	5	8	2	7	2	6	3	5	3
Question E	1	4	8	3	7	2	5	2	5	3
Question F	1	4	9	2	8	2	6	3	6	3
Question G	1	4	8	2	8	2	6	2	5	3
Question H	1	5	8	2	7	2	6	3	5	3
Question I	2	4	8	2	7	2	5	2	5	3
Question J	1	4	9	3	7	2	6	3	5	3
Question K	1	4	8	2	7	2	6	2	6	3
Question L	1	4	8	2	7	1	6	3	5	4
Question M	1	4	8	2	7	1	6	2	5	3
Question N	2	4	8	2	7	2	6	3	5	3
Question O	1	4	8	2	7	1	6	2	5	3

Case H	Arlo	Bex	Cal	Dale	Elsa	Fox	Guy	Ham	Illy	Jay
Question A	1	1	1	1	1	1	1	1	2	1
Question B	4	4	4	5	4	4	4	5	4	4
Question C	8	8	8	8	8	9	8	8	8	9
Question D	2	2	2	2	3	2	2	2	2	3
Question E	7	7	7	7	7	8	8	7	7	7
Question F	5	1	2	2	2	2	2	2	2	2
Question G	6	6	6	6	5	6	6	6	5	6
Question H	2	3	2	3	2	3	2	3	2	3
Question I	5	5	5	5	5	6	5	5	5	5
Question J	3	3	3	3	3	3	3	3	3	3

Inter-Rater Reliability using Inter-Class Correlation (ICC)

If we wish to test for both inter- and intra-rater reliability, we can use the Intraclass Correlation Coefficient (ICC). Cases I and J show example data from a double-blind test on 8 wines (the bottles look identical, with labels removed and replaced with generic labels such as Wine 1, Wine 2, and so forth). And suppose 4 sommeliers or expert wine judges were asked to grade the wines on a scale from 1 (low quality) to 10 (high quality).

In Case I, we see that for each wine, all four judges scored it consistently. For example, Wine 1 is by far the worst, whereas wines 7 and 8 are highly rated by all judges. This would indicate a high level of consistency and reliability across rows. The ICC test returns an Interclass Correlation = 0.9841, the row's p-value = 0.0000, and the column's p-value = 0.8538. This means there is a high level of consistency, as measured by the ICC, and we can reject the null hypothesis of having the same values across rows and fail to reject it for the columns. In other words, all the judges tend to be fairly consistent in their tastes (high ICC), possibly because they all have a similar judging or sommelier training. In addition, the wines differ from one another (p-value of 0.0000 for the rows), and, based on the scores we have now concluded are consistent and reliable, we can say that the wines are certainly of varying quality. In contrast, when comparing the columns (i.e., v the judges have similar judgments.

Case J shows a very different situation. We see that Judge 1 is probably a snob, who considers no wine good. Hence, Judge 1 is internally consistent with himself, or has high intra-rater reliability. In contrast, Judge 4 simply loves wine and scores any and all wines highly. Judge 4 is also internally reliable to himself, but not to the other judges. The computed Interclass Correlation = 0.00149 (low inter-rater consistency and low reliability among the judges) with a row p-value of 0.3958 (we cannot reject the null hypothesis and state that the rows, when taken together, are statistically similar to each other, indicating, in this case, that there is high intra-rater reliability) and a column p-value of 0.0000 (we reject the null hypothesis and state that there is a statistically significant difference among the columns or judges, which means that there is no inter-rater consistency and no reliability in the wine scores).

Case I	Judge 1	Judge 2	Judge 3	Judge 4
Wine 1	1	1	1	1
Wine 2	2	3	3	2
Wine 3	3	3	3	3
Wine 4	6	6	6	6
Wine 5	6	5	5	6
Wine 6	2	2	2	2
Wine 7	8	9	9	9
Wine 8	9	9	9	8

Case J	Judge 1	Judge 2	Judge 3	Judge 4
Wine 1	1	3	5	8
Wine 2	2	3	5	9
Wine 3	3	3	6	9
Wine 4	1	2	6	7
Wine 5	1	2	5	9
Wine 6	1	2	5	9
Wine 7	2	3	4	9
Wine 8	3	1	5	8

Kendall's W Measure of Concordance Inter-rater Reliability Test (With or Without Ties)

Another test of inter-rater reliability is Kendall's W, which can be computed with or without ties. A tie means there are multiple data points with the same value; hence, we must split the difference between them. Regardless, the null hypothesis for these tests is that there is zero agreement (W = 0) among all the judges.

Case K returns a calculated Kendall's W = 1.1068, Kendall's R = 1.124646, and p-value = 0.0000. We reject the null hypothesis and conclude that the judges agree. For instance, we see that Issue 1 is critical for all judges, whereas Issues 3, 7, and 8 are rated lower. All ratings are consistent among all the judges.

In Case L, Kendall's W = 0.2261, Kendall's R = 0.0971, and p-value = 0.1352. This indicates that we cannot reject the null hypothesis and conclude that there is no statistical concordance among the different respondents answering the survey questions.

Finally, in Case M, Kendall's W = 0.0028, Kendall's R = -0.1633, and p-value = 0.9999. This certainly indicates extremely low consistency and reliability among the respondents.

Case K	Issue 1	Issue 2	Issue 3	Issue 4	Issue 5	Issue 6	Issue 7	Issue 8
Judge 1	8	8	2	5	3	5	2	1
Judge 2	8	7	2	6	3	5	1	1
Judge 3	8	7	2	5	3	6	2	1
Judge 4	8	7	3	5	2	5	1	2
Judge 5	8	7	2	6	3	5	1	2
Judge 6	8	8	2	5	3	6	1	2
Judge 7	7	7	3	5	2	5	2	1

Case L	Q1	Q2	Q3	Q4	Q1	Q2	Q3	Q4
Person 1	7	8	5	4	1	7	2	1
Person 2	1	7	10	6	2	6	3	1
Person 3	3	1	7	10	3	5	10	1
Person 4	10	3	1	5	4	4	10	2
Person 5	3	2	1	1	5	3	1	4.5
Person 6	2	6	7.5	2.5	6	2	5	2.5
Person 7	6	10	4	8	7	1	6	1

Case M	Issue 1	Issue 2	Issue 3	Issue 4	Issue 5	Issue 6	Issue 7	Issue 8
Judge 1	5	5	5	5	5	5	5	5
Judge 2	8	8	8	8	7	8	7	8
Judge 3	1	1	1	2	2	1	1	1
Judge 4	5	5	5	5	5	5	5	5
Judge 5	6	7	6	7	6	7	6	7
Judge 6	9	9	9	9	9	9	9	9
Judge 7	2	1	2	2	3	2	2	1

Data Diversity with Shannon, Brillouin, and Simpson Diversity and Homogeneity Test

Another issue regarding data reliability and consistency concerns the randomized and stratified sampling performed. For instance, we may achieve a high level of data consistency and reliability, but if the sampled people are from the same group or category, the data may not be entirely reliable. As an example, suppose we wish to survey voter sentiment on a particular issue in a state. If all the voters selected were Democrats or predominantly Republicans, the data might be skewed in one direction. Hence, to assess the diversity of a randomized and stratified sampling group, we can apply the Shannon, Brillouin, and Simpson indices. In Case N, suppose we have five categories of self-described voters (highly conservative, conservative, moderate, liberal, and highly liberal) and the data grid shows the number of people sampled within each category. The following shows the results of the four samples. The higher the diversity index is relative to the maximum index, the higher the level of diversity. Clearly, we see that Scenario 1 has the highest homogeneity score, and the diversity index is closest to the maximum index value. Scenario 2 has a 94.71% homogeneity score, while Scenarios 3 and 4 have the lowest diversity index relative to the maximum value.

Case N	Scenario 1	Scenario 2	Scenario 3	Scenario 4
Category A	5	5	1	11
Category B	5	8	1	11
Category C	5	6	21	1
Category D	5	2	1	1
Category E	5	4	1	1

Sample 1 Results	Shannon	Brillouin	Simpson
Diversity Index	1.6094	0.5918	0.2000
Max Index	1.6094	0.5918	
Homogeneity	1.0000	1.0000	

Sample 2 Results	Shannon	Brillouin	Simpson
Diversity Index	1.5243	0.5587	0.2320
Max Index	1.6094	0.5918	
Homogeneity	0.9471	0.9441	

Sample 3 Results	Shannon	Brillouin	Simpson
Diversity Index	0.6615	0.2193	0.7120
Max Index	1.6094	0.5918	
Homogeneity	0.4110	0.3706	

Sample 4 Results	Shannon	Brillouin	Simpson
Diversity Index	1.1087	0.3995	0.3920
Max Index	1.6094	0.5918	
Homogeneity	0.6889	0.6751	

Internal Validity

A related issue is that of model validity. When we discuss the validity of a model, we typically mean if the specified model does what it is intended to do. In other words, does the model actually model what we are looking to model? To answer the question, we examine a model's internal and external validity.

The internal validity of a model, such as a multivariate regression, assesses whether the independent variables used are statistically significant; that is, whether the model's internal constructs are valid. We typically use the p-value of a regression to measure this internal validity. The null hypothesis is that each independent variable has no effect on the dependent variable. Hence, low p-values at or below the alpha significance level imply statistical significance and indicate that the independent variable impacts the dependent variable. Hence, a model with only significant independent variables is deemed internally valid.

	Coeff	Std. Error	T-stat	**P-value**	Lower 5%	Upper 95%
Intercept	57.95550	108.79014	0.53273	0.59690	-161.29661	277.20762
VAR X1	-0.00354	0.00352	-1.00656	0.31965	-0.01064	0.00355
VAR X2	0.46437	0.25353	1.83159	**0.01379**	-0.04659	0.97533
VAR X3	25.23770	14.11723	1.78772	**0.02071**	-3.21371	53.68911
VAR X4	-0.00856	0.10156	-0.08433	0.93317	-0.21325	0.19612
VAR X5	16.55792	14.79957	1.11881	**0.03929**	-13.26866	46.38449

External Validity

A statistically significant and internally valid model may or may not have practical significance. This is where external validity comes in. While internal validity examines the individual constructs of the model, external validity assesses the model as a whole and measures how well it explains the predicted variable. Typically, external validity is assessed using various error formulae. The typical adjusted coefficient of determination. The R-square is simply the linear correlation (R) between the actual and predicted values, squared. While R has a domain between –1.00 and +1.00, its squared value will always lie between 0.00 and 1.00. Hence, the R-square is a percentage measure that shows how much of the variation in the dependent variable is explained simultaneously by all the independent variables in the model. The higher the R-squared, the higher the model's external validity. However, in multivariate models, adding exogenous variables, whether or not they are internally valid, will usually increase the R-squared value. This is where the adjusted R-squared comes in. The adjusted R-square accounts for the added independent variables and penalizes the R-square for including too many independent variables that do not statistically significantly increase it. This means that with added extraneous variables, the adjusted R-square may actually decline, making it a more conservative and better estimate of a model's external validity.

In addition, along the lines of penalizing added variables, where holding everything else constant, if the predictive powers of two models are identical but one uses fewer predictor variables, then the more parsimonious model wins out. Based on the theory of parsimony and penalization of too many extraneous variables, other measures of external validity were created, such as the Akaike Information Criterion or the Bayes–Schwarz Criterion. These are relative measures of external model errors and are typically used to compare different model specifications and identify the lower-error scores. The following are additional measures of external validity error. Those denoted with an asterisk * are values that we would rather see increase, versus the remaining error measures, where the lower the error, the higher the external validity of the model.

*R-Squared
*Adjusted R-Squared
*Maximum Likelihood
Akaike Information Criterion (AIC)
Bayes and Schwarz Criterion (BSC)
Hannan–Quinn Criterion (HQC)
Mean Absolute Deviation (MAD)
Mean Absolute Percentage Error (MAPE)
Mean Squared Error (MSE)
Median Absolute Error (MdAE)
Median Absolute Percentage Error (MdAPE)
Root Mean Square Log Error (RMSLE)
Root Mean Square Percentage Error Loss (RMSPE)
Root Mean Squared Error (RMSE)
Root Median Square Percentage Error Loss (RMdSPE)
Sum of Squared Errors (SSE)
Symmetrical Mean Absolute Percentage Error (sMAPE)
Theil's U1 Accuracy (U1)
Theil's U2 Quality (U2)

Predictability and Accuracy: Akaike, Bayes, Hannan–Quinn, Diebold–Mariano, Pesaran–Timmermann

Another concept in data and modeling is that of predictability and accuracy. Multiple methods can be used to measure the accuracy of a predictive model. As previously mentioned, in a multivariate regression setting, we can use the R-square, Akaike Information Criterion, Bayes–Schwarz Criterion and others. As an example, suppose we are comparing the accuracy of two models. One simple way is to look at the model-predicted values and compare them against the historical actuals. The difference would constitute the model's prediction errors. The following shows two example sets of errors. We can see that model 2's errors are much smaller than model 1's. The computed results using BizStats' Forecast Accuracy model show that the second model has much lower error and is therefore the preferred model with a higher level of accuracy. Even if the two models show different levels of forecast accuracy, the next question is whether the two forecasts differ statistically significantly. The Diebold–Mariano Test of Forecast Differences and the Harvey, Leybourne, and Newbold Test allow us to determine if the errors are statistically significant. The null hypothesis tested is that there is no significant difference between the two forecasts. Finally, sometimes the exact forecast accuracy is not in question. Rather, it is the ability to predict directional change that is critical. The Pesaran–Timmerman tests for whether a model can adequately predict and track the directional changes over time. The null hypothesis tested is that the forecast does not track directional changes in the data.

Errors 1	Errors 2
221.4876	0.112161248
-120.1243	0.535868655
88.6704	0.635762518
...	...
...	...
-174.1671	0.234313273
-36.3149	0.530179776

```
Error Measures for Model 1
Maximum Log-Likelihood: -318.173405
Akaike Info Criterion (AIC): 12.926936
AIC Correction (AICC): 15.593603
Bayes and Schwarz Criterion (BSC):
13.118139
Hannan-Quinn Criterion (HQC): 12.999747
Mean Absolute Deviation (MAD): 114.467810
Mean Squared Errors (MSE): 19713.503554
Root Mean Squared Error (RMSE): 140.404785

Error Measures for Model 2
Maximum Log-Likelihood: -41.017947
Akaike Info Criterion (AIC): 1.840718
AIC Correction (AICC): 4.507385
Bayes and Schwarz Criterion (BSC):
2.031920
Hannan-Quinn Criterion (HQC): 1.913529
Mean Absolute Deviation (MAD): 0.475521
Mean Squared Errors (MSE): 0.302051
Root Mean Squared Error (RMSE): 0.549592
```

$$Normal\ N(\mu,\sigma): f(x|\mu,\sigma) = \frac{1}{\sqrt{2\pi\sigma^2}} exp\left[-\frac{(x-\mu)^2}{2\sigma^2}\right]$$

$$f[N_{iid}\ of\ N(\mu,\sigma)] = \prod_{i=1}^{n} f(x_i|\mu_i,\sigma_i) = \left[\frac{1}{\sqrt{2\pi\sigma^2}}\right]^{n/2} exp\left[-\frac{\sum_{i=1}^{n}(x-\mu)^2}{2\sigma^2}\right]$$

$$\text{General Log-Likelihood: } \ln[L(\mu,\sigma)] = -\frac{n}{2}\ln(2\pi\sigma^2) - \frac{1}{2\sigma^2}\sum_{i=1}^{n}(x_i-\mu)^2$$

$$\text{OLS Log-Likelihood: } \ln[L(\mu=0,\sigma=1)] = -\frac{n}{2}\ln(2\pi) - \frac{n}{2}ln\left[\frac{SE}{n}\right] - \frac{n}{2}$$

$$MLE = -\frac{1}{2}Nln(2\pi) - \left(\frac{N}{2}\right)ln\left(\frac{SE}{N}\right) - \frac{N}{2} = -\frac{1}{2}N\left(ln\left(\frac{2\pi SE}{N}\right)+1\right)$$

$$AIC = \frac{-2MLE+2K}{N} = ln\left(\frac{2\pi SE}{N}\right) + \left(\frac{2K+N}{N}\right)$$

$$BIC = \frac{-2MLE+Kln(N)}{N} = ln\left(\frac{2\pi SE}{N}\right) + \frac{Kln(N)+N}{N}$$

$$HQ = \frac{-2MLE+2Kln[ln(N)]}{N} = ln\left(\frac{2\pi SE}{N}\right) + \frac{2Kln[ln(N)]+N}{N}$$

Grubbs Test for Outliers & Mahalanobis Distance

Outliers, as discussed, will impact the validity and consistency of your data. The Grubbs test for outliers is used to test the null hypothesis that all the values are from the same normal population without any outliers. In other words, if we fail to reject the null hypothesis, we can safely state that there are no outliers. To illustrate, suppose we have the two variables below, each with 11 data points. Notice that VAR1 has a clear outlier (bold value, 3).

VAR1: 145, 125, 190, 135, 220, 130, 210, **3**, 165, 165, 150

VAR2: 145, 125, 190, 135, 220, 130, 210, **203**, 165, 165, 150

When we run Grubb's test in BizStats, the results are shown below. We see that for VAR1, the Grubbs statistic for the smallest data point (i.e., 3) exceeds the critical values of all three alpha significance values, indicating that we can reject the null hypothesis and conclude that the value 3 is, indeed, a statistical outlier. In contrast, VAR2's results indicate a Grubbs statistic under the critical limits, which means we cannot reject the null hypothesis and we have to conclude that the data does not have any statistical outliers.

A related test is the Mahalanobis Distance, that measures the distance between point X and a distribution Y, based on multidimensional generalizations of the number of standard deviations X is away from the average of Y. This multidimensional Mahalanobis distance is equivalent to standard Euclidean distance. The null hypothesis tested is that there are no outliers in each of the data rows.

Grubbs Test for Outliers:	VAR1	VAR2
Grubbs Stat (Smallest Data):	**2.523906**	1.245483
Grubbs Stat (Largest Data):	1.229716	1.565597
G Critical @ 0.01:	2.484279	2.484279
G Critical @ 0.05:	2.233908	2.233908
G Critical @ 0.10:	2.088014	2.088014
Minimum:	3.000000	125.0000
Average:	148.9090	167.0909
Maximum:	220.0000	220.0000
Outlier Tested:	3.000000	220.0000

Null: All data values are from the same normal population (no outliers)

Linear & Quadratic Discriminant Analysis

Linear Discriminant Analysis is related to ANOVA and multivariate regression analysis, which attempt to model one dependent variable as a linear combination of other independent variables. Discriminant analysis typically has multiple continuous independent variables and a single categorical dependent variable. The Quadratic Discriminant Analysis is the nonlinear counterpart, where we assume there are nonlinear combinations of the independent variables that best explain the dependent variable.

As an illustration, the following shows part of a dataset used in BizStats, where the dependent variable is the categorical variable. For example, each row may constitute an individual, where the Category may be something like Agree, Neutral, and Agree, while the independent predictor variables X1 to X3 may be years of education, knowledge of the product, experience using the product, and so forth.

In the results, the "True Group" versus "Put into Group" matrix illustrates that, statistically, 68 individuals who should be categorized as Group 1 are indeed put into this group in the raw data, with 13 and 4 others incorrectly put into groups 2 and 3, respectively. This indicates an 80% accuracy. For groups 2 and 3, the grouping accuracy is 72% and 76%, respectively. The linear discriminant function shows that variable X2 (1.2406 and 1.0380 are the highest factors) has the highest impact on whether an individual is in Group 1 and 2, while variable X3 (1.1057 is the highest factor) has the highest impact on whether individuals should be in Group 3. Using this method, certain types of data can be tested to see how the statistically predicted groupings match up against the actual group membership, as an additional layer of data validity checking.

Linear & Quadratic Discriminant Analysis

Category	X1	X2	X3
VAR1	VAR2	VAR3	VAR4
1	10	22	25
1	14	17	66
1	19	33	77
...	......	...	
...	......	...	
2	14	29	12
2	14	25	37
...	......	...	
...	......	...	
3	20	25	12
3	16	18	48

Model Inputs:
VAR1
VAR2; VAR3; VAR4

Linear Discriminant Analysis (LDA)

Group	1	2	3
Count	85	93	66
Prior	0.3484	0.3811	0.2705

Classification Results

		True Group	
Put into Group	1	2	3
1	**68**	16	3
2	**13**	67	13
3	**4**	10	50
Total N	85	93	66
N Correct	68	67	50
Proportion	**0.8000**	**0.7204**	**0.7576**

N: 244
N Correct: 185
Proportion Correct: 0.758197

VAR	1	2	3
Global Mean Vector	15.6393	20.6762	10.5902

	Linear Discriminant Function for Groups		
Betas Group 1	0.6263	**1.2406**	0.6865
Intercept1	-23.0975		
Betas Group 2	0.9966	**1.0380**	0.7956
Intercept2	-25.2063		
Betas Group 3	0.8427	0.7221	**1.1057**
Intercept3	-20.7715		

Principal Component Analysis

Principal Component Analysis is related to another method called Factor Analysis. Principal component analysis makes multivariate data easier to model and summarize. As an example, we start with 9 independent variables that are unlikely to be independent of one another, such that changing the value of one variable will affect another. Recall that multicollinearity can cause bias in a multiple regression model. Both principal component and factor analysis can help identify and eventually replace the original independent variables with a new set of smaller variables that are uncorrelated with one another, while each of these new variables is a linear combination of the original variables. This means most of the variation can be explained with fewer explanatory variables. Similarly, factor analysis is used to examine interrelationships among large numbers of variables and to reduce them to a smaller number of common factors. The method condenses the information contained in the original set of variables into a smaller set of implicit factor variables with minimal information loss. The analysis is based on the correlation matrix and uses principal component analysis, coupled with a varimax rotation, to simplify the factors.

In the next slide, we start with an example of 9 independent variables, which means the factor analysis or principal component analysis results will return a 9×9 matrix of eigenvectors and 9 eigenvalues. Typically, we are only interested in components with eigenvalues > 1. Hence, in the results, we are only interested in the first three or four factors or components (some researchers plot these eigenvalues and call it a scree plot, which can be useful for identifying the kinks in the eigenvalues). Notice that the fourth factor (the fourth column in the figure) returns a cumulative proportion of 72.31%. This means that using these four factors will explain approximately three-quarters of the variation in all the independent factors themselves. Next, we examine the absolute values of the eigenvalues in the matrix. It seems that variables 2, 3, 7, and 8 can be combined into a new variable in factor 1, variables 1 and 9 as the second factor, variable 6 by itself as the third factor, and variable 4 by itself as a new variable. This can be done separately and outside of principal component analysis.

Principal Component Analysis

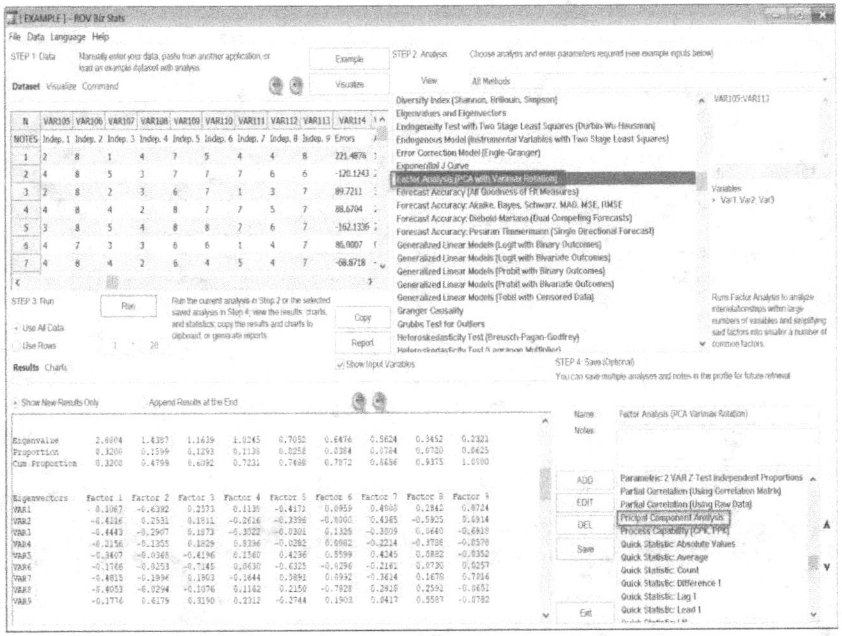

Model Inputs:
VAR105; VAR106; VAR107; VAR108; VAR109; VAR110; VAR111; VAR112; VAR113
Factor Analysis: Eigenvalues and Eigenvectors

Eigenvalue	2.8804	1.4387	1.1639	1.0245	0.7052	0.6476	0.5624	0.3452	0.2321
Proportion	0.3200	0.1599	0.1293	0.1138	0.0258	0.0384	0.0784	0.0720	0.0625
Cum Proportion	0.3200	0.4799	0.6092	0.7231	0.7488	0.7872	0.8656	0.9375	1.0000

Eigenvectors	Factor 1	Factor 2	Factor 3	Factor 4	Factor 5	Factor 6	Factor 7	Factor 8	Factor 9
VAR1	0.1087	-0.6392	0.2573	0.1138	-0.4171	0.0959	0.4808	0.2842	0.0724
VAR2	-0.4116	0.2531	0.1811	-0.2616	-0.3396	-0.0000	0.4365	-0.5925	0.0914
VAR3	-0.4443	-0.2907	0.1873	-0.3022	-0.0301	0.1325	-0.3009	0.0640	-0.6918
VAR4	-0.2156	-0.1355	0.1829	0.8396	-0.0282	0.0082	-0.2214	-0.3788	-0.0578
VAR5	-0.3407	-0.0368	-0.4196	0.1560	0.4236	0.5599	0.4245	0.0882	-0.0352
VAR6	-0.1766	-0.0253	-0.7145	0.0630	-0.6325	-0.0296	-0.2161	0.0730	0.0257
VAR7	-0.4815	-0.1996	0.1803	-0.1644	0.0891	0.0992	-0.3614	0.1678	0.7016
VAR8	-0.4053	-0.0294	-0.1076	0.1162	0.2150	-0.7828	0.2818	0.2591	-0.0651
VAR9	-0.1776	0.6179	0.3190	0.2312	-0.2744	0.1903	0.0417	0.5587	-0.0782

5. Exploratory Data Analysis and the AI Analytics, Sampling and Experimental Design

Core Theme

Starting with the analytics maturity spectrum (descriptive → prescriptive), this section teaches how to translate business questions into tractable analytical problems. It covers data types, quality dimensions, cleaning pipelines, univariate/multivariate EDA (four moments, correlation heatmaps, VIF), and hands-on EDA on the Orchadio dataset, including clustering and anomaly detection. The module also covers probabilistic and nonprobabilistic sampling methods, qualitative research approaches (case study, ethnography, Delphi) and a full catalog of true experimental designs (Designs 0–8, factorial and quasi-experimental).

Module Objectives

Foundations: Data, EDA, and the Analytics Toolkit

Frame Business Problems

Translate ambiguous business questions into analytically tractable problems by defining precise units of analysis, outcome variables, and success metrics.

Assess & Prepare Data

Evaluate datasets for quality dimensions (completeness, accuracy, validity) and implement rigorous cleaning strategies for missing values and outliers.

Conduct Rigorous EDA

Apply univariate and multivariate statistical techniques to surface distributions, patterns, relationships, and anomalies in complex datasets.

Accelerate with AI Tools

Leverage Julius AI and ChatGPT to automate code generation, visualize data instantly, and interpret exploratory findings efficiently.

Communicate Visual Insights

Select appropriate visualization formats for descriptive analytics that clearly communicate insights to executive audiences without "chart junk".

The Analytics Maturity Spectrum

Evolution of Business Value & Analytical Complexity

Descriptive

What happened?

Hindsight. Analyzing historical data to understand past performance.

Dashboards Reports SQL Excel

Diagnostic

Why did it happen?

Insight. Drilling down into data to find root causes and correlations.

Drill-down Discovery Mining Correlations

Predictive

What will happen?

Foresight. Using statistical models to forecast future outcomes.

Regression Forecasting Classification ML Models

Prescriptive

How can we make it happen?

Optimization. Recommending actions to achieve desired goals.

Optimization Simulation Decision Trees Rules

Generative

Create new solutions

Creation. Synthesizing new data, code, or content to accelerate workflows.

LLMs ChatGPT Julius AI Agents

Time to Insight →

From Business Question to Analytical Problem

Translating Strategy into Tractable Analysis

Define the Unit of Analysis

Specify the granular entity (e.g., individual customer, single transaction, daily store sales) that forms the rows of your dataset.

Identify the Outcome Variable (Target)

Determine exactly what you are trying to predict or explain (e.g., churn status (0/1), revenue amount ($), or click probability).

Establish Success Metrics

Define clear quantitative thresholds for model success: Minimum viable accuracy, lift over baseline, or ROI constraints.

Example: "How do we reduce churn?" becomes "Predict which customers (Unit) will cancel service in the next 30 days (Target) with >80% precision (Metric) to target interventions."

Taxonomy of Analytical Methods

Mapping Business Questions to Analytical Techniques

Category	Typical Methods	Data Needs	Key Outputs	Business Example
Descriptive	Aggregation, Summary Statistics, Visualization, Dashboards	Historical, Structured, Transactional	KPI Reports, Histograms, Trends	Monthly sales report by region; customer churn rate calculation.
Diagnostic	Drill-down, Correlation Analysis, Root Cause Analysis	Multi-dimensional, Granular Historical	Heatmaps, Cross-tabs, Anomaly Flags	Why did sales drop in Q3? Investigating regional stockouts.
Predictive	Regression, Time Series Forecasting, Classification (ML)	Labeled Training Data, Time Series History	Probabilities, Forecasts, Risk Scores	Forecasting next month's demand; predicting customer default risk.
Prescriptive	Optimization (LP/IP), Simulation, A/B Testing, Causal Inference	Constraints, Cost Functions, Experimental Data	Optimal Decisions, Treatment Effects	Optimizing inventory levels; determining best price for new product.
Generative	LLMs, Transformers, Diffusion Models, Agents	Unstructured Text, Code, Images, Knowledge Bases	Content, Code, Synthesized Data	Drafting personalized marketing emails; generating SQL queries.

Data Types, Structures, and Sources

Understanding the Raw Material of Analysis

Structured vs. Unstructured Data

Structured: Organized in rows/columns (SQL, Excel); quantitative (numerical) or qualitative (categorical).
Unstructured: Text, images, audio, video; requires processing (NLP, CV) to extract features.

Primary & Secondary Data Sources

Internal Systems: ERP, CRM, transactional logs (Primary).
External: APIs, web scraping, government data, third-party providers (Secondary).

Metadata & Data Lineage

Data about data: definitions, origin, transformations, and ownership. Critical for traceability, compliance, and understanding context.

The Role of AI in Data Collection

Using AI agents to scrape web data, synthesize datasets for training, or automatically tag and structure unstructured inputs.

Key Insight: 80% of enterprise data is unstructured. Unlocking value requires moving beyond simple tables to analyze text (emails, reviews) and images.

Data Quality Dimensions

Key Framework for Assessing and Improving Data Integrity

Dimension	Definition	KPIs / Metrics	Common Checks & SLAs
Completeness	The degree to which all required data is known and present.	% Null Values % Missing Records	Check for nulls in mandatory fields (e.g., Customer ID). SLA: < 0.1% missing critical fields.
Accuracy	The degree to which data correctly describes the "real world" object or event.	Error Rate % Verification Match	Cross-reference with source of truth (e.g., verify address against postal DB).
Consistency	Data values should not conflict across different datasets or systems.	# of Conflicts % Format Compliance	Ensure total sales in CRM matches Accounting system. Standardize date formats (YYYY-MM-DD).
Timeliness	The degree to which data represents reality from the required point in time.	Data Latency Freshness Score	Time difference between event and availability. SLA: Data available within 15 mins of transaction.
Validity	Data must conform to defined business rules or constraints.	% Out of Range % Type Mismatch	Check constraints (e.g., Age > 0). Reject invalid entries at ingestion.

Common Data Problems & Fixes

A Diagnostic Pipeline for Data Quality Assurance

Missing Values

Detection
`NaN, NULL, "", "N/A"`

Incomplete data reduces statistical power and causes model failures.

Fix Strategies

- Impute (Mean/Median)
- KNN / Regression
- Drop Rows (if <5%)

Outliers

Detection
`Z-Score > 3, IQR Rule`

Extreme values skew averages and distort linear regression models.

Fix Strategies

- Winsorization (Cap/Floor)
- Log Transformation
- Remove (if error)

Duplicates

Detection
`Exact or Fuzzy Match`

Repeated records inflate counts and bias frequency analysis.

Fix Strategies

- De-duplicate (Keep First)
- GroupBy & Aggregate
- Fuzzy Matching

Inconsistency

Detection
`Typos, Case, Formats`

Inconsistent categories split groups and break string matching.

Fix Strategies

- Standardize Case (Lower)
- Regex Pattern Matching
- Value Mapping Maps

Univariate EDA: Distributions & Moments

FOUR MOMENTS

CENTRAL TENDENCY (MEAN)

$$\bar{x} = \frac{1}{n}\sum_{i=1}^{n} x_i$$

The arithmetic average of the dataset; sensitive to outliers.

SPREAD (VARIANCE & SD)

$$s^2 = \frac{1}{n-1}\sum_{i=1}^{n}(x_i - \bar{x})^2, s = \sqrt{s^2}$$

Measures dispersion around the mean using squared deviations.

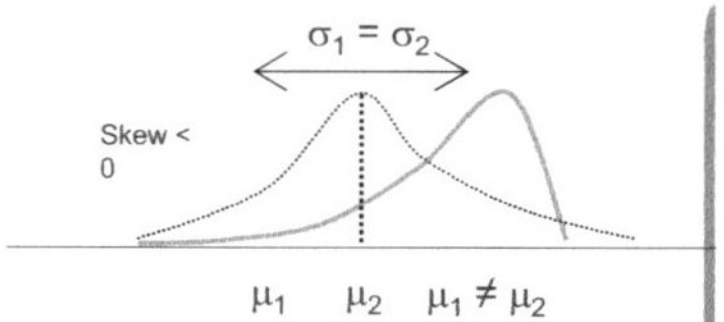

ASYMMETRY (SKEWNESS)

$$\text{Skew} = \frac{n}{(n-1)(n-2)}\sum_{i=1}^{n}\left(\frac{x_i - \bar{x}}{s}\right)^3$$

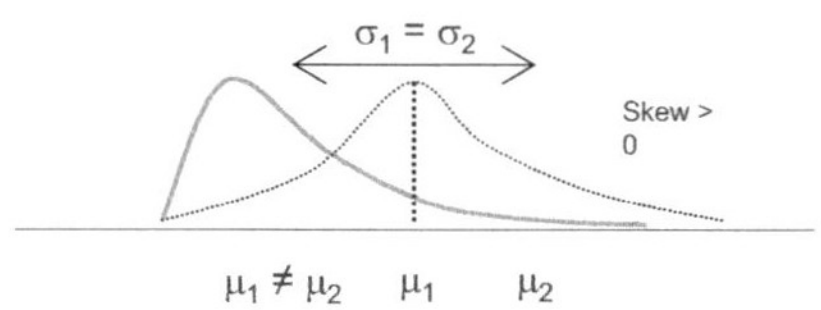

Positive or right skew: tail on right;
Negative or left skew; tail on left.

TAIL THICKNESS (KURTOSIS)

$$\text{Kurt} = \frac{n(n+1)}{(n-1)(n-2)(n-3)}\sum_{i=1}^{n}\left(\frac{x_i - \bar{x}}{s}\right)^4 - 3$$

Excess kurtosis > 0 implies heavy tails (outlier-prone).

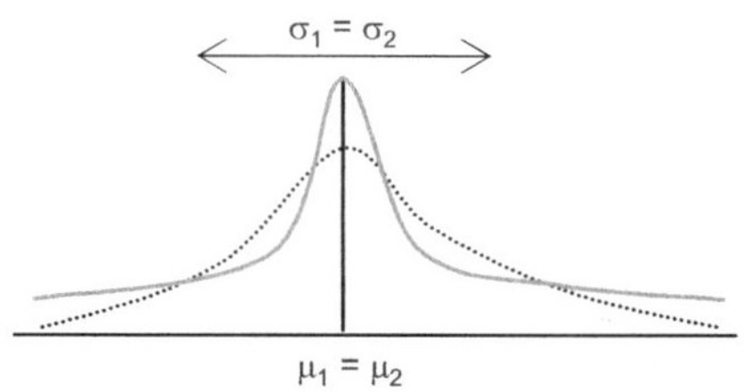

Distribution Shape (Histogram)

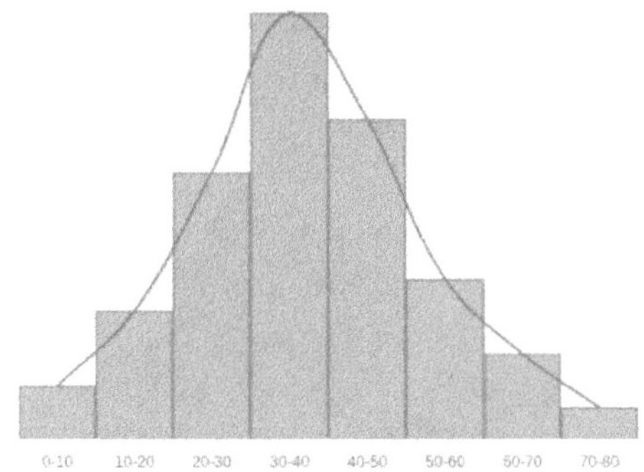

Outliers & Spread (Box Plot)

Multivariate EDA: Relationships

Uncovering Connections, Patterns, and Redundancies

Correlation Heatmap

● Positive   Neutral   ● Negative

	Price	Ad Spend			Quality	Sales
Price	1.00	0.30	0.82	0.45	0.78	-0.65
Ad Spend	0.30	1.00	0.05	-0.20	0.10	0.55
Discount	0.82	0.05	1.00	0.00	0.60	0.15
Season	0.45	-0.20	0.00	1.00	0.25	-0.30
Quality	0.78	0.10	0.60	0.25	1.00	0.40
Sales	-0.65	0.55	0.15	-0.30	0.40	1.00

-1   1

$$r = \frac{n\sum x_i y_i - \sum x_i \sum y_i}{\sqrt{n\sum x_i^2 - \sum(x_i)^2}\sqrt{n\sum y_i^2 - \sum(y_i)^2}}$$

Pearson Correlation Coefficient (r)

$$r = \frac{cov(x,y)}{s_x s_y} = \frac{\sum(x_i-\bar{x})(y_i-\bar{y})}{\sqrt{(x_i-\bar{x})^2}\sqrt{(y_i-\bar{y})^2}}$$

Measures linear relationship strength between -1 (perfect negative) and +1 (perfect positive).

Key Concepts

Multicollinearity: High correlation between predictors (e.g., >0.7) can destabilize regression coefficients.

Statistical vs. Business Relevance: A strong correlation (r=0.9) may be spurious or irrelevant to business goals.

> **Interpretation Tip**
> Look for dark squares off the diagonal. Red indicates variables moving together; blue indicates inverse movement.

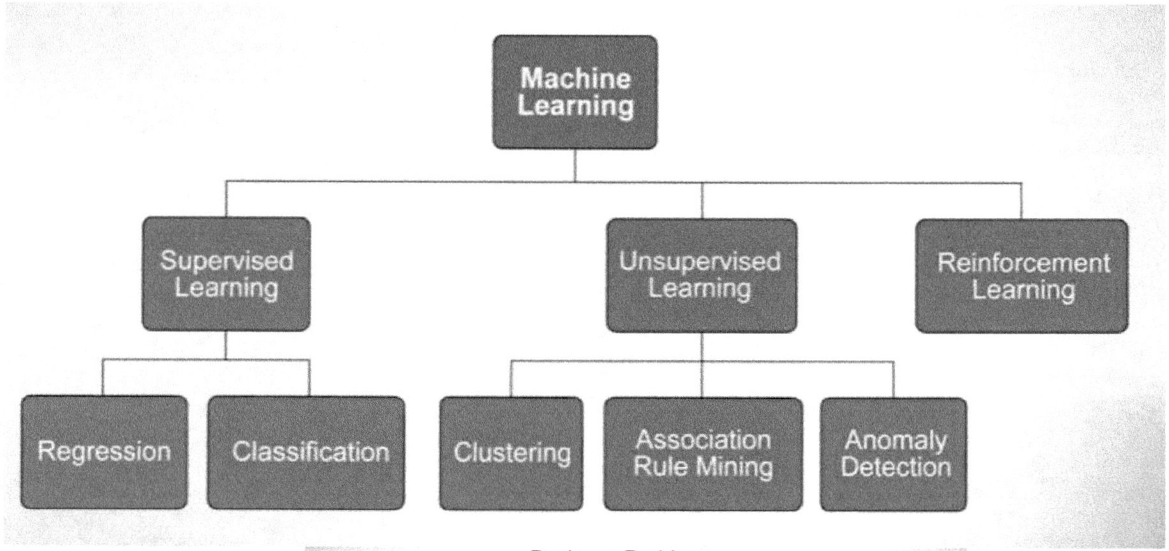
Machine Learning
Supervised Learning
Unsupervised Learning
Reinforcement Learning
Regression
Classification
Clustering
Association Rule Mining
Anomaly Detection

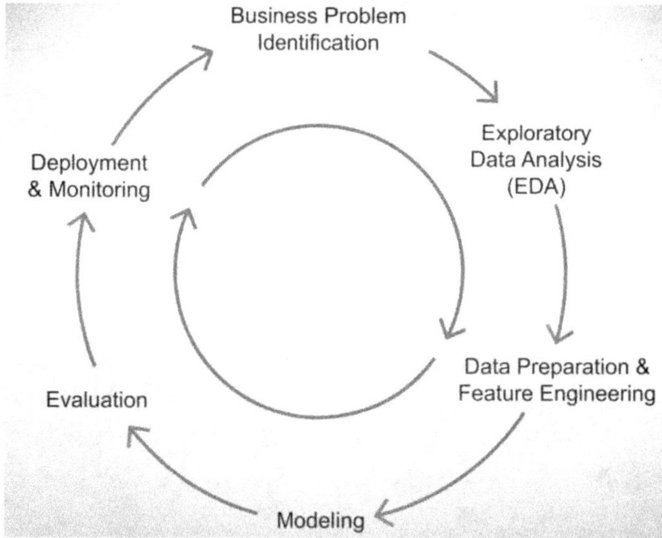
Business Problem Identification
Exploratory Data Analysis (EDA)
Data Preparation & Feature Engineering
Modeling
Evaluation
Deployment & Monitoring

Exploratory Data Analysis (EDA)

EDA helps you answer critical questions, including:

- What's the structure of your data? How are variables distributed? Are there outliers or unexpected values?
- What relationships exist? Do variables correlate in ways that support (or contradict) your hypotheses?
- Are there data quality issues? Are there missing values, measurement errors, or inconsistencies that need addressing?
- Are there sampling biases? Does your dataset accurately represent the population you care about, or are certain groups over- or under-represented?

Anscombe Quartet

Shows several datasets with similar statistical moments but very different shapes—proving that visualization is essential. Failure to run EDA may result in a technically correct model but a practically useless one.

Levels of Measurement: N.O.I.R.

Nominal · Ordinal · Interval · Ratio

Also: 4 Distributional Moments

DATA FILE: 01 - EDA Data

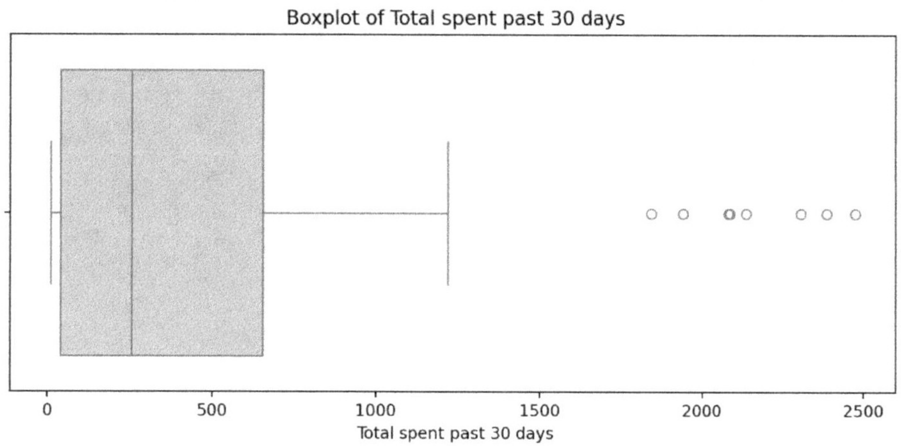

Quick interpretation

- Sample size: 1010 (from the descriptive stats).
- Median spend ≈ 255.05.
- 25th percentile ≈ 40.23, 75th percentile ≈ 653.14 — distribution is right-skewed (long upper tail).
- Minimum ≈ 11.29, maximum ≈ 2476.35 — there are high spend outliers that stretch the range.

Most of the numerical variables show right-skewed distributions—meaning most customers cluster at lower values, with a tail extending toward higher values. This is common in customer behavior data. These patterns highlight significant **heterogeneity in customer behavior**—from light users to highly engaged ones, and from newer customers to long-tenured accounts. The right-skewed distributions and presence of extreme values suggest that customers are not all alike; instead, they behave in distinct ways across spending, activity, and tenure. Recognizing this behavioral diversity is essential. It's what makes segmentation valuable—and it's why clustering can help uncover **natural groupings** within the customer base that reflect meaningful differences in how people engage with the business.

Specific Observations

Total spent past 30 days
Most customers are lower spenders, concentrated below $600 with a median ~$255. A smaller group exceeds $1,000.

N purchases past 30 days
Most customers make fewer than 15 purchases/month, concentrated under 5. A smaller group is highly active (30–50 purchases).

Time & Sessions past 30 days
Most customers show low engagement—limited time, few sessions. A smaller group of highly active users exceeds 200 min or 30+ sessions/month.

Time since first purchase
Most customers are relatively new (past few months). Some accounts go back nearly 900 days.

Age
Roughly symmetric, centered around 40 years old. Most fall between early 30s and mid-40s.

The categorical variables reveal diversity in how customers engage with Orchardio's service. Some behaviors—like delivery frequency—skew toward specific options, while others—like box customization—are more evenly split. Even a balanced distribution is meaningful: it shows that customers are making different choices, rather than behaving uniformly. This variation across membership, delivery preferences, and customization highlights different customer types—exactly what segmentation aims to uncover. When combined with the behavioral heterogeneity seen in the numerical variables, these categorical differences will help clustering surface distinct customer segments based on both what customers do and how they choose to engage.

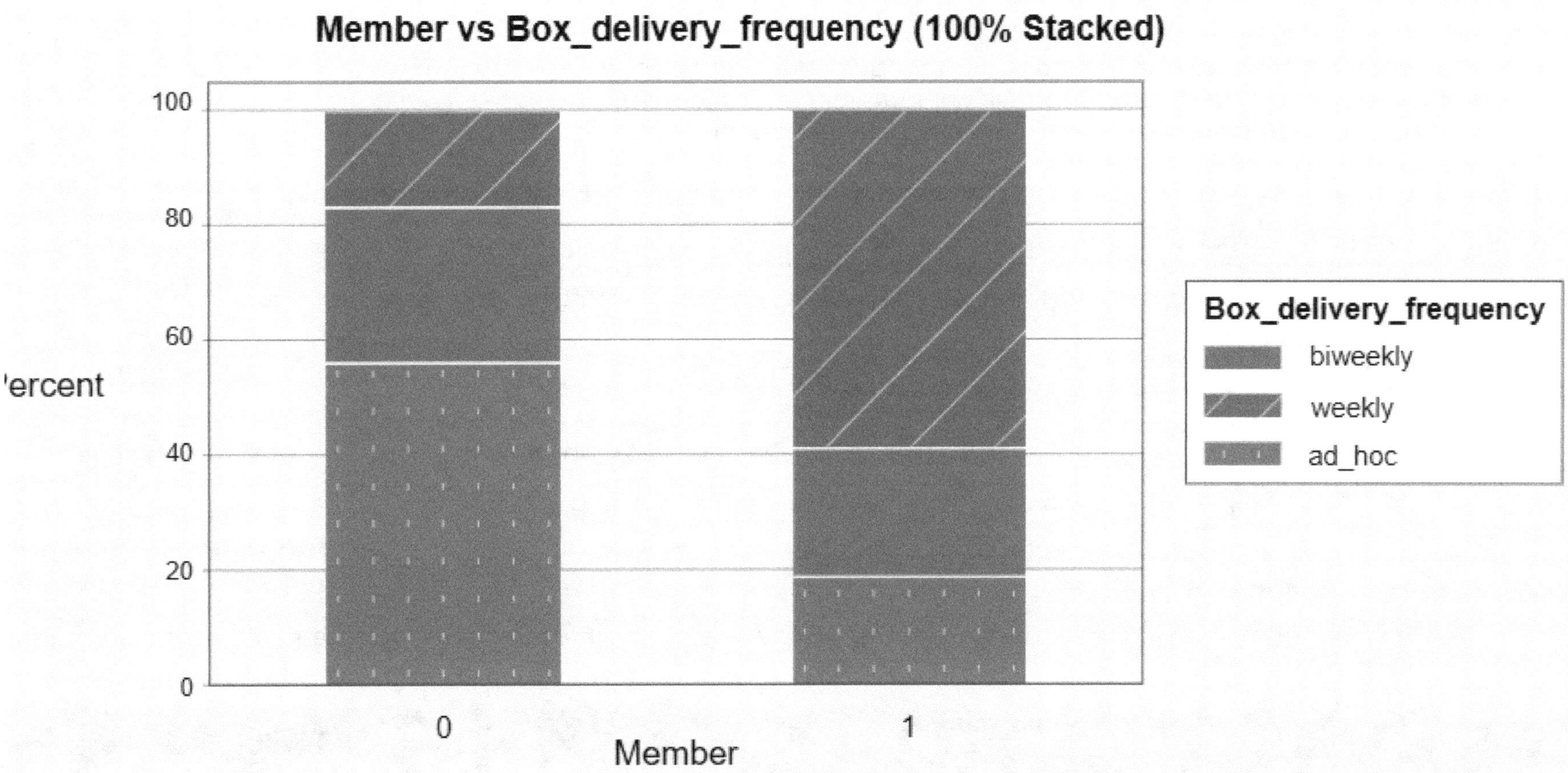
Member vs Box_delivery_frequency (100% Stacked)
100
80
60
40
20
0
'ercent
0
1
Member
Box_delivery_frequency
biweekly
weekly
ad_hoc

EDA: Categorical vs. Categorical

The 100% stacked bar chart normalizes each group to show proportional differences in delivery frequency

Here's what stands out:

- About 56% of **non-members** use ad hoc delivery, with smaller shares using weekly or biweekly.
- Nearly 60% of **members** choose weekly delivery, and very few use ad hoc.

Key Insight

Delivery preferences differ sharply by membership status. Members are far more likely to choose weekly delivery, while non-members mostly choose ad hoc. This suggests that membership is associated with more frequent, regular engagement—a meaningful behavioral difference that could shape how segments are formed and how marketing teams approach each group.

These group-level patterns give us a head start on understanding different types of customer behavior—even before clustering. By identifying which combinations signal higher or lower engagement, you'll be better equipped to interpret the segments we uncover later, and to think ahead about how to personalize messages, offers, or services.

EDA: Numerical vs. Numerical

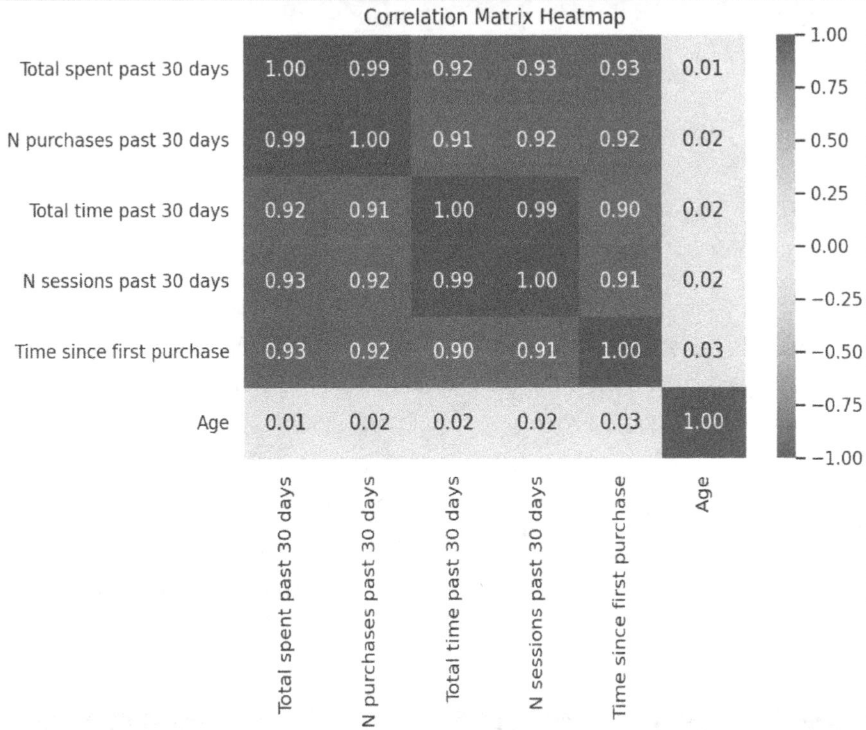

Total spend is extremely highly correlated with:

- N purchases past 30 days (≈ 0.99)
- Total time past 30 days (≈ 0.92)
- N sessions past 30 days (≈ 0.93)
- Time since first purchase (≈ 0.93)
- The engagement / activity metrics are also very highly correlated with each other (0.90+).
- Age has near-zero correlation with all behavioral variables (correlations all around 0.01–0.03), suggesting age is not linearly related to recent spend or activity.

Strong Positive (≈ +1)
Spend, Purchases, Time on Site, and Sessions are all strongly positively correlated. Customers high on one tend to be high on all—revealing consistent light, moderate, or heavy user groups.

Weak / None (≈ 0)
Age has very weak or no correlation with behavioral variables. Customer engagement is not age-dependent in this dataset.

Strong Negative (≈ –1)
There are no strong negative relationships in this dataset.

EDA: Numerical vs. Numerical

Total spend is extremely highly correlated with:

- N purchases past 30 days (≈ 0.99)
- Total time past 30 days (≈ 0.92)
- N sessions past 30 days (≈ 0.93)
- Time since first purchase (≈ 0.93)
- The engagement/activity metrics are also very highly correlated with each other (0.90+).
- Age has near-zero correlation with all behavioral variables (correlations all around 0.01–0.03), suggesting age is not linearly related to recent spend or activity.

Strong Positive (≈ +1)

Spend, Purchases, Time on Site, and Sessions are all strongly positively correlated. Customers high on one tend to be high on all—revealing consistent light, moderate, or heavy user groups.

Strong Negative (≈ –1)

There are no strong negative relationships in this dataset.

Weak / None (≈ 0)

Age has very weak or no correlation with behavioral variables. Customer engagement is not age-dependent in this dataset.

EDA: Categorical vs. Numerical

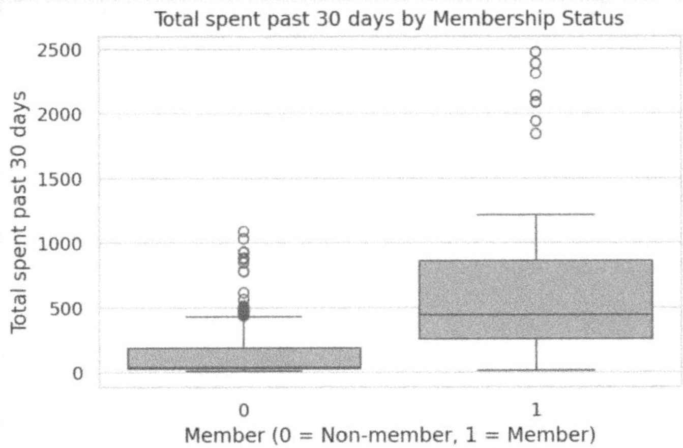

Median: The median spend (shown as the line inside the box) is higher for members than for non-members. This suggests that, on average, members tend to spend more.

Spread and Outliers: Spending among members shows a wide range and includes several high outliers—customers who spend far more than the typical customer. Non-members show a narrower, lower range with fewer high spenders.

Three Engagement Tiers

Highly Engaged, Long-Tenured
Members, weekly delivery customers, and customizers consistently score higher across all behavioral variables—spend, purchases, time, sessions, and tenure. Regular, committed users.

Moderately Engaged, Consistent
Biweekly delivery customers show mid-level engagement. More active than ad hoc users but less than weekly ones. Balanced, steady, and predictable.

Lower-Engagement / Newer
Non-members and ad hoc delivery customers score lower across most behavioral variables—often newer, visit less often, and spend less overall—suggesting a more casual relationship with the service.

These group-level patterns will help you make sense of the clusters once formed—whether tailoring messages, designing features, or identifying strategic opportunities.

Preparing for Cluster Analysis

Z-Score normalization of the data should be done before running cluster analysis. The number of clusters is strategic, but can also be determined analytically by examining the elbow.

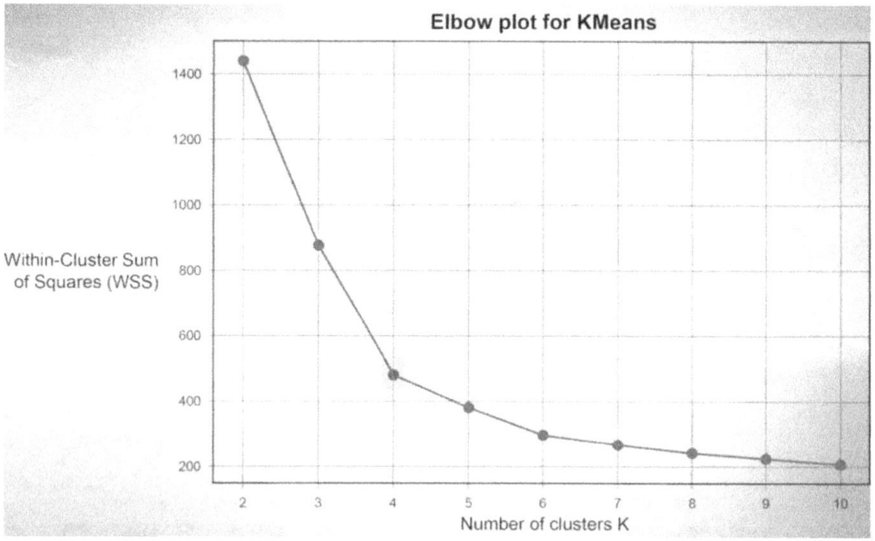

PCA Scatter Plot Interpretation

A PCA scatter plot with K-means after the clusters are formed helps determine whether the selected number of clusters is sufficient and correct.

PC1 – Main Behavior Dimension

Largely an "overall activity/value" axis combining spend, purchases, sessions, time, and tenure. The clean ordering along PC1 shows clusters that mainly differ in intensity of engagement.

PC2 – Secondary Pattern

A smaller secondary pattern—minor contrasts among high/low dimensions. The clean ordering along PC1 confirms that the clusters mainly differ in engagement value.

Preparing for Cluster Analysis

Within each chart, the boxplots for the four clusters appear at different heights, showing that each cluster reflects a distinct level of engagement for each variable.

All five charts (spending, purchases, time on site, sessions, tenure) look nearly identical in shape and order, indicating that the clusters differ consistently across all behavioral dimensions—these behaviors rise and fall together.

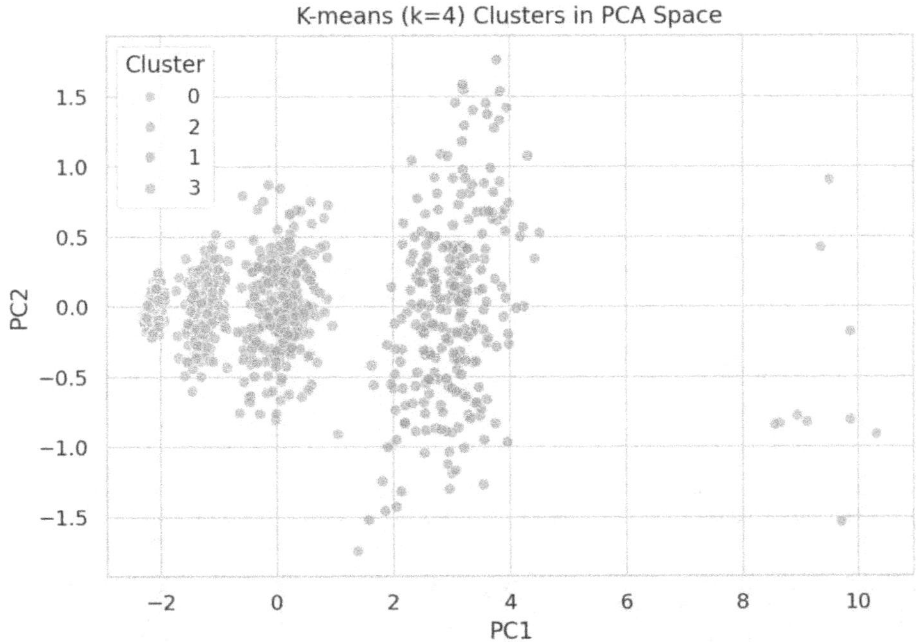

Cluster Profiles

Cluster 0 – Lowest Usage & Value
Customers spend the least, buy the fewest boxes, have the fewest sessions, and the shortest history. Low engagement with behaviors typical of casual or trial use: mostly non-members, ad hoc delivery, little customization.

Cluster 1 – High Usage & Value
Heavy users with high spend, lots of purchases and sessions, and relatively long relationships. Mostly members. Strong weekly delivery usage. Increased customization. Regular, stable customers.

Cluster 2 – Moderate Usage & Value
A clear step up from Cluster 0 on every metric. Moderate spending, purchases, and engagement. Mix of members and non-members. Uses a blend of ad hoc, biweekly, and weekly delivery. Meaningful amount of customization.

Cluster 3 – Extreme VIPs / Super-Users
Tiny group but off-the-charts on ALL five metrics: very high spend, very frequent purchases and sessions, and very long tenure. Entirely members, exclusively weekly users, and all customers can customize.

cluster 4	Total spent past 30 days	N purchases past 30 days	Total time past 30 days	N sessions past 30 days	Time since first purchase
0	101.08	2.18	34.40	3.84	48.53
2	398.56	8.06	107.33	11.96	196.59
1	902.24	17.97	223.86	24.75	400.04
3	2130.21	43.60	453.07	50.90	811.10

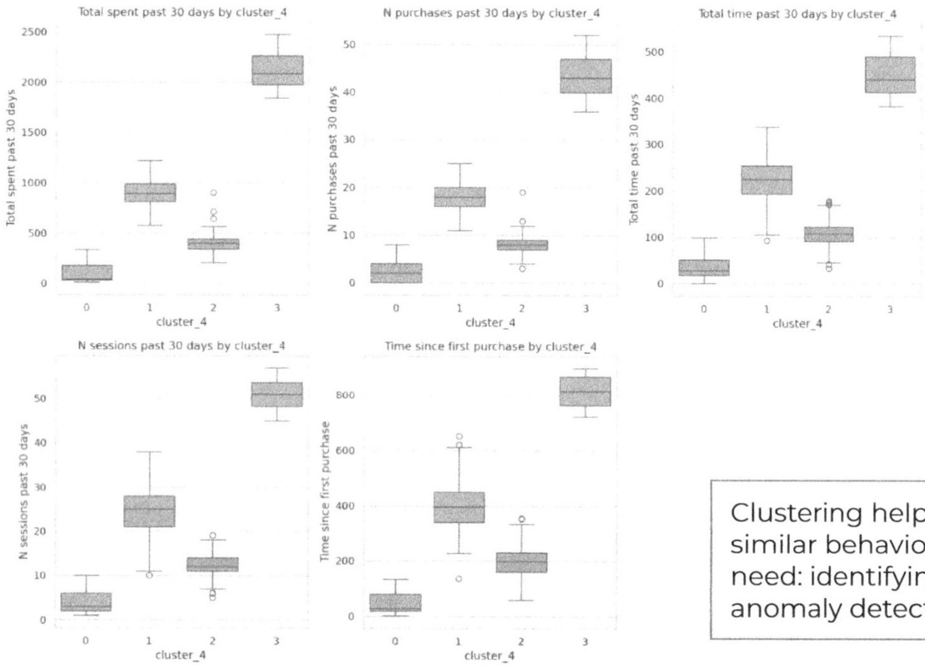

Actions by Cluster

Cluster 0 – "Trial Users"
"Trial users" or "one-time customers." Focus on onboarding, registration, or first-purchase incentives to convert casual visitors into repeat buyers.

Cluster 1 – "Regular Subscribers"
"Regular subscribers" or "steady users." Target for loyalty programs, retention messaging, or value-added features that reward consistency.

Cluster 2 – "Occasional Customers"
"Occasional customers" or "light repeaters." Marketing actions could include nudges toward routine use or introductory personalization features.

Cluster 3 – "Power Users / VIPs"
"Power users" or "VIPs." Marketing actions focus on premium options, exclusive offers, or deep personalization for maximum engagement.

Clustering helps organizations uncover structure in data by grouping similar behaviors. But unsupervised learning can also support the opposite need: identifying cases that don't follow expected patterns. That's where anomaly detection comes in.

Anomaly Detection & Supervised Learning

Anomaly Detection

Anomaly detection is especially valuable because it helps teams flag unusual or emerging behaviors—whether related to fraud, operational failures, quality issues, or shifts in customer activity—so they can respond quickly and effectively. At its core, anomaly detection builds on the same foundations as clustering: understanding what "normal" looks like in order to recognize meaningful deviations.

Supervised Learning

Two common applications of supervised learning:

Classification

Predicts categories. For example: Is this transaction fraudulent or legitimate? Will a customer churn or stay?

Forecasting

Predicts continuous values. For example, how much demand will we see next month? What will revenue look like next quarter?

Data Analysis I

Tools & Techniques Available

Data Analysis & Exploration

- Load and inspect data from various formats (CSV, Excel, JSON)
- Generate descriptive statistics and data summaries
- Data cleaning and preprocessing
- Handle missing values and outliers
- Data type conversions and transformations

Statistical Analysis

- Descriptive statistics (mean, median, std dev, quartiles, etc.)
- Hypothesis testing (t-tests, chi-square, ANOVA, etc.)
- Correlation and covariance analysis
- Regression analysis (linear, logistic, polynomial)
- Time series analysis and forecasting
- Probability distributions and sampling

Data Visualization

- Line plots, scatter plots, histograms, box plots
- Heatmaps and correlation matrices
- Bar charts and pie charts
- Geographic maps (with geopandas and contextily)
- Interactive visualizations (Bokeh, Plotly)
- Multi-panel plots and subplots

Machine Learning

- Classification models (logit, decision trees, random forests)
- Regression models
- Clustering (K-means, hierarchical, DBSCAN, etc.)
- Dimensionality reduction (PCA, t-SNE, UMAP)
- Neural networks and deep learning (TensorFlow/Keras)
- Model evaluation and cross-validation

Data Analysis II

Text & NLP Analysis

- Text preprocessing and tokenization
- Sentiment analysis
- Topic modeling
- Text classification
- Named entity recognition
- Word embeddings and similarity

Time Series Analysis

- Trend analysis and decomposition
- Seasonal analysis
- Autocorrelation and partial autocorrelation
- ARIMA and exponential smoothing models
- Forecasting

Data Export & Reporting

- Save results to CSV, Excel, JSON, or other formats
- Generate summary reports
- Create publication-ready visualizations

Advanced Analytics

- Causal inference
- Anomaly detection
- Network analysis
- Optimization problems
- Bayesian analysis

Early Diagnostics: Collinearity & Patterns

Detecting Regression Assumption Violations Before Modeling

Multicollinearity (VIF)

$$\mathrm{VIF}_j = \frac{1}{1 - R_j^2}$$

Regress squared residuals on predictors. Significant coefficients imply non-constant variance (heteroscedasticity).

Heteroscedasticity (Breusch-Pagan)

$$\hat{\varepsilon}^2 = \delta_0 + \delta_1 x_1 + \cdots + \delta_p x_p + \nu$$

Regress squared residuals on predictors. Significant coefficients imply non-constant variance (heteroscedasticity).

Non-Linearity Detection

$$y = \beta_0 + f(x) + \varepsilon$$

Use LOWESS (Locally Weighted Scatterplot Smoothing) on residual plots to detect curvature missed by linear models.

Residuals vs Fitted (Non-Linearity Check)

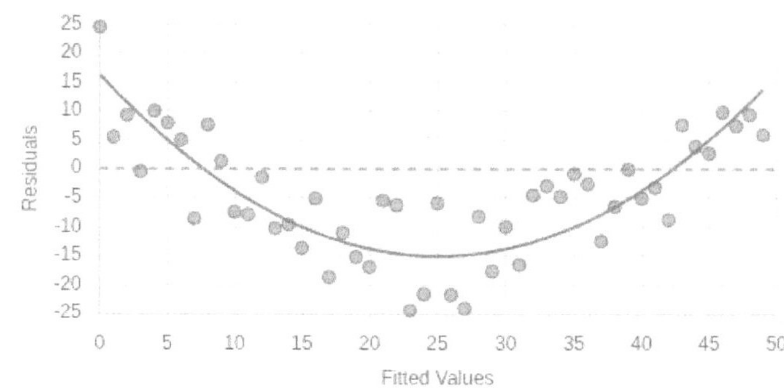

Normal Q-Q Plot (Normality Check)

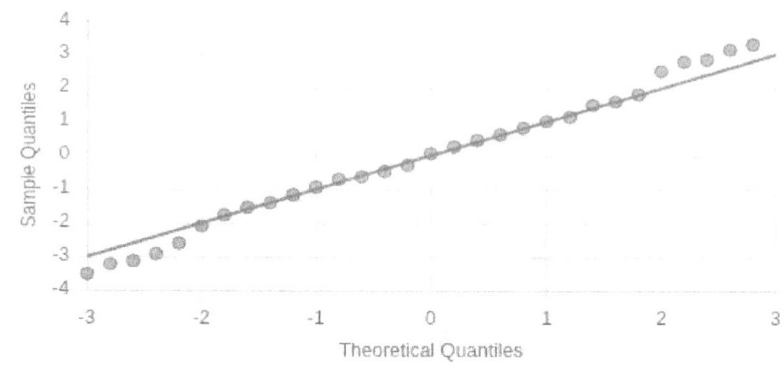

EDA with Julius AI and ChatGPT: HANDS-ON EXAMPLE

Accelerating Exploration with Natural Language Prompts

Natural Language Prompt

Julius AI / ChatGPT

```
User:
Upload 'customer_churn.csv'. 1. Check for
missing values and duplicates. 2. Generate a
summary statistics table for numerical
variables. 3. Create a histogram of
'MonthlyCharges' colored by 'Churn'. 4.
Visualize the relationship between 'Tenure' and
'TotalCharges'.
```

Interpretation Request

Analytical Reasoning

```
User:

Based on the histogram and scatter plot, what
are the key drivers of churn? Are there any
obvious outliers or data quality issues in
'TotalCharges'?
```

Generated Output

Data Quality Check: No duplicates found. 'TotalCharges' has 11 missing values (replaced with 0).
Visualization Generated: Histogram of Monthly Charges by Churn Status.

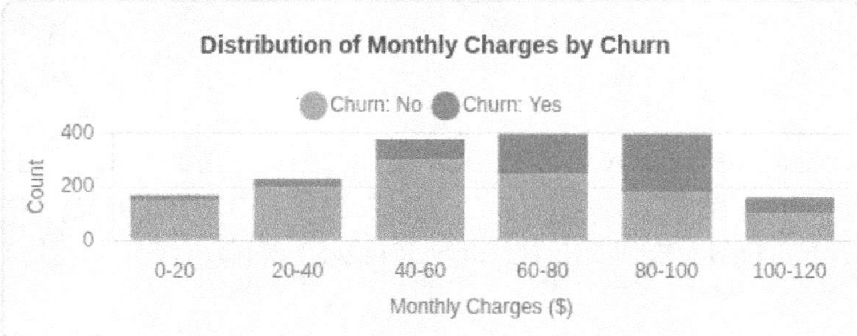

AI Insight:

Customers with higher monthly charges ($70-100) show significantly higher churn rates. The distribution is bimodal. 'Tenure' and 'TotalCharges' have a strong positive correlation, but there's a cluster of customers with high tenure and low charges, likely on legacy plans.

Probabilistic Statistical Sampling

Sampling theory, in its simplest form, states that if a sample is truly representative of the entire population, then the estimated sample statistics should be identical to the corresponding theoretical population parameters. This rationale is based on the Central Limit Theorem and Sampling Distribution Theory.

Top-Down Sampling Approach

- Target Population
- Sampling Frame
- Sampling Technique

Sampling Approaches

- Randomized Sampling Theory
- Simple Random Sampling
- Systematic Sampling
- Stratified Sampling
- Cluster Sampling
- Matched Pairs Sampling
- Multiple Stage Sampling

Nonprobabilistic Statistical Sampling

In nonprobabilistic statistical sampling, some units of the population have zero chance of selection, or the probability of selection cannot be accurately determined. Typically, units are selected based on certain nonrandom criteria, such as quota or convenience. Because selection is nonrandom, nonprobability sampling does not allow the estimation of sampling errors and may be subject to a sampling bias.

Types of Nonprobabilistic Sampling

- Convenience Sampling
- Quota Sampling
- Subject Matter Expert Sampling (Delphi & Likert)

Qualitative Research Approaches (I)

Case Study
Detailed analysis of a specific case, focusing on a specific facet, aspect, subject, process, or activity. The research instruments may include interviews, focus groups, questionnaires, project documentation, physical visits, observations, stories, and surveys.

Phenomenology.
Subjective interpretation of a problem from different points of view. In other words, how individuals feel or perceive a phenomenon. Typically, the researcher would identify a specific phenomenon to study, then find exemplars of this phenomenon and identify subjects who might best fit the profile of having experienced the events. In-depth interviews and focus groups are usually conducted to understand individual and collective experiences. The typical characteristics of these interviews are that they tend to be detailed and lengthy, and may require follow-ups. The researchers are usually experienced in eliciting open-ended responses and highly trained in the phenomenon under study.

Field Research, **Field Studies**, or **Fieldwork**.
Collection of data outside a laboratory or controlled setting, where subjects are observed in their natural state. Researchers typically take extensive notes of certain events, typically with modern videography and computer simulation models. Examples of field research may include observing animals in their original habitats, interacting with other animals, or social scientists observing people in their natural environment, observing, and learning their languages, political leanings, folklore, and social structures.

Qualitative Research Approaches (II)

Ethnographic Research.
Embeds the researcher into an organization or culture to study an entire culture, organization, or group and the interactions within entire groups. Extensive notes and recordings are usually made, and conclusions from the researchers typically include subjective observations and impressions of the interactions.

Grounded Theory (Inductive Reasoning).
Development of theories about the phenomenon that is being researched, grounded in empirical observation. Core theoretical concepts are identified simultaneously as data are gathered. Explanations, causal relationships, associations, or linkages between the theoretical concepts and the empirical data are established. Because each new observation can theoretically lead to a new linkage, the circular process never terminates. The research terminates only when the researcher decides to conclude the study. Grounded theory is an eccentric data analysis approach as it involves simultaneous data collection and data analysis. Researchers hope to reveal value-added insights as more data are gathered and their research direction changes. For this to happen, the data is analyzed from the moment data collection begins and continues until the research ends.

True Experimental Design

The following slides are some sample classical experimental designs in the tradition of Campbell and Stanley, as well as Isaac and Michael. To illustrate each of the design types below, let us assume we wish to determine whether a new math teaching method (e.g., Singapore Math) at a middle school is effective in increasing math aptitude, as measured by standardized test scores. Treatment X is the new math learning method that the students will be exposed to for a specific amount of time. Tests (T) are administered at different times in the various designs. In some designs, a pre-test (T1) is administered to gauge students' math abilities prior to the new teaching method, and a post-test (T2) is later administered to assess the effects of the teaching method.

Design 0: Poor No-Control One-Shot Case Study

Treatment	Post Test
X	T2

Design 0 is a one-shot test, where no pre-tests were administered, only a post-test. This is considered a poor research design as there is no control and it provides no internal validity, making the results highly misleading because there is no basis for comparison. There might exist numerous exogenous effects that can impact T2 that are not considered or controlled for. This might be a good initial rough-cut design to quickly test if a problem is researchable, but no proper or valid conclusions can be drawn.

Design 1: Minimal Control One Group Pre- and Post-Test Design

Pre-Test	Treatment	Post-Test
T1	X	T2

Design 1 includes a pretest as a control for the single tested group. In contrast to Design 0, this design provides a much-needed control or comparison. If the same subjects take T1 and T2, we can eliminate selection bias (different people taking the two tests) and mortality bias (possible loss of subjects over time) only if the experiment is conducted in a time-constrained manner. The difference in scores (T2 – T1) is the test variable subjected to statistical hypothesis tests, such as a parametric t-test for larger sample sizes with interval and ratio data, or a nonparametric Wilcoxon signed-rank test or Mann–Whitney test for smaller sample sizes or when the data are ordinal.

Potential issues with this design include history bias (some students might take external courses to help boost their scores between T1 and T2), maturation bias (students generally get better at a subject the more they practice and learn), testing bias (having a pre-test might increase a student's motivation to do well, or reduce morale and induce test anxiety), instrumentation bias (different pre- and post-test exam types), and outlier bias (there might be extreme cases with super achievers and low test scores in the class, biasing the regression line).

Design 2: Randomized Control Group Pre- and Post-Test Design

Group	Pre-Test	Treatment	Post-Test
Experimental Group	T1	X	T2
Control Group	T1	.	T2

Design 2 introduces a control group and randomization. All conditions are kept identical between the experimental and control groups except for the treatment, which the control group does not receive. Students are randomly assigned to the two groups. The differences T2 – T1 for each group are computed. Compare the two variables to determine whether there is a statistical difference. A parametric pairwise t-test with independent variables and equal variance or a nonparametric two-variable Wilcoxon signed rank test and Mann–Whitney test can be applied.

Design 2: Randomized Control Group Pre- and Post-Test Design (EXTENSION)

Group	Pre-Test	Treatment	Post-Test
Experimental Group 1	T1	X (Method A)	T2
Experimental Group 2	T1	X (Method B)	T2
Control Group	T1	.	T2

Design 2 can be further extended to multiple experimental groups, as shown next. A parametric single-factor ANOVA with multiple treatments or a nonparametric Kruskal–Wallis test can be used to identify differences among all groups simultaneously. In addition, pairwise t-tests or the Wilcoxon and Mann–Whitney tests can be used to compare pairs of experimental groups. The control group is not required in the model when comparing differences between groups. The different groups can also be subjected to different treatment types or treatment levels. Internal validity is strengthened in Design 2, but instrumentation bias (the same tests are administered identically by the same teachers) and maturation bias (different teachers and teaching techniques across groups) may still exist.

Design 3: Randomized Solomon Four Group Design

Group	Pre-Test	Treatment	Post-Test
Pre-Tested	T1	X	T2
Pre-Tested	T1	.	T2
No Pre-Test		X	T2
No Pre-Test		.	T2

Design 3 has four groups, of which two were not subjected to any pre-test, thereby eliminating potential external validity issues (e.g., students not subjected to pre-tests may not feel the extra pressure to perform, may be unmotivated and may underperform due to the added stress of testing). The reduction of a pre-test (T1) removes any additional anxiety, which may create an interaction effect on students' learning experience and eventual test scores (T2), potentially impacting the experimental results.

Design 4: Randomized Control Group Post-Test Only Design

Group	Pre-Test	Treatment	Post-Test
Experimental Group		X	T2
Control Group		.	T2

Design 4 consists of the last two groups of Design 3, where the possible interacting effects of a pre-test are removed. Although this looks similar to Design 0 with a control group, the students are randomly selected. When performed correctly, randomization can be used to assume that both groups have an equal distribution of abilities. Interestingly, in some respects, Design 4 is superior to Design 2 in that the confounding and interacting effects have been removed, and it also reduces cost and time by eliminating the need for a pre-test.

Design 5: Non-Randomized Control Group Pre- and Post-Test Design

Group	Pre-Test	Treatment	Post-Test
Experimental Group	T1	X	T2
Control Group	T1	.	T2

Design 5 is similar to Design 2 except that the students are not randomized but pre-assigned and pre-assembled into the various groups. The same validity threats exist in this design as in Design 2, but the benefits are that these pre-assembled groups are convenient, and we further reduce any added anxiety or stress for the subjects, as their classes are kept intact without any further random redistribution into new cohorts or groups.

Design 6: Counterbalanced Design

Replication	Treatment X(a)	Treatment X(b)	Treatment X(c)	Treatment X(d)
1	A	B	C	D
2	B	D	A	C
3	C	A	D	B
4	D	C	B	A

Design 6 is an enhancement to Design 5: if intact and pre-assembled groups are required and random assignment is not possible, a counterbalanced design might be appropriate. When multiple treatments are tested (a, b, c, d), with one of these treatments serving as a control (no treatment applied), student cohorts (A, B, C, D) can be exposed to each treatment in a rotational fashion. A post-test is administered after each treatment. This design reduces the weakness of nonrandomization in Design 5 but introduces additional biases related to maturation (student fatigue across so many experiments and tests) and interaction or confounding variables (learning materials from one treatment type versus another might create confusion for the students).

Design 7: One Group Time-Series Design

Pre-Test	Treatment	Post-Test
T1, T2, T3, T4	X	T5, T6, T7, T8

Design 7 is similar to Design 1 except that multiple pre- and post-tests are administered over time. This helps control for internal validity issues that exist in Design 1. If the scores T1 to T4 are comparable, and T5 to T8 are comparable, we can state that the internal validity issues of maturation bias and instrumentation bias are reduced. However, the external validity threats of interaction between the pre- and post-tests remain.

Design 8: Control Group Time-Series Design

Group	Pre-Test	Treatment	Post-Test
Experimental Group	T1, T2, T3, T4	X	T5, T6, T7, T8
Control Group	T1, T2, T3, T4	.	T5, T6, T7, T8

Design 8 is like Design 7 except for a new control group. This eliminates any contemporaneous history bias, especially if there is little difference between T5 and T4 in the control group, but the experimental group shows statistically significant gains. Contemporaneous history bias implies that there might be an event (e.g., a Math Olympiad or a math week on television) that could confound the post-test results.

Factorial Design

2 × 2 Factorial Design	Factor A1	Factor A2
Factor B1	...	...
Factor B2	...	...

The classical research designs shown previously apply to single-factor treatments. These designs can be further improved by using a factorial design when more than one factor is tested. The design shown next is a 2 × 2 factorial design in which we test two factors, A and B, and their interaction. Factor A can be the two different math courses; whereas B can be the length of time the courses are taught (one semester versus one academic year), and we can also model the potential interactions among A and B. The Parametric Two-Factor ANOVA model, or regression model, can be used to test this factorial experimental design. Extensions of this Factorial Design might be done with replication. A Two-Factor ANOVA model with Replication can be applied in such instances. If the second factor needs to be controlled, we can apply the ANOVA with the Blocking Variables method. Additional factors beyond this 2 × 2 factorial design can be included, such as an M × N design or even a P × Q × R design, in which MANOVA models and multiple regression (with all factors and all possible combinations of interacting factors as independent variables) can be employed.

Quasi-Experimental Design

Unlike a true experiment, a quasi-experiment does not rely on random assignment. Instead, subjects are assigned to groups based on nonrandom criteria. In fact, Design 6 can be classified as a quasi-experimental design in that subjects were not randomized, and counterbalancing is used to reduce maturation and confounding variables biases. A Latin Cube and Latin Hypercube approach can be used when randomization is impractical and when the sample size is small. A true experimental design requires a larger sample size, proper randomization, and proper designing of the experimental process.

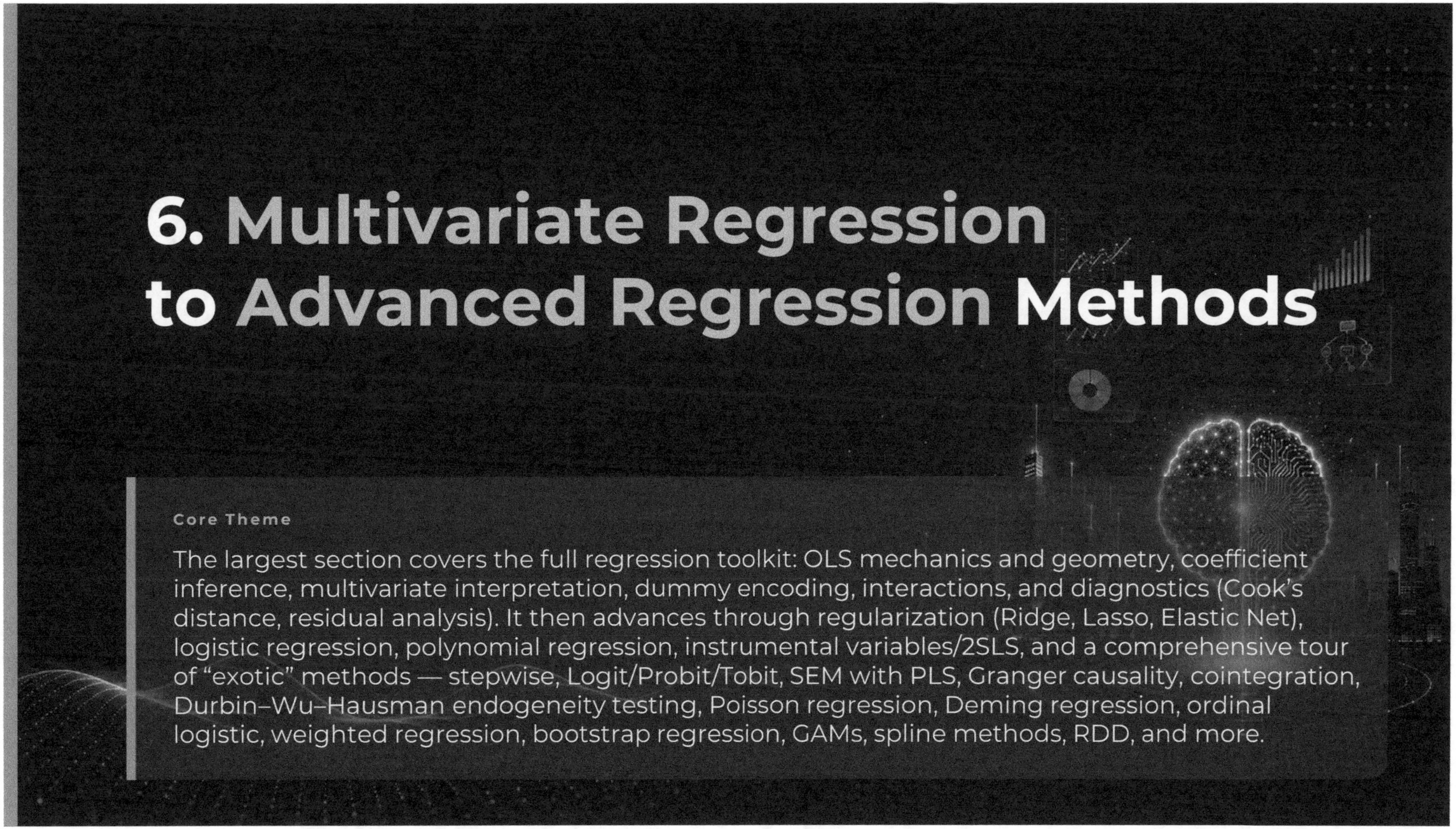
6. Multivariate Regression
to Advanced Regression Methods
Core Theme
The largest section covers the full regression toolkit: OLS mechanics and geometry, coefficient inference, multivariate interpretation, dummy encoding, interactions, and diagnostics (Cook's distance, residual analysis). It then advances through regularization (Ridge, Lasso, Elastic Net), logistic regression, polynomial regression, instrumental variables/2SLS, and a comprehensive tour of "exotic" methods — stepwise, Logit/Probit/Tobit, SEM with PLS, Granger causality, cointegration, Durbin–Wu–Hausman endogeneity testing, Poisson regression, Deming regression, ordinal logistic, weighted regression, bootstrap regression, GAMs, spline methods, RDD, and more.

Module Objectives

Regression Analysis — From Multivariate to Advanced Methods

Build Multivariate Models

Construct, diagnose, and interpret multivariate linear regression models for diverse business problems.

Model Binary Outcomes

Implement logistic regression for classification tasks, interpreting odds ratios and marginal effects.

Capture Nonlinearity

Detect and model nonlinear relationships using polynomial regression, splines, and transformations.

Leverage AI Assistance

Use Julius AI and ChatGPT to accelerate model building, interpretation, and diagnostic workflows.

Select & Regularize Variables

Apply Ridge, Lasso, and Elastic Net to handle high-dimensional data and multicollinearity effectively.

Handle Count & Quantiles

Utilize Poisson/Negative Binomial for count data and quantile regression for distributional insights.

Diagnose Assumptions

rigorous testing of OLS assumptions (linearity, homoscedasticity, normality) and handle violations.

Translate to Business

Convert statistical coefficients and model metrics into actionable business recommendations and impact.

Linear, Nonlinear, Bivariate, and Multivariate Regression

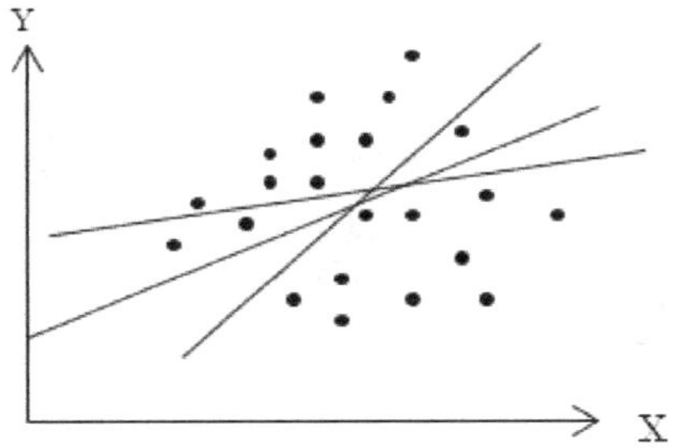

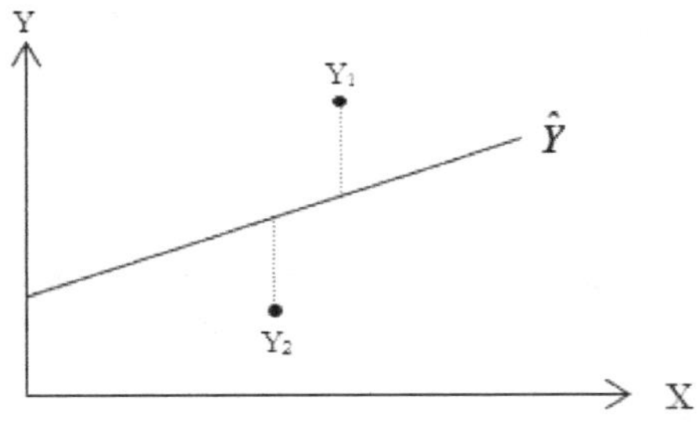

$$Population:\ y_i = \beta_0 + \beta_1 x_{1,i} + \beta_2 x_{2,i} + \cdots + \beta_k x_{k,i} + \varepsilon_i$$

$$Fitted:\ \hat{y}_i = b_0 + b_1 x_{1,i} + b_2 x_{2,i} + \cdots + b_k x_{k,i}$$

$$Matrix:\ \mathbf{y} = \mathbf{X}\beta + \varepsilon \text{ and } \hat{\beta}_{OLS} = (\mathbf{X'X})^{-1}\mathbf{X'y}$$

$Linearity\ in\ parameters: E(y_i) = \beta_0 + \beta_1 x_{1,i} + \beta_2 x_{2,i} + \cdots + \beta_k x_{k,i}$

$No\ autocorrelation\ (random\ independent\ samples):\ cov(\varepsilon_i, \varepsilon_j) = 0$

$No\ multicollinearity\ (independent\ IV):\ (X'X)^{-1}\ is\ invertible\ cov(x_i, \varepsilon) = 0$

$Exogeneity:\ E(\varepsilon|X) = 0\ unbiased\ zero\ conditional\ mean$

$Homoskedasticity:\ var(\varepsilon|X) = \sigma^2\ static\ errors, not\ var(\varepsilon|X) = \sigma_i^2$

$Normality\ and\ spheretincy\ of\ Errors:\ \varepsilon \sim iid\ N(0, \sigma^2)$

$No\ micronumerosity: n > k + 1$

$$\hat{\beta}_1 = \frac{\sum_{i=1}^{n}(X_i - \bar{X})(Y_i - \bar{Y})}{\sum_{i=1}^{n}(X_i - \bar{X})^2} = \frac{cov_{x,y}}{var_x} = \frac{\sum_{i=1}^{n} X_i Y_i - \frac{\sum_{i=1}^{n} X_i \sum_{i=1}^{n} Y_i}{n}}{\sum_{i=1}^{n} X_i^2 - \frac{\left(\sum_{i=1}^{n} X_i\right)^2}{n}}$$

$$\hat{\beta}_0 = \bar{Y} - \hat{\beta}_1 \bar{X}$$

$$\hat{\beta}_2 = \frac{\sum Y_i X_{2,i} \sum X_{3,i}^2 - \sum Y_i X_{3,i} \sum X_{2,i} X_{3,i}}{\sum X_{2,i}^2 \sum X_{3,i}^2 - \left(\sum X_{2,i} X_{3,i}\right)^2}$$

$$\hat{\beta}_3 = \frac{\sum Y_i X_{3,i} \sum X_{2,i}^2 - \sum Y_i X_{2,i} \sum X_{2,i} X_{3,i}}{\sum X_{2,i}^2 \sum X_{3,i}^2 - \left(\sum X_{2,i} X_{3,i}\right)^2}$$

$$OLS: \min_{\beta_0, \beta_1} \sum_{i=1}^{n} \varepsilon_i^2 = \min_{\beta_0, \beta_1} \sum_{i=1}^{n} (y_i - \hat{y}_i)^2$$

$$SST = \sum_{i=1}^{n} (y_i - \bar{y})^2$$

$$SSR = \sum_{i=1}^{n} (\hat{y}_i - \bar{y})^2$$

$$SSE = \sum_{i=1}^{n} (y_i - \hat{y}_i)^2$$

$$SST = SSR + SSE$$

$$R^2 = \frac{SSR}{SST} = 1 - \frac{SSE}{SST} = 1 - \frac{\sum_{i=1}^{n}(y_i - \hat{y}_i)^2}{\sum_{i=1}^{n}(y_i - \bar{y})^2}$$

$$\bar{R}^2 = 1 - \frac{SSE/(n-k-1)}{SST/(n-1)} = 1 - (1 - R^2)\frac{n-1}{n-k-1}$$

$$t = \frac{\hat{\beta}_j}{SE(\hat{\beta}_j)} \qquad SE(\hat{\beta}_j) = \sqrt{\hat{\sigma}^2 (X'X)^{-1}} = \sqrt{\frac{SSE}{n-k-1}(X'X)^{-1}}$$

Data Diagnostics

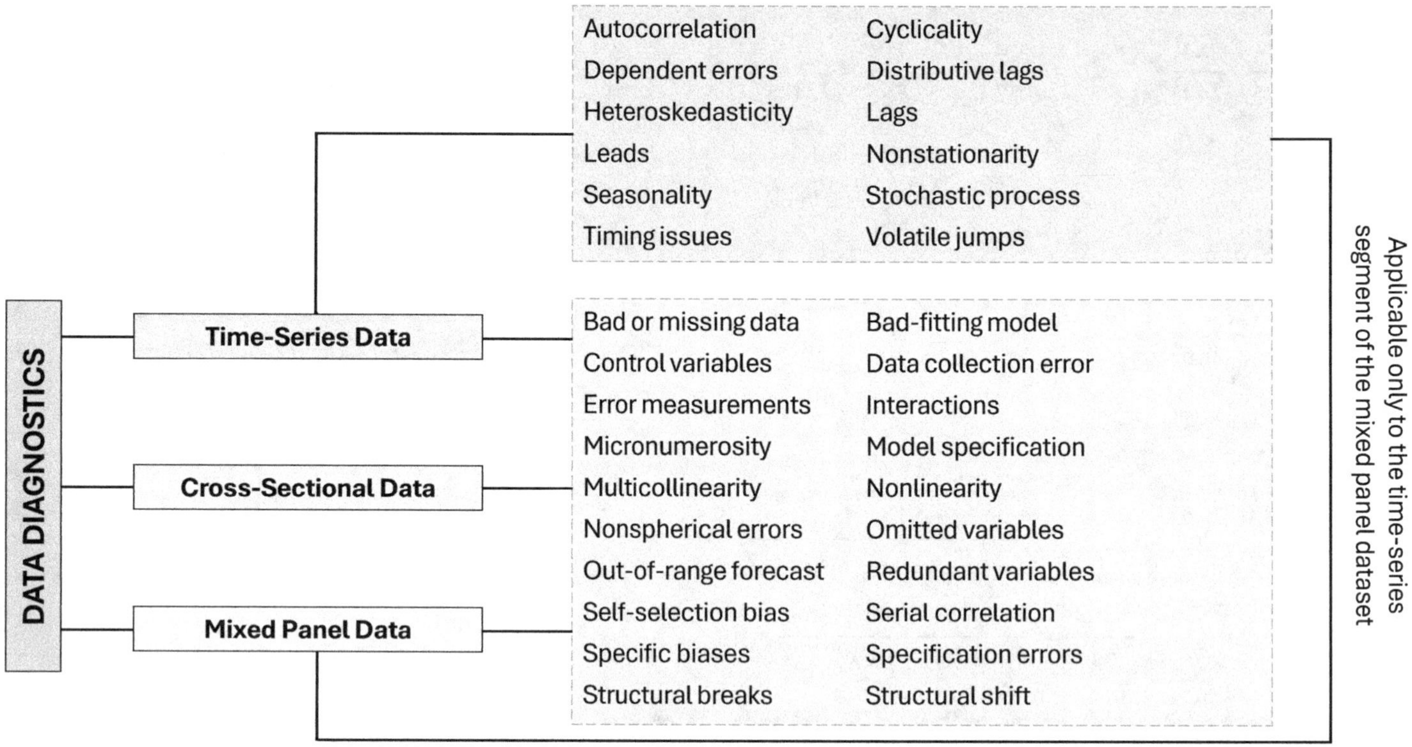

Time-series data is more prevalent in real life, and, therefore, there are more time-series forecast methods as well as error and specification tests for time-series data.

Types of Regression Analysis

10 Families · Organized by purpose and analytical complexity

Linear

OLS, Ridge, Lasso, Elastic Net & more

Logistic

Binary, Multinomial, Ordinal

Polynomial

Any-degree features + CV

GLM

Poisson, Gamma, Tweedie & more

Robust

Huber, RANSAC, Theil-Sen

Non-parametric

KNN, Trees, Forests, SVR

Time Series

ARIMA, VAR, GARCH

Quantile

Conditional quantile prediction

Bayesian

Posterior inference & credible intervals

Spline & Mixed

LOESS, smoothing, mixed effects

Linear Regression

The foundational family — predicting continuous outcomes from one or more features

Simple & Multiple Linear Regression

Models the relationship between one (simple) or several (multiple) predictors and a continuous response using a linear equation.

One predictor **Many predictors** **Continuous output**

Ordinary Least Squares (OLS)

Minimizes the sum of squared residuals to find the best-fit line. The gold-standard method when assumptions (linearity, normality, homoscedasticity) hold.

Unbiased **BLUE estimator**

Ridge Regression (L2 Regularization)

Adds a penalty proportional to the square of coefficients, shrinking them toward zero without eliminating predictors. Best for multicollinearity.

$\lambda \cdot \Sigma\beta^2$ **Multicollinearity** **Keeps all features**

Lasso Regression (L1 Regularization)

Penalizes the absolute values of coefficients, driving some exactly to zero — performing built-in feature selection.

$\lambda \cdot \Sigma|\beta|$ **Sparse models** **Feature selection**

Elastic Net

Combines L1 and L2 penalties — inherits Lasso's sparsity and Ridge's stability. Ideal when many correlated features exist.

L1 + L2 **Best of both** **Grouped selection**

Logistic & Polynomial Regression

Classification via probabilities · Non-linear curve fitting with higher-degree features

Logistic Regression

Binary Logistic Regression

Predicts the probability of one of two classes. Output is passed through a sigmoid function to yield a value between 0 and 1.

0 vs 1 | Sigmoid

Multinomial Logistic Regression

Extends binary logistic to three or more unordered categories using a softmax function over class probabilities.

3+ classes | Softmax

Ordinal Logistic Regression

Used when categories have a natural order (e.g., low / medium / high). Models cumulative probabilities across thresholds.

Ordered classes | Cumulative logit

Polynomial Regression

Polynomial Features (Any Degree)

Adds powers and interactions of features (x^2, x^3...) to a linear model, capturing non-linear relationships without leaving the linear framework.

x^2 x^3 x^n | Non-linear fit

Polynomial Fitting with Cross-Validation

Uses k-fold CV to select the optimal polynomial degree — preventing overfitting that high-degree terms introduce without regularization.

Degree selection | Bias-variance | k-fold CV

Key Insight

Polynomial regression is still a linear model — linear in its parameters. Only the features are non-linear. This means all linear model theory and tools still apply.

Generalized Linear Models (GLM)

Flexible extension of linear regression for non-normal response distributions

Poisson Regression

Models count data (events per unit time/area). Uses a log link and assumes the mean equals the variance.

Count data **Log link**

Negative Binomial

Extends Poisson to handle over-dispersed count data where variance exceeds the mean.

Overdispersion **Extra variance**

Gamma Regression

Models strictly positive, right-skewed continuous responses such as insurance claim costs or reaction times.

Positive values **Right-skewed**

Tweedie Regression

Spans Gaussian, Poisson, and Gamma distributions via a power parameter. Widely used in insurance for modeling zero-inflated continuous losses.

Zero-inflated **Insurance** **Power param p**

Other Exponential Family Distributions

GLMs can model any distribution in the exponential family — Beta for proportions, Inverse Gaussian for survival data, and Binomial for rates.

Beta **Inverse Gaussian** **Binomial**

Robust & Non-parametric Regression

Outlier-resistant methods · Distribution-free, data-driven approaches

Robust Regression

Huber Regression

Acts like OLS for small residuals, but switches to absolute-value loss for large ones — reducing the influence of outliers while remaining efficient.

Hybrid loss **Outlier-robust**

RANSAC Regression

Iteratively fits a model on random subsets of inliers, then evaluates which points fit the model — classifying the rest as outliers. Extremely robust.

Random sampling **Inlier detection**

Theil-Sen Regression

Estimates slope as the median of all pairwise slopes between data points. Highly resistant to outliers — up to 29.3% contamination.

Median slope **Non-parametric**

Non-parametric Regression

K-Nearest Neighbors Regression

Predicts by averaging the outputs of the k nearest training points. No training phase — all computation happens at prediction time.

Lazy learning **Instance-based**

Decision Tree & Random Forest

Tree-based models that split feature space into regions, with forests averaging many trees to reduce variance and improve generalization.

Interpretable **Bagging** **Feature importance**

Gradient Boosting & SVR

Boosting sequentially builds trees to correct errors; SVR finds a hyperplane that lies within an ε-tube around the data.

XGBoost **LightGBM** **Kernel SVR**

Time Series Regression

Sequential data modeling — capturing autocorrelation, seasonality, and volatility

ARIMA Models

AutoRegressive Integrated Moving Average — models time series using its own past values (AR), differencing for stationarity (I), and past forecast errors (MA).

p, d, q params **Stationarity** **Forecasting**

ARIMAX (with Exogenous Variables)

Extends ARIMA by incorporating external predictors (X) alongside the time series itself — useful when external drivers are known (e.g., promotions, weather).

External inputs **Transfer function**

Exponential Smoothing

Applies decreasing weights to past observations. Includes Simple, Double (Holt), and Triple (Holt-Winters) variants for trend and seasonality.

Holt-Winters **Seasonality**

Vector Autoregression (VAR)

Models multiple interdependent time series simultaneously — each variable is regressed on lagged values of all variables in the system.

Multivariate **Granger causality**

GARCH Models

Generalized Autoregressive Conditional Heteroskedasticity — models time-varying volatility clustering, essential in financial and risk modeling.

Volatility **Finance / Risk**

Quantile & Bayesian Regression

Beyond the mean — full distributional modeling with uncertainty quantification

Quantile Regression

Conditional Quantile Prediction

Instead of modeling the conditional mean, quantile regression models any quantile (e.g., 10th, 50th, 90th percentile) of the outcome distribution.

Q10 Q50 Q90 · Pinball loss

Full Distributional Insights

By fitting multiple quantiles, you capture the entire conditional distribution of Y — revealing heteroscedasticity and asymmetric effects that OLS misses.

Heteroscedasticity · Risk modeling · Tails

Applications

Value-at-Risk in finance, growth reference curves in medicine, delivery-time guarantees in logistics, and wage inequality research in economics.

Bayesian Regression

Bayesian Linear Regression

Places prior distributions on coefficients and updates them with data using Bayes' theorem to yield a posterior distribution over parameters — not a single point estimate.

Prior + Likelihood · Posterior

Bayesian Hierarchical Models

Pools information across groups via shared priors — ideal for repeated-measures, nested, or multi-level data where group-level variation matters.

Partial pooling · Multi-level

Posterior Inference & Credible Intervals

MCMC sampling (Stan, PyMC) draws from the posterior, yielding credible intervals that are directly interpretable as probability statements — unlike frequentist CIs.

MCMC · Stan · PyMC · HDI intervals

Spline & Mixed Effects Models

Smooth flexible curves · Group-level variation with random effects

Spline & Smoothing Methods

Cubic Splines

Piecewise cubic polynomials joined at knots with continuous first and second derivatives — producing smooth, flexible fits without global polynomial instability.

Knot placement **Smooth joins**

Smoothing Splines & LOESS

Smoothing splines minimize a penalized fit criterion; LOESS (locally estimated scatterplot smoothing) fits low-degree polynomials to local neighborhoods.

LOESS **Local fitting** **Bandwidth λ**

Kernel Regression

Estimates the conditional expectation by computing a weighted average of nearby points, where weights are determined by a kernel function (Gaussian, Epanechnikov).

Nadaraya-Watson **Bandwidth h**

Mixed Effects Models

Linear Mixed Models (LMM)

Combines fixed effects (population-level) with random effects (group-level deviations in intercepts or slopes) — ideal for repeated-measures and panel data.

Fixed + Random **Panel data**

Generalized Linear Mixed Models (GLMM)

Extends LMM to non-Gaussian outcomes (binary, count) by combining random effects with a GLM link function — for clustered or longitudinal non-normal data.

Non-normal **Clustered**

Hierarchical Regression

Builds models in sequential steps — testing whether adding blocks of predictors significantly improves fit via likelihood ratio tests or F-tests at each stage.

Sequential blocks **Model building**

Specialized Methods & Model Validation

Niche regression families · Rigorous evaluation & comparison frameworks

Specialized Regression Methods

Isotonic & Segmented Regression

Isotonic fits a monotone step function. Segmented (piecewise) regression fits separate linear segments with breakpoints — ideal for structural change detection.

Monotone | Breakpoints | Change detection

Orthogonal & Nonlinear Regression

Orthogonal (Deming) regression minimizes errors in both X and Y — useful when both have measurement error. Nonlinear regression fits arbitrary nonlinear functions via iterative optimization.

Errors in both axes | Curve fitting

Model Validation & Diagnostics

Cross-Validation & Hyperparameter Tuning

k-Fold, leave-one-out, and nested CV estimate generalization error without data leakage; grid/random/Bayesian search optimize hyperparameters.

k-Fold CV | Grid search | LOOCV

Residual Analysis & Diagnostics

Check assumptions: residual vs. fitted plots (linearity), Q-Q plots (normality), scale-location (homoscedasticity), leverage plots (influential points), and VIF (multicollinearity).

Q-Q plots | Cook's distance | VIF

Model Comparison & Selection

Compare models using AIC, BIC, adjusted R^2, likelihood ratio tests, and hold-out set performance. Feature importance via permutation and SHAP values.

AIC · BIC | SHAP | Adj. R^2

Linear, Nonlinear, Bivariate, and Multivariate Regression

Multiple Regression Analysis Data Set

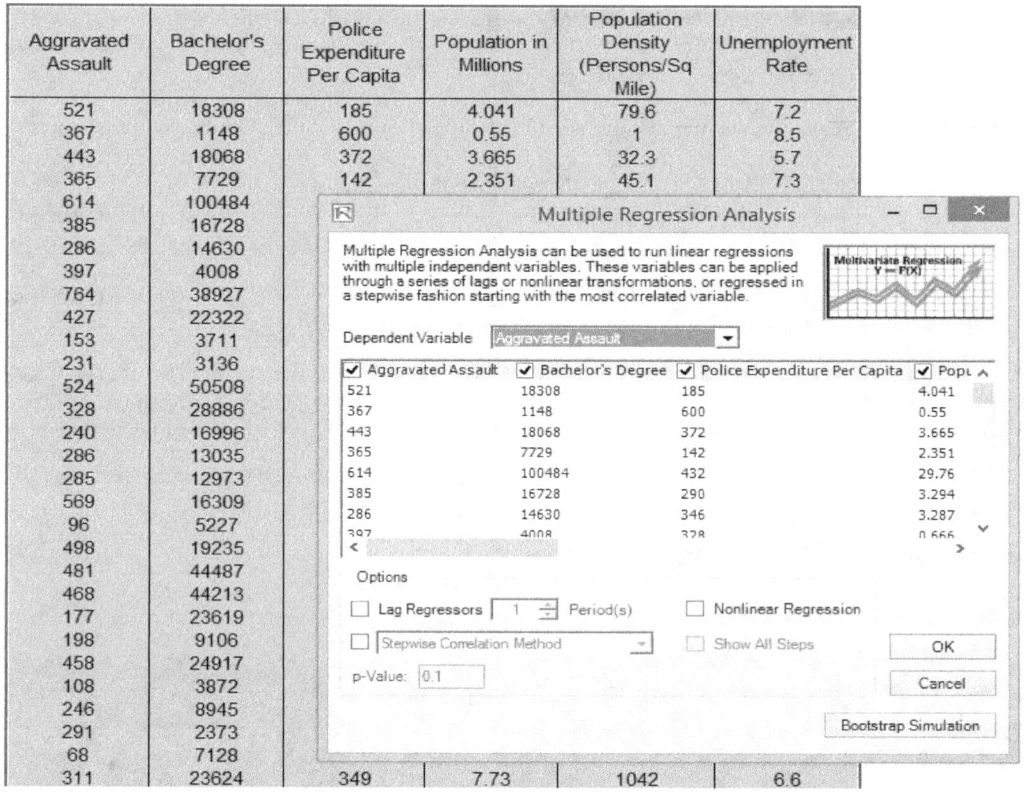

Linear, Nonlinear, Bivariate, and Multivariate Regression

Regression Analysis Report

Regression Statistics

Regression Statistics	
R-Squared (Coefficient of Determination)	0.3272
Adjusted R-Squared	0.2508
Multiple R (Multiple Correlation Coefficient)	0.5720
Standard Error of the Estimates (SEy)	149.6720
Number of Observations	50

The R-Squared or Coefficient of Determination indicates that 0.33 of the variation in the dependent variable can be explained and accounted for by the independent variables in this regression analysis. However, in a multiple regression, the Adjusted R-Squared takes into account the existence of additional independent variables or regressors and adjusts this R-Squared value to a more accurate view of the regression's explanatory power. Hence, only 0.25 of the variation in the dependent variable can be explained by the regressors.

The Multiple Correlation Coefficient (Multiple R) measures the correlation between the actual dependent variable (Y) and the estimated or fitted (Y) based on the regression equation. This is also the square root of the Coefficient of Determination (R-Squared).

The Standard Error of the Estimates (SEy) describes the dispersion of data points above and below the regression line or plane. This value is used as part of the calculation to obtain the confidence interval of the estimates later.

Regression Results

	Intercept	Bachelor's Degree	Police Expenditure Per Capita	Population in Millions	Population Density (Persons/Sq Mile)	Unemployment Rate
Coefficients	57.9555	-0.0035	0.4644	25.2377	-0.0086	16.5579
Standard Error	108.7901	0.0035	0.2535	14.1172	0.1016	14.7996
t-Statistic	0.5327	-1.0066	1.8316	1.7877	-0.0843	1.1188
p-Value	0.5969	0.3197	0.0738	0.0807	0.9332	0.2693
Lower 5%	-161.2966	-0.0106	-0.0466	-3.2137	-0.2132	-13.2687
Upper 95%	277.2076	0.0036	0.9753	53.6891	0.1961	46.3845

Degrees of Freedom	
Degrees of Freedom for Regression	5
Degrees of Freedom for Residual	44
Total Degrees of Freedom	49

Hypothesis Test	
Critical t-Statistic (99% confidence with df of 44)	2.6923
Critical t-Statistic (95% confidence with df of 44)	2.0154
Critical t-Statistic (90% confidence with df of 44)	1.6802

The Coefficients provide the estimated regression intercept and slopes. For instance, the coefficients are estimates of the true; population b values in the following regression equation Y = b0 + b1X1 + b2X2 + ... + bnXn. The Standard Error measures how accurate the predicted Coefficients are, and the t-Statistics are the ratios of each predicted Coefficient to its Standard Error.

The t-Statistic is used in hypothesis testing, where we set the null hypothesis (Ho) such that the real mean of the Coefficient = 0, and the alternate hypothesis (Ha) such that the real mean of the Coefficient is not equal to 0. A t-test is is performed and the calculated t-Statistic is compared to the critical values at the relevant Degrees of Freedom for Residual. The t-test is very important as it calculates if each of the coefficients is statistically significant in the presence of the other regressors. This means that the t-test statistically verifies whether a regressor or independent variable should remain in the regression or it should be dropped.

The Coefficient is statistically significant if its calculated t-Statistic exceeds the Critical t-Statistic at the relevant degrees of freedom (df). The three main confidence levels used to test for significance are 90%, 95% and 99%. If a Coefficient's t-Statistic exceeds the Critical level, it is considered statistically significant. Alternatively, the p-Value calculates each t-Statistic's probability of occurrence, which means that the smaller the p-Value, the more significant the Coefficient. The usual significant levels for the p-Value are 0.01, 0.05, and 0.10, corresponding to the 99%, 95%, and 90% confidence levels.

The Coefficients with their p-Values highlighted in blue indicate that they are statistically significant at the 90% confidence or 0.10 alpha level, while those highlighted in red indicate that they are not statistically significant at any other alpha levels.

Analysis of Variance

	Sums of Squares	Mean of Squares	F-Statistic	p-Value
Regression	479388.49	95877.70	4.28	0.0029
Residual	985675.19	22401.71		
Total	1465063.68			

Hypothesis Test	
Critical F-statistic (99% confidence with df of 5 and 44)	3.4651
Critical F-statistic (95% confidence with df of 5 and 44)	2.4270
Critical F-statistic (90% confidence with df of 5 and 44)	1.9828

The Analysis of Variance (ANOVA) table provides an F-test of the regression model's overall statistical significance. Instead of looking at individual regressors as in the t-test, the F-test looks at all the estimated Coefficients' statistical properties. The F-Statistic is calculated as the ratio of the Regression's Mean of Squares to the Residual's Mean of Squares. The numerator measures how much of the regression is explained, while the denominator measures how much is unexplained. Hence, the larger the F-Statistic, the more significant the model. The corresponding p-Value is calculated to test the null hypothesis (Ho) where all the Coefficients are simultaneously equal to zero, versus the alternate hypothesis (Ha) that they are all simultaneously different from zero, indicating a significant overall regression model. If the p-Value is smaller than the 0.01, 0.05, or 0.10 alpha significance, then the regression is significant. The same approach can be applied to the F-Statistic by comparing the calculated F-Statistic with the critical F values at various significance levels.

Forecasting

Period	Actual (Y)	Forecast (F)	Error (E)
1	521.0000	299.5124	221.4876
2	367.0000	487.1243	(120.1243)
3	443.0000	353.2789	89.7211
4	365.0000	276.3296	88.6704
5	614.0000	776.1336	(162.1336)
6	385.0000	298.9993	86.0007
7	286.0000	354.8718	(68.8718)
8	397.0000	312.6155	84.3845
9	764.0000	529.7550	234.2450
10	427.0000	347.7034	79.2966
11	153.0000	266.2526	(113.2526)
12	231.0000	264.6375	(33.6375)
13	524.0000	406.8009	117.1991
14	328.0000	272.2226	55.7774
15	240.0000	231.7882	8.2118
16	286.0000	257.8862	28.1138
17	285.0000	314.9521	(29.9521)
18	569.0000	335.3140	233.6860
19	96.0000	282.0356	(186.0356)
20	498.0000	370.2062	127.7938
21	481.0000	340.8742	140.1258
22	468.0000	427.5118	40.4882
23	177.0000	274.5298	(97.5298)
24	198.0000	294.7795	(96.7795)
25	458.0000	295.2180	162.7820

RMSE: 140.4048

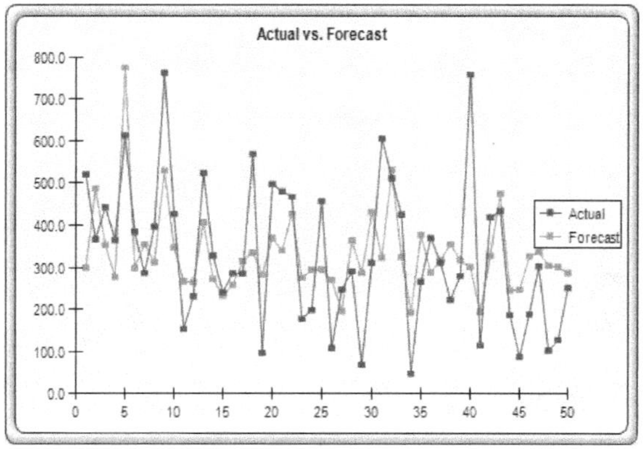

Manual Computations of Bivariate Model

Example: Given the following sales amounts ($ millions) and advertising sizes (measured as linear inches by summing up all the sides of an ad) for a local newspaper, answer the following questions.

Advertising size (inch)	12	18	24	30	36	42	48
Sales ($ millions)	5.9	5.6	5.5	7.2	8.0	7.7	8.4

(a) Which is the dependent variable and which is the independent variable?
The independent variable is advertising size, whereas the dependent variable is sales.

(b) Manually calculate the slope (β_1) and the intercept (β_0) terms.

X	Y	XY	X^2	Y^2
12	5.9	70.8	144	34.81
18	5.6	100.8	324	31.36
24	5.5	132.0	576	30.25
30	7.2	216.0	900	51.84
36	8.0	288.0	1296	64.00
42	7.7	323.4	1764	59.29
48	8.4	403.2	2304	70.56
$\Sigma(X)=210$	$\Sigma(Y)=48.3$	$\Sigma(XY)=1534.2$	$\Sigma(X^2)=7308$	$\Sigma(Y^2)=342.11$

$$\beta_1 = \frac{1534.2 - \frac{210(48.3)}{7}}{7308 - \frac{210^2}{7}} = 0.0845 \quad and \quad \beta_0 = \frac{48.3}{7} - 0.0845\left[\frac{210}{7}\right] = 4.3643$$

(c) What is the estimated regression equation?
$Y = 4.3643 + 0.0845X$ or Sales = 4.3643 + 0.0845(Size)

(d) What would the level of sales be if we purchase a 28-inch ad?
$Y = 4.3643 + 0.0845\ (28) = \$6.73$ million dollars in sales

Note that we only predict or forecast and cannot say for certain. This is only an expected value or on average.

Manual Computation of Coefficient of Determination

The R-squared (R^2), or coefficient of determination, is an error measurement that looks at the percent variation of the dependent variable that can be explained by the variation in the independent variable for a regression analysis. The coefficient of determination can be calculated by:

$$R^2 = 1 - \frac{\sum_{i=1}^{n}(Y_i - \hat{Y}_i)^2}{\sum_{i=1}^{n}(Y_i - \bar{Y})^2} = 1 - \frac{SSE}{TSS}$$

where the coefficient of determination is one less the ratio of the sums of squares of the errors (SSE) to the total sums of squares (TSS). In other words, the ratio of SSE to TSS is the unexplained portion of the analysis, thus, one less the ratio of SSE to TSS is the explained portion of the regression analysis.

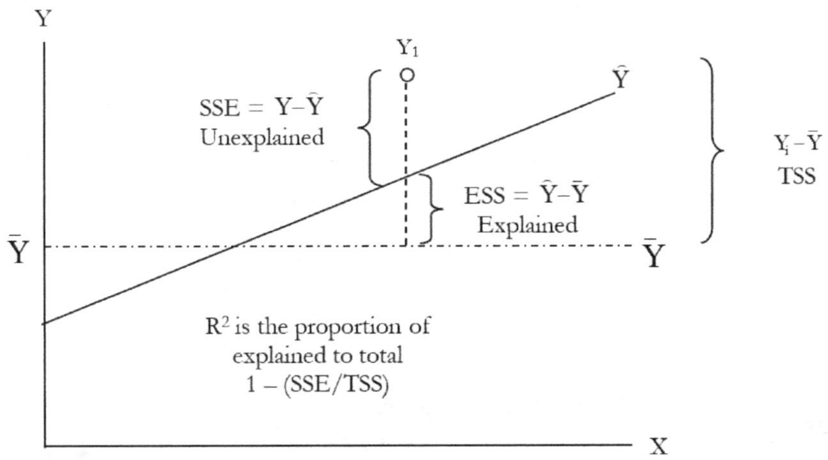

Another related statistic, the adjusted coefficient of determination, or the adjusted R-squared $\bar{R}^2$, corrects for the number of independent variables (k) in a multivariate regression through a degrees of freedom correction to provide a more conservative estimate:

$$\bar{R}^2 = 1 - \frac{\sum_{i=1}^{n}(Y_i - \hat{Y}_i)^2 / (k-2)}{\sum_{i=1}^{n}(Y_i - \bar{Y})^2 / (k-1)} = 1 - \frac{SSE / (k-2)}{TSS / (k-1)}$$

The adjusted R-squared should be used instead of the regular R-squared in multivariate regressions because every time an independent variable is added into the regression analysis, the R-squared will increase; indicating that the percent variation explained has increased. This increase occurs even when nonsensical regressors are added. The adjusted R-squared takes the added regressors into account and penalizes the regression accordingly, providing a much better estimate of a regression model's goodness-of-fit.

$Linearity\ in\ parameters: E(y_i) = \beta_0 + \beta_1 x_{1,i} + \beta_2 x_{2,i} + \cdots + \beta_k x_{k,i}$

$No\ autocorrelation\ (random\ independent\ samples):\ cov(\varepsilon_i, \varepsilon_j) = 0$

$No\ multicollinearity\ (independent\ IV):\ (X'X)^{-1}\ is\ invertible\ cov(x_i, \varepsilon) = 0$

$Exogeneity:\ E(\varepsilon|X) = 0\ unbiased\ zero\ conditional\ mean$

$Homoskedasticity:\ var(\varepsilon|X) = \sigma^2\ static\ errors, not\ var(\varepsilon|X) = \sigma_i^2$

$Normality\ and\ spheretecy\ of\ Errors:\ \varepsilon \sim iid\ N(0, \sigma^2)$

$No\ micronumerosity: n > k + 1$

Regression Interpretation

Regression Statistics		
R-Squared (Coefficient of Determination)		0.8146
Adjusted R-Squared		0.7776
Multiple R (Multiple Correlation Coefficient)		0.9026
Standard Error of the Estimates (SEy)		0.5725
Number of Observations		7
Regression Results		
	Intercept	Ad Size
Coefficients	4.3643	0.0845
Standard Error	0.5826	0.0180
t-Statistic	7.4911	4.6877
p-Value	0.0007	0.0054
Lower 5%	2.8667	0.0382
Upper 95%	5.8619	0.1309

ANOVA

	df	*SS*	*MS*	*F*	*Significance F*
Regression	1	7.2014	7.2014	21.9747	0.0054
Residual	5	1.6386	0.3277		
Total	6	8.8400			

	Coefficients	*Standard Error*	*t Stat*	*P-value*	*Lower 95%*	*Upper 95%*
Intercept	4.3643	0.5826	7.4911	0.0007	2.8667	5.8619
X Variable 1	0.0845	0.0180	4.6877	0.0054	0.0382	0.1309

Example: Given the information from the regression analysis output, interpret the following:

(a) Perform a hypothesis test on the slope and intercept to see if they are *each* significant at a two-tailed alpha (α) of 0.05). The null hypothesis H_0 is such that the slope $\beta_1 = 0$ and the alternate hypothesis H_a is such that $\beta_1 \neq 0$. The t-statistic calculated is 4.6877, which exceeds the t-critical (2.9687 obtained from the t-statistic table at the end of this book) for a two-tailed alpha of 0.05 and degrees of freedom $n - k = 7 - 1 = 6$.[36] Therefore, the null hypothesis is rejected, and one can state that the slope is statistically significantly different from 0, indicating that the regression's estimate of the slope is statistically significant. This hypothesis test can also be performed by looking at the t-statistic's corresponding p-value (0.0054), which is less than the alpha of 0.05, which means the null hypothesis is rejected. The hypothesis test is then applied to the intercept, where the null hypothesis H_0 is such that the intercept $\beta_0 = 0$ and the alternate hypothesis H_a is such that $\beta_0 \neq 0$. The t-statistic calculated is 7.4911, which exceeds the critical t value of 2.9687 for $n - k$ $(7 - 1 = 6)$ degrees of freedom, so, the null hypothesis is rejected indicating that the intercept is statistically significantly different from 0, meaning that the regression's estimate of the intercept if statistically significant. The calculated p-value (0.0007) is also less than the alpha level, which means the null hypothesis is also rejected.

(b) Perform a hypothesis test to see if both the slope and intercept are significant as a whole. In other words, if the estimated model is statistically significant at an alpha (α) of 0.05. The simultaneous null hypothesis H_0 is such that $\beta_0 = \beta_1 = 0$ and the alternate hypothesis H_a is $\beta_0 \neq \beta_1 \neq 0$. The calculated F-value is 21.9747, which exceeds the critical F-value (5.99 obtained from the table at the end of this book) for k (1) degrees of freedom in the numerator and $n - k$ $(7 - 1 = 6)$ degrees of freedom for the denominator, so the null hypothesis is rejected indicating that both the slope and intercept are simultaneously significantly different from 0 and that the model as a whole is statistically significant. This result is confirmed by the p-value of 0.0054 (significance of F), which is less than the alpha value, thereby rejecting the null hypothesis and confirming that the regression as a whole is statistically significant.

(c) Using Risk Simulator's regression output, interpret the R^2 value. How is it related to the correlation coefficient? The calculated R^2 is 0.8146, meaning that 81.46% of the variation in the dependent variable can be explained by the variation in the independent variable. The R^2 is simply the square of the correlation coefficient, that is, the correlation coefficient between the independent and dependent variable is 0.9026.

Bivariate Functional Forms and Specifications

Regression models can also take many functional forms or specifications. For instance, a linear regression will take the form of $Y = \beta_0 + \beta_1 X_1 + \beta_2 X_2 ... + \beta_n X_n + \varepsilon$ whereas a nonlinear regression can take the standard form of $Y = \beta_0 + \beta_1 ln(X_1) + \beta_2 ln(X_2) ... + \beta_n ln(X_n) + \varepsilon$. However, there are other functional forms depending on the relationship of the variables. Typically, to test for functional form specifications, we revert to using a single independent variable at a time. The following are the most commonly used bivariate functional forms:

Linear	$Y = \beta_0 + \beta_1 X_1 + \varepsilon$
Linear Log	$Y = \beta_0 + \beta_1 ln(X_1) + \varepsilon$
Reciprocal	$Y = \beta_0 + \beta_1 (1/X_1) + \varepsilon$
Quadratic	$Y = \beta_0 + \beta_1 X_1 + \beta_2 X_1^2 + \varepsilon$
Log Linear	$ln(Y) = \beta_0 + \beta_1 X_1 + \varepsilon$
Log Reciprocal	$ln(Y) = \beta_0 + \beta_1 (1/X_1) + \varepsilon$
Log Quadratic	$ln(Y) = \beta_0 + \beta_1 X_1 + \beta_2 X_1^2 + \varepsilon$
Double Log	$ln(Y) = \beta_0 + \beta_1 ln(X_1) + \varepsilon$
Logistic	$Y/(1 - Y) = \beta_0 + \beta_1 X_1 + \varepsilon$

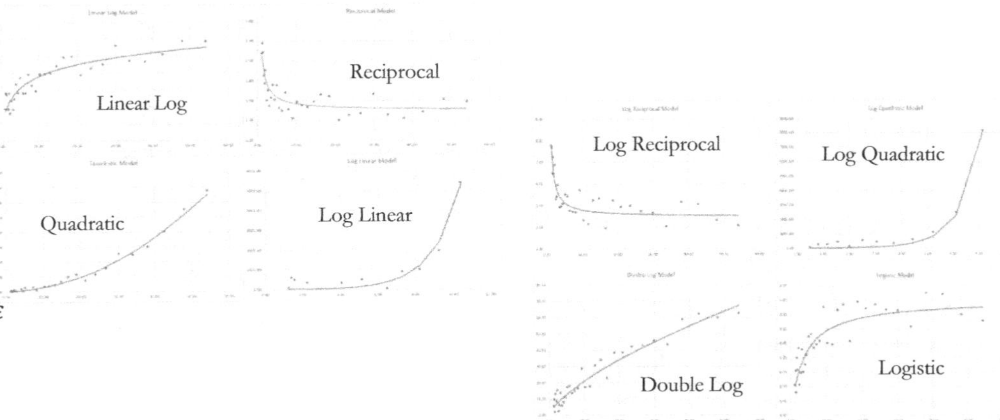

These functional forms are tested with one dependent variable and one independent variable. In the case of multivariate regressions, simply run the pairwise models and take the resulting functional forms and combine them into a more complex multivariate structure, with the understanding that when combining different functional forms, some previously statistically significant functions may drop out of the comprehensive model and integrate with other functions in the larger model.

Bivariate Functional Forms Specification with BizStats

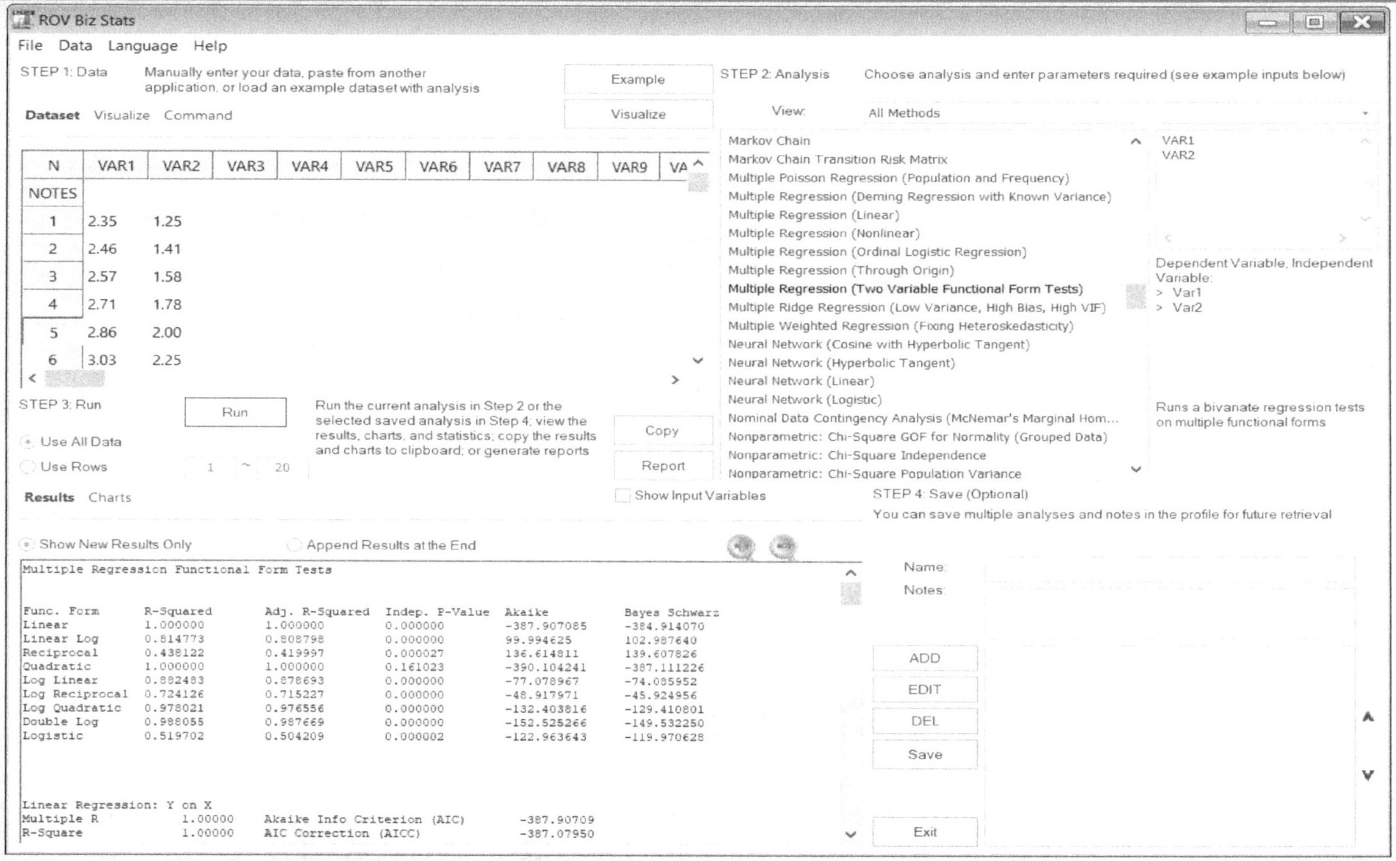

Simple Linear Regression

Intuition, Mechanics, and Goodness of Fit

The Linear Model

$$y_i = \beta_0 + \beta_1 x_i + \varepsilon_i$$

Ordinary Relationship between predictor x and outcome y with intercept β_0, slope β_1, and error term ε.

OLS Criterion (Minimize SSE)

$$\min_{\beta_0,\beta_1} \sum_{i=1}^{n} \varepsilon_i^2 = \min_{\beta_0,\beta_1} \sum_{i=1}^{n} (y_i - \hat{y}_i)^2$$

Ordinary Least Squares finds the line that minimizes the sum of squared vertical distances (residuals).

GOODNESS OF FIT

$$R^2 = 1 - \frac{\text{SSE}}{\text{SST}} = 1 - \frac{\sum (y_i - \hat{y}_i)^2}{\sum (y_i - \bar{y})^2}$$

Proportion of variance in y explained by x. Ranges from 0 to 1.

OLS Fit: Minimizing Residuals

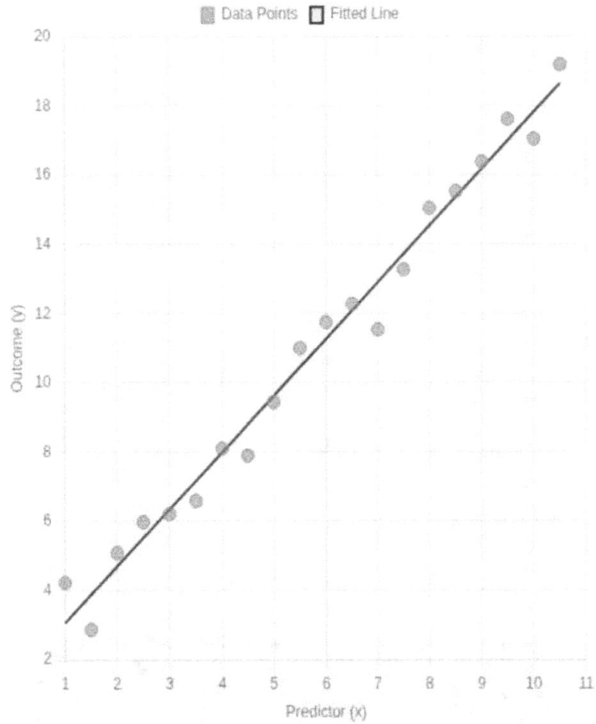

The black line represents the best fit $\hat{y} = \beta_0 + \beta_1 x$. The blue dots represent the data points.

OLS and Geometry

Closed Form Solution & Projection Interpretation

Closed Form Solution (Normal Equations)

$$\hat{\beta} = (X'X)^{-1}X'y$$

Derived by minimizing the sum of squared residuals. Requires X'X to be invertible (no perfect multicollinearity).

Orthogonality Condition

$$X'\hat{\varepsilon} = 0 \text{ where } \hat{\varepsilon} = y - X\hat{\beta}$$

Residuals are orthogonal to every predictor in X. This means no linear information remains in the residuals.

Projection Matrix (Hat Matrix)

$$\hat{y} = X(X'X)^{-1}X'y = Hy$$

H projects the observed vector y onto the column space of X. Projected y is the closest point in the span of X to y.

Geometric Interpretation

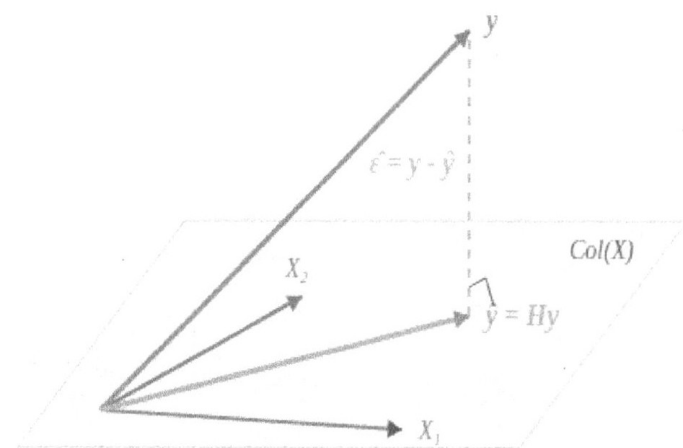

Key Insight: OLS finds the coefficient vector beta such that the residual vector epsilon is perpendicular (orthogonal) to the plane spanned by the predictors X1 and X2. This minimizes the Euclidean distance epsilon squared.

Inference for Coefficients

Evaluating Significance and Uncertainty in Regression Models

Standard Errors (SE)

Measures the precision of the estimate $SE(\hat{\beta})$. Smaller standard errors imply higher precision, which is achieved through larger sample sizes (n) and greater variation in the predictor variable (X).

t-Statistic & Hypothesis Testing

Tests the null hypothesis that the coefficient is zero ($H_0: \beta=0$). Calculated as the ratio of the coefficient to its standard error: $t=\hat{\beta} / SE(\hat{\beta})$. A larger absolute t-value generally indicates significance.

Interpreting p-values

The probability of observing the test statistic if the null hypothesis were true. A low p-value (typically < 0.05) suggests that the relationship is unlikely to be due to random chance.

Confidence Intervals Formula

Defines the range of plausible values for the true population parameter with a specific confidence level (e.g., 95%): $\hat{\beta}_j \pm t_{(\alpha \cdot /2df)} \cdot SE(\hat{\beta}_j)$. If the interval excludes 0, the effect is significant.

Practical vs. Statistical Significance: With very large datasets, tiny coefficients can be statistically significant (low p-value) but functionally irrelevant to business outcomes.

Multivariate Regression & Model Fit

Interpreting Coefficients, Significance, and Diagnostics

The Linear Model

$$y = \beta_0 + \beta_1 x_1 + \cdots + \beta_K x_K + \varepsilon$$

Estimates the **partial effect** of each predictor (x) on the outcome (y), holding all other variables constant.

Adjusted R-Squared

$$R^2_{adj} = 1 - (1 - R^2)\frac{n-1}{n-k-1}$$

Penalizes model complexity. Unlike standard R^2, it only increases if a new variable improves the model more than chance.

F-Statistic

F = MST / MSE

Tests the global null hypothesis: Do **any** of the predictors have a non-zero relationship with the outcome?

Model Output: Predicting Customer Lifetime Value (CLV)

N = 1,450 Adj. R^2 = 0.684 Prob(F) < 0.001

VARIABLE	COEFF (Β)	STD. ERROR	T-STATISTIC	P > |T|	CONF. INTERVAL [95%]
Intercept (Constant)	1250.45	85.20	14.67	0.000 ***	[1083.2, 1417.6]
Avg_Monthly_Spend ($)	12.45	0.85	14.64	0.000 ***	[10.78, 14.12]
Tenure_Months	45.20	3.10	14.58	0.000 ***	[39.12, 51.28]
Support_Calls (Count)	-8.30	12.40	-0.67	0.503	[-32.65, 16.05]
Web_Visits_Last_30d	0.15	0.08	1.87	0.061	[-0.01, 0.31]
High_Income_Dummy	320.10	45.50	7.03	0.000 ***	[230.8, 409.4]

Signif. codes: '***' 0.001 '**' 0.01 '*' 0.05 '.' 0.1

Interpretation: "Avg_Monthly_Spend" has a significant positive effect; "Support_Calls" is not statistically significant.

Encoding Categories & Interactions

Handling Qualitative Variables and Moderation Effects

Dummy Variable Encoding

$$D_j = \begin{cases} 1 & \text{if category } j \\ 0 & \text{otherwise} \end{cases}$$

For a categorical variable with **k** levels, we create **k-1** binary dummy variables to avoid perfect multicollinearity (dummy variable trap).

Interaction Model

$$y = \beta_0 + \beta_1 x + \beta_2 z + \beta_3 (x \cdot z) + \varepsilon$$

Here, the effect of **x** on **y** depends on the value of **z.** This models the moderation effects where relationships are not constant.

Marginal Effect Interpretation

$$\frac{\partial y}{\partial x} = \beta_1 + \beta_3 z$$

The slope of **y** with respect to **x** is no longer just β_1; it changes linearly with the moderator variable **z**.

Dummy Coding Example (Region)

Original Category	Is_North (D1)	Is_South (D2)	Is_East (D3)
North	1	0	0
South	0	1	0
East	0	0	1
West (Base)	0	0	0

Interaction Effect Visualization

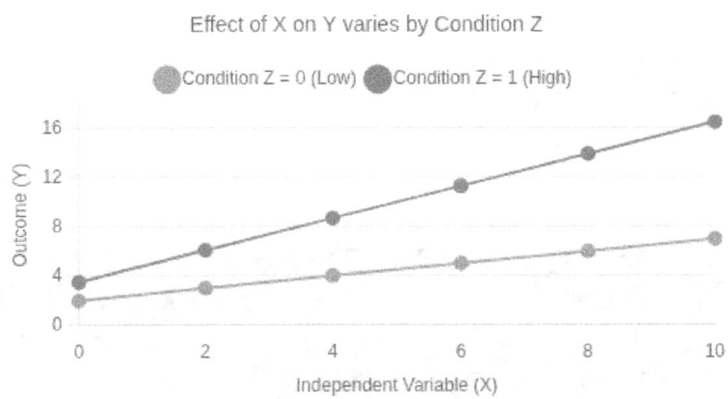

Regression Diagnostics & Influence

Validating OLS Assumptions and Identifying Outliers

Diagnostic Panel

1. Residuals vs Fitted

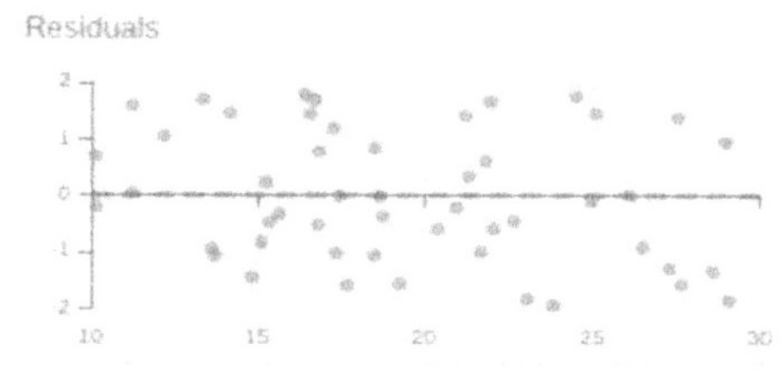

2. Normal Q-Q

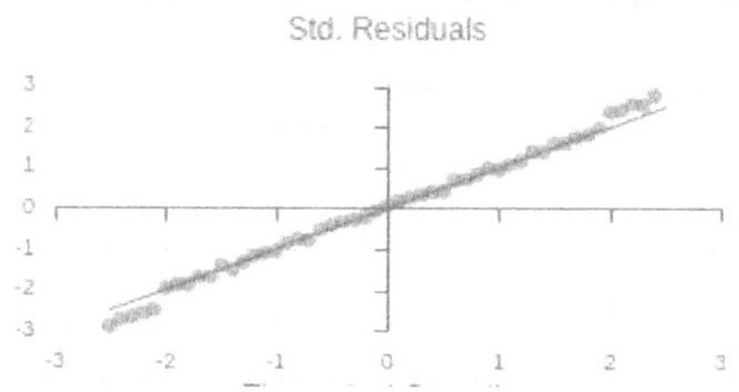

3. Residuals vs Leverage (Cook's Distance)

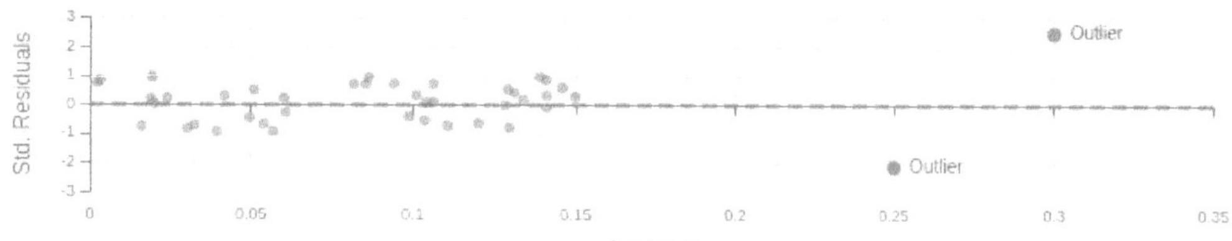

Cook's Distance (D)

$$D_i = \frac{e_i^2}{p \cdot \text{MSE}} \cdot \left[\frac{h_{ii}}{(1 - h_{ii})^2}\right]$$

OLS Assumptions

- **Linearity:** Residuals should have mean 0 vs. fitted values (no curve).
- **Homoscedasticity:** Constant variance (no "funnel" shape).
- **Normality:** Residuals follow normal distribution (Q-Q line).
- **Independence:** No correlation between error terms.

Variable Selection & Information Criteria

Strategies for Model Complexity and Feature Selection

Akaike Information Criterion (AIC)

$$\text{AIC} = 2k - 2\ln(\hat{L})$$

Estimates prediction error. k is predictors, L is likelihood. Lower values indicate better trade-off between fit and complexity.

Bayesian Information Criterion (BIC)

$$\text{BIC} = k\ln(n) - 2\ln(\hat{L})$$

Similiar to AIC but penalizes complexity more heavily as sample size n increases. Prefers simpler models.

K-Fold Cross-Validation Error

$$\text{CV}_{(k)} = \frac{1}{k}\sum_{i=1}^{k} \text{MSE}_i$$

Robust estimation of out-of-sample performance by averaging error across k validation folds.

Model Complexity vs. Error

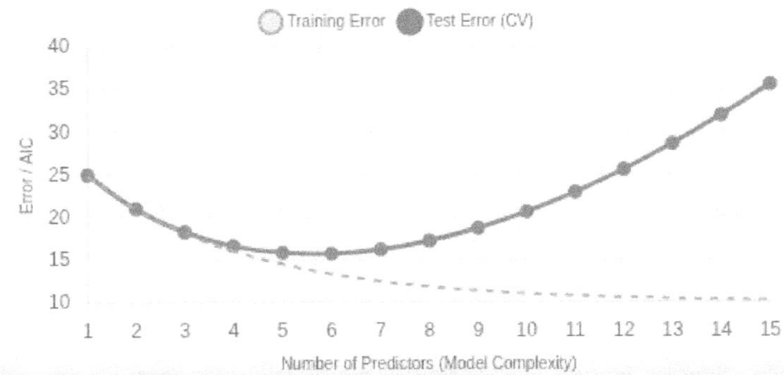

Selection Algorithms

Forward Selection

Start with null model. Iteratively add the most significant predictor (lowest p-value) until no improvement.

Backward Elimination

Start with the full model. Iteratively remove the least significant predictor (highest p-value) until all are significant.

Stepwise Regression

Hybrid approach. At each step, consider adding the best variable and removing any that became insignificant.

Regularized Regression: Ridge, Lasso, Elastic Net

Handling Multicollinearity and Overfitting via Penalization

Ridge Regression (L2 Penalty)

$$\min_{\beta} \sum_{i=1}^{n} (y_i - x_i^T \beta)^2 + \lambda \sum_{j=1}^{p} \beta_j^2$$

Shrinks coefficients toward zero (L2 norm) to reduce variance. Handles multicollinearity well but doesn't perform variable selection (coefficients ≠ 0).

Lasso Regression (L1 Penalty)

$$\min_{\beta} \sum_{i=1}^{n} (y_i - x_i^T \beta)^2 + \lambda \sum_{j=1}^{p} |\beta_j^2|$$

Uses L1 norm to shrink coefficients. Can force some coefficients exactly to zero, performing automatic variable selection.

Elastic Net

$$\min_{\beta} \text{RSS} + \lambda_1 \left\| \beta \right\|_1 + \lambda_2 \|_{\beta}^{\|22}$$

Combines L1 and L2 penalties. Useful when predictors are correlated (groups related features together).

Tuning Parameter (λ)

Choose λ via k-Fold Cross-Validation

Controls strength of regularization. High λ = high bias/low variance; Low λ = low bias/high variance.

Lasso Coefficient Paths

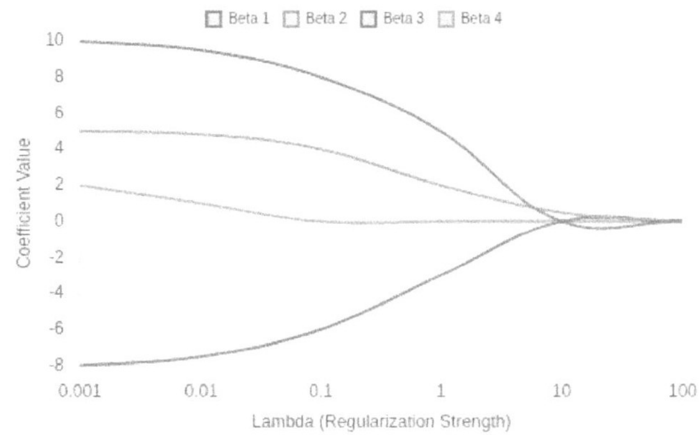

Bias-Variance Tradeoff

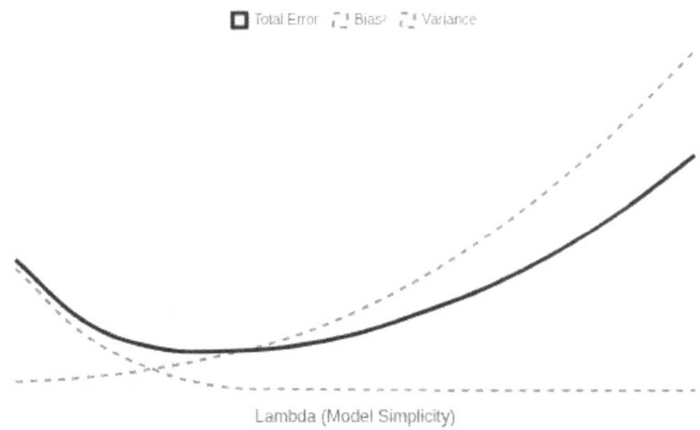

Logistic Regression & Classification Metrics

Modeling Binary Outcomes and Evaluating Model Performance

Probability Mapping (Sigmoid Function)

$$P(y| = 1x) = \sigma(z) = \frac{1}{1 + e^{-z}} \text{ where } z = X\beta$$

Transforms linear output into a probability between 0 and 1.

Linear Relationship (Log-Odds)

$$\ln\left(\frac{p}{1-p}\right) = \beta_0 + \beta_1 x_1 + \cdots + \beta_k x_k$$

The logit transformation linearizes the relationship between predictors and the outcome.

Evaluation Metrics

$$\text{Precision} = \frac{TP}{TP+FP}, \ \text{Recall} = \frac{TP}{TP+FN}$$

$$F1 = 2 \cdot \frac{\text{Precision} \cdot \text{Recall}}{\text{Precision} + \text{Recall}}$$

Balancing sensitivity (Recall) and correctness (Precision) for imbalanced classes.

The Logistic Function

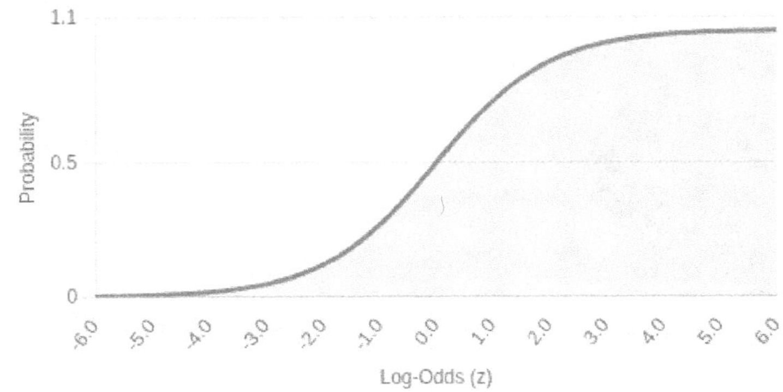

ROC Curve & AUC

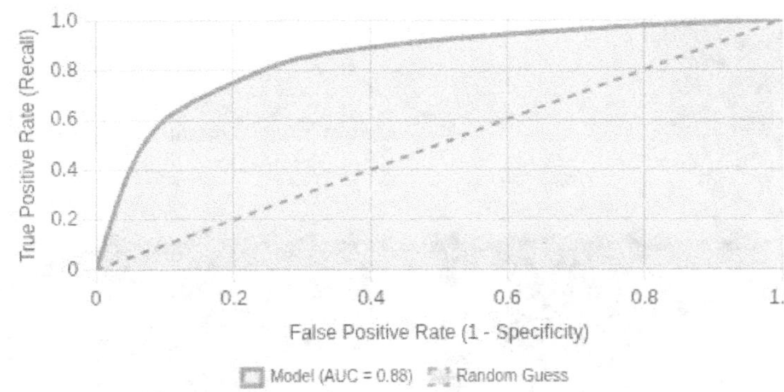

Specialized Regression Models

Polynomial, Quantile, and Count Data Methods

Nonlinear Relationships (Polynomial)

$$y_i = \beta_0 + \beta_1 x_i + \beta_2 x_i^2 + \cdots + \beta_d x_i^d + \varepsilon_i$$

Extends linear models to capture curvature. Higher degrees (d) increase flexibility but risk overfitting.

Robust Estimation (Quantile Regression)

$$\min_{\beta} \sum_{i=1}^{n} \rho_\tau (y_i - x_i'\beta)$$

Minimizes weighted absolute deviations to model conditional quantiles (e.g., median $\tau = 0.5$), not just the mean.

$$\log(\lambda_i) = \beta_0 + \beta_1 x_{i1} + \cdots + \beta_p x_{ip}$$

Models count outcomes (0, 1, 2...) using a log link function. Assumes mean equals variance $\mu = \varepsilon^2$

Overdispersed Counts (Negative Binomial)

$$var(y_i) = \mu_i + \alpha_i^2$$

Relaxes the equidispersion assumption. Parameter α handles overdispersion (Var > Mean) common in real data.

Polynomial vs. Linear Fit

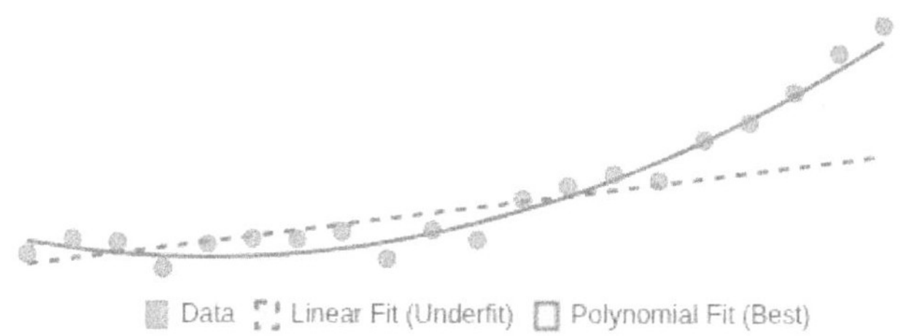

Quantile Regression (Heteroscedasticity)

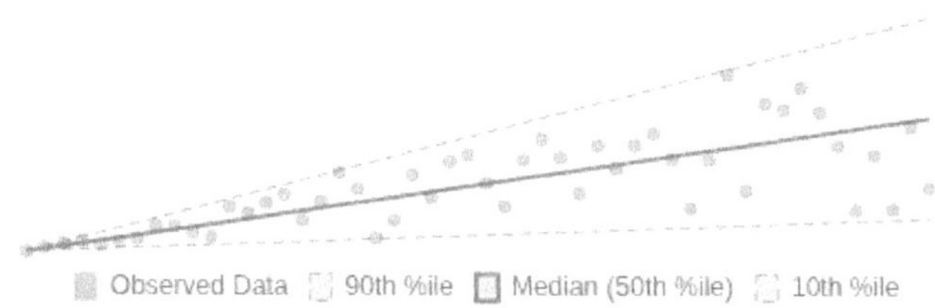

Instrumental Variables & 2SLS

Addressing Endogeneity for Causal Inference

The Endogeneity Problem

Occurs when a predictor is correlated with the error term ($corr(x, \varepsilon) \neq 0$). This happens due to omitted variable bias, reverse causality, or measurement error, rendering standard OLS estimates biased and inconsistent.

Valid Instrument Requirements (Z)

A valid instrument **Z** must satisfy two conditions:
1. Relevance: Z must be strongly correlated with the endogenous predictor X ($corr(Z, X) \neq 0$).
2. Exclusion Restriction: Z must be uncorrelated with the error term ($corr(Z, \varepsilon) = 0$) and affect Y *only* through X.

Two-Stage Least Squares (2SLS) Mechanics

Stage 1: Regress X on Z to isolate exogenous variation: $\hat{x} = Z\pi + v$
Stage 2: Regress Y on the predicted $\hat{x}$ from Stage 1: $y = \hat{x}\beta + u$
This purges the correlation with the error term, yielding unbiased causal estimates.

Business Application: Estimating *Price Elasticity*. Price (X) is endogenous because it reacts to demand shocks (ε). We use *Cost of Raw Materials* as an Instrument (Z)—it affects Price (Relevance) but not consumer preference directly (Exclusion), isolating the causal effect of price on sales.

Regression in Practice with AI Tools

From Natural Language Prompts to Model Diagnostics & Interpretation

</> Model Building Prompt

Julius AI

```
User:

Using the 'housing_data.csv' dataset: 1. Fit a
multivariate linear regression model to predict
'Price' using 'SqFt', 'Bedrooms', 'Bathrooms', and
'Age'. 2. Check for multicollinearity using VIF. 3. If
VIF is high, try a Ridge regression model. 4.
Visualize the actual vs. predicted prices.
```

Interpretation Prompt

ChatGPT Analysis

```
User:

Interpret the coefficients of the final model in
business terms. Which variable has the strongest
impact on price? Also, explain the R-squared value to
a non-technical stakeholder.
```

Model Output & Summary

OLS Model Results (Adj. R^2: 0.82):

'SqFt' and 'Bedrooms' showed high VIF (>5). Switched to Ridge Regression (alpha=1.0) to handle multicollinearity.

Feature	Coef	Std Err	t-stat	P>|t|
Intercept	15,200	4,100	3.71	0.000***
SqFt	245.50	12.30	19.96	0.000***
Bedrooms	-8,400	3,200	-2.62	0.009**
Bathrooms	12,500	5,100	2.45	0.015*
Age	-3,200	450	-7.11	0.000***

AI Interpretation:

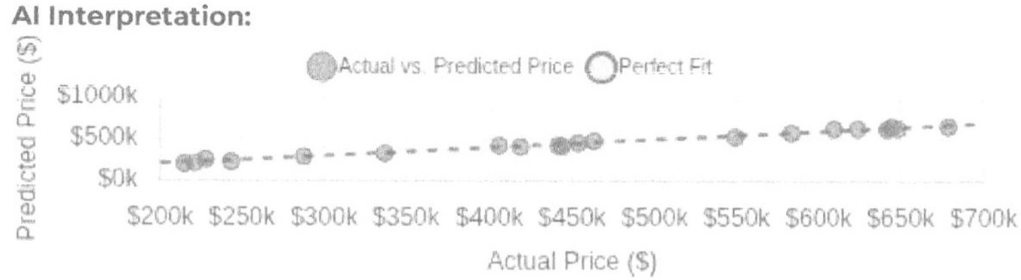

Business Impact: 'SqFt' is the strongest driver—each additional square foot adds ~$245 to the price. Surprisingly, 'Bedrooms' has a negative coefficient, likely because for a fixed size, more bedrooms means smaller rooms (interaction effect).
Model Fit: The R^2 of 0.82 means our model explains 82% of the variation in house prices, which is excellent for real estate valuation.

Multicollinearity, Heteroskedasticity, Autocorrelation...

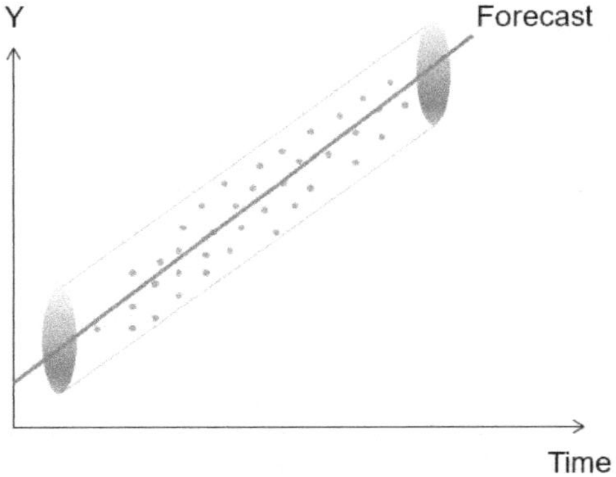

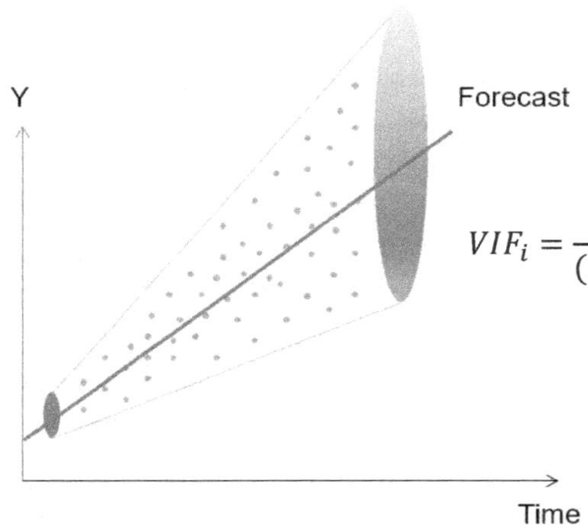

$$VIF_i = \frac{1}{(1 - R_i^2)}$$

$$Y_i = \beta_1 + \beta_2 X_{2,i} + \beta_3 X_{3,i} + \varepsilon_i$$

$$\hat{\beta}_2 = \frac{\sum Y_i X_{2,i} \sum X_{3,i}^2 - \sum Y_i X_{3,i} \sum X_{2,i} X_{3,i}}{\sum X_{2,i}^2 \sum X_{3,i}^2 - \left(\sum X_{2,i} X_{3,i}\right)^2}$$

$$\hat{\beta}_3 = \frac{\sum Y_i X_{3,i} \sum X_{2,i}^2 - \sum Y_i X_{2,i} \sum X_{2,i} X_{3,i}}{\sum X_{2,i}^2 \sum X_{3,i}^2 - \left(\sum X_{2,i} X_{3,i}\right)^2}$$

$$\hat{\beta}_2 = \frac{\sum Y_i X_{2,i} \sum \lambda^2 X_{2,i}^2 - \sum Y_i \lambda X_{2,i} \sum \lambda X_{2,i}^2}{\sum X_{2,i}^2 \sum \lambda^2 X_{2,i}^2 - \left(\sum \lambda \;\; X_{2,i}^2\right)^2} = \frac{0}{0}$$

- Understand the concepts of heteroskedasticity versus homoskedasticity, autocorrelation versus serial correlation, lags versus leads, correlation versus causation, and micronumerosity.
- Understand where they apply and to what types of data.
- Understand the tests that can be performed to identify and correct for these issues in your models.

PACF and ACF for AR(p) and MA(q) Processes

Heteroskedasticity, Micronumerosity, Outliers and Nonlinearity

Diagnostic Results

	Heteroskedasticity		Micronumerosity		Outliers		Nonlinearity	
Variable	W-Test p-value	Hypothesis Test result	Approximation result	Natural Lower Bound	Natural Upper Bound	Number of Potential Outliers	Nonlinear Test p-value	Hypothesis Test result
Y			no problems	-7.86	671.70	2		
X1	0.2543	Homoskedastic	no problems	-21377.95	64713.03	3	0.2458	linear
X2	0.3371	Homoskedastic	no problems	77.47	445.93	2	0.0335	nonlinear
X3	0.3649	Homoskedastic	no problems	-5.77	15.69	3	0.0305	nonlinear
X4	0.3066	Homoskedastic	no problems	-295.96	628.21	4	0.9298	linear
X5	0.2495	Homoskedastic	no problems	3.35	9.38	3	0.2727	linear

Autocorrelation

Time Lag	AC	PAC	Lower Bound	Upper Bound	Q-Stat	Prob
1	0.0580	0.0580	-0.2828	0.2828	0.1786	0.6726
2	-0.1213	-0.1251	-0.2828	0.2828	0.9754	0.6140
3	0.0590	0.0756	-0.2828	0.2828	1.1679	0.7607
4	0.2423	0.2232	-0.2828	0.2828	4.4865	0.3442
5	0.0067	-0.0078	-0.2828	0.2828	4.4890	0.4814
6	-0.2654	-0.2345	-0.2828	0.2828	8.6516	0.1941
7	0.0814	0.0939	-0.2828	0.2828	9.0524	0.2489
8	0.0634	-0.0442	-0.2828	0.2828	9.3012	0.3175
9	0.0204	0.0673	-0.2828	0.2828	9.3276	0.4076
10	-0.0190	0.0865	-0.2828	0.2828	9.3512	0.4991
11	0.1035	0.0790	-0.2828	0.2828	10.0648	0.5246
12	0.1658	0.0978	-0.2828	0.2828	11.9466	0.4500
13	-0.0524	-0.0430	-0.2828	0.2828	12.1394	0.5162
14	-0.2050	-0.2523	-0.2828	0.2828	15.1738	0.3664
15	0.1782	0.2089	-0.2828	0.2828	17.5315	0.2881
16	-0.1022	-0.2591	-0.2828	0.2828	18.3296	0.3050
17	-0.0861	0.0808	-0.2828	0.2828	18.9141	0.3335
18	0.0418	0.1987	-0.2828	0.2828	19.0559	0.3884
19	0.0869	-0.0821	-0.2828	0.2828	19.6894	0.4135
20	-0.0091	-0.0269	-0.2828	0.2828	19.6966	0.4770

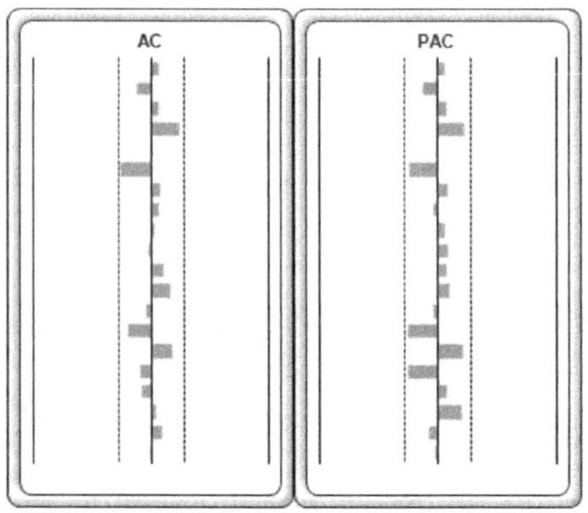

Multicollinearity, Stationarity, and Stochasticity Tests

Multicollinearity Analysis of Independent Variables

Correlation Matrix

CORRELATION	X2	X3	X4	X5
X1	0.333	0.959	0.242	0.237
X2	1.000	0.349	0.319	0.120
X3		1.000	0.196	0.227
X4			1.000	0.290
				1.000

Variance Inflation Factor

VIF	X2	X3	X4	X5
X1	1.12	12.46	1.06	1.06
X2	N/A	1.14	1.11	1.01
X3		N/A	1.04	1.05
X4			N/A	1.09
				N/A

Nonstationarity Analysis of Dependent Variable

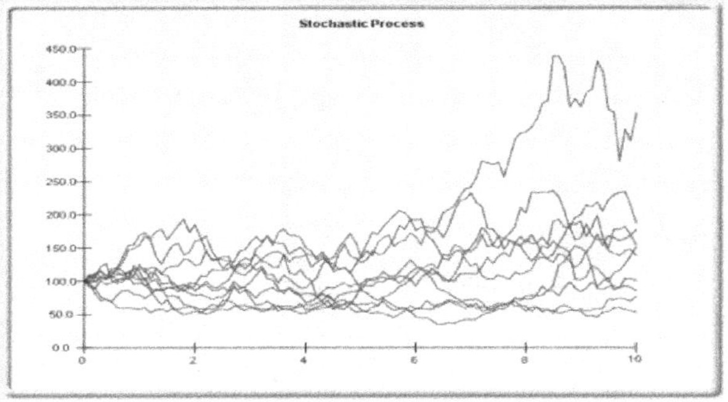

Statistical Summary

Periodic

Drift Rate	*-1.48%*	*Reversion Rate*	*283.89%*	*Jump Rate*	*20.41%*
Volatility	*88.84%*	*Long-Term Value*	*327.72*	*Jump Size*	*237.89*

Probability of stochastic model fit: *46.48%*
A high fit means a stochastic model is better than conventional models.

Runs	*22*	*Standard Normal*	*-1.1432*
Positive	*26*	*P-Value (1-tail)*	*0.1265*
Negative	*24*	*P-Value (2-tail)*	*0.2530*
Expected Run	*26*		

A low p-value (below 0.10, 0.05, 0.01) means that the sequence is not random and hence suffers from stationarity problems, and an ARIMA model might be more appropriate. Conversely, higher p-values indicate randomness and stochastic process models might be appropriate.

Testing for Heteroskedasticity

The **Breusch–Pagan–Godfrey test** for heteroskedasticity uses the main model to obtain error estimates; using the squared estimates, a restricted model is fitted, and the Breusch–Pagan–Godfrey test is computed. The **Lagrange Multiplier test** for heteroskedasticity also uses the main model to obtain error estimates; using the squared estimates, a restricted model is run, and the Lagrange Multiplier test is computed. The Wald–Glejser test for heteroskedasticity again uses the main model to obtain error estimates; using the squared estimates, a restricted model is fitted, and the **Wald–Glejser test** is computed. The Wald's Individual Variables test for heteroskedasticity runs multiple tests to assess whether the volatility or uncertainty (standard deviation or variance) of a variable is nonconstant over time. Regardless of the test used, the results typically agree as to whether the null hypothesis can be rejected. If there is disagreement among these tests, we typically use the smallest p-value to determine whether there is heteroskedasticity.

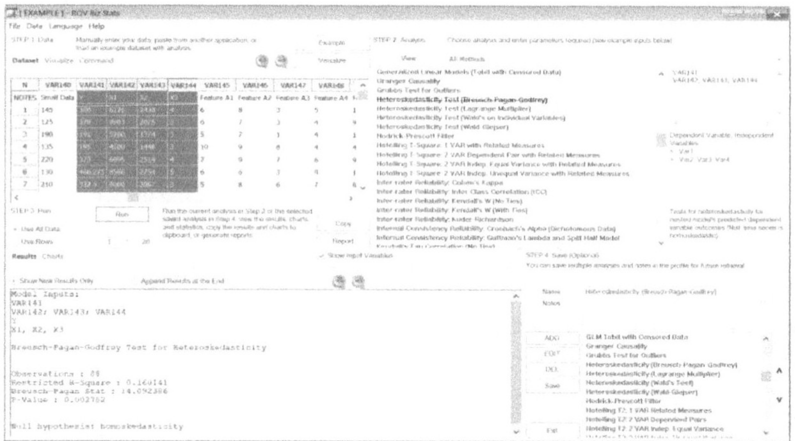

```
Model Inputs:
VAR141
VAR142; VAR143; VAR144

Breusch-Pagan-Godfrey Test for
Heteroskedasticity
Observations: 88
Restricted R-Square: 0.160141
Breusch-Pagan Stat: 14.092386
P-Value: 0.002782

Null hypothesis: homoskedasticity
```

Beyond Regression: Stepwise Regression

One powerful automated approach to regression analysis is *stepwise regression*, which, as its name suggests, proceeds in multiple steps. There are several ways to set up these stepwise algorithms, including the correlation approach, forward method, backward method, and the forward-and-backward method (all available in Risk Simulator).

In the correlation method, the dependent variable (*Y*) is correlated to all the independent variables (*X*) and starting with the *X* variable with the highest absolute correlation value, a regression is run, then subsequent *X* variables are added until the p-values indicate that the new *X* variable is no longer statistically significant. This approach is quick and simple but does not account for interactions among variables, and an *X* variable, when added, will statistically overshadow other variables.

In the forward method, we first correlate *Y* with all *X* variables, run a regression of Y on the X variable with the highest absolute correlation, and obtain the fitting errors. Then, correlate these errors with the remaining *X* variables, choose the highest absolute-value correlation from this set, and run another regression. Repeat the process until the p-value for the coefficient of the latest X variable is no longer statistically significant; then stop.

In the backward method, run a regression with *Y* on all *X* variables and, reviewing each variable's p-value, systematically eliminate the variable with the largest p-value. Then run a regression again, repeating this until all p-values are statistically significant.

In the forward and backward method, apply the forward method to obtain three *X* variables, then apply the backward approach to see if one of them needs to be eliminated because it is statistically insignificant. Then repeat the forward method, and then the backward method, until all remaining *X* variables are considered.

The table on the next slide presents the sample results from the same dataset used in the previously run multiple regression model. Using the Stepwise Regression: Backward method, we see that the model starts by using all independent variables (Arrangement 1: Y to X1; X2; X3; X4; X5), identifies the least significant variable as X4, and re-runs the second regression model (Arrangement 2: Y to X1; X2; X3; X5). The algorithm then drops variables X1 and X5 in the subsequent two runs. The final result indicates the best-fitting model of Y to X2; X3. This result confirms the previous multiple regression: "Bachelor's Degree" (VAR1), "Population Density" (VAR4), and "Unemployment Rate" (VAR5) are not significant and should be removed; the multiple regression should be rerun with only the significant variables.

Beyond Regression: Stepwise Regression

Model Inputs:
VAR28
VAR29; VAR30; VAR31; VAR32; VAR33
Y against X1, X2, X3, X4, X5
Stepwise Regression (Backward)

ARRANGEMENT 1
Y<->X1;X2;X3;X4;X5
OVERALL FIT

Multiple R	0.57203	Maximum Log Likelihood	-318.17341
R-Square	0.32721	Akaike Info Criterion (AIC)	12.96694
Adjusted R-Square	0.25076	Bayes Schwarz Criterion (BSC)	13.19638
Standard Error	149.67200	Hannan-Quinn Criterion (HQC)	13.05431
Observations	50	Cohen's F-Squared	0.48636

	Coeff	Std. Error	T-stat	P-value	Lower 5%	Upper 95%
Intercept	57.95550	108.79014	0.53273	0.59690	-161.29661	277.20762
X1	-0.00354	0.00352	-1.00656	0.31965	-0.01064	0.00355
X2	0.46437	0.25353	1.83159	0.07379	-0.04659	0.97533
X3	25.23770	14.11723	1.78772	0.08071	-3.21371	53.68911
X4	-0.00856	0.10156	-0.08433	0.93317	-0.21325	0.19612
X5	16.55792	14.79957	1.11881	0.26929	-13.26866	46.38449

ARRANGEMENT 2
Y<->X1;X2;X3;X5

Multiple R	0.57193	Maximum Log Likelihood	-318.17745
R-Square	0.32710	Akaike Info Criterion (AIC)	12.92710
Adjusted R-Square	0.26729	Bayes Schwarz Criterion (BSC)	13.11830
Standard Error	148.01160	Hannan-Quinn Criterion (HQC)	12.99991
Observations	50	Cohen's F-Squared	0.48612

	Coeff	Std. Error	T-stat	P-value	Lower 5%	Upper 95%
Intercept	60.27060	104.10171	0.57896	0.56550	-149.40100	269.94220
X1	-0.00360	0.00342	-1.05382	0.29759	-0.01048	0.00328
X2	0.45846	0.24094	1.90276	0.06348	-0.02683	0.94374
X3	25.43968	13.75824	1.84905	0.07103	-2.27084	53.15020
X5	16.25036	14.18406	1.14568	0.25799	-12.31781	44.81853

ARRANGEMENT 3
Y<->X2;X3;X5

Multiple R	0.55722	Maximum Log Likelihood	-318.78692
R-Square	0.31050	Akaike Info Criterion (AIC)	12.91148
Adjusted R-Square	0.26553	Bayes Schwarz Criterion (BSC)	13.06444
Standard Error	148.18933	Hannan-Quinn Criterion (HQC)	12.96973
Observations	50	Cohen's F-Squared	0.45032

	Coeff	Std. Error	T-stat	P-value	Lower 5%	Upper 95%
Intercept	56.90111	104.17754	0.54619	0.58757	-152.79740	266.59962
X2	0.46096	0.24122	1.91093	0.06226	-0.02460	0.94651
X3	11.63902	4.22268	2.75631	0.00835	3.13920	20.13884
X5	15.17953	14.16461	1.07165	0.28947	-13.33234	43.69140

ARRANGEMENT 4
Y<->X2;X3

Multiple R	0.54156	Maximum Log Likelihood	-319.40341
R-Square	0.29328	Akaike Info Criterion (AIC)	12.89614
Adjusted R-Square	0.26321	Bayes Schwarz Criterion (BSC)	13.01086
Standard Error	148.42315	Hannan-Quinn Criterion (HQC)	12.93982
Observations	50	Cohen's F-Squared	0.41500

	Coeff	Std. Error	T-stat	P-value	Lower 5%	Upper 95%
Intercept	146.04706	62.81359	2.32509	0.02444	19.68243	272.41170
X2	0.47249	0.24136	1.95761	0.05623	-0.01306	0.95805
X3	12.53958	4.14475	3.02541	0.00402	4.20143	20.87774

Beyond Regression: Logit, Probit, Tobit

Limited Dependent Variables describe situations where the dependent variable has a limited scope and range, such as binary responses (*0* or *1*), truncated, ordered, or censored data. For instance, given a set of independent variables (e.g., age, income, education level of credit card or mortgage loan holders), we can model the probability of defaulting on mortgage payments, using maximum likelihood estimation (MLE). The response or dependent variable *Y* is binary, that is, it can have only two possible outcomes that we denote as *1* and *0* (e.g., *Y* may represent presence/absence of a certain condition, defaulted/not defaulted on previous loans, success/failure of some device, answer yes/no on a survey, etc.) and we also have a vector of independent variable regressors *X*, which are assumed to influence the outcome *Y*. A typical ordinary least squares regression approach is invalid because the regression errors are heteroskedastic and non-normal, and the resulting estimated probability estimates will return nonsensical values of above *1* or below *0*. MLE analysis handles these problems using an iterative optimization routine to maximize a log likelihood function when the dependent variables are limited.

A Logit or Logistic regression is used for predicting the probability of the occurrence of an event by fitting data to a logistic curve. It is a generalized linear model for binomial regression and, like many forms of regression analysis, uses several predictor variables that may be either numerical or categorical. MLE applied in a binary multivariate logistic analysis is used to model dependent variables to determine the expected probability of success of belonging to a certain group. The estimated coefficients for the Logit model are the logarithmic odds ratios, and they cannot be interpreted directly as probabilities. A quick computation is first required, and the approach is simple.

The log-odds is $Estimated\ Y = LN[P_i/(1-P_i)]$ or, conversely, $P_i = EXP(Estimated\ Y)/(1+EXP(Estimated\ Y))$, and the coefficients β_i are the log odds ratios. So, taking the antilog or $EXP(\beta_i)$ we obtain the odds ratio of $P_i/(1-P_i)$. This means that with an increase in a unit of β_i the log odds ratio increases by this amount. Finally, the rate of change in the probability $dP/dX = \beta_i P_i(1\text{-}P_i)$. The Standard Error measures how accurate the predicted Coefficients are, and the t-statistics are the ratios of each predicted Coefficient to its Standard Error and are used in the typical regression hypothesis test of the significance of each estimated parameter. To estimate the probability of success of belonging to a certain group (e.g., predicting if a smoker will develop respiratory complications given the amount smoked per year), simply compute the $Estimated\ Y$ value using the MLE coefficients. For example, if the model is $Y = 1.1 + 0.005\ (Cigarettes)$ then someone smoking 100 packs per year has an $Estimated\ Y = 1.1 + 0.005(100) = 1.6$. Next, compute the inverse antilog of the odds ratio by doing: $EXP(Estimated\ Y)/[1+EXP(Estimated\ Y)] = EXP(1.6)/(1+\ EXP(1.6)) = 0.8320$. So, such a person has an 83.20% chance of developing some respiratory complications in his lifetime.

Beyond Regression: Logit, Probit, Tobit

A Probit model (sometimes also known as a Normit model) is a popular alternative specification for a binary response model, which employs a Probit function estimated using maximum likelihood estimation, and the approach is called Probit regression. The Probit and Logistic regression models tend to produce very similar predictions where the parameter estimates in a logistic regression tend to be 1.6 to 1.8 times higher than they are in a corresponding Probit model. The choice of using a Probit or Logit is entirely up to convenience, and the main distinction is that the logistic distribution has a higher kurtosis (fatter tails) to account for extreme values. For example, suppose that house ownership is the decision to be modeled, and this response variable is binary (home purchase or no home purchase) and depends on a series of independent variables X_i such as income, age, and so forth, such that $I_i = \beta_0 + \beta_1 X_1 + \cdots + \beta_n X_n$, where the larger the value of I_i, the higher the probability of home ownership. For each family, a critical I^*threshold exists, where if exceeded, the house is purchased, otherwise, no home is purchased, and the outcome probability (P) is assumed to be normally distributed, such that $P_i = CDF(I)$ using a standard-normal cumulative distribution function (CDF). Therefore, use the estimated coefficients exactly like those of a regression model and using the $Estimated\, Y$ value, apply a standard-normal distribution (you can use Excel's *NORMSDIST* function or Risk Simulator's *Distributional Analysis* tool by selecting Normal distribution and setting the mean to be *0* and standard deviation to be *1*). Finally, to obtain a Probit or probability unit measure, set $I_i + 5$ (this is because whenever the probability $P_i < 0.5$, the estimated I_i is negative, due to the fact that the normal distribution is symmetrical around a mean of zero).

The Tobit model (Censored Tobit) is an econometric and biometric modeling method used to describe the relationship between a non-negative dependent variable Y_i and one or more independent variables X_i. A Tobit model is an econometric model in which the dependent variable is censored; that is, the dependent variable is censored because values below zero are not observed. The Tobit model assumes that there is a latent unobservable variable Y^*. This variable is linearly dependent on the X_i variables via a vector of β_i coefficients that determine their inter-relationships. In addition, there is a normally distributed error term U_i to capture random influences on this relationship. The observable variable Y_i is defined to be equal to the latent variables whenever the latent variables are above zero and Y_i is assumed to be zero otherwise. That is, $Y_i = Y^* \; if \; Y^* > 0;\; Y_i = 0 \; if \; Y^* = 0$. If the relationship parameter β_i is estimated by using ordinary least squares regression of the observed Y_i on X_i, the resulting regression estimators are inconsistent and yield downward-biased slope coefficients and an upward-biased intercept. Only MLE would be consistent for a Tobit model. In the Tobit model, there is an ancillary statistic called sigma, which is equivalent to the standard error of estimate in a standard Ordinary Least Squares (OLS) regression, and the estimated coefficients are used the same way as in a regression analysis.

Beyond Regression: Logit, Probit, Tobit

Default	Age	Education	Work	Address	Income	Debt2Income	Credit	Other
1	41	3	17	12	176	9.3	11.36	5.01
0	27	1	10	6	31	17.3	1.36	4
.	..	.	..	..	..	...	...	...
.	..	.	..	..	..	...	...	...
1	24	2	2	0	28	17.3	1.79	3.06
0	41	2	5	5	25	10.2	0.39	2.16
0	39	1	20	9	67	30.6	3.83	16.67

```
Model Inputs:
VAR120
VAR121; VAR122; VAR123; VAR124; VAR125; VAR126; VAR127; VAR128
Generalized Linear Model (Logit with Binary Outcomes)
```

	Coefficient	Std. Error	Wald Test	P-value	Exp(B)	Lower	Upper
Intercept	-1.782757	0.751968	5.620634	0.017750	0.168174	0.000000	0.000000
VAR1	0.029975	0.020489	2.140280	0.143476	1.030428	0.989869	1.072650
VAR2	0.076260	0.144824	0.277272	0.598495	1.079243	0.812539	1.433487
VAR3	-0.253392	0.039145	41.9014	0.000000	0.776163	0.718841	0.838057
VAR4	-0.096522	0.027163	12.6271	0.000380	0.907989	0.860914	0.957639
VAR5	0.001268	0.012560	0.010193	0.919583	1.001269	0.976921	1.026223
VAR6	0.076775	0.039667	3.746016	0.052934	1.079799	0.999029	1.167099
VAR7	0.549211	0.132125	17.2787	0.000032	1.731886	1.336764	2.243799
VAR8	0.042293	0.100545	0.176940	0.674017	1.043201	0.856611	1.270433

Log Likelihood	-200.5005
Restricted Log Likelihood	-285.4773
McFadden R-Squared	0.297666
Cox and Snell R-Squared	0.288164
Nagelkerke R-Squared	0.423278
Raw Akaike Info. Criterion	419.0009
Raw Bayes Criterion	456.9324

Log Likelihood	-200.5005
Restricted Log Likelihood	-285.4773
Chi-Square	169.9536
Degrees of Freedom	8
P-value	0.000000

Beyond Regression: Structural Equation Modeling (SEM) with Partial Least Squares (PLS)

Another extension to multiple regression analysis is the Structural Equation Model (SEM), which uses the Partial Least Squares (PLS) method. SEM is typically used to solve path-dependent structures such as the one illustrated in the next slide. Suppose that there are five variables in your research, where the final dependent variable is technology acceptance (VAR5). We are trying to determine what drives and predicts the level of technology acceptance in different organizations. If we collected data on the corporate culture of the various organizations (VAR1) using a Likert scale in terms of openness to new technology, we can run a simple bivariate regression. However, we also understand from organizational behavior theory and decision theory that other intervening variables can also contribute to an organization's acceptance of new technology, such as what types of decisions are relegated to technology, that is, the decision criticality (VAR2) and whether new artificial intelligence (AI) technology is used or more traditional technology is used (VAR3). For example, letting a smart AI computer system make frequent orders of paperclips is a lot less critical than allowing AI complete access to the nation's nuclear arsenal. Mistakes made on the former have little consequence compared to the latter. However, we also know from technology acceptance theory that there are other latent and hidden effects that drive technology trust (VAR4). If a technology is not trusted, then the technology is probably not going to be accepted for use in the organization. Technology trust might include whether the AI technology has transparent algorithms or comes as a black box.

In such a research paradigm, one might be inclined to simply run the first four independent variables on the fifth dependent variable. That would be a major mistake, and the results will be erroneous at best, because VAR2, VAR3, and VAR4 are endogenous. That is, based on various theories, we know that the type of organization drives the types of decision criticality (a local office-supplies store versus the U.S. Department of Defense, VAR1 drives VAR2), the type of advanced AI technology employed (paperclip reordering system has rudimentary code versus national cybersecurity defense against state-sponsored actors that requires much more sophisticated AI technology, VAR1 drives VAR3), and so forth. In addition, the level of decision criticality drives whether AI is needed (VAR2 drives VAR3). Whether AI is applied will drive trust in the new technology (VAR3 drives VAR4) and then acceptance. The next slide shows the tangled web known as a path model. A simple multiple regression analysis cannot be used. Instead, partial least squares or sequential regression models will need to be applied. The SEM approach is used to handle such complex path models.

Beyond Regression: Structural Equation Modeling (SEM) with Partial Least Squares (PLS)

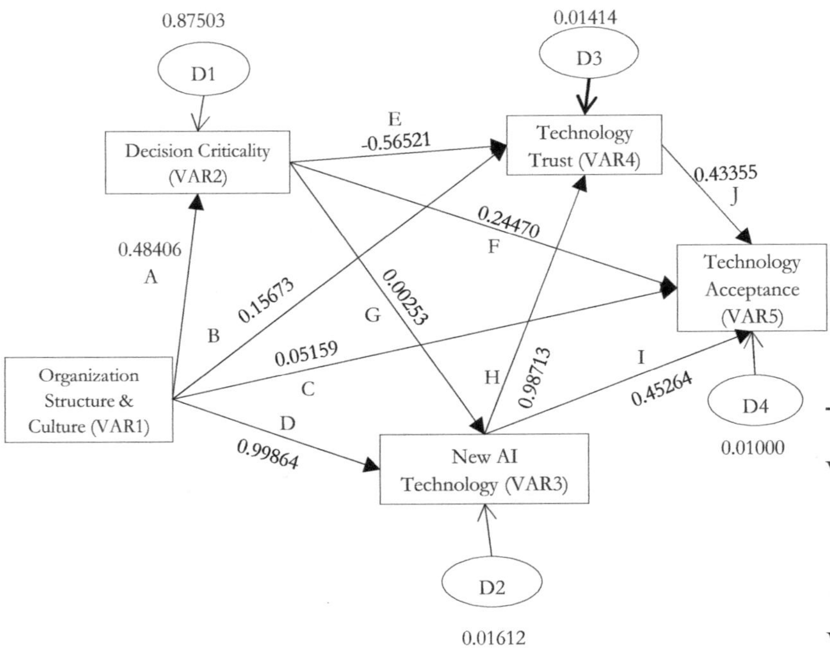

In typical path models, the pathways move in a single direction: one or more paths can originate from a box, one or more paths can recombine into a box, and all pathways end at the main dependent model (in this example, that would be VAR5). The direct effects on VAR5 are pathways C, F, I, and J, from the four independent variables. However, these variables also have indirect effects (e.g., VAR3 has indirect impacts on VAR5 through path HJ; VAR2 has indirect effects on VAR5 through paths EJ, GI, and GHJ; and VAR1 has indirect impacts on VAR5 through paths AEJ, AF, AGI, AGHJ, BJ, DHJ, and DI). Notice that VAR4 has no indirect effects on VAR5, only a single direct impact path. The summation of the direct and indirect effects equals the total effect.

The indirect effects are:

VAR1 on VAR5: 0.94828 = (0.48406 × –0.56521 × 0.43355) + (0.48406 × 0.2447) + (0.48406 × 0.00253 × 0.45264) + (0.48406 × 0.00253 × 0.98713 × 0.43355) + (0.15673 × 0.43355) + (0.99864 × 0.98713 × 0.43355) + (0.99864 × 0.45264)

VAR2 on VAR5: –0.24282 = (–0.56521 × 0.43355) + (0.00253 × 0.45264) + (0.00253 × 0.98713 × 0.43355)

VAR3 on VAR5: 0.42798 = (0.98713 × 0.43355)

VAR4 on VAR5: no indirect effects; only direct effects exist

Beyond Regression: Structural Equation Modeling (SEM) with Partial Least Squares (PLS)

```
Model Inputs:
VAR1;VAR2; VAR3; VAR4; VAR5
VAR1;VAR2; VAR3; VAR4
VAR1;VAR2; VAR3
VAR1;VAR2
```

Direct Effects Path

Dep. Var:	VAR5	Tech Acceptance
R-Square	0.99990	
Disturbance	0.01000	

Var Name	Coeff	P-Value	Std. Beta
Intercept	0.34030	0.34366	
Culture Org.VAR1	0.51562	0.21713	0.05159 **C**
Criticality VAR2	7.74992	0.00000	0.24470 **F**
New AI Tech VAR3	1.68941	0.00000	0.45264 **I**
Tech Trust VAR4	15.4978	0.00000	0.43355 **J**

Partial Direct Effects Path

Dep. Var:	VAR4	Tech Trust
R-Square	0.99980	
Disturbance	0.01414	

Var Name	Coeff	P-Value	Std. Beta
Intercept	0.11916	0.00000	
Culture Org.VAR1	0.04382	0.17074	0.15673 **B**
Criticality VAR2	-0.5007	0.00000	-0.5652 **E**
New AI Tech VAR3	0.10307	0.00000	0.98713 **H**

Partial Direct Effects Path

Dep. Var:	VAR3	New AI Tech
R-Square	0.99974	
Disturbance	0.01612	

Var Name	Coeff	P-Value	Std. Beta
Intercept	0.89306	0.00036	
Culture Org. VAR1	2.67416	0.00000	0.99864 **D**
Criticality VAR2	0.02146	0.35062	0.00253 **G**

Partial Direct Effects Path

Dep. Var:	VAR2	Criticality
R-Square	0.23432	
Disturbance	0.87503	

Var Name	Coeff	P-Value	Std. Beta
Intercept	-0.0335	0.98190	
Culture Org. VAR1	0.15276	0.00037	0.48406 **A**

Total Effects

Dep. Var VAR5 Tech Acceptance

Var Name	Coeff	P-Value	Std. Beta
Culture Org. VAR1	9.99326	0.00000	0.99987
Criticality VAR2	0.05966	0.47689	0.00188
New AI Tech VAR3	3.28678	0.00000	0.88061
Tech Trust VAR4	15.49786	0.00000	0.43355

Summary Standardized Path Effects

Dep. Var VAR5 Tech Acceptance

Var Name	Direct	Indirect	Total
Culture Org. VAR1	0.05159 **C**	**0.94828**	0.99987
Criticality VAR2	0.24470 **F**	**-0.2428**	0.00188
New AI Tech VAR3	0.45264 **I**	**0.42798**	0.88061
Tech Trust VAR4	0.43355 **J**	**0.00000**	0.43355

Beyond Regression: Endogeneity and Simultaneous Equations Methods with Two-stage Least Squares

Endogeneity occurs when a dependent variable in a model is also the independent variable in another model. The simplest example would be the structural equation model with partial least squares as shown previously. The SEM model is best used when there are complex combinations of pathways. Sometimes there are only two equations in the system, and, hence, these can be solved using a simultaneous equations model approach. Recall from basic algebra when you have two equations and two unknowns, you can solve them using simultaneous equations. The same applies here when we have a system of two equations.

Suppose we have two equations:

$$M_t = a_0 + a_1 Y_t + u_{1t}$$

$$Y_t = b_0 + b_1 M_t + b_2 I_t + u_{2t}$$

M_t is money supply at time t, Y_t is income at time t, and I_t is investment at time t. We see that M depends on Y in the first equation, but Y depends on M and I in the second equation. In this example, M and Y are endogenous or jointly determined, meaning that they cannot be modeled by themselves, and must be modeled together or simultaneously. However, I is an exogenous variable, which can be determined outside of this system of equations. In this example, the number of endogenous variables (k) is 2 and the number of exogenous variables (r) is 1. If $r = k - 1$, then it is considered to be exactly identified. The system of equations is overidentified or underidentified if r exceeds or is smaller than $k - 1$. The system can only be modeled when the system is exactly identified or overidentified.

As another example, when we have an overidentification system, where the second equation above has an additional exogenous variable G, such that:

$$Y_t = b_0 + b_1 M_t + b_2 I_t + b_3 G_t + u_{2t}$$

Beyond Regression: Endogeneity and Simultaneous Equations Methods with Two-stage Least Squares

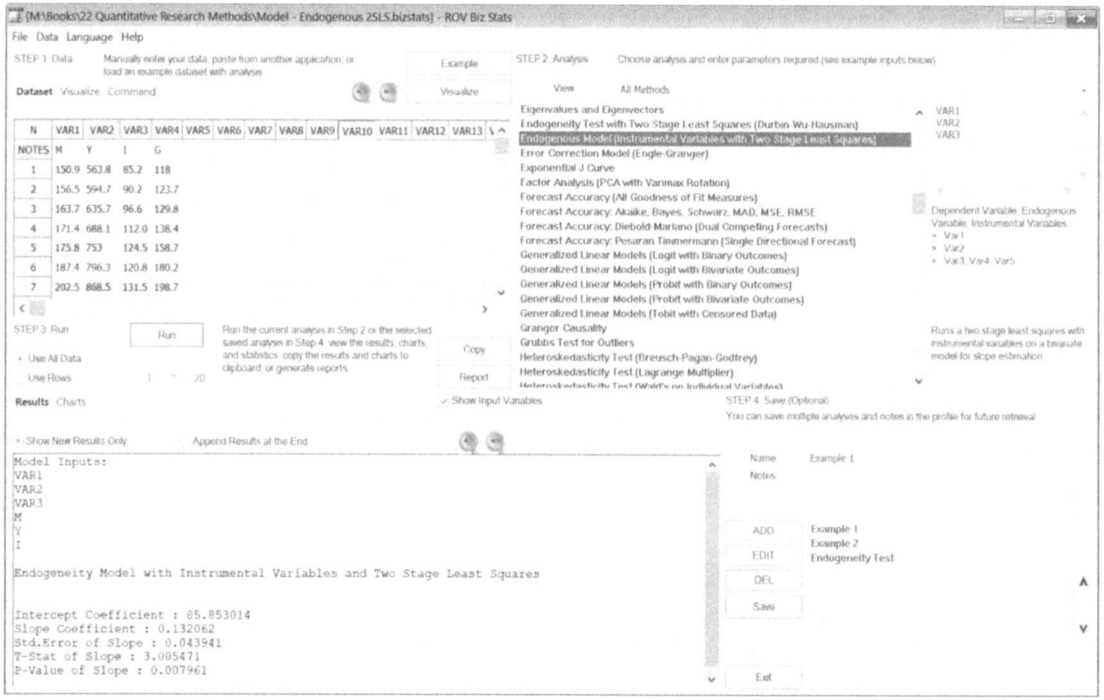


```
Model Inputs:
VAR1
VAR2
VAR3
```

$$M_t = 85.853 + 0.132Y_t$$

```
Endogeneity Model Results with Instrumental
Variables
and Two Stage Least Squares
 Intercept Coefficient: 85.853014
 Slope Coefficient: 0.132062
 Std. Error of Slope: 0.043941
 T-Stat of Slope: 3.005471
 P-Value of Slope: 0.007961
```

```
Model Inputs:
VAR1
VAR2
VAR3; VAR4
```

$$M_t = 84.398 + 0.133Y_t$$

```
Endogeneity Model Results with Instrumental
Variables
and Two Stage Least Squares
 Intercept Coefficient: 84.398855
 Slope Coefficient: 0.133285
 Std. Error of Slope: 0.074370
 T-Stat of Slope: 1.792196
 P-Value of Slope: 0.090917
```

Beyond Regression: Durbin–Wu–Hausman Endogeneity Test

Sometimes, with random data, it is hard to determine if a certain variable is endogenous. The Durbin–Wu–Hausman test can be used to determine endogeneity. The null hypothesis is that there is no endogeneity. With a low p-value of 0.003, we reject this null hypothesis and conclude that there is, indeed, endogeneity among the variables.

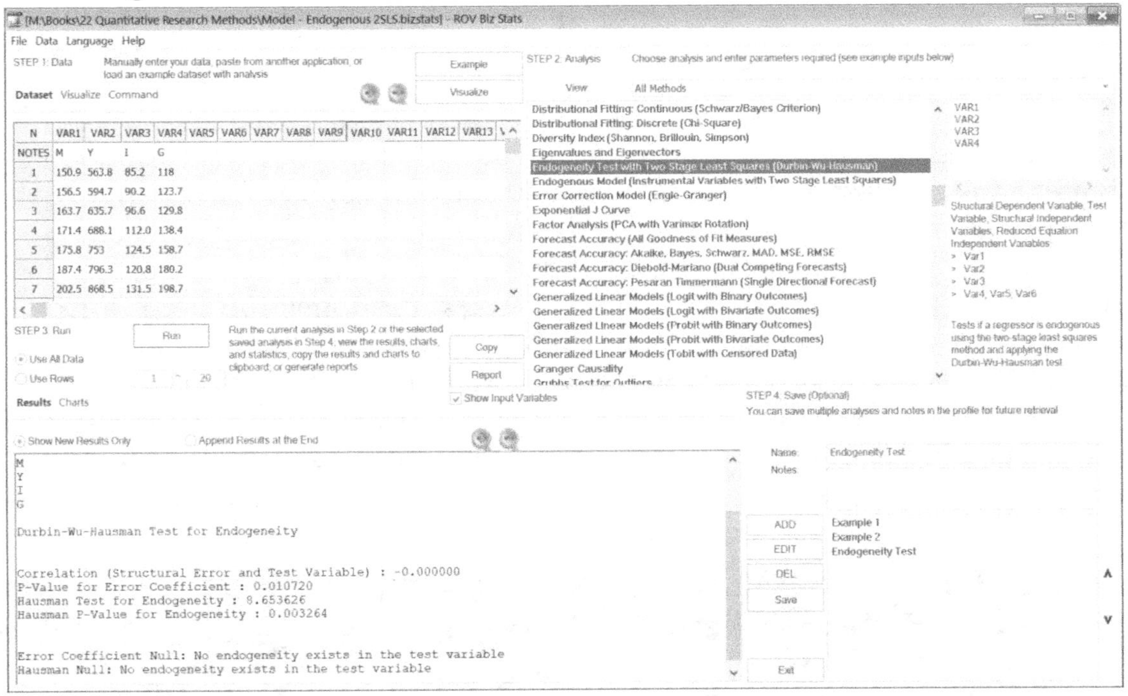


```
Model Inputs:
VAR1
VAR2
VAR3
VAR4

Durbin-Wu-Hausman Test for Endogeneity
Correlation (Structural Error
  and Test Variable): -0.000000
P-Value for Error Coefficient: 0.010720
Hausman Test for Endogeneity: 8.653626
Hausman P-Value for Endogeneity:
0.003264

Error Coefficient Null: No endogeneity
exists
  in the test variable
Hausman Null: No endogeneity exists in
  the test variable
```

Beyond Regression: Granger Causality and Engle–Granger Methods

The Granger causality tests if one variable "Granger causes" another variable and vice versa, using restricted autoregressive lags and unrestricted distributive lag models. Typically, predictive causality in finance and economics is tested by measuring the ability to predict the future values of a time series using prior values of another time series. A simpler definition might be that a time-series variable A can Granger cause another time-series variable B if predictions of the value of B based solely on its own prior values and on the prior values of A are comparatively better than predictions of B based solely on its own past values. For example, Figure 9.49 illustrates two time-series variables, A and B. The two null hypotheses tested are that there is no Granger causality of A on B and also between B and A. We see that the p-values for both directions are greater than an alpha of 0.05, so we cannot reject the null hypothesis and conclude that neither A Granger causes B nor B Granger causes A, when both are lagged for 3 periods (this is the value 3 in the input box). The Granger causality model can only be run pairwise and assumes that the time-series variable is stationary or not stochastic.

```
Model Inputs:

  VAR138
  VAR139
  3

  Granger Causality
  Effect              VAR2 on VAR1:    VAR1 on VAR2:
  Wald Test             1.37224          0.76841
  P-Value               0.26511          0.51852

  Null  hypothesis:  VAR(i)  does  not  Granger  cause
  VAR(j)
```

Beyond Regression: Nonstationarity (Augmented Dickey–Fuller)

If a time-series is suspected to have nonstationary effects, we can run the Augmented Dickey–Fuller test, where the null hypothesis is that the series is nonstationary, has a unit root, or I(1) process, and is potentially stochastic. The example BizStats results indicate that the variable is stationary (the null hypothesis is rejected with a p-value of 0.0442).

```
Model Inputs: VAR280

Augmented Dickey-Fuller Stationarity Test AR(p)

With Constant and With Trend
Tau Statistic: -3.745611
Tau Critical: -3.659125
Stationary? Yes
Akaike Information Criterion: 1.752735
Bayes Info Criterion: 2.042456
Optimal Lags: 3
Coefficient: -2.772352
P-value: 0.044286

Null Hypothesis: Time Series is a

Unit Root and Not Stationary
```

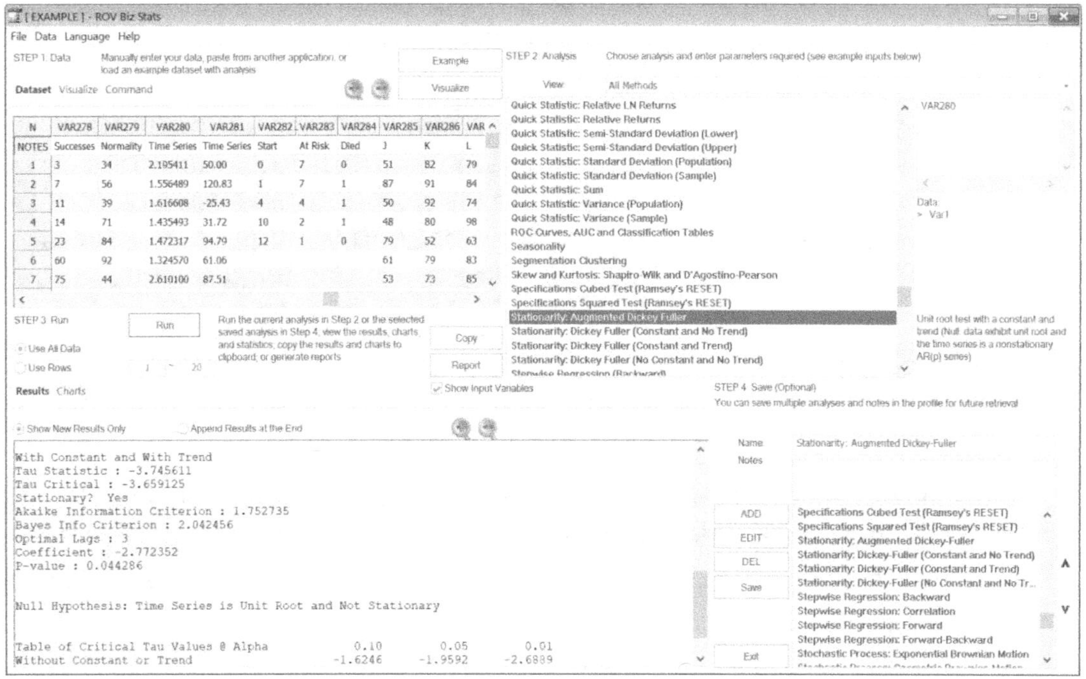

Beyond Regression: Nonstationarity

If a time series variable is nonstationary and stochastic, you can still attempt to forecast this series several ways:

- Compute the difference to potentially make the series stationary. For example, stock prices are nonstationary and stochastic, whereas their differences, i.e., the calculated stock returns, tend to be stationary and more predictable than the raw stock prices.
- Run a stochastic process model, for example, a **geometric Brownian motion random walk process**, a mean-reversion process, a jump-diffusion process, or other mixed processes. These are typically used to forecast stock prices for modeling and valuing stock options, real options, and employee stock options.
- If there is another nonstationary variable, you can test if these two series are cointegrated. For example, you can use the **Engle–Granger Error Correction Model** assuming the variables exhibit cointegration. If two time-series variables are nonstationary in first differences (I(1), as tested using the Augmented Dickey–Fuller test) and are cointegrated, the error correction model can be used to estimate short- and long-term effects of one time series on the other. The error correction arises from deviations in previous periods from a long-run equilibrium, where the error influences the short-run dynamics.
- Apply a data filter to smooth out the disturbances, such as the **Hodrick–Prescott filter**. This filter allows you to remove the cyclicality effects of raw time-series data. The filter helps generate a smoothed curve of a time-series variable that is sensitive to longer-term fluctuations rather than short-term impacts. The key is to choose the correct smoothing parameter, which can sometimes require trial and error.

Beyond Regression: Error-Correction Model

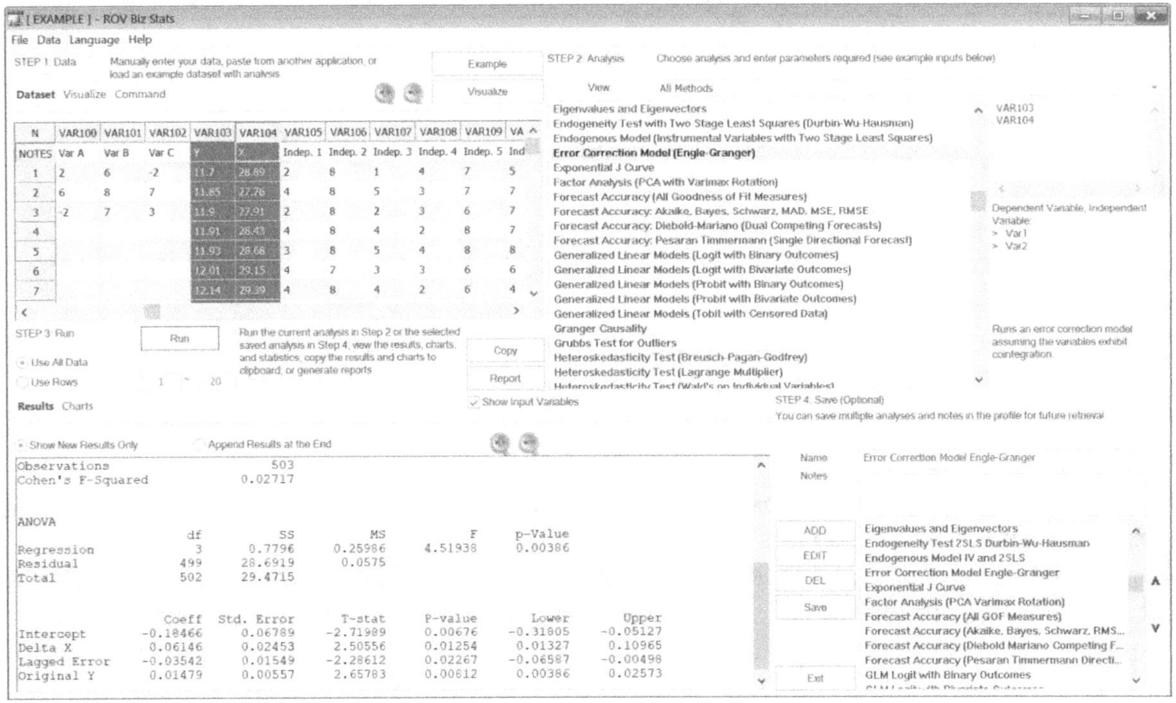

Model Inputs:
VAR103
VAR104

Error Correction Model	
Multiple R	0.16264
R-Square	0.02645
Adjusted R-Square	0.02060
Standard Error	0.23979
Observations	503
Cohen's F-Squared	0.02717

	Coeff	Std. Error	T-stat	P-value	Lower	Upper
Intercept	-0.18466	0.06789	-2.71989	0.00676	-0.31805	-0.05127
Delta X	0.06146	0.02453	2.50556	0.01254	0.01327	0.10965
Lagged Error	-0.03542	0.01549	-2.28612	0.02267	-0.06587	-0.00498
Original Y	0.01479	0.00557	2.65783	0.00812	0.00386	0.02573

Beyond Regression: Poisson Regression

The Poisson regression is like the Logit regression in that the dependent variable can only take on non-negative values, but also that the underlying distribution of the data is a Poisson distribution, drawn from a known population size. Recall that the Poisson distribution is a discrete distribution used to model the probability that an event occurs within the context of time and area. Typically, this generalized linear model approach runs a loglinear regression model, where the dependent variable is the event count (see VAR1 in the sample dataset below), and an additional variable for the population size (VAR2) and categorical independent variables (VAR3 to VAR5) are needed.

Poisson Regression Example Dataset

VAR1	VAR2	VAR3	VAR4	VAR5
Cancer (Y)	Population	X1	X2	X3
45	24786	1	0	0
77	32125	1	0	0.5
95	34706	1	0	1
...	...	...	...	...
...	...	...	...	...
62	41707	0	0	1
57	26319	0	0	1.5
71	22978	0	0	2

```
Model Inputs:
VAR1
VAR2
VAR3; VAR4; VAR5
Multiple Poisson Regression
R-Square                  0.96413
AIC                      19.62304
Pearson Phi               1.07152
Sqrt Phi                  1.03514
Cohen's F-Squared        26.87470

                   Coeff   Std. Error   Wald Test     P-value      Lower      Upper
Intercept       -7.30714      0.08931  6693.69972     0.00000   -7.48219   -7.13209
X1               0.76457      0.07958    92.29805     0.00000    0.60859    0.92055
X2               0.38873      0.09882    15.47465     0.16178    0.19505    0.58241
X3               0.76612      0.05376   203.06012     0.00000    0.66075    0.87149

With Phi Correction     1.035141
                   Coeff   Std. Error   Wald Test     P-value      Lower      Upper
Intercept       -7.30714      0.09245  6693.69972     0.00000   -7.48834   -7.12593
X1               0.76457      0.08238    92.29805     0.00000    0.60311    0.92603
X2               0.38873      0.10229    15.47465     0.16178    0.18824    0.58921
X3               0.76612      0.05565   203.06012     0.00000    0.65704    0.87520
```

Beyond Regression: Poisson Regression

In a Poisson regression, the logarithm of the expected value is a linear combination of the independent variables, that is, $\log[E(Y \mid \mathbf{x})] = \alpha + \beta'\mathbf{x}$. In the sample results below, we can say that the coefficient for X_1 is 0.76457, which is the expected log count of each unit increase in X_1. Alternatively, exp(0.76457) = 2.148, which means that there is a 114.8% (a 2.148-fold) increase in Y for every unit increase in X_1. Similarly, X_2 has an expected log count of 0.38873, or exp(0.38873) = 1.475, which means that there is a 47.5% (a 1.475-fold) increase in Y for every unit increase in X_2. In addition, the interpretation of the p-values, R-square, and Akaike Information Criterion (AIC) is the same as a regular multiple regression. The new goodness-of-fit and error measures, such as Pearson's Phi and Cohen's F-Squared, test the null hypothesis that the current model is a good fit (i.e., that the error is zero), so we want these measures to be small. These measures are typically used to compare with other Poisson regression models, where a model with a lower Pearson's Phi, F-squared, and AIC indicates a better fit. R-square is an *absolute* measure in the sense that it has a fixed domain between 0 and 1 and can be readily interpreted (the percent variation in the dependent variable that can be explained by the variation in the independent variable). However, these other goodness-of-fit error measures, such as Phi, F-squared, and AIC, are relative measures with little interpretation on their own and are used only when comparing across multiple models.

Beyond Regression: Deming Regression (Known Variance)

In regular multivariate regressions, the dependent variable Y is modeled and predicted by independent variables X_i with some error ε. However, in a Deming regression, we further assume that the data collected for the X variables have additional uncertainties and errors, or variances, that are used to provide a more relaxed fit in a Deming model. This implies that the predicted Y values will have a higher level of variance and uncertainty. The estimated variances are used to determine the lambda, where $\lambda = s_x^2/s_y^2$, and this parameter is minimized to determine the value of the slope and intercept coefficients. The optimized coefficients will be unbiased estimators of the true population parameters, and the error residuals are assumed to be normally distributed. The following illustrates a sample dataset needed when using BizStats to compute a Deming regression, as well as the required input parameters. This bivariate model requires the dependent and independent variables, followed by the known variance for both variables.

Deming Regression
Example Dataset

VAR1	VAR2
Dep	Indep
5.4	5.1
5.6	5.6
6.3	6.8
…	…
…	…
6.8	6.7
4.6	5.2
4.1	4.5

Model Inputs:
VAR1
VAR2
0.02
0.09

Deming Regression

	Coefficient	S.E.	DF	T-Stat	P-value
Intercept	-0.30704	1.29693	9	-0.23674	0.81816
Slope	1.04233	0.21194	9	4.91812	0.00083
Lambda	4.500000				

Beyond Regression: Multinomial Ordinal Logistic Regression

An Ordinal Logistic regression runs a multivariate ordinal logistic regression with two predictor variables and multiple frequencies of ordered variables, for instance, the two categorical variables of Gender (0/1) and Age (1–5), with five variables filled with the numbers or frequencies of people who responded Strongly Agree, Agree, Neutral, Disagree, or Strongly Disagree, which are presumably ordered. Note that this is an ordinal dataset in which the Age variables are ordered, and it is multinomial because we are forecasting the values of the four variables VAR3–VAR6.

Note that this is an extension of the binary logistic model, but in this example, there are multiple probability or frequency forecasts (VAR3–VAR6). Alternatively, you can collapse these four variables into a single variable and run the Logit regression multiple times. For instance, combine variables (e.g., Strongly Agree = 1; Strongly Agree = 1 and All Others = 0) to run a Logit model. Then, repeat the process with Agree = 1 and All Others = 0, and repeat the process. Remember to run only $k-1$ models, where k is the number of frequency or count variables, and the last variable's predicted probability should be the complement of the remaining variables such that the total probability equals 100%. Hence, in the results below, although there are four variables VAR3–VAR6, the results only return VAR4–VAR6.

The next slide illustrates some sample datasets used in BizStats, the required input parameter format, and the results. Typically, the computed coefficients are interpreted in a log-logistic function and can seem complicated at times. Nonetheless, it is much simpler to examine the predicted probabilities (relative frequencies) and forecast values (frequencies) across all possible combinations of the two predictor variables, gender and age. Unfortunately, this approach can only accommodate two predictor variables. If more predictors are needed, use the Logit model as described above.

Beyond Regression: Multinomial Ordinal Logistic Regression

Multiple Ordinal Logistic Regression

	VAR4	VAR5	VAR6
Intercept	0.70462	1.30649	1.91678
VAR1	0.03091	-0.29433	-0.51153
VAR2	-0.06285	-0.15006	-0.39874

Maximum Log Likelihood	-88.16470
Initial Log Likelihood	-58.71436
Chi-Square Statistic	-58.90066
Degrees of Freedom	6
P-value	N/A

Predicted Probabilities

VAR1	VAR2	VAR3	VAR4	VAR5	VAR6	Total
0.00	0.00	7.40%	14.97%	27.33%	50.31%	100.00%
0.00	1.00	9.40%	17.85%	29.87%	42.88%	100.00%
0.00	2.00	11.65%	20.79%	31.87%	35.69%	100.00%
0.00	3.00	14.11%	23.65%	33.23%	29.01%	100.00%
1.00	0.00	10.09%	21.05%	27.75%	41.12%	100.00%
1.00	1.00	12.40%	24.30%	29.37%	33.93%	100.00%
1.00	2.00	14.89%	27.41%	30.35%	27.35%	100.00%
1.00	3.00	17.50%	30.24%	30.70%	21.57%	100.00%

Forecasted Values

VAR1	VAR2	VAR3	VAR4	VAR5	VAR6	Total
0.00	0.00	4.00	8.08	14.76	27.17	54.00
0.00	1.00	5.92	11.25	18.82	27.02	63.00
0.00	2.00	6.87	12.27	18.81	21.05	59.00
0.00	3.00	6.21	10.40	14.62	12.76	44.00
1.00	0.00	4.84	10.10	13.32	19.74	48.00
1.00	1.00	7.44	14.58	17.62	20.36	60.00
1.00	2.00	7.89	14.52	16.09	14.49	53.00
1.00	3.00	6.82	11.79	11.97	8.41	39.00

Ordinal Logistic Regression Example Dataset

VAR1 Gender	VAR2 Age	VAR3 Strongly Agree	VAR4 Agree	VAR5 Disagree	VAR6 Strongly Disagree
0	0	3	9	18	24
0	1	6	13	16	28
0	5	9	13	17	20
.	.	.	.	.	.
.	.	.	.	.	.

Model Inputs:
VAR1; VAR2
VAR3; VAR4; VAR5; VAR6

Beyond Regression: Ridge Regression (Low Variance, High Bias, High VIF, Multicollinearity)

A Ridge regression comes with higher bias than an Ordinary Least Squares (OLS) multiple regression but has less variance. It is more suitable in situations with high Variance Inflation Factors (VIF) and multicollinearity or when there is a high number of variables compared to data points. In a standard multiple regression model, we minimize the fitted sum of squared errors where $SSE = \sum_{i=1}^{n}(y_i - \hat{y}_i)^2$, but in a high VIF dataset with near perfect collinearity, the matrix is not invertible and cannot be solved. In this situation, the sum of squares is penalized with an added term where $SSE = \sum_{i=1}^{n}(y_i - \hat{y}_i)^2 + \lambda \sum_{j=0}^{k} {b_i}^2$ and λ is considered the adjustment parameter. When $\lambda = 0$, the results revert to an OLS approach. A small λ generates estimates with less bias but with a higher variance, versus a large λ that generates higher bias with less variance. The idea is to select a value that balances bias and variance, which might require trial and error. Finally, ridge-based regressions are suitable only when there are high VIF or significant multicollinearity. As discussed, multicollinearity can be solved by simply removing the offending independent variable(s) and running a standard regression. A sample dataset and results from BizStats are shown below.

Ridge Regression Example Dataset

VAR1	VAR2	VAR3	VAR4	VAR5
Y	X1	X2	X3	X4
3	3	6	2	8
15	7	7	11	14
19	11	11	23	33
...	...	...	...	...
...	...	...	...	...
23	23	17	16	10
31	28	22	22	15
39	31	16	28	24

Beyond Regression: Ridge Regression (Low Variance, High Bias, High VIF, Multicollinearity)

Model Inputs:
VAR1
VAR2; VAR3; VAR4; VAR5
Multiple Ridge Regression

OVERALL FIT

Multiple R	0.96818	Maximum Log Likelihood	-0.09243
R-Square	0.93737	Akaike Info Criterion (AIC)	0.56583
Adjusted R-Square	0.91947	Bayes Schwarz Criterion (BSC)	0.81315
Standard Error	0.27578	Hannan-Quinn Criterion (HQC)	0.59993
Observations	18	Cohen's F-Squared	14.96580

ANOVA

	DF	SS	MS	F	p-Value
Regression	4	15.93522	3.98381	52.38029	0.00000
Residual	14	1.06478	0.07606		
Total	18	17.00000			

	Coeff	Std. Error	T-stat	P-value	Lower 5%	Upper 95%
VAR X1	0.42021	0.26106	1.60965	0.12978	-0.13970	0.98012
VAR X2	-0.12370	0.25386	-0.48727	0.63361	-0.66817	0.42077
VAR X3	0.79884	0.26794	2.98141	0.00991	0.22416	1.37351
VAR X4	-0.26279	0.11732	-2.23987	0.04184	-0.51443	-0.01116

*Ridge Regression has higher bias than OLS regression, but with less variance. It is more suitable in situations with high VIF and multicollinearity or a high number of variables compared to data points.

Lambda	0.00000	0.00170	0.01700	0.17000	1.70000	17.00000	170.00000
VAR X1	0.41543	0.41602	0.42020	0.42021	0.36398	0.25379	0.07428
VAR X2	-0.37140	-0.36783	-0.33685	-0.12370	0.23040	0.23845	0.07251
VAR X3	1.11241	1.10725	1.06388	0.79884	0.39040	0.22834	0.07024
VAR X4	-0.38094	-0.37902	-0.36284	-0.26279	-0.09478	0.01508	0.02177

Beyond Regression: Weighted Regression (Heteroskedastic Model)

A Multiple Weighted regression runs a Multivariate Regression on Weighted Variables (also known as weighted least squares, or WLS) to correct for heteroskedasticity in all the variables. The weights used to adjust these variables are the user input standard deviations. As mentioned, the standard OLS approach minimizes the sum of squares of the errors $SSE = \sum_{i=1}^{n}(y_i - \hat{y}_i)^2$, but in a weighted least squares approach, we add an additional weight variable w_i such that we have $SSE = \sum_{i=1}^{n} w_i(y_i - \hat{y}_i)^2$. Similarly, in matrix notation, the standard regression's $B = (X'X)^{-1}(X'Y)$ becomes $B = (X'WX)^{-1}(X'WY)$. These weights are used as an additional input variable to the model in situations where the errors are heteroskedastic.

The following provides an example dataset and results from BizStats using a weighted regression model. Notice that a new input variable called standard deviation is required.

Finally, the regression results will show $1/Stdev$ as a representation of the weighted intercept and $X/Stdev$ as a representation of the weighted X variable. These variables can be used exactly as in a standard regression model to determine the predicted dependent variable's values. In fact, the results from a WLS should be relatively close to those in an OLS model.

Beyond Regression: Weighted Regression (Heteroskedastic Model)

Weighted Regression

Example Dataset

VAR1	VAR2	VAR3
Y	X	Stdev
266.7	2.60269	60.5
342.5	3.62434	68.3
418.1	4.31749	81.4
…	…	98.8
608.3	5.92693	110.6
798.3	6.62007	145.6
950.6	0.00637	173.1
916.5	8.92266	238.3

Model Inputs:
VAR221
VAR222
VAR223

Multiple Weighted Regression

OVERALL FIT

Multiple R	0.99552	Maximum Log Likelihood	-5.59816
R-Square	0.99107	Akaike Info Criterion (AIC)	2.14954
Adjusted R-Square	0.98809	Bayes Schwarz Criterion (BSC)	2.17933
Standard Error	0.56252	Hannan-Quinn Criterion (HQC)	1.94861
Observations	8	Cohen's F-Squared	110.93199

ANOVA

	DF	SS	MS	F	p-Value
Regression	2	210.61	105.31	332.79596	0.00000
Residual	6	1.90	0.32		
Total	8	212.51			

	Coeff	Std. Error	T-stat	P-value	Lower 5%	Upper 95%
X1/Stdev	126.84523	11.82915	10.72311	0.00004	97.90035	155.79012
1/Stdev	-100.84543	53.29659	-1.89216	0.10733	-231.25749	29.56662

Beyond Regression: Bootstrap Regression

Bootstrap regression is the process of re-running hundreds to thousands of the same regression model via resampled data to generate the best consensus forecasts. The idea is that in a random selection of data, taking the average forecast of an ensemble of models provides a more accurate prediction than a single sample. This is the same concept as the wisdom of the crowd. Risk Simulator provides variations of this bootstrap regression by resampling the residual errors as well as generating probabilistic Monte Carlo simulation assumptions as a result. Bootstrapping works well in situations where the dataset consists of independent and identically distributed (*i.i.d.*) data points. This means that the sequential order of the data points is not important in fitting the underlying process. For example, if we sufficiently resample rows of data (one row may consist of multiple columns of independent variables) with replacement, the fitted parameters will be distributed around the true population parameters. Because we assume that order is not important, bootstrap regression is typically used in cross-sectional data only. In addition, there might be situations where bootstrap regression is problematic, especially when the data points are not *i.i.d.* such as when the data points are clumpy or sensitive to extreme values.

In a traditional Empirical Bootstrap, given the original data of i rows of observations of k independent variables, $(Y_i, X_{ij}, \ldots X_{ik})$, we resample and generate a new set of *i.i.d.* observations $(Y_i^*, X_{ij}^*, \ldots X_{ij}^*)$ with replacement, such that for each l, $P(Y_l^* = Y_i, X_l^* = X_i) = \frac{1}{n}\ \forall\, i = 1, \ldots, n$. Each time, we generate n new observations (typically less than the original total number of observations) from the original dataset and the regression is run to obtain the coefficients. The process is then repeated B times in the bootstrap. The fitted coefficients $\hat{\beta}_i$ will be approximately normally distributed around the true values of β_i. This method is fast and effective but can run afoul if the original sample size is small and certain data elements are highly susceptible to extreme values. For example, if certain influential and outlier data points are not resampled, the estimated regression equation may increase the spread or the skew of the final coefficients' distributions. This methodology is available in *Risk Simulator | Forecasting | Multiple Regression | Bootstrap Regression | Random X Case Resampling*.

An alternative approach is Parametric Residual Bootstrap (sometimes also known as the wild residual bootstrap), which helps reduce the impact of influential outlier data points. Using the residuals from the regression $e_i = Y_i - \hat{\beta}_0 - \hat{\beta}_i X_i$, we generate *i.i.d.* $\hat{e}_i^*, \ldots, \hat{e}_n^*$. Then, we fix the covariates $X_i^* = X_i$ for each i and resample only the value of Y_i using the residual e_i. The bootstrap sampling is then obtained by $Y_i^* = \hat{\beta}_0 + \hat{\beta}_i X_i + \Phi_i e_i$, where $\Phi \sim N(0,1)$. The *i.i.d.* normal random variable is applied to reduce any heteroskedasticity issues in the event the variance of the error is unstable over time. This approach is preferred when there are influential outliers or heteroskedasticity issues in the data, whereas the empirical bootstrap approach is preferred in almost all other cases. This is available in *Risk Simulator | Forecasting | Multiple Regression | Bootstrap Regression | Fixed X Parametric Residual Resampling*.

Summary of Exotic Regression Methods

Bayesian Regression
Used when you want to incorporate prior beliefs about parameters and update them with data, producing a full probability distribution for coefficients (not just point estimates). You specify a prior $p(\beta)$ and a likelihood $p(y \mid X, \beta)$, and compute the posterior $p(\beta \mid y, X)$ using Bayes' rule. It's especially useful with small samples, hierarchical structure, or when uncertainty quantification matters. Computation is often done via MCMC or variational inference.

Bootstrap Regression
Used to assess the stability and uncertainty of regression estimates by repeatedly resampling the data and refitting the model. You draw many bootstrap samples, compute $\hat{\beta}^{(b)}$ for each sample b, and use the empirical distribution of $\hat{\beta}^{(b)}$ to estimate standard errors, confidence intervals, and bias. It is helpful when analytic standard errors are unreliable, or assumptions are questionable. It can be applied to OLS, logistic regression, and many other models.

Cointegration Test (Engle–Granger)
Used to test whether two (or more) nonstationary time series share a stable long-run relationship, even though each series individually has a unit root. In the Engle–Granger approach, you first estimate the long-run regression $y_t = \alpha + \beta x_t + u_t$, then test whether residuals u_t are stationary using an ADF-type test. If $u_t \sim I(0)$while $x_t, y_t \sim I(1)$, the series are cointegrated. If cointegration exists, an Error Correction Model is typically used next.

Cox Regression (Survival Regression)
Used for time-to-event outcomes (e.g., time until failure, death, churn) when some observations are censored. The Cox proportional hazards model specifies $h(t \mid X) = h_0(t)\exp(X\beta)$, separating the baseline hazard from covariate effects. It estimates how predictors multiplicatively change the hazard rate without requiring you to fully specify $h_0(t)$. It's widely used in medical, reliability, and customer analytics.

Deming Regression
Used when both the predictor X and response Y are measured with error, which violates ordinary least squares assumptions. Unlike OLS, it fits a line by minimizing squared *orthogonal* distances from data points to the line. The fit is weighted by the ratio of measurement error variances in X and Y. This is common in lab calibration and method-comparison studies.

Difference-in-Differences Regression (DiD)
A quasi-experimental method used to estimate a treatment's causal effect by comparing outcome changes over time between treated and control groups. The key assumption is parallel trends: in the absence of treatment, treated and control would have evolved similarly. A standard model is $Y_{it} = \beta_0 + \beta_1 Post_t + \beta_2 Treat_i + \beta_3(Treat_i \times Post_t) + \varepsilon_{it}$where β_3 is the estimated treatment effect. It's common in policy evaluation, program impact, and business interventions.

Summary of Exotic Regression Methods

Discriminant Analysis (LDA / QDA)
Used to classify observations into two or more groups using continuous predictors and a categorical outcome. LDA assumes each class is normally distributed with a shared covariance matrix Σ, leading to a linear decision boundary; QDA allows class-specific covariance matrices Σ_k, producing nonlinear boundaries. Classification is based on a discriminant score, e.g. $\delta_k(x) = x^\top \Sigma^{-1}\mu_k - \frac{1}{2}\mu_k^\top \Sigma^{-1}\mu_k + \ln \pi_k$.It is related to regression/ANOVA in that it models group separation using linear combinations of predictors.

Elastic Net Regression
Used when you have many predictors, especially correlated ones, and want both shrinkage and variable selection. It combines Lasso and Ridge penalties: $\min_\beta \sum(y_i - x_i^\top \beta)^2 + \lambda(\alpha \parallel \beta \parallel_1 + (1-\alpha) \parallel \beta \parallel_2^2)$.The Ridge component helps keep groups of correlated variables together, while the Lasso component can set some coefficients exactly to zero. It's widely used in high-dimensional prediction problems.

Endogeneity Test (Durbin–Wu–Hausman using 2SLS)
Used to test whether a regressor is endogenous (correlated with the error term), which would bias OLS estimates. A common approach is to run a first-stage regression using instruments, obtain residuals, and include them in the structural equation; significance implies endogeneity. Conceptually, it compares OLS vs IV/2SLS estimates and checks whether the difference is systematic. This is a core diagnostic step before committing to IV methods.

Endogenous Model (Instrumental Variables with 2SLS)
Used when a regressor is endogenous and you have valid instruments that affect the regressor but not the outcome error term. In 2SLS, you first predict the endogenous regressor from instruments (and exogenous controls), then regress the outcome on that predicted regressor:
Stage 1: $X_{end} = Z\pi + X_{exo}\gamma + u$,
Stage 2: $y = \hat{X}_{end}\beta + X_{exo}\theta + \varepsilon$.
This isolates the variation in X_{end} that is plausibly exogenous. Validity depends heavily on instrument relevance and exclusion.

Error Correction Model (ECM, Engle–Granger)
Used after cointegration is established, to model short-run dynamics while enforcing long-run equilibrium. The model includes an "error correction term" (ECT) that measures last period's deviation from equilibrium, e.g.

$$\Delta y_t = \alpha + \lambda(y_{t-1} - \beta x_{t-1}) + \sum \phi_i \Delta y_{t-i} + \sum \psi_i \Delta x_{t-i} + \varepsilon_t.$$

The coefficient λ captures the speed of adjustment back toward the long-run relationship. ECMs are common in macro/finance where levels are nonstationary but tied together long-run.

Summary of Exotic Regression Methods

Generalized Additive Models (GAMs)
Used to model nonlinear relationships flexibly while preserving additivity across predictors. A GAM typically has the form

$$g(E[Y \mid X]) = \beta_0 + f_1(X_1) + \cdots + f_p(X_p),$$

where $f_j(\cdot)$ are smooth functions (often splines) learned from data. This gives more flexibility than linear regression without going fully "black box." GAMs are popular when interpretability of each predictor's shape matters.

Granger Causality
Used to test whether lagged values of one time series improve prediction of another time series beyond its own lags. A common setup is

$$y_t = c + \sum_{i=1}^{p} a_i y_{t-i} + \sum_{i=1}^{p} b_i x_{t-i} + \varepsilon_t,$$

and you test $H_0: b_1 = \cdots = b_p = 0$. Rejection suggests "Granger causality," meaning predictive (not necessarily structural) causality. It's widely used in econometrics and finance for lead–lag relationships.

Lasso Regression
Used when you want automatic variable selection and coefficient shrinkage in one step. It minimizes squared error plus an L_1 penalty $\lambda \parallel \beta \parallel_1$, which can drive some coefficients exactly to zero. This makes it useful in sparse, high-dimensional settings. It can be sensitive when predictors are highly correlated (often motivating Elastic Net).

Linear Regression (OLS)
Used to model a linear relationship between a continuous outcome and one or more predictors. It assumes $y = X\beta + \varepsilon$ and estimates $\hat{\beta}$ by minimizing $\sum(y_i - x_i^{\top}\beta)^2$. OLS is simple, interpretable, and often a baseline model. Its reliability depends on assumptions like linearity, exogeneity, and error behavior.

Logistic Regression
Used to model the probability of a binary outcome (0/1) as a function of predictors. It models the log-odds as linear: $\log\frac{p}{1-p} = X\beta$, with $p = P(Y = 1 \mid X)$. Coefficients interpret as changes in log-odds (or odds ratios after exponentiation). It is a workhorse for classification with strong interpretability.

Multinomial Logistic Regression
Used when the outcome has more than two unordered categories (e.g., choose A/B/C). It models each non-reference category via

$$\log\frac{P(Y = k \mid X)}{P(Y = K \mid X)} = X\beta_k, k = 1, \ldots, K - 1.$$

Predicted probabilities across categories sum to 1, enabling multi-class classification. Common in choice modeling and segmentation.

Summary of Exotic Regression Methods

Nonparametric Regression (Kernel & Local)
Used when you don't want to assume a fixed parametric relationship between X and Y. Instead, it estimates $m(x) = E[Y \mid X = x]$ directly from local neighborhoods, e.g. kernel smoothing:

$$\widehat{m}(x) = \frac{\sum K_h(x - X_i)Y_i}{\sum K_h(x - X_i)}.$$

This allows the data to shape the curve but can require more data and careful bandwidth selection. It's great for exploratory modeling and flexible fits.

Ordinal Regression (Proportional Odds)
Used when the outcome is ordered categories (e.g., low/medium/high) and you want the model to respect ordering. A common specification is the proportional odds model:

$$\log \frac{P(Y \leq j \mid X)}{P(Y > j \mid X)} = \theta_j - X\beta.$$

It assumes the effect of predictors is consistent across thresholds ("parallel lines"). It's common in survey and rating-scale modeling.

Partial Least Squares (PLS) Regression
Used when predictors are many and collinear, and you want dimension reduction targeted toward predicting Y. PLS constructs latent components as linear combinations of X that maximize covariance with Y. Then Y is regressed on these components rather than the raw predictors. It's often used in chemometrics, marketing analytics, and high-dimensional settings.

Poisson Regression
Used for modeling count outcomes (0,1,2,...) as a function of predictors. It assumes $Y \sim$ Poisson (μ) with $\log(\mu) = X\beta$, making effects multiplicative on the expected count. It is the standard GLM for counts but can struggle with overdispersion. In practice it's often paired with checks or alternatives (negative binomial).

Poisson Regression (Exposure & Population Offset)
Used when counts depend on an underlying exposure such as time at risk, population size, or number of trials. You include an offset term so the model predicts rates:

$$\log(\mu_i) = X_i\beta + \log(\text{exposure}_i).$$

This makes interpretation about incidence rates rather than raw counts. Common in epidemiology, insurance frequency, event modeling.

Quantile Regression
Used to model conditional quantiles of Y (median, 90th percentile, etc.) instead of the conditional mean. It estimates β_τ by minimizing the check-loss $\sum \rho_\tau(y_i - x_i^\top \beta)$, where $\rho_\tau(u) = u(\tau - 1[u < 0])$. This is useful when effects differ in the tails or when you care about risk/inequality. It is robust to certain outlier patterns compared to OLS.

Summary of Exotic Regression Methods

Regression Discontinuity Design (RDD)
A quasi-experimental method that identifies causal effects by exploiting a cutoff in a running variable. The key idea is that units just above and below the cutoff are comparable, so a jump at the threshold is attributed to treatment. A common local linear specification is

$$Y_i = \alpha + \tau D_i + \beta_1(R_i - c) + \beta_2(R_i - c)D_i + \varepsilon_i,$$

$D_i = 1[R_i \geq c]$.Validity depends on no manipulation around the cutoff and smooth potential outcomes.

Ridge Regression
Used when predictors are highly correlated or when p is large, to stabilize estimates and reduce variance. It adds an L_2 penalty $\lambda \parallel \beta \parallel_2^2$, shrinking coefficients toward zero but typically not to exactly zero. Ridge often improves prediction when multicollinearity inflates OLS variance. It is a common baseline regularization method.

Robust Regression (Huber)
Used when outliers or heavy-tailed errors would overly influence OLS. It replaces squared loss with a robust loss $\rho(\cdot)$ that grows more slowly for large residuals (e.g., Huber). This down-weights extreme observations rather than letting them dominate the fit. It's useful for messy real-world data or when you suspect contamination.

Spatial Regression
Used when observations are spatially located and neighboring units are correlated, violating independence assumptions. Common forms include a spatial lag model $y = \rho Wy + X\beta + \varepsilon$ or a spatial error model $\varepsilon = \lambda W\varepsilon + u$, where W encodes neighborhood weights. These models separate covariate effects from spatial spillovers/dependence. They are common in real estate, epidemiology, and regional economics.

Spline Regression
Used to model nonlinear relationships by stitching together low-degree polynomials while enforcing smoothness at knots. It represents the relationship using spline-basis functions (e.g., B-splines) so the curve can bend where needed without becoming overly wiggly. This is a structured alternative to fully nonparametric methods. Splines are building blocks of GAMs.

Stepwise Regression
Used to select a subset of predictors in a multiple regression when many candidates exist. Variants include forward selection, backward elimination, and combined forward/backward, often using p-values or information criteria (AIC/BIC) to decide adds/drops. It can be quick and practical, but it may overfit or yield unstable variable choices. It's best treated as a heuristic rather than definitive inference.

Stepwise Regression (Backward)
Starts with all predictors, then iteratively removes the least significant variable (largest p-value) and refits. The process continues until all remaining predictors meet a significance criterion (or improve an information criterion). This can be effective when you believe most variables matter but want to simplify. Results can still be sensitive to collinearity and sampling noise.

Summary of Exotic Regression Methods

Stepwise Regression (Correlation)
Begins by correlating Y with each candidate X, selecting the strongest correlation first and building the model incrementally. It adds variables until newly added variables become insignificant. This is fast and intuitive but can be misleading because correlations ignore joint effects and interactions. Strong predictors added early may "mask" others.

Three-Stage Least Squares (3SLS)
Used for simultaneous equation systems where regressors are endogenous and error terms are correlated across equations. It combines 2SLS to address endogeneity with a GLS step to exploit cross-equation correlation for efficiency. This can improve estimates when the system structure is correct. It's common in structural econometric modeling.

Through-Origin Regression (No Intercept)
Used when theory or measurement implies the regression line should pass through zero. The model is $y = X\beta + \varepsilon$ with no constant term, so predictions are forced to be 0 when all predictors are 0. This is appropriate in some physical or production settings but can be dangerous if the true intercept isn't actually zero. Fit statistics can also behave differently, so interpretation needs care.

Tobit Regression
Used when the dependent variable is censored (e.g., values pile up at a lower bound like 0). It assumes an underlying latent variable $y_i^* = x_i^\top \beta + \varepsilon_i$, but observed y_i is censored, such as $y_i = \max(c, y_i^*)$. Estimation uses the censored normal likelihood rather than OLS. It's common for expenditures, demand, and limited outcomes.

Two-Stage Least Squares (2SLS)
Used to handle endogeneity using instrumental variables that shift regressors without directly affecting the outcome error term. In stage 1, endogenous regressors are predicted using instruments; in stage 2, the outcome is regressed on those fitted values. This produces consistent estimates under valid instruments, though standard errors must account for the two-stage procedure. It's foundational in causal econometrics.

Vector Autoregression (VAR)
Used for multivariate time series where each variable depends on its own lags and the lags of other variables. A VAR(p) is $y_t = A_1 y_{t-1} + \cdots + A_p y_{t-p} + \varepsilon_t$, with y_t a vector and A_j coefficient matrices. VARs are used for forecasting and impulse response analysis (shock propagation). They require stationarity or differencing/cointegration when nonstationary.

Weighted Least Squares (WLS)
Used when observations have different error variances (heteroskedasticity), so OLS is inefficient and standard errors can be misleading. WLS gives higher weight to more precise observations by minimizing $\sum w_i (y_i - x_i^\top \beta)^2$, often with $w_i \propto 1/\sigma_i^2$. It can improve both estimation and inference when weights are correctly specified. It is common in meta-analysis and models with known measurement variance.

7. AI-Powered Prediction, Classification, and Clustering

Core Theme

This section covers the machine learning paradigm end-to-end: supervised vs. unsupervised learning, train/validation/test splits, cross-validation, decision trees (Gini, entropy, pruning), Random Forests, Gradient Boosting (XGBoost, LightGBM), SVMs, KNN, and neural network foundations (perceptrons, backpropagation). Unsupervised methods include K-Means, hierarchical clustering, Gaussian mixture models, and PCA for dimensionality reduction. Model interpretability (SHAP, PDP) and practical implementation through AI tools are emphasized throughout.

Module Objectives

AI-Powered Prediction, Classification, and Clustering

Implement Tree Methods

Master Decision Trees, Random Forests, and Gradient Boosting (XGBoost, LightGBM) for robust prediction.

Advanced Classification

Apply Support Vector Machines (SVM) and K-Nearest Neighbors (KNN) to model complex boundaries.

Neural Networks Basics

Understand the foundations of Perceptrons, activation functions, and feedforward network architectures.

Clustering & Reduction

Build unsupervised workflows using K-Means, DBSCAN, and Principal Component Analysis (PCA).

Rigorous Evaluation

Assess model performance using Precision, Recall, F1-score, ROC-AUC, and confusion matrices.

Interpretability & SHAP

Unbox black-box models using SHAP values, feature importance, and partial dependence plots.

Business Deployment

Translate raw model probabilities into actionable business strategies like targeting and scoring.

AI-Accelerated Workflow

Leverage Julius AI and ChatGPT to accelerate model training, tuning, and explanation tasks.

The Machine Learning Paradigm

Learning Types & The End-to-End Workflow

Supervised Learning

Models learn mapping from input X to output Y using labeled training data.

`Regression, Classification, Gradient Boosting`

Unsupervised Learning

Models discover hidden patterns, structures, or groupings in unlabeled data.

`Clustering (K-Means), PCA, Anomaly Detection`

Semi-Supervised

Combines a small amount of labeled data with a large amount of unlabeled data.

`Self-training, Label Propagation, SSL`

Standard ML Development Pipeline

1. Define
Problem framing & success metrics

2. Prepare
Cleaning, splitting & engineering

3. Select
Algorithm choice & baseline

4. Train
Fitting model & tuning hyperparams

5. Evaluate
Validation metrics & error analysis

6. Deploy
Integration & monitoring

Data Splits and Cross-Validation

Evaluating Model Performance & Ensuring Generalization

Holdout Method

Splitting data into distinct sets to simulate unseen data for evaluation.

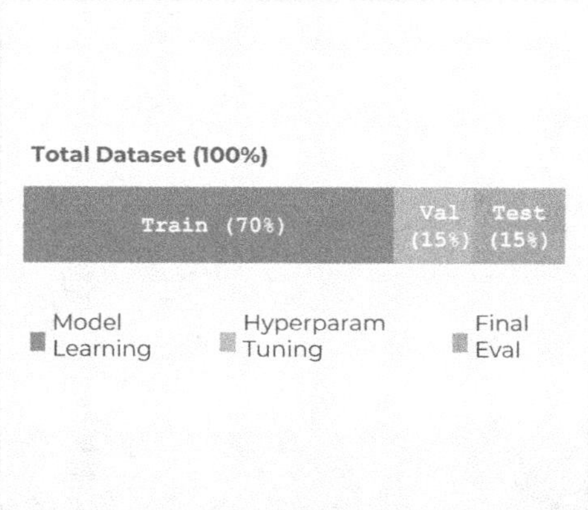

K-Fold Cross-Validation

Iterative splitting to use all data for both training and validation.

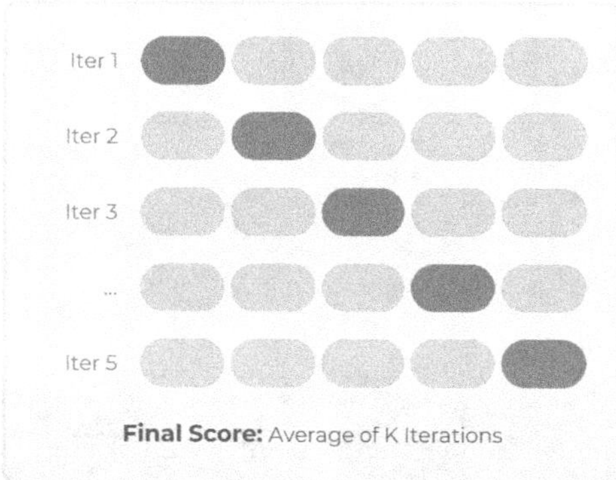

Stratification

Preserving the percentage of samples for each class across splits.

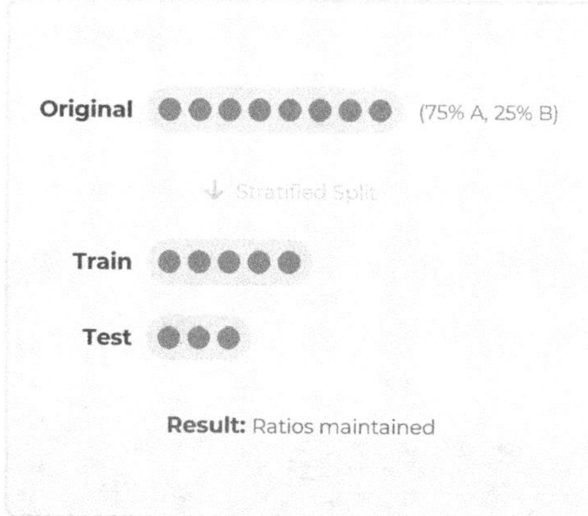

Decision Trees: Splitting & Pruning

Optimizing Tree Structure for Classification

Gini Impurity (CART)

$$I_G(p) = 1 - \sum_{k=1}^{K} p_k^2$$

Measures the probability of misclassifying a randomly chosen element. Lower is purer (0 = pure node).

Entropy (ID3, C4.5)

$$H(S) = -\sum_{k=1}^{K} p_k \log_2(p_k)$$

Measure of impurity or disorder. High entropy implies a uniform mix of classes; zero implies a single class.

Information Gain

$$IG(S, A) = H(S) - \sum_{v \in Values(A)} \frac{|S_v|}{|S|} H(S_v)$$

The reduction in entropy achieved by splitting dataset S on attribute A. Used to select the best split.

Regularization & Pruning Parameters

Max Depth, Min Samples Leaf, CCP Alpha

Controls overfitting by limiting tree growth or removing weak branches (Cost-Complexity Pruning).

Impurity Measures (Binary Classification)

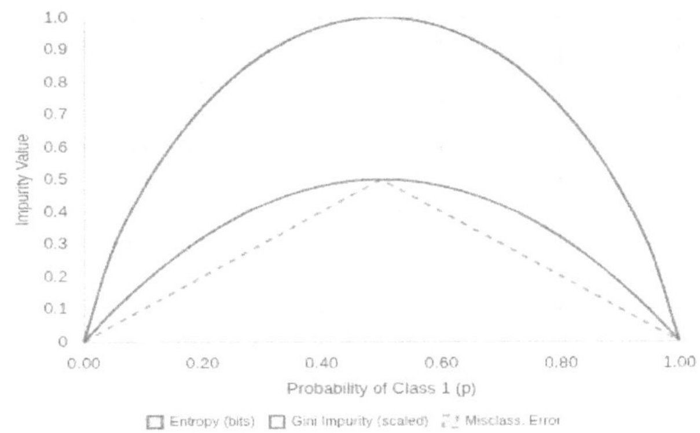

The Need for Pruning: Bias-Variance

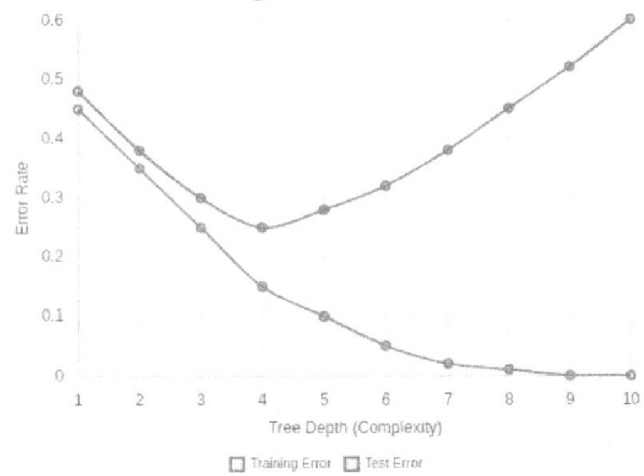

Ensembles: Random Forests

Bagging, Feature Randomness, and OOB Error Analysis

OOB Error vs. Number of Trees

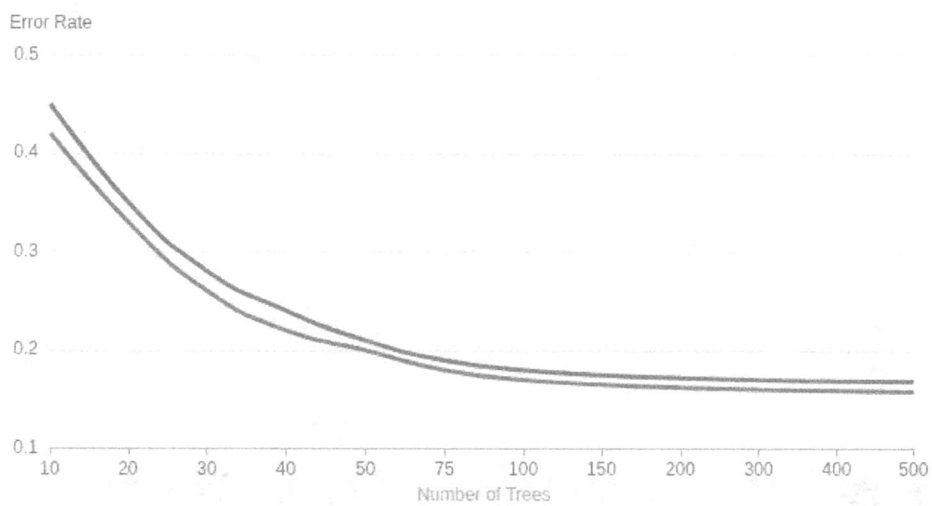

Feature Randomness

$$m \approx \sqrt{p}$$

Unlike standard decision trees that check all features at a split, Random Forests consider only a random subset (m) of total features (p). This **decorrelates** the trees.

Core Mechanics

Bagging (Bootstrap Aggregating): Training each tree on a random sample of data drawn *with replacement*. Reduces variance and helps avoid overfitting.

Out-of-Bag (OOB) Error: Data points not used in the training of a specific tree act as an internal validation set. The OOB error often converges to the leave-one-out cross-validation error.

Key Insight

Increasing the number of trees does not cause overfitting in Random Forests; the error rate stabilizes.

Gradient Boosting Machines (GBM)

XGBoost, LightGBM, and Sequential Learning

Sequential Additive Training

Unlike Random Forests which build trees in parallel, GBMs build trees sequentially. Each new tree focuses on correcting the residuals (errors) made by the previous ensemble of trees.

Gradient Descent Optimization

The model minimizes a differentiable loss function (e.g., Log Loss for classification) by adding weak learners that follow the negative gradient direction.

Regularization & Efficiency (XGBoost/LightGBM)

Modern implementations include advanced regularization (L1/L2) and system optimizations (histogram-based splitting) to handle large datasets efficiently while preventing overfitting.

Key Hyperparameters to Tune

`Learning Rate` (shrinkage): Step size for weight updates (lower requires more trees).
`N Estimators`: Number of boosting rounds (trees) to build.
`Max Depth`: Controls tree complexity; deeper trees capture more interactions but risk overfitting.

Model Interpretation: PDP and SHAP

From "Black Box" to Transparent, Actionable Insights

PDP & ICE Plot: Feature Effect

Feature: "Tenure" vs. Probability

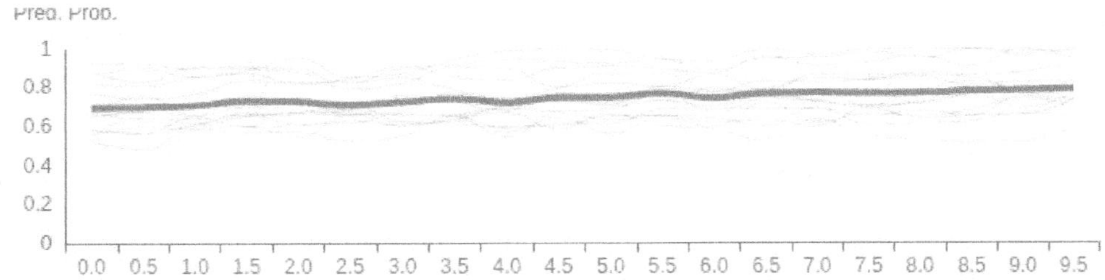

SHAP Beeswarm Summary

Global Feature Importance & Direction

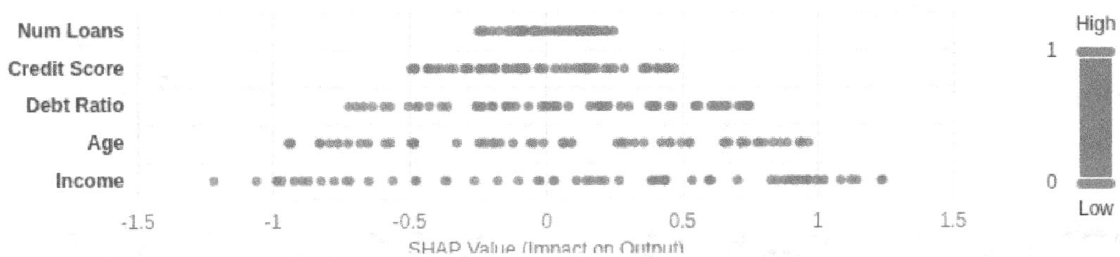

Partial Dependence (PDP/ICE)

PDP (Thick Line): Shows the marginal effect of a feature on the predicted outcome, averaged across all instances.

ICE (Thin Lines): Displays the functional relationship for *individual* observations, revealing heterogeneity (interactions) that averages might hide.

SHAP Values

$$f(x) = \phi_0 + \sum_{j=1}^{M} \phi_j$$

Based on cooperative game theory (Shapley values), SHAP guarantees consistency and local accuracy.

Reading the Beeswarm

X-axis: Impact on model output (SHAP value).
Color: Feature value (Red = High, Blue = Low).
Example: If "High Income" (Red) dots are on the right, higher income increases the prediction.

Support Vector Machines & Kernels

Maximizing Margins and Handling Non-Linearity

Objective: Maximize Margin

$$\min_{w,b} \frac{1}{2}\|w\|^2 + C\sum_{i=1}^{n}\xi_i$$

Minimize weights ($||w||^2$) to maximize margin, plus penalty (C) for misclassified points (ξ_i).

Constraints

$$y_i(w \cdot x_i + b) \geq 1 - \xi_i, \xi_i \geq 0$$

Ensure data points lie on the correct side of the margin boundary, allowing slack (ξ_i).

Decision Function

$$f(x) = \text{sign}\left(\sum_{i=1}^{n} \alpha_i y_i K(x_i, x) + b\right)$$

Classification depends only on support vectors where $\alpha_i > 0$.

Kernel Trick (RBF)

$$K(x, x') = \exp(-\|\gamma x - x'\|^2)$$

Projects data into infinite dimensions to separate non-linear patterns.

The SVM Hyperplane & Margins

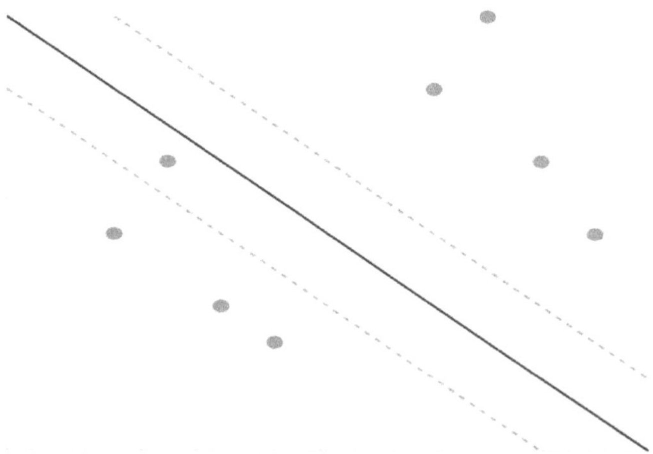

Why Kernels? (Non-Linear Data)

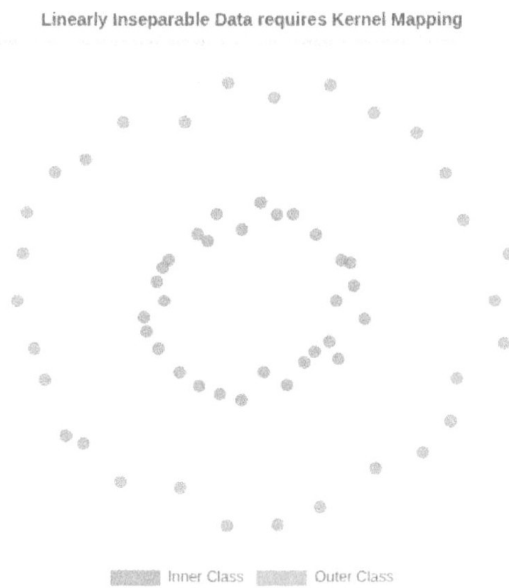

K-Nearest Neighbors (KNN)

Distance-Based Classification & Regression

Distance Metrics Matter

KNN relies on calculating "closeness" between data points. Common metrics include **Euclidean** (straight line, sensitive to scale) and **Manhattan** (grid-like, robust to high dimensions). **Cosine similarity** is often used for text/sparse data.

The Curse of Dimensionality

As the number of features increases, the volume of the space increases exponentially, making data sparse. Distance becomes less meaningful in high dimensions, often requiring dimensionality reduction (like PCA) beforehand.

Tuning K with Cross-Validation

Choosing 'k' is critical: small 'k' leads to low bias/high variance (overfitting/noise sensitivity), while large 'k' leads to high bias/low variance (underfitting/smooth boundaries). Use k-fold cross-validation to find the optimal 'k'.

Key Insight: Scaling features (Standardization/Normalization) is mandatory for KNN, as distance calculations are heavily influenced by the magnitude of variables.

Neural Networks: Foundations

Perceptrons, Backpropagation, and Activation Functions

The Perceptron Model

$$\hat{y} = \varphi\left(\sum_{i=1}^{n} w_i\, x_i + b\right)$$

A linear combination of inputs passed through a non-linear activation function φ.

Key Activation Functions

$$\mathrm{ReLU}(z) = \max(0, z), \sigma(z) = \frac{1}{1 + e^{-z}}$$

ReLU handles vanishing gradients in deep nets; Sigmoid maps outputs to probabilities (0,1).

Backpropagation (Learning)

$$w_{\text{new}} = w_{\text{old}} - \eta \cdot \frac{\partial \mathcal{L}}{\partial w}$$

Updating weights by moving opposite to the gradient of the loss function $\mathcal{L}$ with learning rate η.

Activation Function Profiles

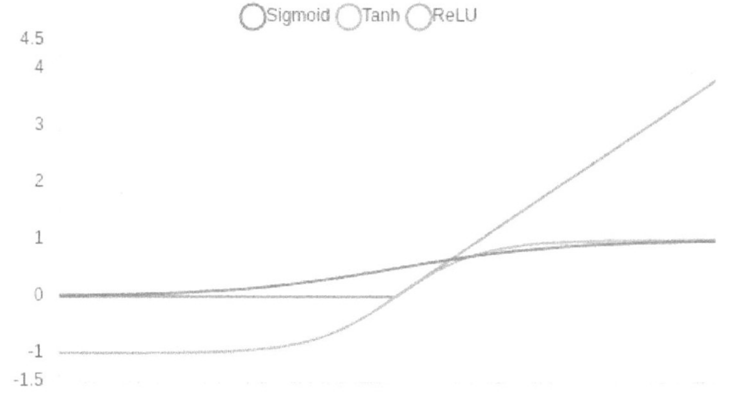

Perceptron Architecture

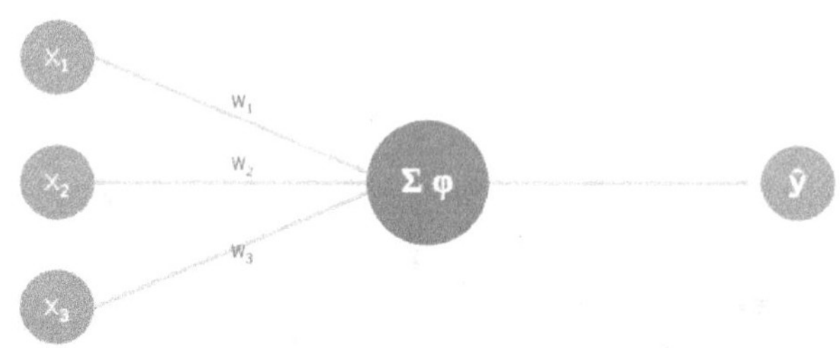

Clustering & Evaluation

Unsupervised Learning Algorithms and Validation Metrics

K-Means Objective (Inertia)

$$\min_{C} \sum_{k=1}^{K} \sum_{x_i \in C_k} ||x_i - \mu_k||^2$$

Minimize the within-cluster sum of squares (WCSS). Partition n observations into K clusters defined by centroids μ.

Hierarchical Clustering

$$d(A, B) = min/\max/avg\{d(a,b): a \in \mathrm{A}, \mathrm{b} \in \mathrm{B}$$

Builds a hierarchy of clusters using Agglomerative (bottom-up) or Divisive strategies, visualized via Dendrograms.

DBSCAN (Density-Based)

Parameters: ε (neighborhood radius), MinPts (min points). Identifies core samples in high-density areas and expands clusters. Capable of finding arbitrary shapes and filtering noise.

Cluster Validity (Silhouette Score)

$$s(i) = \frac{b(i) - a(i)}{\max(a, (i) b(i))}$$

a(i): mean intra-cluster distance. b(i): mean nearest-cluster distance. Range: [-1, 1]. Higher is better.

The Elbow Method (Finding Optimal K)

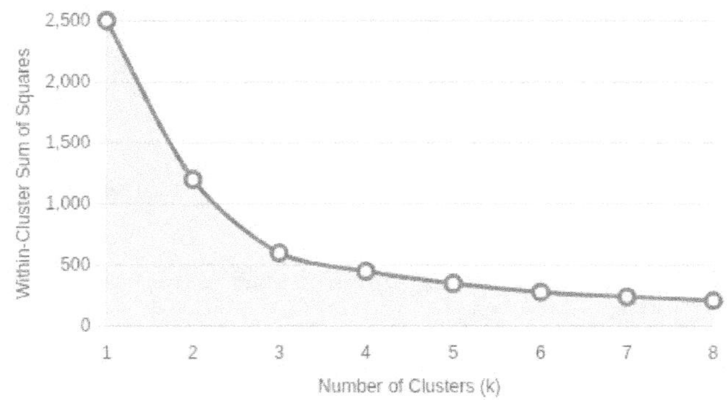

Silhouette Analysis by Cluster Count

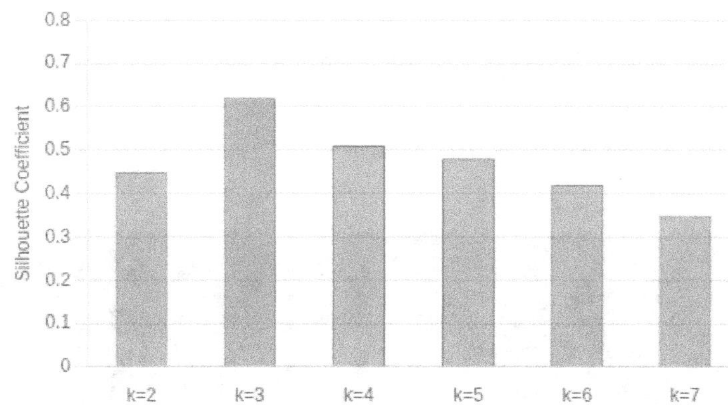

Dimensionality Reduction (PCA) and Business Use

Simplifying Complexity for Actionable Insights

PCA Eigendecomposition

Principal Component Analysis transforms correlated variables into a set of linearly uncorrelated orthogonal axes (principal components) via eigendecomposition of the covariance matrix.

Variance Explained & Selection

Eigenvalues indicate the amount of variance captured by each component. A scree plot helps identify the optimal number of components to retain the signal while discarding noise.

Business Applications in Segmentation

Reduces hundreds of behavioral metrics into core "personas" for customer segmentation. This enables more effective targeting and resource allocation by focusing on dominant patterns.

Key Insight: PCA is crucial before clustering (like K-Means) to handle the "curse of dimensionality" and ensure distances are calculated on meaningful, uncorrelated features rather than noise.

ARTIFICIAL INTELLIGENCE

Artificial Intelligence (AI) is a broad catch-all term for a group of artificial intelligence technologies used to simulate intelligence. The science of AI was established in the 1950s to determine whether inorganic robots could exhibit human-level intelligence. Significant interest in AI resurfaced around the same time that Big Data computing capacity became more widely available to researchers and businesses, enabling them to apply the science to a variety of practical applications. Manufacturing robots, smart assistants, proactive healthcare management, illness mapping, automated financial investing, virtual travel-booking agents, social media monitoring, conversational marketing bots, natural language processing tools, and inventory supply chain management are all examples of commercially feasible AI applications.

The timeline of AI and Data Science development reveals a long journey in which mathematical statistics evolved into applied statistics, data science, artificial intelligence, and machine learning (ML). For instance, in 1962, John Tukey's work as a mathematical statistician can be considered one of the early seminal works in data analytics. In 1977, the International Association for Statistical Computing (IASC) was founded to link traditional statistical methodology, modern computer technology, and domain experts' knowledge to convert data into information and knowledge. Database marketing set a trend in 1994, and by 1996, the term "Data Science" first appeared at the International Federation of Classification Societies in Japan. The inaugural topic was entitled "Data Science, Classification, and Related Methods." In 1997, Jeff Wu gave an inaugural lecture titled simply "Statistics = Data Science?" In 2001, William Cleveland published "Data Science: An Action Plan for Expanding the Technical Areas of the Field of Statistics." He put forward the notion that data science was an independent discipline and identified several areas in which he believed data scientists should be educated: multidisciplinary investigations; models and methods for data analysis; computing with data; pedagogy; tool evaluation; and theory. By 2008, the term "data scientist" was often attributed to Jeff Hammerbacher and D. J. Patil, then of Facebook and LinkedIn, respectively, and in 2010, the term "data science" had fully infiltrated the vernacular. Between 2011 and 2012, job listings for "data scientist" increased by 15,000%. Around 2016, data science started to be entrenched in Machine Learning and Deep Learning. This implies that AI/ML techniques are solidly grounded in traditional mathematical statistics, with smart algorithmic steps wrapped around these methods.

The term AI typically conjures the nebulous concept of machine learning, which, in reality, is a subset of AI in which a computer system is programmed to identify and categorize external real-world stimuli. AI can be loosely defined as the ability of machines to perform tasks that normally require human intelligence—for example, recognizing patterns, learning from experience, drawing conclusions, making predictions, or taking action—whether digitally or as the smart software behind autonomous physical systems. AI processes most appropriate for data science, quantitative research analytics, prediction, and forecasting modeling include Machine Learning (ML), Natural Language Processing (NLP), and Robotic Process Automation (RPA).

Whereas AI, in general, involves the use of algorithms exhibiting "smart" behavior, the use of AI algorithms in Machine Learning (ML)— that detect patterns and use them for prediction and decision making—can be broadly divided into supervised and unsupervised methods. *Supervised* learning means that the correct answers are provided by humans to train the algorithm, whereas *unsupervised* learning does not include the correct results. Supervised algorithms are taught patterns using past data and then detect them automatically in new data. For example, a multiple regression on the dependent variable, Y and one or more independent variables, X_i. Because the results (dependent variable) are provided, this is considered a supervised ML algorithm. In contrast, unsupervised algorithms are programmed to detect new and interesting patterns in completely new data. Without supervision, the algorithm is not expected to surface specific correct answers; instead, it looks for logical patterns within raw data. For example, a factor analysis where there are multiple independent variables X_i but the a priori groupings of these variables are not known would be considered an unsupervised method.

AI MACHINE LEARNING

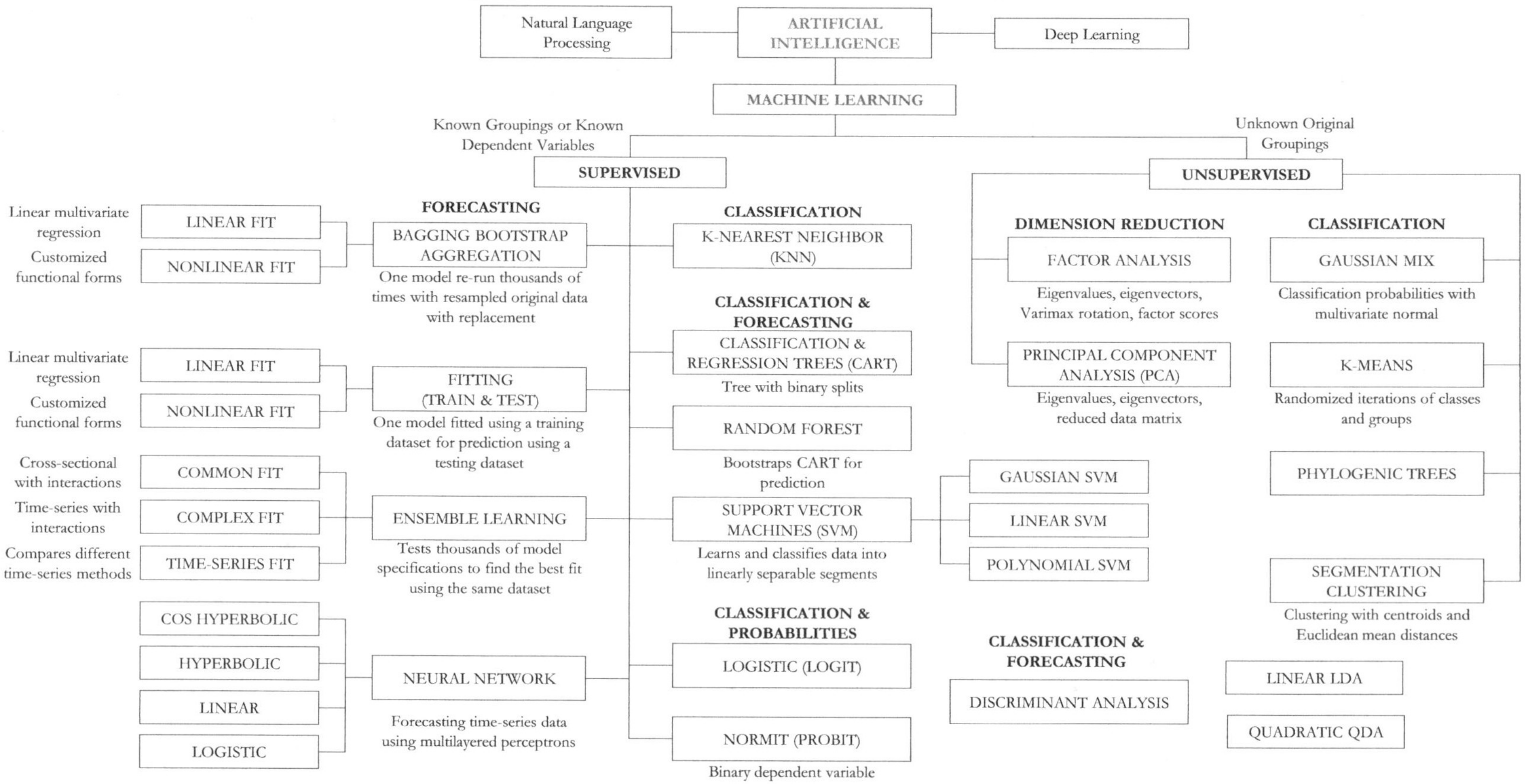

AI MACHINE LEARNING: BAGGING LINEAR FIT BOOTSTRAP (SUPERVISED)

This method applies a Bootstrap Aggregation (Bagging) Linear Fit Model of hundreds of models via resampled data to generate the best consensus forecasts. The idea is that in a random selection of data, taking the average forecast of an ensemble of models provides a more accurate prediction than a single sample. In a typical multivariate linear regression, the relationship structure and characteristics of a dependent variable and how it depends on other independent exogenous variables can be modeled. The model can be used to understand the relationship among these variables as well as for the purposes of forecasting and predictive modeling. The accuracy and goodness of fit for this model can also be determined. Similar to a linear multivariate regression model, we first train the algorithm using the training dependent and training independent variables, which will identify the optimized parameters to use on the testing dataset. Then, the dataset is resampled, and the algorithm is again run. This process is repeated or bootstrapped hundreds of times, and the output forecasts will be a consensus of all these bootstrapped models.

In an ensemble forecast, we would apply different models to the same dataset, whereas in a bagging or bootstrap aggregation approach, we use the same model but applied multiple times to a random selection of the existing dataset. The latter's algorithm is trivial. Suppose we have a dependent response variable Y and k number of predictor independent variables $\mathbf{X} = X_1, X_2, \ldots, X_k$, each with N rows of data. Then, we would initialize B, the number of bootstrap models to be fitted, as well as n, the number of data rows to use in the bootstrap, where $n < N$. Starting with $B = 1$, we take a bootstrap resampling of n data rows and fit the model; specifically, we sample with replacement, to fit $\mathbf{X}_B$ to Y_B and obtain a forecast fit $\hat{f}_B(\mathbf{X})$. Repeat the process applying a resampling with replacement and generating the aggregate consensus forecast. Recall that this bootstrap approach assumes that the model is correctly specified, and we are simply re-running the same model specification on resampled data. In contrast, the Ensemble Learning methods such as the AI/ML Ensemble Common Fit and the Ensemble Complex Fit will take the same dataset and apply hundreds or even thousands of models to test for the best-fitting model specification.

```
Model Inputs:
VAR373          Training Y (1 variable)
VAR374:VAR375   Training X (≥ 1 variables)
VAR380:VAR381   Testing X (matches Training X's number of variables)
1000            Number of Bootstraps (1-1000)
45              Number of Data Points (< number of data rows)
0               Testing Y (optional, 1 variable)
VAR442          Forecast Save Location (optional, 1 variable)
```

```
AI Machine Learning: Bagging Linear Fit Bootstrap (Supervised)

Period  Forecast (F)  Min Forecast  Max Forecast
   1      380.4235      283.1699      523.8427
   2      425.6080      314.7315      615.5356
   3      418.1381      309.9623      603.3895
   .        . .           . .           . .
  30      349.5307      277.0782      440.0635
```

AI MACHINE LEARNING: BAGGING LINEAR FIT BOOTSTRAP (SUPERVISED)

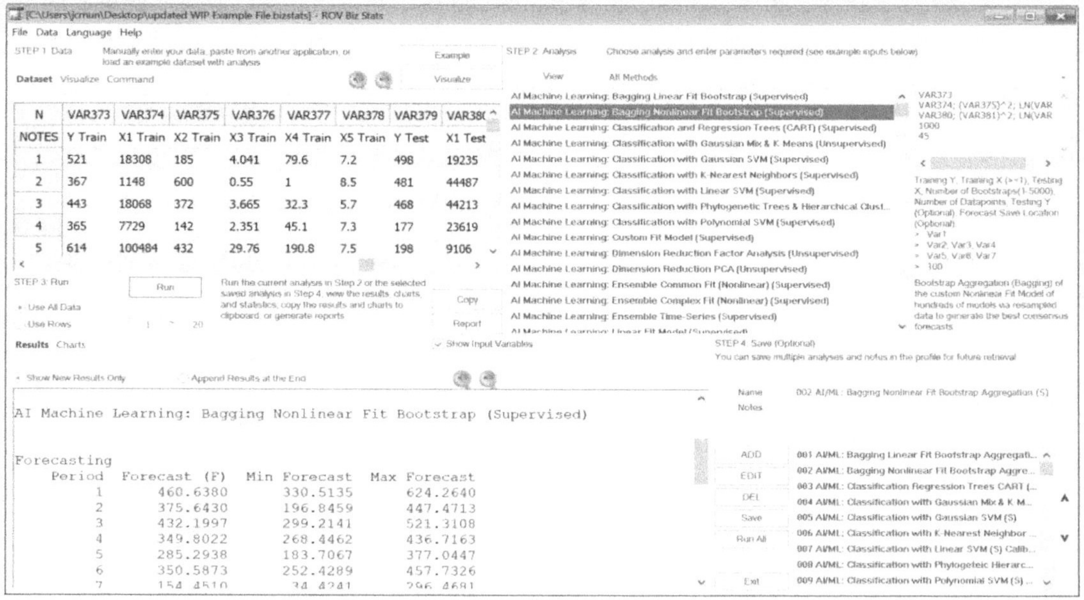

Model Inputs:

VAR373	Training Y (1 variable)
VAR374; (VAR375)^2; LN(VAR376)	Training X (≥ 1 var(s), customized)
VAR380; (VAR381)^2; LN(VAR382)	Testing X (match Training X)
1000	Number of Bootstraps (1-1000)
45	Number of Data Points (< rows)
VARX	Testing Y (optional, 1 variable)
VARX	Forecast Save Location (optional)

AI Machine Learning: Bagging Nonlinear Fit Bootstrap (Supervised)

Period	Forecast (F)	Min Forecast	Max Forecast
1	460.6380	330.5135	624.2640
2	375.6430	196.8459	447.4713
3	432.1997	299.2141	521.3108
4	349.8022	268.4462	436.7163
.	. .	. .	. .
30	378.2814	294.0299	466.1581

AI MACHINE LEARNING: CLASSIFICATION AND REGRESSION TREES CART (SUPERVISED)

The Classification and Regression Trees (CART) model generates branches and subgroups of the categorical dependent Y variable using characteristic X variables. CART is typically used for data mining and constitutes a supervised machine learning approach. This is a classification approach when the dependent variable is categorical, and the tree is used to determine the class or group within which a target testing variable is most likely to fall. The data is split into branches along a tree, and each branch split will be determined using Gini coefficients and information loss coefficients based on the questions asked along the way. Specifically, $Gini = 1 - \sum_{i=1}^{c} p_i^2$. If this Gini index is 0, it means the data are perfectly classified. Therefore, using a recursive algorithm, we can apply the splits that have the lowest Gini index. The final structure looks like a tree with its many branches. Additional splitting and stopping rules are applied along the way, and the terminal branches will provide predictions of the target testing variable.

The next slide provides a visual illustration and the results of a CART model. Simply enter the variables you need to classify and enter the number of clusters desired. The CART model then generates if-then-else rules that are simple to understand and implement as a forecasting tool. The tree can identify patterns that are oftentimes obscured in the complex interactions of the data.

The CART algorithm runs the optimal splits according to the Gini coefficient and then retests the regression tree against the actual Training Y variable to identify its accuracy. If a different set of Testing X variables is entered, it will also project and classify the relevant groupings. The sample data shows the information on 10 individuals, where each individual's preferred transportation mode is the dependent variable (a categorical variable 1, 2, 3 for bus, train, or car). The independent predictors are the individuals' gender (1, 2 for male or female), whether the person owns a car (1, 0 for yes or no), the cost of transportation (1, 2, 3 for cheap, medium, or expensive), and the individual's income level category (1, 2, 3 for low, medium, or high). The tree provides a good visual, with all the relevant splits and Gini coefficients. The tree is then used to back-fit the original data. For the example data, the first individual who ended up taking the Bus (Transportation Mode = 1) has the following dependent variable values: Gender = 1, Car Ownership = 0, Transportation Cost = 1, and Income Level = 1. We start from the top of the tree and see that for cost = 1, we take the first right branch, then going down the next level, we take the right branch where travel cost = 1. Then, we take the left branch where gender = 1. The path is bolded for easier identification. This happens to be the terminal branch, which means the model predicts that the transport mode is 1, corresponding to the original data. All rows of data are fed through this tree according to their own pathways.

```
Model Inputs:
VAR433          Training Y (1 variable)
VAR434:VAR437   Training X (≥ 1 variables)
VAR438:VAR441   Testing X (optional, match Training X's # of variables)
VAR442          Forecast save location (optional, 1 variable)
```

AI MACHINE LEARNING: CLASSIFICATION AND REGRESSION TREES CART (SUPERVISED)

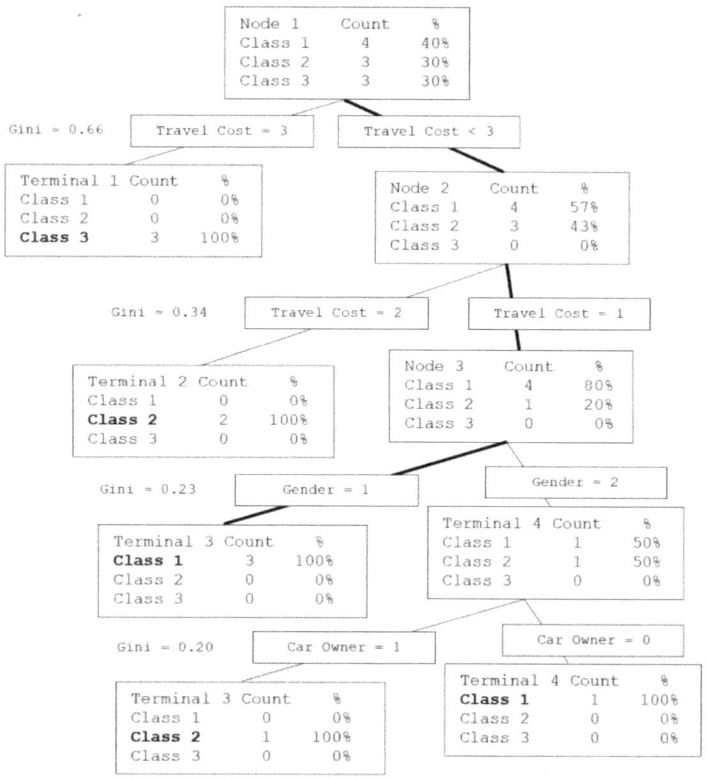

The complete results from the algorithm are shown next. The CART method will return the various unique numerical categories in the Training Y set, and, in this example, we have three categories: 1, 2, and 3. It will show the fit of the training dataset, where here we see the actuals versus CART predicted results, with a perfect 100% accuracy match in each category. The actual categories based on the training set are shown, together with the model's predicted categorization. This fitted model and its comparison to actuals allow one to see the accuracy of the model. Then, using this fitted model, if the optional Testing X variables are provided, the algorithm takes this testing dataset and computes the predicted categories.

```
AI Machine Learning: Classification Regression Tree
(Supervised)

     Category      Actual     Predicted     Accuracy
        1            4            4          100.00%
        2            3            3          100.00%
        3            3            3          100.00%

       Training Dataset
      Actual      Forecast            Testing Dataset
Forecast
        1.00          1.00              1.00
        1.00          1.00              1.00
        2.00          2.00              2.00
        1.00          1.00              1.00
        1.00          1.00              1.00
        2.00          2.00              . .
```

	Actual Category is X	Actual Category is Not X
Predicted Category is X	True Positive (TP)	False Positive (FP)
Predicted Category is Not X	False Negative (FN)	True Negative (TN)
	Positive Sensitivity Recall = TP/(TP+FN)	Negative Specificity = TN/(TN+FP)

AI MACHINE LEARNING: CLASSIFICATION WITH GAUSSIAN MIX & K-MEANS SEGMENTATION (UNSUPERVISED)

The AI Machine Learning Gaussian Mix with K-Means Segmentation model assumes multiple overlaying normal distributions. This is an unsupervised machine learning method that is applicable when we do not know where the clusters come from initially. Typically, the dataset has n rows of data with m columns of multidimensional-space characteristics, and where we typically have $1 \leq m \leq 4$. The results show the probabilities of a certain value belonging to a particular cluster. When there is a single cluster, we would typically perform a distributional fitting routine such as a Kolmogorov–Smirnov model, but when there are multiple such k normal distribution clusters (with μ_k, COV_k mean and covariance), the total probability density is a linear function of the densities across all these clusters, where $p(x) = \sum_{k=1}^{k} \pi_k G(x|\mu_k, COV_k)$ and π_k is the mix-coefficient for the k-th distribution. An expectations maximization algorithm is used to estimate the maximum likelihood function of the fit, while the Bayes Information Criterion is used to automatically select the best covariance parameters.

A Gaussian Mix is related to the K-Means approach and is fairly simple and uses some Naïve Bayes and likelihood estimations. Sometimes the results are not as reliable as, say, a supervised Support Vector Machine (SVM) method. This is because of the Gaussian Mix's unsupervised algorithm, which may not converge. Run the same model several times to see if the model converges (i.e., the results will be the same each time when you click Run). If the results are not identical, try increasing the number of iterations and test again. If the results obtained are not as expected, reduce the number of variables, and increase the number of rows and try again with a higher iteration. The best model is the one with the maximum log-likelihood value (be careful here as log-likelihood is typically a negative value, which means a model with –100 is better than a model with a –300 log-likelihood measure). Alternatively, try the unsupervised AI/ML Segmentation Clustering methodology, which is typically more reliable. Whenever possible and if the data allow for it, the recommendation is to use the supervised SVM methods or the unsupervised AI/ML Segmentation Clustering method.

The results will show both the K-Means Clustering as well as the Gaussian Mix models. As mentioned, if the same model is re-run several times and the results remain the same, the model has converged; otherwise, add more iterations and try again. If the model converges, use the results from that run. If convergence is not achieved, either apply a different method completely or re-run the same model several times and select the one with the maximum log-likelihood value. Also, when the cluster means of K-Means and Gaussian Mix are close to each other, the results are relatively reliable. These means usually do not equal each other as they run different algorithms.

```
Model Inputs:
VAR416:VAR419   The variables to classify
5               The number of clusters to group the data into
1000            Max iterations (Optional=100, Allowed: 1-5000)
VARX            Location to save the forecasted categories
```

AI MACHINE LEARNING: CLASSIFICATION WITH GAUSSIAN MIX & K-MEANS SEGMENTATION (UNSUPERVISED)

```
AI Machine Learning: Classification with Gaussian Mix & K-Means (Unsupervised)
Log-Likelihood:      -532.6046
K-Means Average:
                          X1          X2          X3          X4
Cluster 1            12.3800    246.6000     67.2000     27.7800
Cluster 2             2.9500     62.7000     53.9000     11.5100
Cluster 3             7.5077    170.3846     71.4615     22.6154
Cluster 4            11.8000    300.8571     68.7143     28.8571
Cluster 5             5.5900    112.4000     65.6000     17.2700

Gaussian Mix Average:
                          X1          X2          X3          X4
Cluster 1            12.1347    248.1784     67.3133     27.5988
Cluster 2             2.9546     62.8118     53.9251     11.5229
Cluster 3             7.8164    171.4283     71.0373     22.6710
Cluster 4            11.8121    298.4321     68.9918     29.1794
Cluster 5             5.6117    112.3859     65.5904     17.2776

K-Means Count :
          Cluster 1   Cluster 2   Cluster 3   Cluster 4   Cluster 5
             10          10          13          7           10

Gaussian Mix Probabilities for Each Row :
          Cluster 1   Cluster 2   Cluster 3   Cluster 4   Cluster 5
           0.9981      0.0000      0.0019      0.0000      0.0000
           1.0000      0.0000      0.0000      0.0000      0.0000
           0.0032      0.0000      0.0000      0.9968      0.0000
           0.0000      0.0000      1.0000      0.0000      0.0000
           0.0235      0.0000      0.0000      0.9765      0.0000
           0.0013      0.0000      0.9850      0.0136      0.0000
            . . .       . . .       . . .       . . .       . . .
           0.0000      1.0000      0.0000      0.0000      0.0000
           0.0000      0.0000      1.0000      0.0000      0.0000

K-Means Assignments for Each Row
             1
             1
             4
             3
             4
             3
             .
             3
```

The K-Means and Gaussian Mix cluster means are provided for the requested 5 clusters (shown as rows in the results) for each of the 4 independent variables (shown as columns). Then, the K-Means counts of the number of states in each category are provided, as are the K-Means assignments of these states into the various categories. The Gaussian Mix results also provide the probabilities that a certain state falls within a specific category. For instance, the results show that there are 10 rows in Cluster 1, 10 in Cluster 2, and so forth. The Gaussian Mix probabilities show that there is a 99.81% chance the first row's data fall into Cluster 1, the second row's data has a 100% chance of being in Cluster 1, the third row's data has a 99.68% chance of being in Cluster 4, and so forth You can also run the analysis using AI/ML Cluster Segmentation but be aware that similar rows will be clustered together although the numbering of the clusters may differ due to the different algorithms used. For example, Cluster 1 may be called Cluster 5, and so on.

AI MACHINE LEARNING: CLASSIFICATION WITH K-NEAREST NEIGHBORS (SUPERVISED)

The K-Nearest Neighbor (KNN) algorithm is used to classify and segregate the data into groups. Another name for this method is the k-dimensional tree structure, useful for partitioning data points into a few small dimensions. Simply enter the variables you need to classify and enter the number of clusters desired. KNN results will show the testing points and identify the nearest neighbors. For example, in the first row of the testing data, we have the values 4, 7, 5 and this numerical sequence, as compared to all the other data, is most closely related to 4, 8, 5 (this can be either in the testing set or the training set).

```
Model Inputs:
VAR105:VAR107      Training X (≥ 1 variable)
VAR108:VAR110      Testing X (match Training X's number of variables)
```

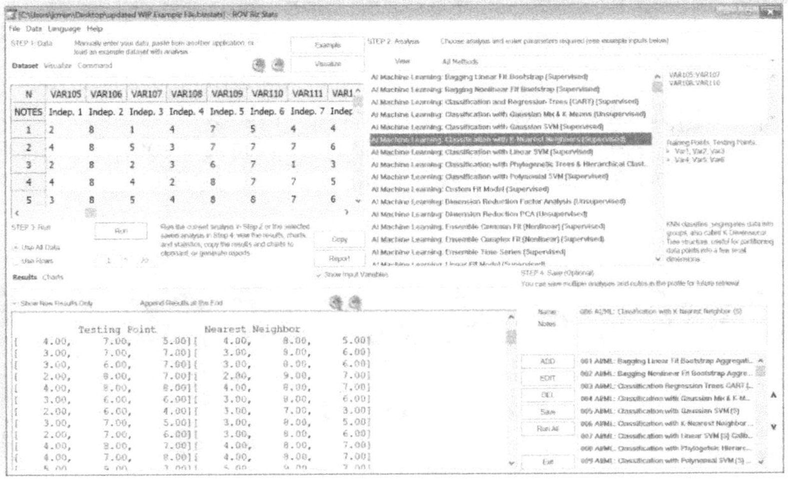

```
AI Machine Learning: Classification with
K-Nearest Neighbors (Supervised)


  Testing Points            Nearest Neighbor
[4.00,  7.00,  5.00]     [4.00,  8.00,  5.00]
[3.00,  7.00,  7.00]     [3.00,  8.00,  6.00]
[3.00,  6.00,  7.00]     [3.00,  8.00,  6.00]
[2.00,  8.00,  7.00]     [2.00,  9.00,  7.00]
[4.00,  8.00,  8.00]     [4.00,  8.00,  7.00]
[3.00,  6.00,  6.00]     [3.00,  8.00,  6.00]
 . . .   . . .   . . .     . . .   . . .   . . .
[5.00,  8.00,  3.00]     [5.00,  8.00,  3.00]
[4.00,  7.00,  4.00]     [4.00,  8.00,  4.00]
[5.00,  5.00,  6.00]     [5.00,  8.00,  5.00]
```

AI MACHINE LEARNING: CLASSIFICATION WITH PHYLOGENETIC TREES & HIERARCHICAL CLUSTERING (UNSUPERVISED)

In this method, the algorithm runs phylogenetic trees for data classification by applying a hierarchical clustering algorithm. Phylogenetic trees are typically used in biomedical and genetic research, such as looking at DNA sequences. This method is unsupervised, and the algorithm is applied to figure out how to cluster a set of data that is unordered without being provided with any training data having the correct responses. The result is a hierarchical cluster with multiple fully nested sets where the smallest sets are the individual elements of the set, and the largest set is the entire dataset.

To apply a phylogenetic tree using hierarchical clustering, the dataset is typically a set of sequences or distance matrices. Simply enter the variables you need to classify and enter the number of clusters desired. The input variable is a sample genetic DNA sequence, and the results show a hierarchical 5-level phylogenetic tree. The 5-level tree (vertical lines indicate branching events, and there are 5 vertical lines starting from the first branch to the longest path).

Model Inputs:

VAR462	Genetic Chain
0	Chain Name (Optional)
1	Distance Type (Optional, 1-5)

	DNA Sequence	Names	DNA Sequence	Names
I	CGGTTGGGAGCT	A	AGGCGGTGCGGG	
J	AGGTCGTGAGGT	B	GGGCGGGGCGGG	
K	TGGGTGCGAGTT	C	GGGCGCTGCGGG	
L	ACGTTTGGGTGA	D	GGACGGAGGCTG	
M	AAGGTTGGGGAA	E	GGGTGGGAGCTG	
N	GTCTTTCGGGTG	F	AGGAGGCTGATG	
O	CACTTGCGGGGG	G	TGGCGGATGATG	
P	GCGCGGTGCAGC	H	TGGGTGCGAGTT	

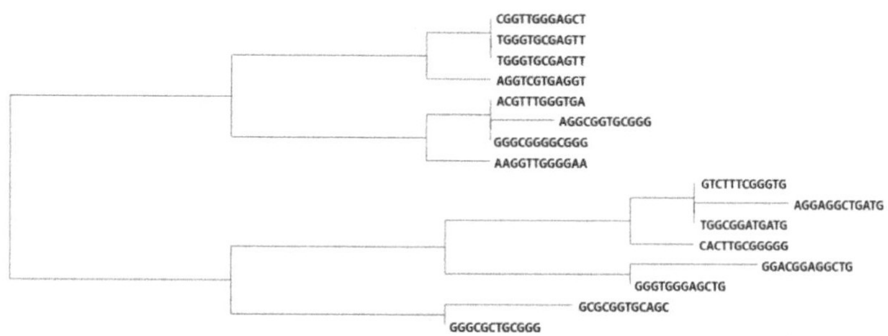

AI MACHINE LEARNING: CLASSIFICATION WITH SUPPORT VECTOR MACHINES SVM (SUPERVISED)

Support Vector Machines (SVM) is a class of supervised machine learning algorithms used for classification. The term "machine" in SVM might be a misnomer in that it is only a vestige of the term "machine learning." SVM methods are simpler to implement and run than complex neural network algorithms. In supervised learning, we typically start with a set of training data. The algorithm is trained using this dataset (i.e., the parameters are optimized and identified), and then the same model parameters are applied to the testing set, or to a new dataset never before seen by the algorithm. The training dataset comprises m data points, placed as rows in the data grid, where there is an outcome or dependent variable y_i, followed by one or more independent predictors x_i for $i = 1, \ldots, m$. Each of the dependent (also known as predictor or feature) variables has n dimensions (number of columns). In contrast, there is only a single y_i variable, with a binary outcome (e.g., 1 and 0, or 1 and 2, indicating if an item is in or out of a group). Note that the training set can also be used as the testing set, and the results will typically yield a high level of segregation accuracy. However, in practice, we typically use a smaller subset of the testing dataset as the training dataset and unleash the optimized algorithm on the remaining testing set. One of the few limiting caveats of SVM methods is a requirement that there exists some n-dimensional hyperplane that separates the data.

The hyperplane is defined by an equation $f(x) = w \cdot x + b = 0$, which completely separates the training dataset into two groups. The parameters w (the normal vector to the hyperplane) and b (an offset parameter such as a virtual intercept) can be scaled as needed, to adjust the forecast back into the original two groups. Applying some analytical geometry, we see that the parameters are best fitted by applying an internal optimization routine to minimize $\frac{1}{2} w \cdot w$, which reduces to a Lagrangian problem where we maximize the likelihood of $\mathcal{L}(\alpha, \beta) = \frac{1}{2} f(w) + \sum_j \alpha_j g_j(w) + \sum_k \beta_k h_k(w)$, where all parameters are positive.

SVM algorithms are best used in conjunction with a kernel density estimator, and the three most commonly used are the Gaussian, Linear, and Polynomial kernels. Try each of these approaches and see which fits the data the best by reviewing the accuracy of the results.

- **Gaussian SVM:** Applies a normal kernel estimator $exp\left[-\frac{1}{2}\left|x_i - x_j\right|^2 / \sigma^2\right]$.
- **Linear SVM:** Applies a standard linear kernel estimator $x_i \cdot x_j$.
- **Polynomial SVM:** Applies a polynomial (e.g., quadratic nonlinear programming) kernel density estimator such as $\left|a x_i \cdot x_j + b\right|^c$.

AI MACHINE LEARNING: CLASSIFICATION AND REGRESSION TREES CART (SUPERVISED)

The same procedure applies to all three SVM subclasses. To get started, we use an example dataset where the weights and sizes of 40 fruits were measured. These fruits were either apples or oranges. Recall that SVMs are best used for separations into two groups. The data grid shows VAR408 with the alphanumeric category of the dependent or classified variable (apples or oranges). However, the SVM algorithms require numerical inputs, hence, the dependent groupings have been coded to a numerical value of 1 and 2 in VAR407 (bivariate numerical categories). VAR405 and VAR406 are the predictors or features set (the weights and sizes of the fruits) that we will use as the training set to calibrate and fit the model. These are the first two sets of inputs in the model. Note that we have VAR407 entered in the first row as the training dependent variable and in the second row, VAR405; VAR406 as the training independent variables (predictor feature set). To get started, we use the default Sigma, Lambda, and Omega values of 2, 1000, and 0.5. Depending on the SVM subclass, only some or all three of these will be used. Start with the defaults and change as required. The main variable that impacts the results is the Omega, which is a value between 0 and 1. If you set the Calibrate Option to 1, it will test various Omega values and shows the accuracy levels of each. Select the Omega value with the highest accuracy and rerun the model.

Model Inputs:

VAR407	Training dependent variable (1)
VAR405; VAR406	Training independent variables (≥ 1)
2.00	Sigma
1000.00	Lambda
0.50	Omega (this is tested for accuracy)
1.00	Calibrate (1 = calibrate Omega, 0 = do not)
VAR409; VAR410	Testing independent variables
VAR411	Paste the forecast results (optional, can be empty)
VAR412	Paste the grouped results (optional, can be empty)

AI Machine Learning: Classification with Gaussian SVM (Supervised)

Accuracy	85%	85%	85%	100%	100%	100%	100%	100%	100%	100%
Omega	0.10	0.20	0.30	0.40	0.50	0.60	0.70	0.80	0.90	1.00

Forecast	Group	Forecast (Test Vars)	Group (Test Vars)
1.013598	1.00	1.013598	1.00
1.013860	1.00	1.013860	1.00
0.922405	1.00	0.922405	1.00
0.709851	2.00	0.709851	2.00
1.016426	1.00	1.016426	1.00
. . .	. .	. . .	. .
0.670190	2.00	0.670190	2.00

AI MACHINE LEARNING: CLASSIFICATION WITH SUPPORT VECTOR MACHINES SVM (SUPERVISED)

The results provide a series of forecast values and forecast groups for the training set as well as for the testing dataset, showing the numerical segmentation results and the final resulting groups. Note that the example results indicate relatively high goodness of fit to the testing dataset at 95% fit. This fit applies to the training dataset and assuming the same data structure holds, the testing dataset should also have a fit that is close to this result. Typically, only the testing dataset's forecast values and grouping membership are important to the user; hence, you can optionally enter the location in the data grid to save the results, for example, VAR411 and VAR412. If these inputs are left empty, the results will not be saved in the data grid, and they will only be available in the results area.

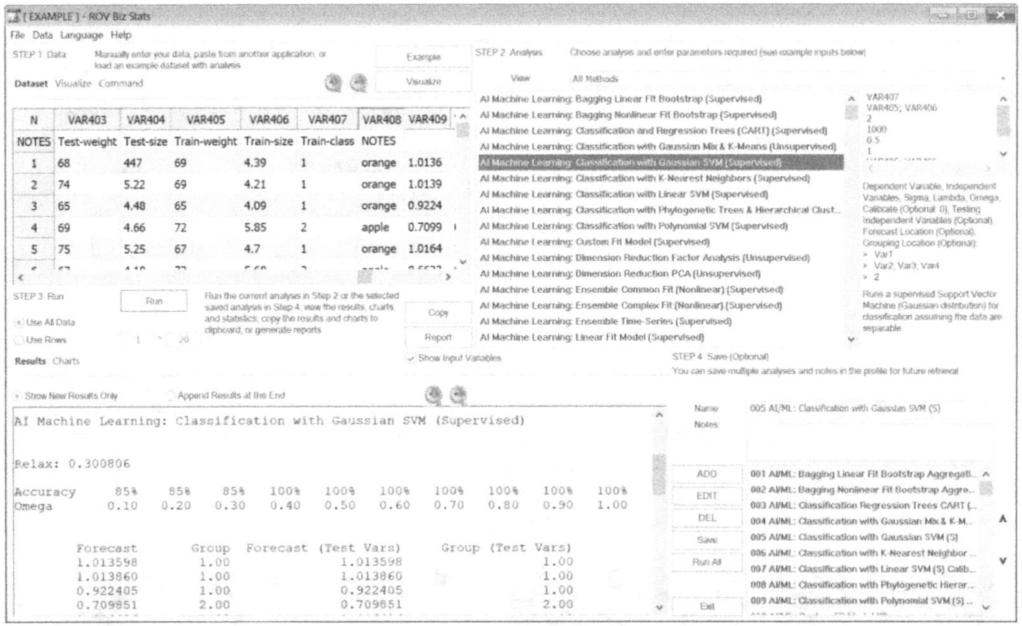

AI MACHINE LEARNING: CUSTOM FIT MODEL (SUPERVISED)

The AI Machine Learning Custom Fit model is applicable in forecasting time-series and cross-sectional data for modeling relationships among variables. It allows you to create custom-fit multiple regression models. Econometrics refers to a branch of business analytics, modeling, and forecasting techniques for modeling the behavior of or forecasting certain business, financial, economic, physical science, and other variables. Running the Custom Fit model is like regular econometric regression analysis except that the dependent and independent variables can be modified before a regression is run. For more detailed explanations of regression models, see the sections on Linear and Nonlinear Multivariate Regression and Regression Analysis, as well as the associated sections on pitfalls of regression modeling.

As usual, the standard practice is to divide your data into training and testing sets. The training set (one dependent with one or more independent variables) is used to train the algorithm and obtain the best-fitting parameters. In this model, you can create your custom equations. Note that only one variable is allowed as the Training Y Dependent Variable, whereas multiple variables are allowed in the Training X Independent Variables section, separated by a semicolon (;), and that basic mathematical functions can be used (e.g., LN, LOG, LAG, +, -, /, *, TIME, RESIDUAL, DIFF). For instance, you can use your training set's dependent variable as VAR373 and independent variables VAR374; (VAR375)^2; LN(VAR376), and so forth. You need to use the same functional form for the testing set's independent variables as well (but with the same or different variables), otherwise, the model will not run properly. For example, a complementary set of testing independent variables would be VAR380; (VAR381)^2; LN(VAR382). Notice that the same functional form is used but applied to different variables. Applying it to the same variables would be the same as running a customized econometric model instead.

The algorithm also allows you to optionally enter known testing set dependent values. Sometimes these are known and sometimes they are unknown and are to be forecasted. If the values are unknown, simply leave the input empty or enter a 0 in the input if you wish to enter the next input, which is the forecast results save location in the data grid.

```
Model Inputs:
VAR373                             Training set dependent variable
VAR374; (VAR375)^2; LN(VAR376)     Training set custom independent variable(s)
VAR380; (VAR381)^2; LN(VAR382)     Testing set independent (match training set)
{VARx or 0 or empty}               Testing set dependent (optional or 0)
{VARxx or empty}                   Forecast results save location (optional)
```

AI MACHINE LEARNING: CUSTOM FIT MODEL (SUPERVISED)

The interpretation of the results would be similar to that of the basic econometric analysis. The goodness-of-fit results and parameter estimates pertain to the training dataset, whereas the forecast values are based on the testing dataset when applied to the fitted parameters. Sometimes, you may wish to hold some data back from the training dataset and apply it to the testing dataset to assess the model's accuracy and forecasting ability, as well as to view forecast errors. In other words, the optional testing set's dependent variable can be used, and because these known values are applied, forecast errors can also be generated as a result. For example, the VARx value above can be set to VAR379.

```
AI Machine Learning: Custom Fit Model (Supervised)

Multiple R                0.64492     Maximum Log-Likelihood                -314.63844
R-Square                  0.41593     Akaike Info Criterion (AIC)             12.74554
Adjusted R-Square         0.37783     Bayes Schwarz Criterion (BSC)           12.89850
Standard Error          136.39035     Hannan-Quinn Criterion (HQC)            12.80379
Observations                   50     Cohen's F-Squared                        0.71211

                   Coeff  Std. Error       T-stat      P-value
Intercept      160.13054    37.08823      4.31756      0.00008
VAR X1          -0.00320     0.00186     -1.72599      0.09106
VAR X2           0.00102     0.00034      2.96002      0.00485
VAR X3         145.42613    38.41272      3.78588      0.00044

ANOVA
                   DF            SS           MS           F         p-Value
Regression          3     609356.63    203118.88    10.91900         0.00002
Residual           46     855707.05     18602.33
Total              49    1465063.68

Forecasting
              Period         Forecast (F)
                 1             456.4715
                 2             379.5395
                 3             436.1389
                 .               . .
                30             379.7052
```

AI MACHINE LEARNING: DIMENSION REDUCTION PRINCIPAL COMPONENT ANALYSIS (UNSUPERVISED)

Principal component analysis, or PCA, makes multivariate data easier to model and summarize. To understand PCA, suppose we start with *N* variables that are unlikely to be independent of one another, such that changing the value of one variable will change another variable. PCA modeling will replace the original *N* variables with a new set of *M* variables that are less than *N* but are uncorrelated to one another, while at the same time, each of these *M* variables is a linear combination of the original *N* variables so that most of the variation can be accounted for using fewer explanatory variables.

PCA is a way of identifying patterns in data and recasting the data in such a way as to highlight their similarities and differences. Patterns of data are very difficult to find in high dimensions when multiple variables exist, and higher dimensional graphs are very difficult to represent and interpret. Once the patterns in the data are found, they can be compressed, and the number of dimensions is now reduced. This reduction of data dimensions does not mean much reduction in loss of information. Instead, similar levels of information can now be obtained by a fewer number of variables.

PCA is a statistical method that is used to reduce data dimensionality using covariance analysis among independent variables by applying an orthogonal transformation to convert a set of correlated variables data into a new set of values of linearly uncorrelated variables named principal components. The number of computed principal components will be less than or equal to the number of original variables. This statistical transformation is set up such that the first principal component has the largest possible variance accounting for as much of the variability in the data as possible, and each subsequent component has the highest variance possible under the constraint that it is orthogonal to or uncorrelated with the preceding components. Thus, PCA reveals the internal structure of the data in a way that best explains the variance in the data. Such a dimensional reduction approach is useful to process high-dimensional datasets while still retaining as much of the variance in the dataset as possible. PCA essentially rotates the set of points around their mean to align with the principal components. Therefore, PCA creates variables that are linear combinations of the original variables. The new variables have the property that the variables are all orthogonal. Factor analysis is similar to PCA, in that factor analysis also involves linear combinations of variables using correlations, whereas PCA uses covariance to determine eigenvectors and eigenvalues relevant to the data using a covariance matrix. Eigenvectors can be thought of as preferential directions of a dataset or main patterns in the data. Eigenvalues can be thought of as quantitative assessments of how much a component represents the data. The higher the eigenvalues of a component, the more representative it is of the data.

As an example, PCA is useful when running multiple regression or basic econometrics when the number of independent variables is large or when there is significant multicollinearity in the independent variables. It can be run on the independent variables to reduce the number of variables and to eliminate any linear correlations among the independent variables. The extracted revised data obtained after running PCA can be used to rerun the linear multiple regression or linear basic econometric analysis. The resulting model will usually have slightly lower R-squared values but potentially higher statistical significance (lower p-value). Users can decide to use as many principal components as required based on the cumulative variance.

Suppose there are k variables, X_k, there are exactly k principal components, $Z_i \in i = 1...k$, and $Z_i = w_{i,1}X_1 + w_{i,2}X_2 + ... + w_{i,k}X_k$, where $w_{i,k}$ are the weights or component loadings. The first principal component Z_1 is a linear combination that best explains the total variation, while the second principal component Z_2 is orthogonal or uncorrelated to the first and explains as much as it can of the remaining variation in the data, and so forth, all the way until the final Z_k component.

AI MACHINE LEARNING: DIMENSION REDUCTION PRINCIPAL COMPONENT ANALYSIS (UNSUPERVISED)

Related to another method called Factor Analysis, PCA makes multivariate data easier to model and summarize. An example where we start with 5 independent variables that are unlikely to be independent of one another, such that changing the value of one variable will change another variable. Recall that this multicollinearity effect can cause biases in a multiple regression model. Both principal component and factor analysis can help identify and eventually replace the original independent variables with a new set of smaller variables that are less than the original but are uncorrelated to one another, while, at the same time, each of these new variables is a linear combination of the original variables. This means most of the variation can be accounted for by using fewer explanatory variables. Similarly, factor analysis is used to analyze interrelationships within large numbers of variables and simplifies said factors into a smaller number of common factors. The method condenses information contained in the original set of variables into a smaller set of implicit factor variables with minimal loss of information. The analysis is related to the principal component analysis by using the correlation matrix and applying principal component analysis coupled with a varimax matrix rotation to simplify the factors.

For example, if we have 5 independent variables, which means the factor analysis or principal component analysis results will return a 5×5 matrix of eigenvectors and 5 eigenvalues. Typically, we are only interested in components with eigenvalues >1. Hence, in the results, we are only interested in the first three or four factors or components (some researchers would plot these eigenvalues and call it a scree plot, which can be useful for identifying where the kinks are in the eigenvalues). Notice that the first and second factors (the first two result columns) return a cumulative proportion of 69.88%. This means that using these two factors will explain approximately 70% of the variation in all the independent factors themselves. Next, we look at the absolute values of the eigenvalue matrix. It seems that variables 1 and 3 can be combined into a new variable in factor 1, with variables 4 and 5 as the second factor. This can be done separately and outside of principal component analysis. Notice that the results are not as elegant with only 5 variables. The idea of PCA and Factor Analysis is that the more variables you have, the better the algorithm will perform in terms of reducing the number of data variables or the data dimensionality size.

```
Eigenvalues (Arranged and Ranked):
2.4180        1.0760        0.8665        0.6003          0.0393

Proportions Ranked:
48.36%        21.52%        17.33%        12.01%          0.79%

Cum Proportions Ranked:
48.36%        69.88%        87.21%        99.21%        100.00%

Eigenvectors (Arranged and Ranked):
0.5820       -0.3560       -0.1169        0.1485          0.7063
0.3759        0.1935        0.6864       -0.5911          0.0257
0.5770       -0.3868       -0.1066        0.0858         -0.7062
0.3228        0.6483        0.2073        0.6563         -0.0429
0.2878        0.5157       -0.6789       -0.4364          0.0021

Revised Data:
-0.0652        0.0004       -0.1386       -0.0046          0.0010
 0.0740        0.2294        0.2263       -0.4869          0.0050
  . .           . .           . .           . .             . .
-0.0141       -0.0306        0.1469       -0.1321          0.0151
```

NOTE: The results of multiple linear regressions to illustrate how orthogonality works in PCA. For instance, the first multiple regression is run using the original dataset (VAR28 against VAR29:VAR33). The second regression is run based on the revised PCA data (VAR28 against the converted data). Notice that the goodness-of-fit measures such as R-square, Adjusted R-square, Multiple R, and Standard Error of the Estimates are identical. The estimated coefficients will differ because different data were used in each situation. Some of the variables are not significant in the models because this is only meant as an illustration of the PCA method and not about calibrating a good regression model. In fact, using the reduced model, the Adjusted R-square of only using two variables is 23% as opposed to 25% using all 5 independent variables in the original dataset. This showcases the power of PCA, where fewer variables are used while retaining a high level of variability explained.

AI MACHINE LEARNING: DIMENSION REDUCTION FACTOR ANALYSIS (UNSUPERVISED)

This method runs Factor Analysis to analyze interrelationships within large numbers of variables and simplifies said factors into a smaller number of common factors. The method condenses information contained in the original set of variables into a smaller set of implicit factor variables with minimal loss of information. The analysis is related to Principal Component Analysis (PCA) by using the correlation matrix and applying PCA coupled with a Varimax matrix rotation to simplify the factors. The same results interpretation is used for Factor Analysis as for PCA. For instance, an example where we start with 9 independent variables that are unlikely to be independent of one another, such that changing the value of one variable will change another variable. Factor analysis helps identify and eventually replace the original independent variables with a new set of fewer variables that are less than the original but are uncorrelated to one another, while, at the same time, each of these new variables is a linear combination of the original variables. This means most of the variation can be accounted for by using fewer explanatory variables. Factor analysis is therefore used to analyze interrelationships within large numbers of variables and simplifies said factors into a smaller number of common factors. The method condenses information contained in the original set of variables into a smaller set of implicit factor variables with minimal loss of information. The data input requirement is simply the list of variables you want to analyze (separated by semicolons for individual variables or separated by a colon for a contiguous set of variables, such as VAR105:VAR113 for all 9 variables).

```
Model Inputs:
  VAR105:VAR113    The list of variables to analyze
```

AI MACHINE LEARNING: DIMENSION REDUCTION FACTOR ANALYSIS (UNSUPERVISED)

We started with 9 independent variables, which means the factor analysis results will return a 9×9 matrix of eigenvectors and 9 eigenvalues. Typically, we are only interested in components with eigenvalues >1. Hence, in the results, we are only interested in the first four factors or components. Notice that the first four factors (the first four result columns) return a cumulative proportion of 72.31%. This means that using these four factors will explain 72.31% of the variation in all the independent factors themselves. Next, we look at the absolute values of the eigenvalue matrix. It seems that variables 2, 3, 7, 8 can be combined into a new variable in factor 1, with variables 1 and 9 as the second factor, and so forth.

Factor Analysis (Eigenvalues and Eigenvectors)

Eigenvalue	2.8804	1.4387	1.1639	1.0245	0.7052	0.6476	0.5624	0.3452	0.2321
Proportion	0.3200	0.1599	0.1293	0.1138	0.0258	0.0384	0.0784	0.0720	0.0625
Cumulative	0.3200	0.4799	0.6092	**0.7231**	0.7488	0.7872	0.8656	0.9375	1.0000

Eigenvectors	Fact1	Fact2	Fact3	Fact4	Fact5	Fact6	Fact7	Fact8	Fact9
VAR1	0.1087	**-0.6392**	0.2573	0.1138	-0.4171	0.0959	0.4808	0.2842	0.0724
VAR2	**-0.4116**	0.2531	0.1811	-0.2616	-0.3396	-0.0000	0.4365	-0.5925	0.0914
VAR3	**-0.4443**	-0.2907	0.1873	-0.3022	-0.0301	0.1325	-0.3009	0.0640	-0.6918
VAR4	-0.2156	-0.1355	0.1829	0.8396	-0.0282	0.0082	-0.2214	-0.3788	-0.0578
VAR5	-0.3407	-0.0368	-0.4196	0.1560	0.4236	0.5599	0.4245	0.0882	-0.0352
VAR6	-0.1766	-0.0253	-0.7145	0.0630	-0.6325	-0.0296	-0.2161	0.0730	0.0257
VAR7	**-0.4815**	-0.1996	0.1803	-0.1644	0.0891	0.0992	-0.3614	0.1678	0.7016
VAR8	**-0.4053**	-0.0294	-0.1076	0.1162	0.2150	-0.7828	0.2818	0.2591	-0.0651
VAR9	-0.1776	**0.6179**	0.3190	0.2312	-0.2744	0.1903	0.0417	0.5587	-0.0782

AI MACHINE LEARNING: ENSEMBLE COMMON FIT (NONLINEAR) (SUPERVISED)

This algorithm computes thousands of possible nonlinear and interaction models (suitable for cross-sectional data for pattern recognition); it calibrates the best model with the training dataset and forecasts outcomes using the testing dataset. In other words, it performs an ensemble learning approach.

```
Model Inputs:
VAR373          Training Y (1 variable)
VAR374:VAR378   Training X (≥ 1 variables)
VAR380:VAR384   Testing X (optional, match Training X's # of variables)
VAR379          Forecast Save Location (optional, 1 variable)
0.10            P-value Threshold (optional, default at 0.1)
0               Time Series Lags (optional positive integer, default at 0)
```

The sample results illustrate the ensemble algorithm where over 1,593 combinations of linear, nonlinear, interacting, and mixed models were tested, and the 10 best models are shown. The models are selected based on the independent variables' p-values ≤ 0.10 and ranked by Adjusted R-squares. A stricter p-value can be entered if required.

```
Number of Dependent Variables Tested: 5
Number of Econometric Models Tested: 1593
Number of Best Models Shown: 20
    ADJ R-SQ    MODEL
     0.39034    VAR1;VAR2;LN(VAR3)
     0.38540    LN(VAR3)+LN(VAR5);LN(VAR2)
     0.37892    VAR2*VAR5;LN(VAR3)
      . . .        . . .
     0.34489    LN(VAR2)+LN(VAR5);LN(VAR3)
     0.33791    LN(VAR3)+LN(VAR5)+LN(VAR4);LN(VAR2)

Top Model Result: VAR1;VAR2;LN(VAR3)
Multiple R           0.65396      Maximum Log-Likelihood          -314.13076
R-Square             0.42767      Akaike Info Criterion (AIC)       12.80523
Adjusted R-Square    0.39034      Bayes Schwarz Criterion (BSC)     13.03467
Standard Error     135.01252      Hannan-Quinn Criterion (HQC)      12.89260
Observations                      Cohen's F-Squared                  0.74723

                    Coeff  Std. Error    T-stat    P-value
Intercept        59.91680    60.90323   0.98380    0.33036
VAR1             -0.00308     0.00181  -1.70238    0.09543
VAR2              0.70340     0.22372   3.14406    0.00292
LN(VAR3)        138.21002    37.29707   3.70565    0.00056

ANOVA                DF          SS          MS           F     p-Value
Regression            3   626558.21   208852.74    11.45756     0.00001
Residual             46   838505.47    18228.38
Total                49  1465063.68
```

AI MACHINE LEARNING: ENSEMBLE COMPLEX FIT (NONLINEAR) (SUPERVISED)

Using an ensemble learning approach, this model computes thousands of possible nonlinear and interaction models (suitable for time-series data for pattern recognition); it calibrates the best model with the training dataset and forecasts outcomes using the testing dataset.

```
Model Inputs:
VAR373              Training Y (1 variable)
VAR374:VAR378       Training X (≥ 1 variables)
VAR380:VAR384       Testing X (optional, match Training X's # of variables)
VAR379              Forecast Save Location (optional, 1 variable)
0.10                P-value Threshold (optional, default=0.1)
0                   Time Series Lags (optional positive integer, default=0)
0                   Autoregressive AR(p) (optional positive integer, default=0)
```

The results illustrate the complex ensemble model where thousands of combinations of linear, nonlinear, interacting, time-series (lags, rate, and differences), and mixed models were tested, and the best model is shown. The models are selected based on the independent variables' p-values ≤ 0.10 and ranked by Adjusted R-squares. A stricter p-value can be entered if required.

```
Combination List: (14 Variables)

LN(VAR1);DIFF(VAR1);LN(RATE(VAR1));DIFF(VAR2);RATE(VAR2);LN(VAR3);DIFF(VAR4);RATE(VAR5);
LN(RATE(VAR5));VAR1*VAR4;VAR1*VAR5;VAR3*VAR4;VAR3*VAR5;VAR4*VAR5

Multiple R              0.90820    Maximum Log-Likelihood          -273.52980
R-Square                0.82483    Akaike Info Criterion (AIC)       11.40938
Adjusted R-Square       0.75270    Bayes Schwarz Criterion (BSC)     11.64103
Standard Error         85.79084    Hannan-Quinn Criterion (HQC)      11.49727
Observations                 49    Cohen's F-Squared                  4.70880

                       Coeff  Std. Error      T-stat     P-value
Intercept         3664.81960   805.12137     4.55188     0.00006
LN(VAR1)          -321.07588    83.62231    -3.83960     0.00051
DIFF(VAR1)          -0.00469     0.00144    -3.26953     0.00247
LN(RATE(VAR1))     138.86285    31.87150     4.35696     0.00012
DIFF(VAR2)           0.83499     0.36471     2.28944     0.02839
RATE(VAR2)        -137.48661    77.44510    -1.77528     0.08480
LN(VAR3)           286.43034    66.04043     4.33720     0.00012
DIFF(VAR4)          -0.35191     0.05970    -5.89427     0.00000
RATE(VAR5)        -497.73236   156.06627    -3.18924     0.00306
LN(RATE(VAR5))     431.68094   163.34071     2.64283     0.01234
VAR1*VAR4            0.00004     0.00001     3.46983     0.00143
VAR1*VAR5           -0.00193     0.00077    -2.49557     0.01759
VAR3*VAR4           -0.15513     0.04131    -3.75557     0.00065
VAR3*VAR5            8.92027     2.57281     3.46713     0.00145
VAR4*VAR5            0.03743     0.01553     2.40975     0.02152
```

AI MACHINE LEARNING: ENSEMBLE TIME-SERIES (SUPERVISED)

This algorithm computes and calibrates an ensemble of different time-series forecast models, selects the best combination, and generates forecasts for the single historical time-series variable. An ensemble of time-series forecast methods such as Holt–Winters, deseasonalized forecasts, ARIMA, and others are applied, the best model combinations are used, and the consensus forecasts are provided. A visual representation of the back-fitting and forecast fit is also provided in the results. An alternative is to run each of these models manually in BizStats.

```
Model Inputs:
VAR64 Historical time series (1 variable)
4     Seasonality (e.g., 1, 4, 12, 250, 365)
8     Forecast periods (positive integer)
VARX  Forecast save location (optional, 1 variable)
```

Another related process is the Combinatorial Fuzzy Logic method available in BizStats. The term fuzzy logic is derived from fuzzy set theory to deal with reasoning that is approximate rather than accurate—as opposed to crisp logic, where binary sets have binary logic, fuzzy logic variables may have a truth value that ranges between 0 and 1 and is not constrained to the two truth values of classic propositional logic. Fuzzy weighting schema is used together with a combinatorial method to yield time-series forecast results.

```
BEST RMSE: 249.495091
Auto ARIMA(Autoregressive Integrated Moving Average)
 ARIMA(P,D,Q) Adj R-Sq     AIC         SC      DW Stat        Iter.   Rank
     3,2,0    0.975310   10.9575    11.1463   3.00222          0       1
     3,3,0    0.974249   12.8944     13.077   3.08095          0       2
     3,0,0    0.810734   13.2187    13.4148   3.13092          0       3
      . .       . . .      . . .      . . .    . . .
     0,3,2    0.647397   14.3629    14.5100   1.88313         15      20

 ARIMA (P, D, Q): 3, 2, 0
 R-Squared (Coefficient of Determination)        0.9806010
 Adjusted R-Squared                              0.9753100
 Multiple R (Multiple Correlation Coefficient)   0.9902530
 Standard Error of the Estimates (SEy)           478.74859
 Number of Observations                          15
 Akaike Information Criterion (AIC)              10.957458
 Schwarz Criterion (SC)                          11.146272
 Log-Likelihood                                 -78.180937
 Durbin-Watson (DW) Statistic                    3.0022200

                 Intercept        AR(1)         AR(2)        AR(3)
  Coefficients   27.051029    -1.097853     -1.155977    -1.254295
  Standard Error 19.571112     0.052945      0.069607     0.067098
  t-Statistic     1.382192   -20.735646    -16.607232   -18.693438
  p-Value         0.194334     0.000000      0.000000     0.000000
```

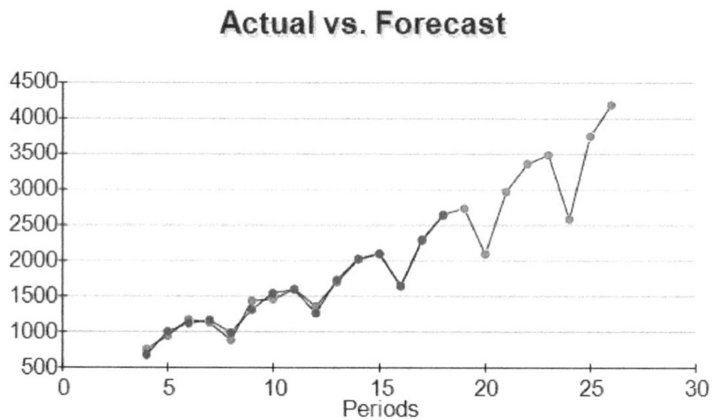

AI MACHINE LEARNING: LINEAR FIT MODEL (SUPERVISED)

Multivariate linear regression is used to model the relationship structure and characteristics of a certain dependent variable as it depends on other independent exogenous variables. Using the modeled relationship, we can forecast the future values of the dependent variable. The accuracy and goodness of fit for this model can also be determined. Linear and nonlinear models can be fitted in the multiple regression analysis. Similar to the custom fit model, running the Linear Fit model is like regular regression analysis except that we first train the algorithm using the training dependent and training independent variables, which will identify the optimized parameters to use on the testing dataset.

Similar to the custom fit model explained previously, we divide the dataset into a training set and a testing set. The example uses VAR373 as the training dependent variable and VAR374; VAR375 as the training independent variables, making this a form of supervised learning. Using these training data, the model is calibrated, and the parameters estimated. Then, the testing independent variables are entered, such as VAR380; VAR381. Please note that there can only be a single dependent variable versus one or more independent variables. Also, the number of independent variables in the testing set and training set must match.

The algorithm also allows you to optionally enter known testing set dependent values. Sometimes these are known and sometimes they are unknown and are to be forecasted. If the values are unknown, simply leave the input empty or enter a 0 in the input if you wish to enter the next input, which is the forecast results save location in the data grid.

```
Model Inputs:
VAR373                 Training set dependent variable
VAR374; VAR375         Training set independent variable(s)
VAR380; VAR381         Testing set matching dependent variable(s)
{VARx or 0 or empty}   Testing set dependent variable (optional or 0)
{VARxx or empty}       Forecast results save location (optional)
```

The results interpretation would be similar to the multiple linear regression. The goodness-of-fit results and fitted parameter estimations pertain to the training dataset, whereas the forecast values are based on the testing dataset when applied to these fitted parameters. Sometimes, you may wish to hold some data back from the training dataset and apply it to the testing dataset to test the accuracy of the model and its ability to forecast, as well as to view the forecast errors. In other words, the optional testing set's dependent variable can be used and because these known values are applied, forecast errors can also be generated as a result. For example, the VARx value above can be set to VAR379.

Training Fit Results

Multiple R	0.50677	Maximum Log-Likelihood	-320.66137
R-Square	0.25681	Akaike Info Criterion (AIC)	12.94645
Adjusted R-Square	0.22519	Bayes Schwarz Criterion (BSC)	13.06118
Standard Error	152.20473	Hannan-Quinn Criterion (HQC)	12.99014
Observations	50	Cohen's F-Squared	0.34556

	Coeff	Std. Error	T-stat	P-value	Std. Beta
Intercept	138.07546	64.40980	2.14370	0.03726	
VAR X1	0.00266	0.00105	2.52933	0.01484	0.33735
VAR X2	0.52024	0.24598	2.11499	0.03976	0.28209

Forecasting

Period	Forecast (F)
1	375.5419
2	420.4133
3	413.4408
4	319.5842
.	. . .
30	347.6475

AI MACHINE LEARNING: MULTIVARIATE DISCRIMINANT ANALYSIS (LINEAR) (SUPERVISED)

A Linear Discriminant Analysis (LDA) approach classifies a categorical dependent Training Y variable using one or more characteristic Training X variables. This supervised method applies maximum linear discriminant ratios (i.e., the ratio of between-class variance to within-class variance), which allows a clear separation or groupings of the Testing X variable. In other words, the separations are obtained through the maximization of $ss_{between}/ss_{within}$ or the sum of squares ratio of a linear combination $w_x x + w_y y + w_z z$. The optimized coefficient results help identify how each of the independent variables contributes towards the categorization. The group assignment will be based on the maximum estimated impact scores. To run the model, enter the variables you need to classify and enter the number of clusters desired. For instance, the required model inputs look like the following:

```
Model Inputs:
VAR444          Training Y (1 variable)
VAR445:VAR447   Training X (≥ 1 variables)
VAR448:VAR450   Testing X (optional, match Training X's # of variables)
VAR451          Forecast save location (optional, 1 variable)
```

The results are self-explanatory in that the group counts are provided, as well as the model's classification ("Put Into Group") compared to the actual group ("True Group") or the training dataset's dependent variable. For instance, we see in the original data of 244 rows (N = 244 or 85 + 93 + 66), that 34.84% were in category 1, 38.11% in category 2, and 27.05% in category 3. Out of the 85 originally in category 1 from the training dataset, the model selected 68 of these into group 1, 13 into group 2, and 4 into group 3, which means there is an 80% accuracy (68/85). In total, there were 185 correctly grouped values out of 244, providing a 75.82% accuracy. The groups' means are also shown, as are the estimated coefficients for the three groups. Recall that LDA uses a linear discriminant model to maximize the sums of squares ratio, and we can use these coefficients in the same manner. For example, suppose the first row for the testing dataset has the following: 15, 18, 16. We can then apply the three groups' coefficients and select the one with the highest discriminant value. Therefore, this first line item belongs to group 3. All other rows of testing data are computed in a similar fashion and categorized appropriately.

$$-23.0975 + 0.6263 \times 15 + 1.2406 \times 18 + 0.6865 \times 16 = 19.6118$$

$$-25.2063 + 0.9966 \times 15 + 1.0380 \times 18 + 0.7956 \times 16 = 21.1563$$

$$-20.7715 + 0.8427 \times 15 + 0.7221 \times 18 + 1.1057 \times 16 = 22.5580$$

AI MACHINE LEARNING: MULTIVARIATE DISCRIMINANT ANALYSIS (LINEAR) (SUPERVISED)

AI Machine Learning: Multivariate Discriminant Analysis (Linear) (Supervised)

Group	1	2	3
Count	**85**	**93**	**66**
Prior	**0.3484**	**0.3811**	**0.2705**

Classification Results		True Group	
Put Into Group	1	2	3
1	**68**	16	3
2	**13**	67	13
3	**4**	10	50
Total N	**85**	93	66
N Correct	**68**	67	50
Proportion	**0.8000**	0.7204	0.7576

N: **244**
N Correct: **185**
Proportion Correct: **0.758197**

VAR	1	2	3
Global Mean Vector	15.6393	20.6762	10.5902

Means of Features in Groups			
1	12.5176	24.2235	9.0235
2	18.5376	21.1398	10.1398
3	15.5758	15.4545	13.2424

Linear Discriminant Function for Groups			
Betas1	**0.6263**	**1.2406**	**0.6865**
Intercept1	**-23.0975**		
Betas2	**0.9966**	**1.0380**	**0.7956**
Intercept2	**-25.2063**		
Betas3	**0.8427**	**0.7221**	**1.1057**
Intercept3	**-20.7715**		

Forecast Group
3
3
2
3
2
1
1

AI MACHINE LEARNING: MULTIVARIATE DISCRIMINANT ANALYSIS (QUADRATIC) (SUPERVISED)

This approach classifies the categorical dependent variable Y using the characteristic X variables via Quadratic Discriminant Analysis (QDA). This method is similar to LDA, but the covariance matrix is used in the group assignment as well as the estimated coefficients because LDA assumes homoskedasticity in the prediction errors, whereas QDA allows for some heteroskedasticity. This allows for second-order and second-moment approximations to calibrate the relevant group assignments. To get started, enter the variables you need to classify and the desired number of clusters.

```
Model Inputs:
VAR444          Training Y (1 variable)
VAR445:VAR447   Training X (≥ 1 variables)
VAR448:VAR450   Testing X (optional, match Training X's # of variables)
VAR452          Forecast Save Location (optional, 1 variable)
```

Notice that the forecasted classification groups for the QDA model below are identical to the LDA model shown previously. While the LDA model's category can be easily predicted using a multiple regression equation and selecting the category with the highest likelihood, QDA requires the inclusion of the inverse covariance matrix. This means you will have to rely on the presented results and will not be able to readily compute the likelihood results directly.

Quadratic Discriminant Analysis (QDA)

Group	1	2	3
Count	85	93	66
Prior	0.3484	0.3811	0.2705

Classification Results

	True Group		
Put Into Group	1	2	3
1	68	16	3
2	14	68	14
3	3	9	49
Total N	85	93	66
N Correct	68	68	49
Proportion	0.8000	0.7312	0.7424

N : 244
N Correct : 185
Proportion Correct : 0.758197

VAR	1	2	3
Global Mean Vector	15.6393	20.6762	10.5902

Means of Features in Groups

1	12.5176	24.2235	9.0235
2	18.5376	21.1398	10.1398
3	15.5758	15.4545	13.2424

Quadratic Discriminant Function for Groups

Betas1	0.4466	1.0833	0.7536
Intercept1	-24.4522		
Betas2	1.4812	1.1286	0.5873
Intercept2	-33.5319		
Betas3	0.7866	0.9877	0.9219
Intercept3	-25.2082		

Forecast Group
3
3
2
3
2
1
1

AI MACHINE LEARNING: NEURAL NETWORK (SUPERVISED)

Commonly used to refer to a network or circuit of biological neurons, modern usage of the term *neural network* often refers to artificial neural networks that consist of artificial neurons, or nodes, recreated in a software environment. Such networks attempt to mimic the neurons in the human brain in ways of thinking and identifying patterns and, in our situation, identifying patterns for the purposes of forecasting time-series data.

Note that the number of hidden layers in the network is an input parameter and will need to be calibrated with your data. Typically, the more complicated the data pattern, the higher the number of hidden layers you would need and the longer it would take to compute. It is recommended that you start at 3 layers. The testing period is simply the number of data points used in the final calibration of the Neural Network model, and we recommend using at least the same number of periods you wish to forecast as the testing period.

- **Linear:** Applies a linear function, where $f(x) = x$.
- **Nonlinear Logistic:** Applies a nonlinear logistic function, where $f(x) = (1 + e^{-x})^{-1}$.
- **Nonlinear Cosine with Hyperbolic Tangent:** Applies a nonlinear cosine with hyperbolic tangent function,

  where $f(x) = \cos[(e^{x} - e^{-x})(e^{x} + e^{-x})^{-1}]$.
- **Nonlinear Hyperbolic Tangent:** Applies a nonlinear hyperbolic tangent function, where:

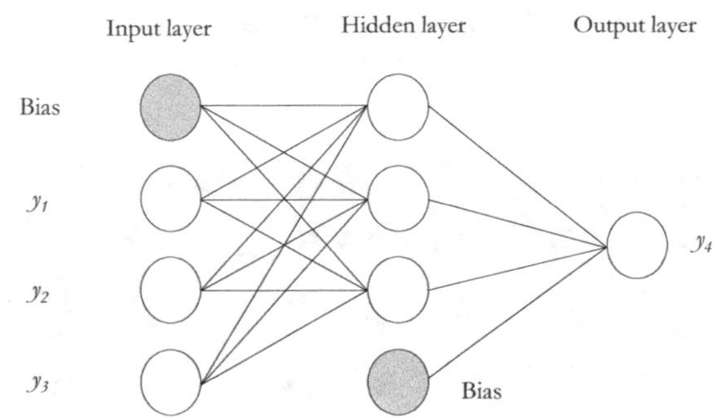

AI MACHINE LEARNING: NEURAL NETWORK (SUPERVISED)

The historical time-series data is entered as the first variable, VAR227. Then, 3 perceptron layers are requested, and 20 data points are used as the testing set. The dataset has 420 data points and entering 2 indicates that we use the first 400 of these data to perform training and calibration on the model, leaving the last 20 data points for testing the model. On completion of the testing, the model is then used to forecast the next future 2 data points. The number of forecast periods has to be ≥1. Finally, the model is run through internal multiphasic optimization routines. Setting this to 1 (for "yes") makes it slightly longer to run but provides a more accurate calibration of the results. A chart is also provided in the results to visually examine how good the forecast fit is.

```
Model Inputs:
VAR227    Historical time-series data to fit
3         Number of perceptron layers
20        Testing data points to withhold
2         Number of periods to forecast
1         Apply multiphased optimization (1=Apply, 0=Do not apply)

   Neural Network (Cosine with Hyperbolic Tangent)
   Sum of Squared Errors (Training): 0.740693
   RMSE (Training): 0.043194
   Sum of Squared Errors (Modified): 167.402055
   RMSE (Modified): 2.893113
```

Forecasting Period	Actual (Y)	Forecast (F)	Error (E)
401	650.0200	665.1658	-15.1458
402	662.4900	660.0630	2.4270
403	660.2300	658.6152	1.6148
404	662.3800	659.7383	2.6417
.	. . .	. . .	. . .
420	664.8100	667.3111	-2.5011
421		668.0264	
422		668.9191	

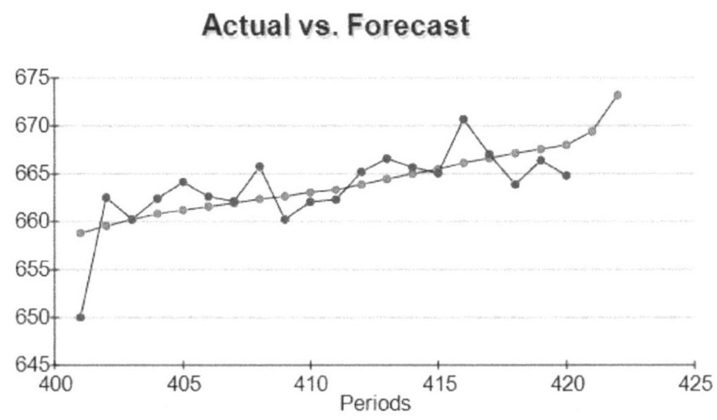

AI MACHINE LEARNING: LOGISTIC BINARY CLASSIFICATION (SUPERVISED)

Limited dependent variables techniques are used to forecast the probability of something occurring given some independent variables (e.g., predicting if a credit line will default given the obligor's characteristics such as age, salary, credit card debt levels; or the probability a patient will have lung cancer based on age and number of cigarettes smoked annually, and so forth). The dependent variable is limited (i.e., binary 1 and 0 for default/cancer, or limited to integer values 1, 2, 3, etc.). Traditional regression analysis will not work as the predicted probability is usually less than 0 or greater than 1, and many of the required regression assumptions are violated (e.g., independence and normality of the errors). We also have a vector of independent variable regressors, X, which are assumed to influence the outcome, Y. A typical ordinary least squares regression approach is invalid because the regression errors are heteroskedastic and non-normal, and the resulting estimated probability estimates will return nonsensical values of above 1 or below 0. This analysis handles these problems using an iterative optimization routine to maximize a log-likelihood function when the dependent variables are limited.

The AI Machine Learning Logistic Binary Classification regression is used for predicting the probability of occurrence of an event by fitting data to a logistic curve. It is a Generalized Linear Model used for binomial regression, and, like many forms of regression analysis, it makes use of several predictor variables that may be either numerical or categorical. Maximum Likelihood Estimation (MLE) is applied in a binary multivariate logistic analysis to determine the expected probability of success of belonging to a certain group.

```
Model Inputs:
VAR421          Training set dependent variable (binary data 0/1)
VAR422:VAR425   Training set independent variables
VAR427:VAR430   Testing set (optional, match independent variables)
VAR432          Forecast probability's save location (optional)
```

The estimated coefficients for the Logistic model are the logarithmic odds ratios and cannot be interpreted directly as probabilities. A quick computation is first required. Specifically, the Logit model is defined as Estimated Y or ($\hat{Y}$) using $\hat{Y} = ln[P_i/(1 - P_i)]$ or, conversely, $P_i = e^{\hat{Y}}/(1 + e^{\hat{Y}})$, and the coefficients β_i are the log odds ratios. So, taking the antilog or e^{β_i} we obtain the odds ratio of $P_i/(1 - P_i)$. This means that with an increase in a unit of β_i, the log odds ratio increases by this amount. Finally, the rate of change in the probability is $dP/dX = \beta_i P_i(1 - P_i)$. The Standard Error measures how accurate the predicted Coefficients are, and the t-Statistics are the ratios of each predicted Coefficient to its Standard Error and are used in the typical regression hypothesis test of the significance of each estimated parameter. To estimate the probability of success of belonging to a certain group (e.g., predicting if a smoker will develop chest complications given the amount smoked per year), simply compute the estimated $\hat{Y}$ value using the MLE coefficients. For example, if the model is $\hat{Y} = 1.1 + 0.005\ (Cigarettes)$, then for someone smoking 100 packs per year, $\hat{Y} = 1.1 + 0.005(100) = 1.6$. Next, compute the inverse antilog of the odds ratio by doing: $e^{\hat{Y}}/[1 + e^{\hat{Y}}] = e^{1.6}/(1 + e^{1.6}) = 0.8320$. So, such a person has an 83.20% chance of developing some chest complications in his or her lifetime.

AI MACHINE LEARNING: LOGISTIC BINARY CLASSIFICATION (SUPERVISED)

The results interpretation is similar to that of a standard multiple regression, with the exception of computing the probability. For example, the first row of the testing variable's data points are 9, 26, 69, 6.7, which means that the $\hat{Y} = -2.047190 - 0.201097(9) - 0.062159(26) + 0.024845(69) + 0.158885(6.7) = -2.6944$. Next, we can compute the inverse antilog of the odds ratio by doing: $e^{\hat{Y}}/[1 + e^{\hat{Y}}] = e^{-2.6944}/(1 + e^{-2.6944}) = 6.33\%$. The remaining rows are similarly computed.

In addition, the results also return a confusion matrix, which lists the true responses based on the training set's dependent variable and the predicted responses. The matrix shows the various positivity and recall rates as well as the specificity, prevalence of false positives, and false negatives. True Positive (TP) is where the actual is 1 and the predicted is 1, and we see that 67.37% of the dataset was predicted correctly as a true positive. The same interpretation applies to False Negatives (FN), False Positives (FP), and True Negatives (TN). In addition, Positive Sensitivity Recall is TP/(TP+FN) and it measures the ability to predict positive outcomes. Negative Specificity is TN/(TN+FP) and it measures the ability to predict negative outcomes. Event Prevalence is the amount of Actual Y=1 and it measures the positive outcomes in the original data. False Positives is FP/(FP+TP) or Type I error. False Negatives is FN/(FN+TN) or Type II error. Positive Precision is TP/(TP+FP) and it measures the accuracy of a predicted positive outcome. Negative Precision is TN/(TN+FN) and it measures the accuracy of a predicted negative outcome. The Accuracy of the overall prediction is the % of TP and TN. Finally, the results show the Receiver Operating Characteristic (ROC) curve. It plots the Positive Sensitivity Rate against the Negative Specificity, where the area under the curve (AUC) is another measure of the accuracy of the classification model. The ROC plots the model's performance at all classification thresholds. AUC ranges from 0%–100%, where 100% indicates a perfect fit. The ROC is available by clicking on the Charts subtab in BizStats while the AUC result is shown as one of the accuracy measures in the Confusion Matrix section.

Generalized Linear Model (Logit with Binary Outcomes)

	Coefficient	Std. Error	Wald Test	P-value	Exp(B)
Intercept	**-2.047190**	0.301976	45.9592	0.000000	0.129097
VAR1	**-0.201097**	0.030500	43.4731	0.000000	0.817833
VAR2	**-0.062159**	0.021873	8.075710	0.004486	0.939734
VAR3	**0.024845**	0.005846	18.0607	0.000021	1.025156
VAR4	**0.158885**	0.019759	64.6603	0.000000	1.172203

Log-Likelihood	-214.8162
Restricted Log-Likelihood	-285.4773
McFadden R-squared	0.247519
Cox and Snell R-squared	0.246212
Nagelkerke R-squared	0.361656
Raw Akaike Info. Criterion	439.6324
Raw Bayes Criterion	460.7054
Chi-Square	141.3222
Degrees of Freedom	4
P-value	0.000000

Positive Sensitivity Recall	49.61%
Negative Specificity	91.64%
Event Prevalence	25.80%
False Positives	32.63%
False Negatives	16.05%
Positive Precision	67.37%
Negative Precision	83.95%
Accuracy	80.80%
ROC Curve's AUC Measure	72.61%

Confusion Matrix

True Response	Predicted Response y = 1	Predicted Response y = 0
y = 1	**True Positive TP**	**False Negative FN**
y = 0	**False Positive FP**	**True Negative TN**

True Response	Predicted Response **y = 1**	Predicted Response y = 0
y = 1	**64**	65
y = 0	31	340

True Response	Predicted Response **y = 1**	Predicted Response y = 0
y = 1	**67.37%**	16.05%
y = 0	32.63%	83.95%

Forecast Y	Probability
-2.6944	**6.33%**
-4.1365	1.57%
-0.5931	35.59%
0.6639	66.01%
-2.7523	6.00%
-0.6550	34.19%

AI MACHINE LEARNING: NORMIT PROBIT BINARY CLASSIFICATION (SUPERVISED)

The AI Machine Learning Normit Probit model is a popular alternative specification for the Logistic binary response model. It employs a Normit-Probit function estimated using maximum likelihood estimation and is also sometimes called a Probit regression. The Probit and logistic regression models tend to produce very similar predictions where the parameter estimates in a logistic regression tend to be 1.6 to 1.8 times higher than they are in a corresponding Probit model. The choice of using a Probit or Logit is entirely up to convenience, and the main distinction is that the logistic distribution has a higher kurtosis (fatter tails) to account for extreme values. For example, suppose that house ownership is the decision to be modeled, and this response variable is binary (home purchase or no home purchase) and depends on a series of independent variables X_i such as income, age, and so forth, such that $I_i = \beta_0 + \beta_1 X_1 + \cdots + \beta_n X_n$, where the larger the value of I_i, the higher the probability of homeownership. For each family, a critical threshold I^* exists, where, if exceeded, the house is purchased, otherwise, no home is purchased, and the outcome probability (P) is assumed to be normally distributed, such that $P_i = CDF(I)$ using a standard-normal cumulative distribution function (CDF). Therefore, use the estimated coefficients exactly like that of a regression model and, using the estimated $\hat{Y}$, apply a standard-normal distribution to compute the probability.

```
Model Inputs:
VAR421          Training set dependent variable (binary data 0/1)
VAR422:VAR425   Training set independent variables
VAR427:VAR430   Testing set (optional, match independent variables)
VAR432          Forecast probability's save location (optional)
```

The results interpretation is similar to that of a standard multiple regression and the AI/ML Logistic Binary Classification model, with the exception of computing the probability, which, in the case of a Normit Probit model, requires a standard normal distribution. For example, the first row of the testing variable's data points are 9, 26, 69, 6.7, 3.92, which means that the $\hat{Y} = -1.218323 - 0.113973(9) - 0.033448(26) + 0.013898(69) + 0.092666(6.7) = -1.5339$ (rounded). Next, we can compute the normal cumulative distribution function $\Phi(-1.5339) = 6.25\%$. The resulting forecasted probability for Normit is typically fairly close to the Logit result seen previously. The remaining rows are similarly computed. Finally, the ROC, AUC, and Confusion Matrix results such as positivity, specificity, false positives, false negatives, and so forth, are also computed and their interpretations are identical to the AI/ML Logistic Binary Classification model.

AI MACHINE LEARNING: NORMIT PROBIT BINARY CLASSIFICATION (SUPERVISED)

Generalized Linear Model (Probit with Binary Outcomes)

	Coefficient	Std. Error	Wald Test	P-value	Lower	Upper
Intercept	**-1.218323**	0.170237	51.2172	0.000000	-1.551982	-0.884664
VAR1	**-0.113973**	0.016800	46.0252	0.000000	-0.146900	-0.081046
VAR2	**-0.033448**	0.012279	7.419795	0.006451	-0.057515	-0.009381
VAR3	**0.013898**	0.003350	17.2135	0.000033	0.007333	0.020464
VAR4	**0.092666**	0.010965	71.4226	0.000000	0.071176	0.114157

Log-Likelihood	-214.3784
Restricted Log-Likelihood	-285.4773
McFadden R-squared	0.249053
Cox and Snell R-squared	0.247531
Nagelkerke R-squared	0.363593
Raw Akaike Info. Criterion	438.7567
Raw Bayes Criterion	459.8298
Chi-Square	142.1979
Degrees of Freedom	4
P-value	0.000000

Positive Sensitivity Recall	54.26%
Negative Specificity	89.49%
Event Prevalence	25.80%
False Positives	35.78%
False Negatives	15.09%
Positive Precision	64.22%
Negative Precision	84.91%
Accuracy	80.40%
ROC Curve's AUC Measure	72.40%

Forecast Y	Probability
-1.5339	**6.25%**
-2.3330	0.98%
-0.3424	36.60%
0.3504	63.70%
-1.5894	5.60%
-0.3880	34.90%
-0.7630	22.27%
-0.5542	28.97%
-1.4084	7.95%
0.8985	81.55%

Confusion Matrix

True Response	Predicted Response y = 1	Predicted Response y = 0
y = 1	True Positive TP	False Negative FN
y = 0	False Positive FP	True Negative TN

True Response	Predicted Response y = 1	Predicted Response y = 0
y = 1	70	59
y = 0	39	332

True Response	Predicted Response y = 1	Predicted Response y = 0
y = 1	64.22%	15.09%
y = 0	35.78%	84.91%

ROC Curve

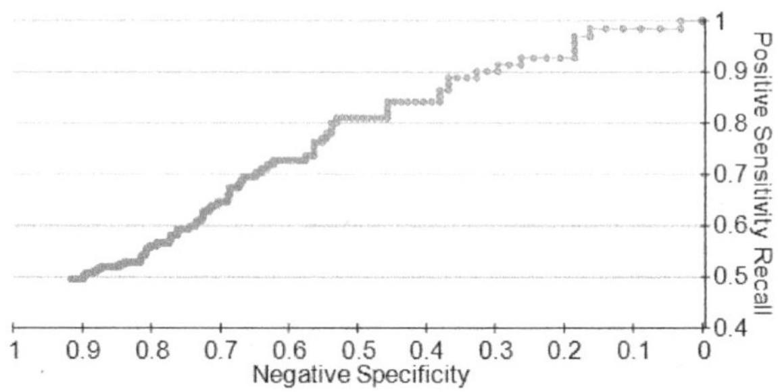

AI MACHINE LEARNING: RANDOM FOREST (SUPERVISED)

In this approach, bootstraps of regression trees are run multiple times with different combinations of data points and variables to develop a consensus forecast of group assignments. Using a single set of Training Y and Training X variables, the data and variables are bootstrapped and resampled. Each resampling will be run in the CART or classification and regression tree model, and the consensus categorization results will be generated. The benefit of random forests is that it provides a consensus forecast (wisdom of the crowd) through a resampling with replacement of both the variables and the data points. However, the individual CART model and tree process will no longer be available. To get started with this approach, enter the variables you need to classify and enter the number of clusters desired.

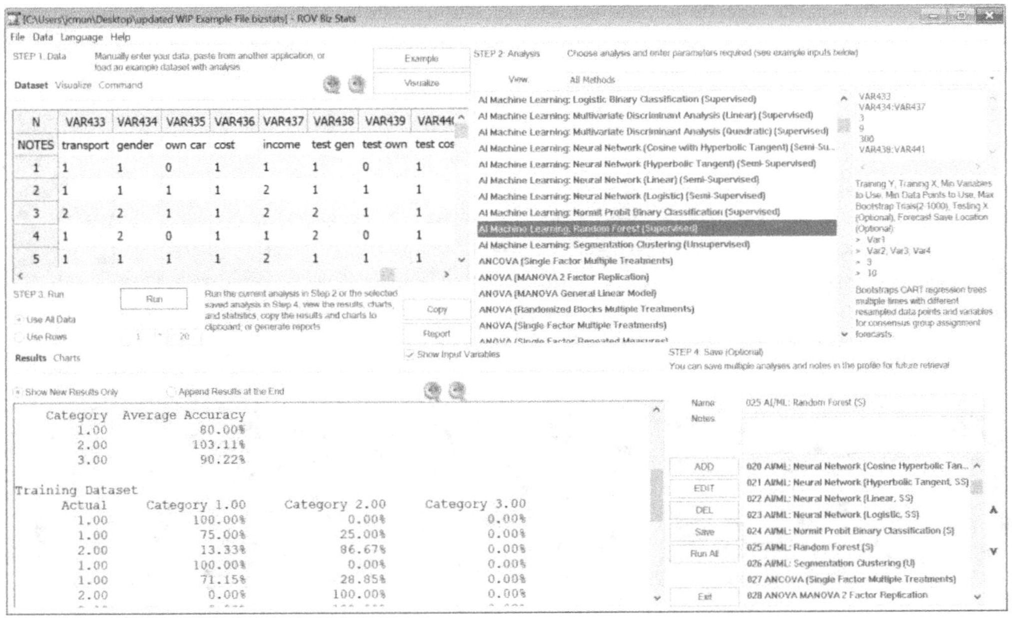

Model Inputs:

VAR433	Training Y (1 variable)
VAR434:VAR437	Training X (≥ 1 variables)
3	Min variables (< the total X variables)
9	Min data points (< total number of rows)
300	Max Bootstrap trials (2-1000)
VAR438:VAR441	Testing X (optional)
VARX	Forecast save location (optional)

AI MACHINE LEARNING: RANDOM FOREST (SUPERVISED)

Suppose we apply the entire dataset and bootstrapped it (i.e., minimum variables is 4 and the minimum data points to use is 10, which means the entire dataset is utilized), the results will be identical to the AI/ML Classification and Regression Tree CART model. Recall that the CART results had 100% for all three categories. In this random forest model, if we only apply a minimum of 3 variables with 9 data rows, we see the results shown next. Hundreds of CART models are bootstrapped, and the averages of the results are obtained. The testing dataset's categorization shows that the highest probability events are in categories 1, 1, 2, 1, 1, 2, 2, 3, 3, 3, which also corresponds to the single CART model results.

AI Machine Learning: Random Forest (Supervised)

Category	Average Accuracy
1.00	80.00%
2.00	103.11%
3.00	90.22%

Training Dataset

Actual	Category 1	Category 2	Category 3
1.00	100.00%	0.00%	0.00%
1.00	75.00%	25.00%	0.00%
2.00	13.33%	86.67%	0.00%
1.00	100.00%	0.00%	0.00%
1.00	71.15%	28.85%	0.00%
2.00	0.00%	100.00%	0.00%
2.00	0.00%	100.00%	0.00%
3.00	0.00%	10.45%	89.55%
3.00	0.00%	0.00%	100.00%
3.00	0.00%	0.00%	100.00%

Testing Dataset

Category 1	Category 2	Category 3
100.00%	0.00%	0.00%
75.00%	25.00%	0.00%
13.33%	86.67%	0.00%
100.00%	0.00%	0.00%
75.00%	25.00%	0.00%
0.00%	100.00%	0.00%
0.00%	100.00%	0.00%
0.00%	10.45%	89.55%
0.00%	0.00%	100.00%
0.00%	9.33%	90.67%

AI MACHINE LEARNING: SEGMENTATION CLUSTERING (UNSUPERVISED)

Taking the original dataset, we run some internal algorithms (a combination of k-means hierarchical clustering and other methods-of-moments to find the best-fitting groups or natural statistical clusters) to statistically divide or segment the original dataset into multiple groups. Segment this dataset into as many groups as you wish. This technique is valuable in a variety of settings including marketing (market segmentation of customers into various customer relationship management groups etc.), physical sciences, engineering, and others.

VAR415 shows the various states, whereas VAR416:VAR419 provides the characteristics in terms of each state's number of murders, number of assaults, the state population in millions, and number of breaking-and-entering events. Using these numerical values (VAR416:VAR419), the states can be segmented into various groups.

```
Model Inputs:
VAR416:VAR419  Variables to cluster
0              Optional (0=Show All Clusters Up To X, 1=Show Cluster X)
5              Cluster X
```

The results from cluster analysis shown next generate clusters of multiple groups partitioned based on data similarity for exploratory data analysis and data mining (e.g., machine learning, pattern recognition, image analysis, bioinformatics, etc.). The objects in the same cluster are more similar to each other than to those in other clusters. In addition, cluster analysis can be used to discover data structures without providing an explanation or interpretation of the relationship among variables. The results will show the cluster membership number as well as the centroid's mean values and counts of members within each cluster subgroup. For example, if we need to segregate the data into 3 segments, we see that one segment has Alaska, Alabama, Arizona, and so forth, while the second segment includes states like Arkansas and so forth (i.e., the 3 Cluster result shows 1, 1, 1, 2, 1, and so forth, indicating that the first three sample rows are categorized into Cluster 1, followed by Cluster 2, and then Cluster 1, etc.). These segments group similar characteristics together as cohorts, where states within these cohorts have the highest amounts of statistical similarities.

AI MACHINE LEARNING: SEGMENTATION CLUSTERING (UNSUPERVISED)

Segmentation Clustering

Sample	X1	X2	X3	X4	Cluster #	2	3	4	5
1	13.20	236.00	58.00	21.20		1	**1**	1	1
2	10.00	263.00	48.00	44.50		1	**1**	1	1
3	8.10	294.00	80.00	31.00		1	**1**	1	2
4	8.80	190.00	50.00	19.50		1	**2**	3	1
5	9.00	276.00	91.00	40.60		1	**1**	1	2
..	..	...	...	...		.	.	.	.
46	8.50	156.00	63.00	207.00		1	3	4	5
47	4.00	145.00	73.00	26.20		2	2	3	4
48	5.70	81.00	39.00	9.30		2	2	2	3
49	2.60	53.00	66.00	10.80		2	2	2	3
50	6.80	161.00	60.00	15.60		1	2	3	4

Cluster Centroids [1]

No. of Clusters	2	3	4	5
1	10.70	11.95	12.14	11.89
2	7.22	7.32	3.94	11.80
3		8.50	10.65	2.95
4			8.50	9.34
5				8.50

Cluster Centroids [2]

No. of Clusters	2	3	4	5
1	234.89	261.95	268.94	232.07
2	95.48	113.50	77.53	300.86
3		156.00	155.71	62.70
4			156.00	133.33
5				156.00

Cluster Centroids [3]

No. of Clusters	2	3	4	5
1	68.74	69.00	67.82	67.07
2	61.78	63.43	57.00	68.71
3		63.00	70.94	53.90
4			63.00	69.72
5				63.00

Cluster Centroids [4]

No. of Clusters	2	3	4	5
1	33.24	28.63	28.22	27.74
2	15.23	16.56	12.69	28.86
3		207.00	21.81	11.51
4			207.00	18.63

Cluster Counts

No. of Clusters	2	3	4	5
1	27	19	17	14
2	23	30	15	7
3		1	17	10
4			1	18
5				1

8. Forecasting, Predictive Modeling, and Time Series Analytics

Core Theme

This module teaches time series decomposition (trend, seasonality, noise), stationarity diagnostics (ACF, PACF, Dickey–Fuller), and classical forecasting methods (moving averages, exponential smoothing, Holt-Winters). It progresses through ARIMA and SARIMA modeling, model selection via information criteria, ARIMAX with external regressors, ML-based forecasting (feature engineering, Prophet), time-series cross-validation (expanding vs. sliding windows), and forecast uncertainty quantification with prediction intervals.

Module Objectives

Forecasting and Time Series Analytics

Decompose & Diagnose

Decompose time series data into trend, seasonality, and noise components; diagnose stationarity and identify appropriate forecasting methods based on data characteristics.

Classical Modeling (ARIMA)

Build, evaluate, and optimize ARIMA/SARIMA and regression-based forecasting models for structured time series data with clear seasonality.

ML-Based Forecasting

Apply machine learning methods including gradient boosting (XGBoost) and Prophet to handle complex time series problems with external regressors.

Uncertainty & Quantification

Quantify forecast uncertainty using prediction intervals, communicate risks effectively to decision-makers, and integrate outputs into planning cycles. Add a Monte Carlo simulation to the mix for forecast uncertainty.

Forecasting Methods

FORECASTING METHODS

Quantitative Forecasting

Cross-Sectional Data

All Data Types
- Auto Econometrics
- Basic Econometrics
- Custom Distribution
- Monte Carlo Simulation
- Multiple Regression
- Stepwise Regression

Binary Dependents
- MLE Logit/Probit/Tobit

Mixed Panel Data
- ARIMA
- Auto ARIMA
- Auto Econometrics
- Basic Econometrics
- Custom Distribution
- Monte Carlo Simulation
- Multiple Regression
- Stepwise Regression

Time-Series Data

Stationary Data
- ARIMA
- Auto ARIMA
- Auto Econometrics
- Basic Econometrics
- Combinatorial Fuzzy Logic
- Cubic Spline
- Custom Distribution
- J-Curve
- Markov Chain
- Monte Carlo Simulation
- Multiple Regression
- Neural Network
- S-Curve
- Stepwise Regression
- Time-Series Forecast
- Trendlines

Nonstationary
- GARCH (E/M/T/GJR)
- Stochastic Processes

Qualitative Forecasting
- Custom Distribution
- Delphi Method
- Fuzzy Sets
- Management Assumptions
- Monte Carlo Simulation
- Subject Matter Experts
- Stepwise Regression

NOTES

- Econometrics and regression methods require at least one independent variable. Time-index and binary dummy variables can be used to model time-series and seasonal models.
- Fuzzy sets return fuzzy numbers.
- GARCH is for estimating volatility based on prices as inputs.
- MLE requires the dependent variable to be truncated or limited (e.g., binary), and independent variables can take on any form. In contrast, econometrics and regression methods cannot have binary values for their dependent variables (however, they can take binary dummy variables as independent variables).
- Mixed panel data are data with both time-series and cross-sectional elements in a large matrix.

Time Series Components & Decomposition

Separating Trend, Seasonality, and Noise for Analysis

Core Components

T_t : Trend , S_t : Seasonality , E_t : Error/Noise

Time series data (y_t) is typically broken down into these three fundamental unobservable components.

Additive Decomposition

$$y_t = T_t + S_t + E_t$$

Use when: The magnitude of seasonal fluctuations is roughly constant over time (variance is independent of the trend level).

Multiplicative Decomposition

$$y_t = T_t \times S_t \times E_t$$

Use when: The seasonal fluctuations grow or shrink proportionally with the trend.

Transformation Strategy

$$\log(y_t) = \log(T_t) + \log(S_t) + \log(E_t)$$

Log-transforming multiplicative data allows you to use additive decomposition methods.

Trend Extraction

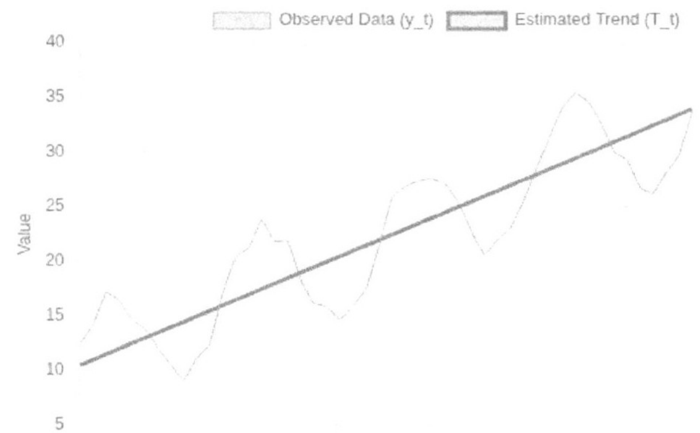

Seasonality & Residuals

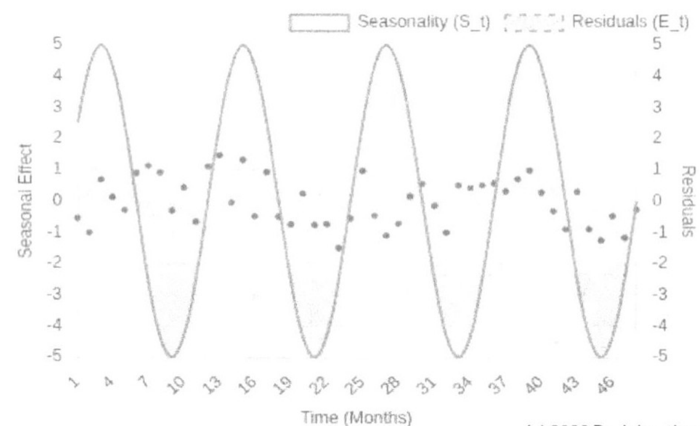

Stationarity, ACF, and PACF

Foundations for Time Series Identification

Non-Stationary vs. Differenced Series

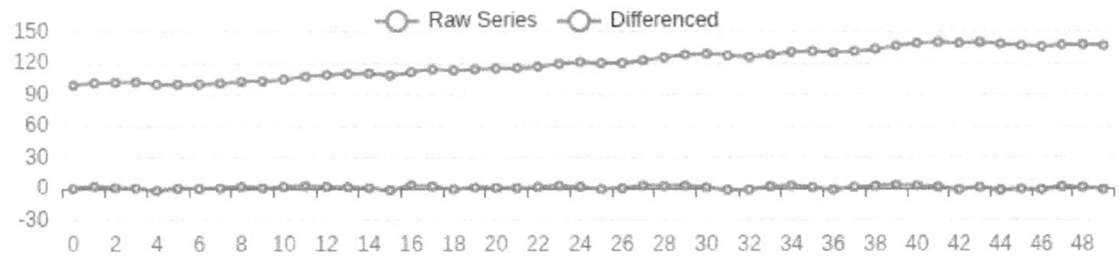

ACF (Autocorrelation)

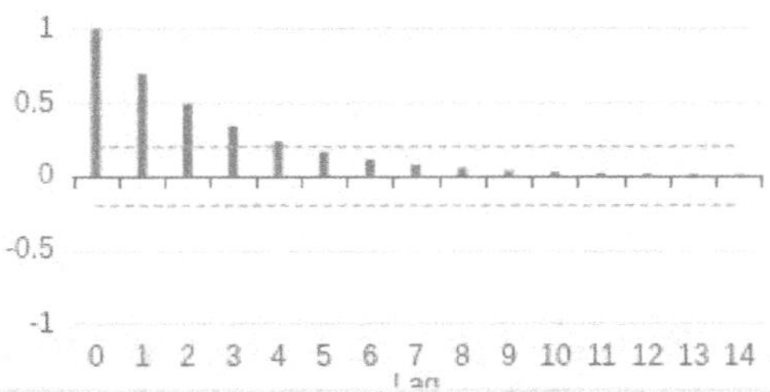

PACF (Partial Autocorrelation)

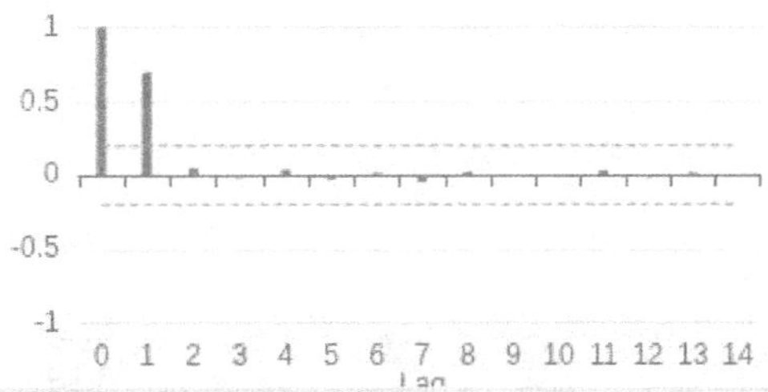

Stationarity

A time series is stationary if its statistical properties (mean, variance) do not change over time. Most models (e.g., ARIMA) assume stationarity.

$$E[y_t] = \mu, Var(y_t) = \sigma^2$$

Differencing Operation

Transforming a non-stationary series to stationary by removing trends.

$$\Delta y_t = y_t - y_{t-1}$$

Log transform is used to stabilize increasing variance.

Model ID with Correlograms

Rule of Thumb

AR(p): ACF tails off, PACF cuts off after lag p.
MA(q): ACF cuts off after lag q, PACF tails off.

Moving Averages & Exponential Smoothing

Classical Forecasting Methods for Trend & Seasonality

Simple Moving Average (SMA)

$$\hat{y}_{t+1} = \frac{1}{k}\sum_{i=0}^{k-1} y_{t-i}$$

Averages the last *k* observations.
Smooths noise but lags behind trends.

Simple Exponential Smoothing (SES)

$$\hat{y}_{t+1} = \alpha y_t + (1-\alpha)\hat{y}_t$$

Weighted average where weight decay exponentially. Best for level data without trend (0< α < 1]

Holt's Linear Trend Method

$$\hat{y}_{t+h} = l_t + hb_t$$

Adds a trend component (b_t) to level (l_t). Captures trend but no seasonality.

Holt-Winters (Seasonal)

$$\hat{y}_{t+h} = l_t + hb_t + s_{t+h-m(k+1)}$$

Speed smoothing: Level (α), Trend(β), and Seasonality(γ). Handles complex seasonal patterns.

Smoothing Effect (SMA vs Raw)

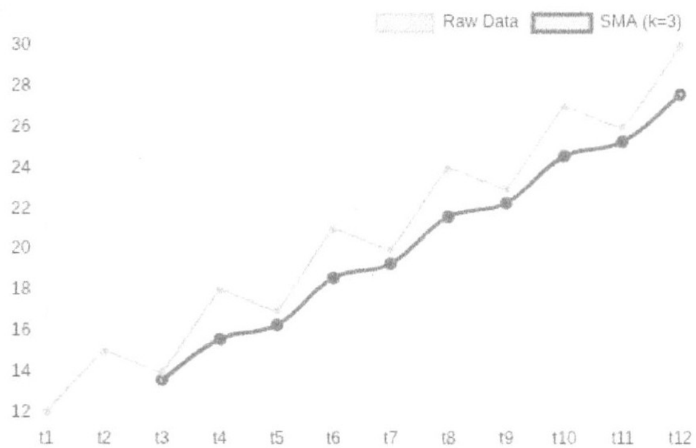

Trend & Seasonality (Holt-Winters)

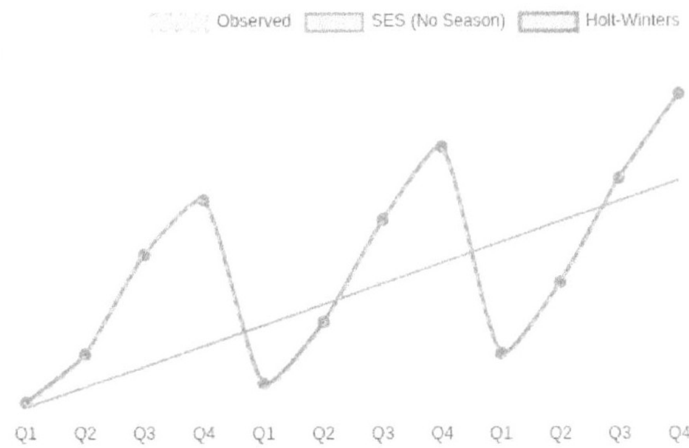

Time Series Forecasting

Classical Forecasting Methods for Trend & Seasonality

The eight most common time-series models, segregated by seasonality and trend, are listed below. For instance, if the data variable has no trend or seasonality, then a single moving-average model or a single exponential-smoothing model would suffice. However, if seasonality exists but no discernible trend is present, either a seasonal additive or seasonal multiplicative model would be better, and so forth.

	NO SEASONALITY	WITH SEASONALITY
WITHOUT TREND	Single Moving Average	Seasonal Additive
	Single Exponential Smoothing	Seasonal Multiplicative
WITH TREND	Double Moving Average	Holt–Winters Additive
	Double Exponential Smoothing	Holt–Winters Multiplicative

Year	Quarter	Period	Sales
2010	1	1	$684.20
2010	2	2	$584.10
2010	3	3	$765.40
2010	4	4	$892.30
2011	1	5	$885.40
2011	2	6	$677.00
2011	3	7	$1,006.60
2011	4	8	$1,122.10
2012	1	9	$1,163.40
2012	2	10	$993.20
2012	3	11	$1,312.50
2012	4	12	$1,545.30
2013	1	13	$1,596.20
2013	2	14	$1,260.40
2013	3	15	$1,735.20
2013	4	16	$2,029.70
2014	1	17	$2,107.80
2014	2	18	$1,650.30
2014	3	19	$2,304.40
2014	4	20	$2,639.40

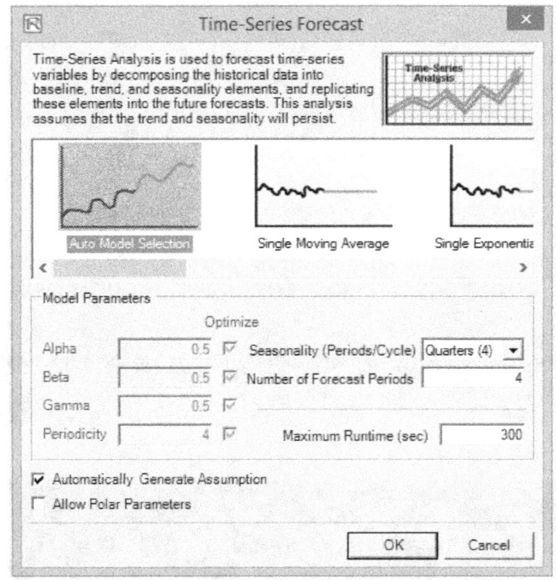

ARIMA Modeling

AutoRegressive Integrated Moving Average: Structure & Components

AutoRegressive Component AR(p)

$$y_t = c + \phi_1 y_{t-1} + \phi_2 y_{t-2} + \cdots + \phi_p y_{t-p} + \varepsilon_t$$

Predicts current value based on past values (lags). ϕ_1 are coefficients.

Moving Average Component MA(q)

$$y_t = \mu + \varepsilon_t + \theta_1 \varepsilon_{t-1} + \cdots + \theta_q \varepsilon_{t-q}$$

Predicts current value based on past forecast errors. θ_1 are coefficients.

Full ARIMA(p,d,q) Model

$$\left(1 - \sum_{i=1}^{p} \phi_i L^i\right)(1 - L)^d y_t = \left(1 + \sum_{j=1}^{q} \theta_j L^j\right)\varepsilon_t$$

Combines AR(p), Differencing (d), and MA(q). is the lag operator where $L^k y_t = y_{t-k}$.

Model Parameters

AutoRegressive Order: Number of lag observations included in the model.

Integrated Order: Number of times raw observations are differenced to achieve stationarity.

Moving Average Order: Size of the moving average window (lagged forecast errors).

Process Flow

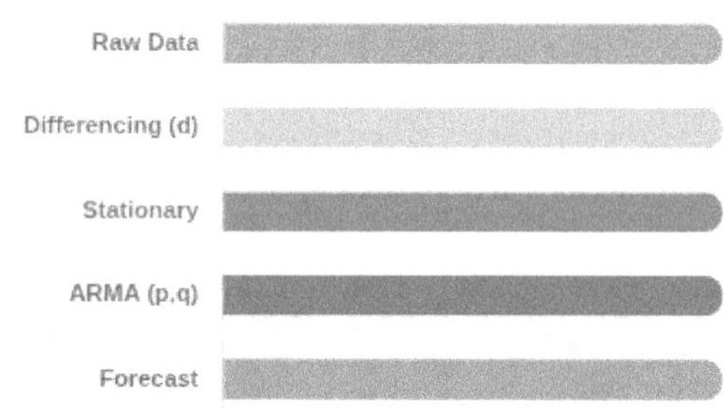

Seasonal ARIMA (SARIMA)

Modeling Seasonality in Time Series Data

SARIMA Notation: (p,d,q) × (P,D,Q)s

Extends ARIMA by adding seasonal components. The notation represents non-seasonal orders (p,d,q) and seasonal orders (P,D,Q) with period s.

$ARIMA(1,1,1)(1,1,1)_{12}$

Identifying Seasonal Patterns

Use Autocorrelation Function (ACF) and Partial ACF plots to detect seasonality. Look for significant spikes at lag multiples of s (e.g., 12, 24, 36 for monthly data).

Seasonal Differencing (D)

Apply seasonal differencing (D=1) to remove seasonal trends before modeling. This involves subtracting the observation from the same season in the previous cycle: $y_t - y_{t-s}$.

Practical Application

For monthly retail sales with a yearly cycle (s=12), a common starting model is **$SARIMA(0,1,1)(0,1,1)_{12}$**. This captures the trend via first differencing and seasonality via seasonal differencing and moving averages.

Model Selection & Diagnostics

Validating Forecast Reliability and Parsimony

Information Criteria Comparison (AIC/BIC)

Select models that balance fit with simplicity. AIC (Akaike) and BIC (Bayesian) penalize complexity to prevent overfitting; lower values indicate a better trade-off.

Residual Analysis & White Noise

Examine residuals for remaining patterns. A valid model produces residuals that resemble "white noise": zero mean, constant variance, and no significant autocorrelation.

Ljung-Box Test

A formal statistical test to check if autocorrelation exists in residuals across multiple lags. A high p-value (>0.05) confirms the residuals are random and the model is adequate.

Key Insight: Never rely solely on training error (RMSE). A model with low training error but structured residuals has missed signal (underfitting) or captured noise (overfitting).

Regression-Based Forecasting (ARIMAX)

Incorporating External Drivers & Events into Time Series

ARIMAX: External Regressors

Extends ARIMA by including exogenous variables (X) that drive the outcome (e.g., Price, Promotion, Weather). This transforms the model from purely historical to causal, allowing for "what-if" scenario planning.

Distributed Lag Models

Captures time-delayed effects where an action today impacts results over future periods. For example, a marketing campaign launched at time *t* may boost sales at *t*, *t+1*, and *t+2* (carryover effect).

Structural Breaks & Indicators

Uses dummy/indicator variables (0 or 1) to account for distinct events like holidays, policy changes, or system outages. This prevents outliers from distorting the underlying trend and seasonality estimates.

```
Model Structure: yt = ARIMA(p,d,q) + β1x1,t + β2x2,t-k + εt
```

Machine Learning for Forecasting

Beyond Classical Methods: Feature Engineering & Automation

Feature Engineering for Temporal Data

Transform time series into supervised learning problems by creating lag features (y_{t-1}, y_{t-7}), rolling statistics (moving average, rolling SD), and calendar features (day of week, month, holiday flags).

Gradient Boosting & Random Forests (GBM/RF)

Powerful for capturing non-linear relationships and interactions. Can handle multiple seasonality and external regressors easily but require careful cross-validation to avoid look-ahead bias.

Prophet: Automated Forecasting at Scale

An additive regression model ($y(t) = g(t) + s(t) + h(t) + \varepsilon(t)$) designed by Facebook. Automatically detects changepoints in trends, handles multiple seasonality, and is robust to missing data and outliers.

Key Advantage: ML models can incorporate hundreds of external features (weather, promotions, economic indicators) more naturally than classical ARIMA models.

Time Series Cross-Validation

Evaluating Performance While Respecting Temporal Order

Expanding Window

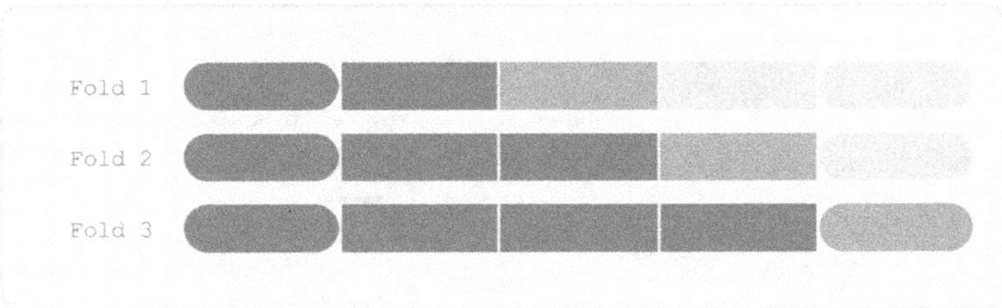

Training Data · Test (Forecast) · Unseen Future

Use Case: When older data remains relevant and you want to maximize training information.

Sliding Window (Walk-Forward)

Fixed Window · Test (Forecast) · Ignored Data

Use Case: When data distributions drift rapidly and old history is less predictive (concept drift).

Prevent Data Leakage

Standard k-fold CV shuffles data randomly. In time series, this allows "future" data to predict the "past," creating unrealistically high accuracy.

Horizon Alignment

Ensure the gap between training end and test start matches your real-world deployment latency (e.g., if you forecast 7 days ahead, gap must be 7).

Rolling Origin Evaluation

Simulate the exact process of re-training (or re-fitting) the model each day/week as new data arrives to estimate true production error.

Forecast Evaluation & Uncertainty

Key Metrics for Accuracy and Risk Quantification

Scale-Dependent Errors MAE & RMSE

$$\text{MAE} = \frac{1}{n}\sum_{t=1}^{n}|y_t - \hat{y}_t| \qquad \text{RMSE} = \sqrt{\frac{1}{n}\sum_{t=1}^{n}(y_t - \hat{y}_t)^2}$$

MAE measures average magnitude; RMSE penalizes large errors more heavily.

Percentage Errors MAPE & sMAPE

$$\text{MAPE} = \frac{100}{n}\sum\left|\frac{y_t - \hat{y}_t}{y_t}\right| \qquad \text{sMAPE} = \frac{200}{n}\sum\frac{|y_t - \hat{y}_t|}{|y_t| + |\hat{y}_t|}$$

Useful for comparing across different scales; sMAPE handles near-zero values better.

Relative Accuracy THEIL'S U

$$RA = \frac{1}{n}\sum_{t=1}^{n}\left(1 - \left|\frac{y_t - \hat{y}_t}{y_t}\right|\right) \times 100\%$$

Quantifying Uncertainty Prediction Intervals

$$U = \sqrt{\frac{\sum_{t=1}^{n-1}\left(\frac{\hat{y}_{t+1} - y_{t+1}}{y_t}\right)^2}{\sum_{t=1}^{n-1}\left(\frac{y_{t+1} - y_t}{y_t}\right)^2}}$$

Defines the range (e.g., 95%) within which the future value is expected to fall.

Forecast with Prediction Intervals

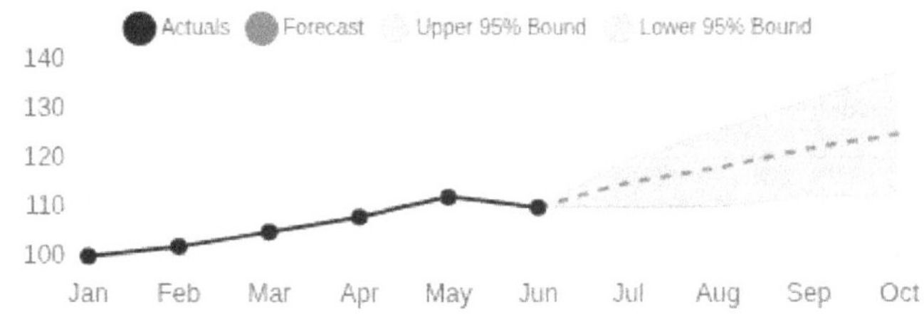

Visualizing the expanding cone of uncertainty for future periods.

Residual Distribution

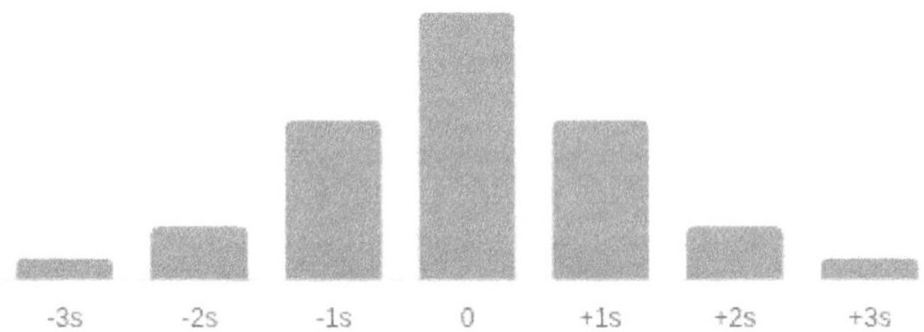

Checking if errors are normally distributed (crucial for interval validity).

Forecasting with AI Tools: HANDS-ON APPLICATION

Automating ARIMA & Prophet Models via Natural Language

Model Building Prompt

Julius AI

```
User:

I've uploaded 'daily_sales.csv'. 1. Convert 'date' to
datetime and set as index. 2. Fit a Facebook Prophet
model to forecast sales for the next 90 days. 3.
Include weekly seasonality and US holidays. 4. Plot
the forecast with confidence intervals and calculate
MAPE.
```

Scenario Analysis

ChatGPT / Analyst

```
User:

Based on the forecast plot, when is the next peak
demand period? Also, run a stress test: What happens
to the Q4 forecast if the trend growth rate decreases
by 10% due to a recession?
```

Generated Forecast Output

Model Status: Prophet model fitted successfully with 365 days of training data.
Accuracy Metric: MAPE on validation set is 4.2%.
Forecast Horizon: 90 days (solid line) with 95% confidence intervals (shaded).

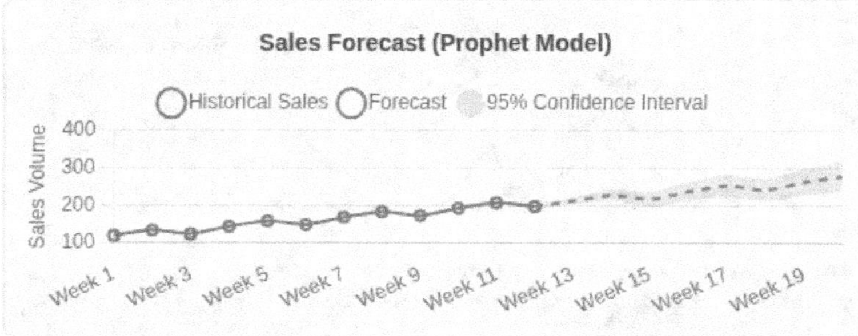

AI Interpretation:

The forecast identifies a strong weekly cycle peaking on Fridays. The next major demand surge is predicted for the Thanksgiving holiday window (Nov 24-28). The confidence interval widens significantly after 60 days, indicating higher uncertainty in long-range planning.

9. Risk-Based Simulation and Prescriptive Analytics Optimization

Core Theme

Moving from correlation to causation, this section covers the potential outcomes framework, experiment design (hypotheses, metrics, randomization units, sample sizing), and common pitfalls (p-hacking, novelty effects, interference). The prescriptive half introduces linear/integer programming for optimization, Monte Carlo simulation for uncertainty quantification, and decision trees for sequential decision-making.

Probability Distributions

COMMONLY USED DISTRIBUTIONS

TRIANGULAR
Looks like a triangle, continuous values, tails end at min and max with most likely as its peak. Can be skewed or symmetrical, with negative excess kurtosis (truncated tails). Examples: sales forecasts, subject matter estimates, management assumptions.

NORMAL
Continuous bell curve, a.k.a. Gaussian distribution, infinite tails on both ends, requires mean and standard deviation as inputs. Symmetrical with zero skew and zero excess kurtosis. Examples: stock returns, height, weight, IQ (most are truncated normal with limits).

UNIFORM
Flat continuous area with equal probability of occurrence at any point between the minimum and maximum. Symmetrical with zero skew and negative excess kurtosis (fixed end points). Examples: business forecasts and economic forecasts.

BINOMIAL
Discrete events with two mutually exclusive and independent outcomes with fixed probability of success at each successive trial. Symmetrical and approaches normal distribution with high number of trials. Example: tossing a coin multiple times.

POISSON
Discrete events occurring independently with the same average rate of repetition and measured in time (hours, days, weeks) or space (area). Examples: sales forecasts, subject matter estimates, management assumptions. Approaches normal with high average rates.

CUSTOM
Empirically fitted discrete distribution when little data is available or when other theoretical distributions fail. Suitable for Delphi methods, can be multimodal or irregular. Examples: subject matter estimates, management assumptions, and qualitative estimates that are converted numerically.

LESS COMMONLY USED BUT IMPORTANT DISTRIBUTIONS

BERNOULLI
Single discrete trial version of Binomial (e.g., simulating success or failure of projects).

BETA 4
Highly flexible continuous distribution capable of taking on multiple shapes and scales.

DISCRETE UNIFORM
Range of discrete events with equal probability of occurrence (e.g., rolling a six-sided die).

EXPONENTIAL 2
High probably of low values, low probability of continuous high values (e.g., wait time).

GUMBEL
Tail-end extreme value simulations of continuous outcomes (e.g., market crashes).

LOGNORMAL
Variables with continuous non-negative and non-zero values (e.g., stock prices).

STUDENT'S T
Continuous-normal with fat tails or higher probability of extremes (e.g., risky returns).

WEIBULL 3
Continuous mean time before failure and reliability estimates (e.g., MTBF of an engine).

OTHER DISTRIBUTIONS: Arcsine, Beta, Beta 3, Cauchy, Chi-square, Cosine, Double Log, Erlang, Exponential, F, Fréchet, Gamma, Geometric, Gumbel Min, Gumbel Max, Hypergeometric, Laplace, Logistic, Lognormal 3, Negative Binomial, Parabolic, Generalized Pareto, Pareto, Pascal, Pearson V, Pearson VI, Pert, Power, Power 3, Rayleigh, Standard-Normal, Standard-T, Weibull

Probability Relationships

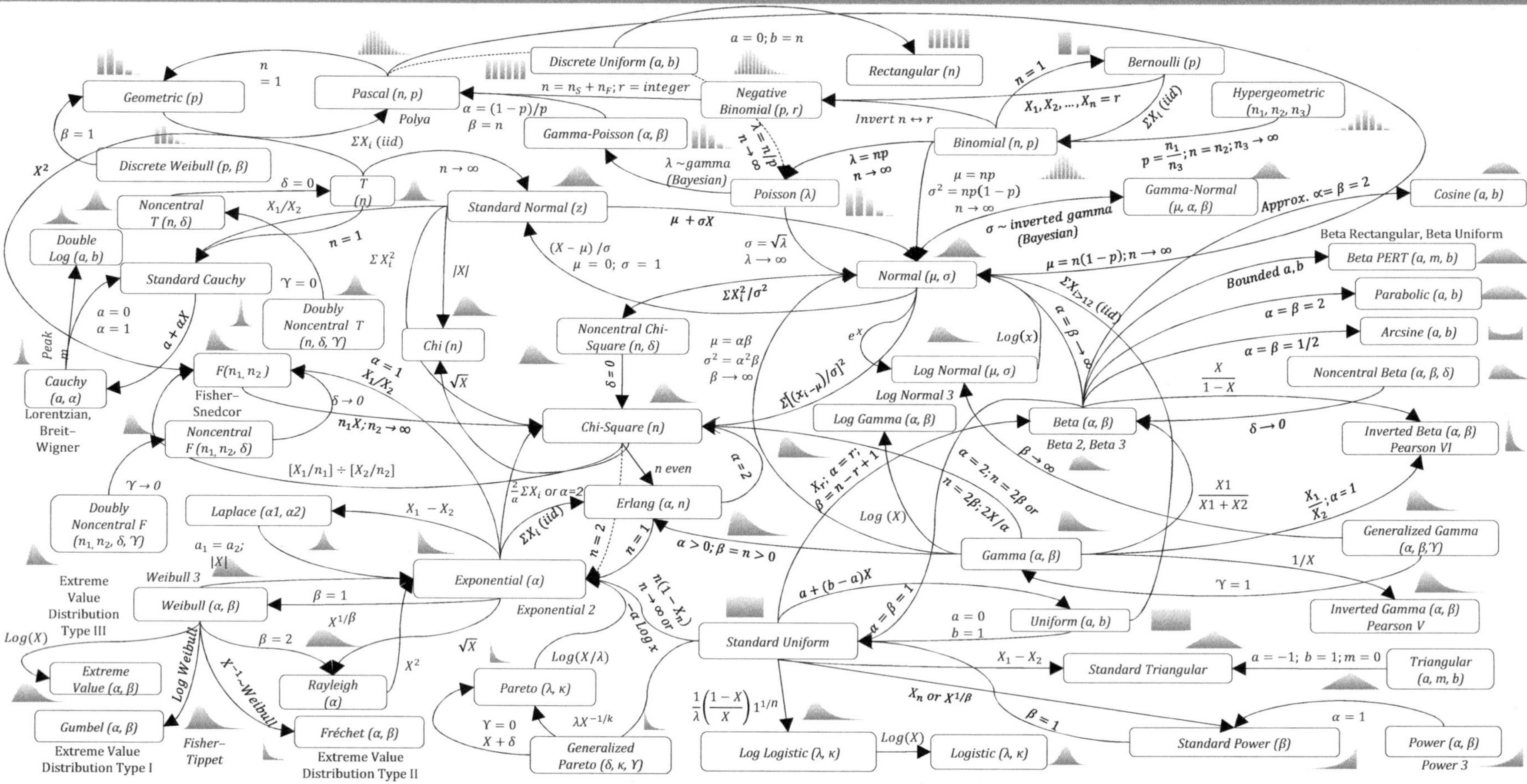

Simulation, Scenario, Tornado, Bootstrap, and Delphi Custom

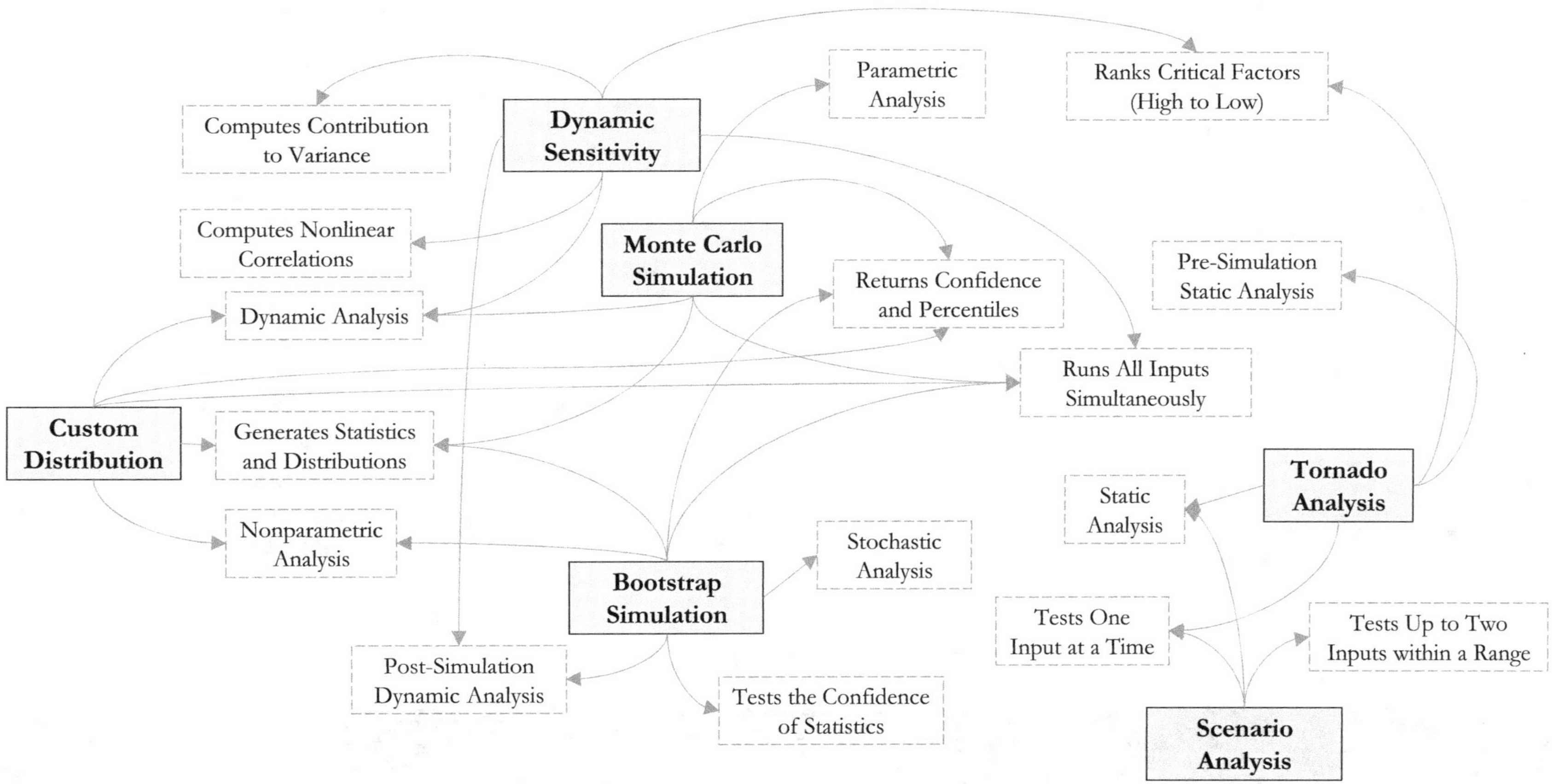

Tornado, Spider, Sensitivity, Scenario, and Fitting

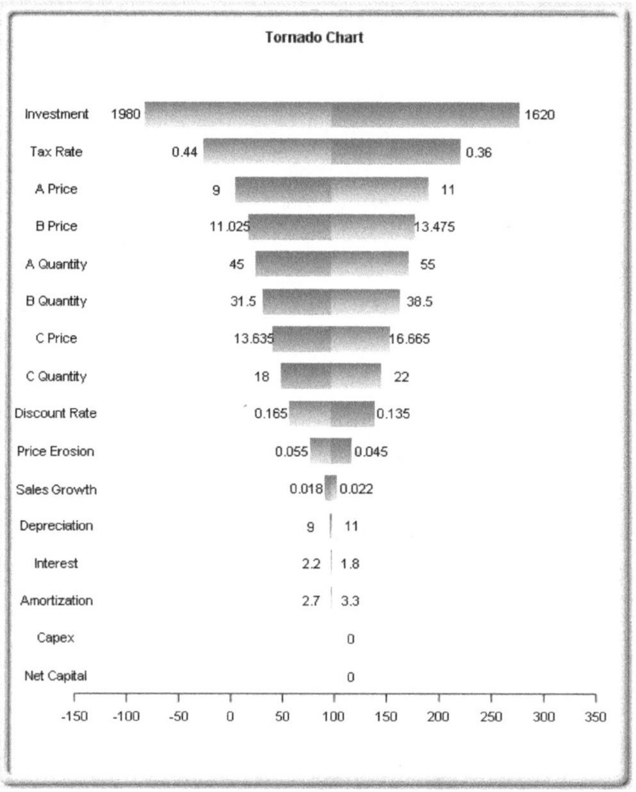

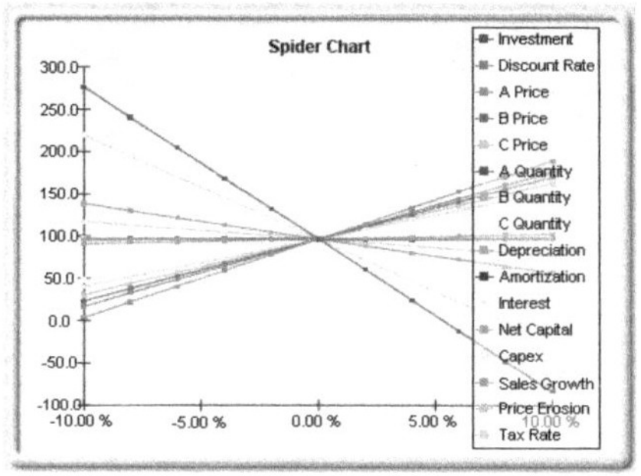

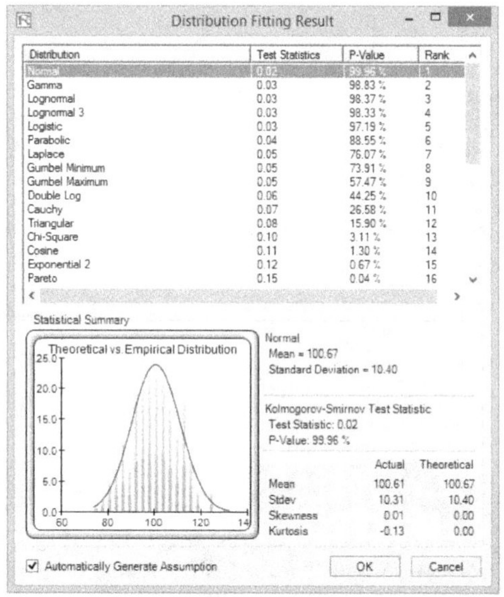

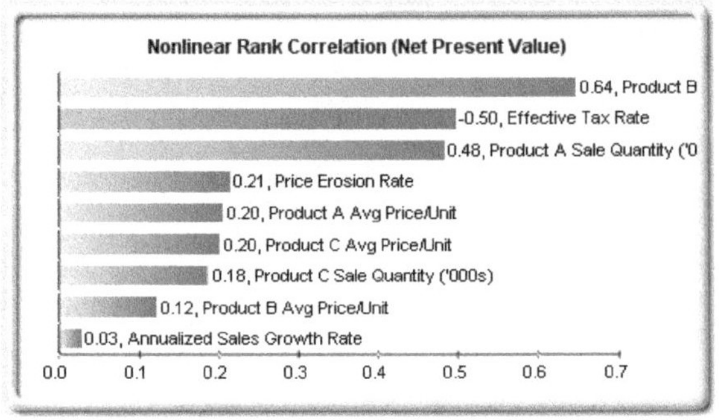

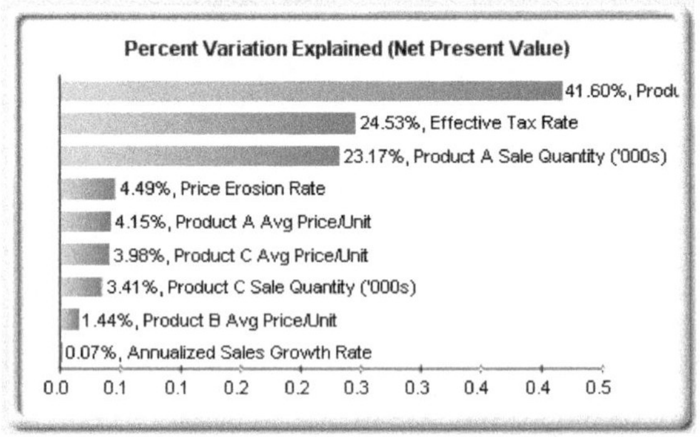

Efficient Frontier and Portfolio Optimization

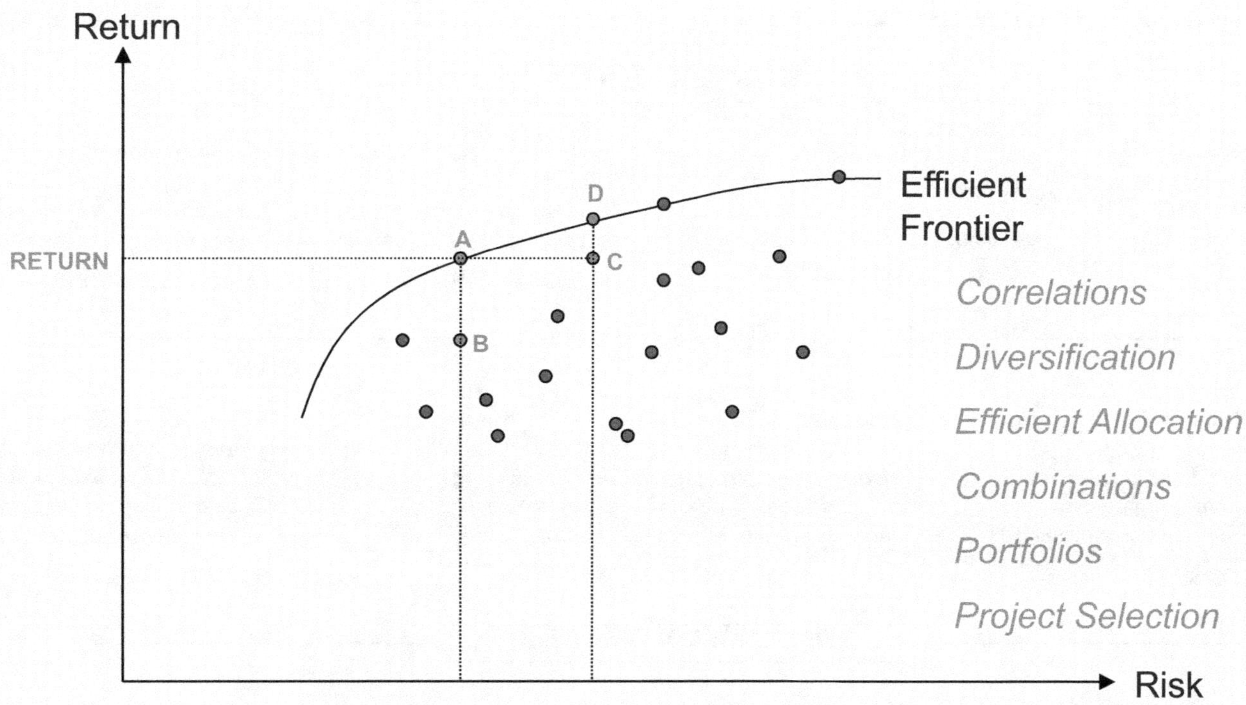

Optimization

OPTIMIZATION METHODS

STATIC

Runs optimization by iteratively changing the decision variables based on their allowed ranges to maximize or minimize the objective, while satisfying the constraints and restrictions imposed in the model.

DYNAMIC

Runs a Monte Carlo risk simulation, and the selected statistic (e.g., mean, Value at Risk, or percentile) is inserted into the model before optimization is run. This statistic accounts for uncertainties and variability in the inputs and model.

STOCHASTIC

Replicates dynamic optimization multiple times (i.e., simulate thousands of trials, statistics used in lieu of single-point-estimates, optimization run with multiple iterations, and the process is repeated multiple times). Distributions of decision variables are the result.

OPTIMIZATION INPUTS

OBJECTIVE

The outcome that is to be minimized (e.g., cost, schedule, error) or maximized (e.g., net income, profitability).

CONSTRAINT

Limitations or restrictions in the model (e.g., resource, budget, schedule, management constraints, risk).

DECISION

Variables or decisions you have control over (e.g., go or no-go decisions, % budget portfolio allocations).

ASSUMPTION

Uncertain variables to be simulated in dynamic and stochastic optimization (e.g., returns, demand).

EFFICIENT FRONTIER

Running multiple optimizations where each successive run perturbs and changes the constraints by some set amount to maximize or minimize the objective outcome while still satisfying the constraints and restrictions. The outcome is a set of multiple points that are the most optimal and efficient, and, when connected by a line, constitutes the efficient investment frontier, representing the best-bang-for-the-buck, where given the requisite constraints and restrictions, each point along the frontier is a portfolio of the best that can be achieved given the set of decision variables. The steep part of the frontier indicates it is better to pursue the higher constraint portfolio whereas, conversely, flat frontiers indicate diminishing marginal returns, and any additional resources provided to the portfolio will not significantly increase its overall portfolio objective.

10. Text Analytics, NLP, Unstructured Data, Ethics, and Governance

Core Theme

The last section covers the NLP pipeline from preprocessing (tokenization, stemming, lemmatization) through feature extraction (BoW, TF-IDF), sentiment analysis (VADER, ABSA), NER, topic modeling (LDA), text clustering, and embeddings (Word2Vec through BERT). It introduces RAG architecture and LLM-enabled NLP pipelines. The module then pivots to AI strategy — maturity models, build-vs-buy decisions, organizational readiness — and closes with ethics (algorithmic fairness, the impossibility theorem), regulatory landscape (GDPR, EU AI Act), responsible AI governance, executive communication, a course synthesis playbook, and a capstone project brief.

Module Objectives

Text Analytics, NLP, and Unstructured Data

Text Preprocessing

Master the cleaning pipeline: tokenization, stop word removal, stemming, lemmatization, and normalization.

Sentiment & Topic Modeling

Apply VADER/ML for sentiment analysis and Latent Dirichlet Allocation (LDA) to discover hidden topics.

Information Extraction

Utilize Named Entity Recognition (NER) to extract structured entities like people, organizations, and dates.

Embeddings & Vector Space

Understand and apply Word2Vec, GloVe, and sentence embeddings for semantic similarity and clustering.

RAG & GenAI Integration

Implement Retrieval-Augmented Generation (RAG) workflows to combine vector search with LLM capabilities.

Predictive Text Features

Transform unstructured text into actionable features to enhance regression and classification models.

Text as Business Data & Preprocessing

Structuring Unstructured Information for Analysis

Unstructured Data Sources

Business insights are hidden in customer reviews, social media posts, support tickets, earnings call transcripts, regulatory filings, and internal communications.

Preprocessing Pipeline

Transform raw text into analytical features through a standard sequence: Tokenization → Stop Word Removal → Stemming/Lemmatization → Normalization.

Tokenization — **Stop Words** — **Lemmatization** — **Normalize**

AI Tip: Use ChatGPT to design domain-specific preprocessing strategies (e.g., preserving financial tickers like $AAPL or hashtags like #AI) and verify cleaning steps.

BoW and TF-IDF: Feature Extraction

Transforming Text into Numerical Vectors for Machine Learning

Term Frequency (TF)

$$tf_{t,d} = \frac{\text{count}(t, d)}{\sum_{t' \in d} \text{count}(t', d)}$$

Measures how frequently a term *t* appears in document *d*. Often normalized by document length.

Inverse Document Frequency (IDF)

$$idf_t = \log\left(\frac{N}{1 + df_t}\right)$$

Measures informativeness. *N* is total documents; *dft* is number of documents containing *t*. Penalizes common words.

TF-IDF Score

$$tf - idf_{t,d} = tf_{t,d} \times idf_t$$

High score = Term is frequent in this document but rare across the corpus (high signature value).

Matrix Sparsity

$$\text{Sparsity} = 1 - \frac{\text{NNZ}}{M \times V}$$

Bag-of-Words matrices are mostly zeros. NNZ = Non-Zero elements, V = Vocabulary size.

Impact of IDF on Common vs. Rare Words

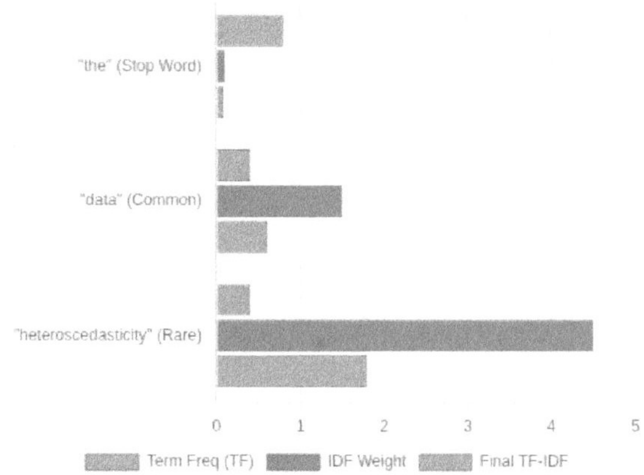

Visualizing Matrix Sparsity (Document-Term Matrix)

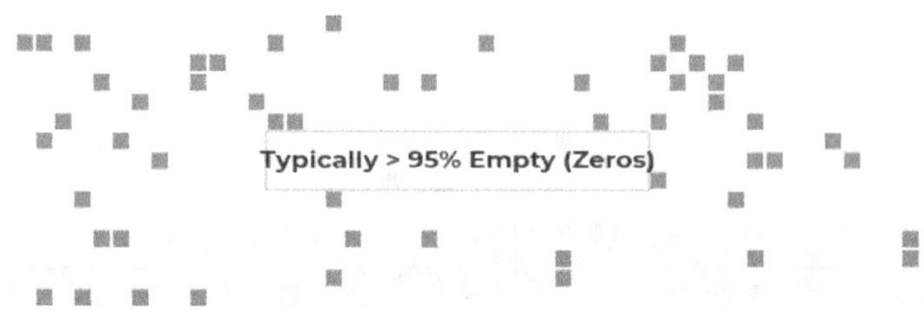

Sentiment Analysis Methods

Approaches to Quantifying Emotional Tone in Text

Rule-Based Approaches (Lexicon-Based)

Uses curated dictionaries (e.g., VADER, AFINN) to score words by polarity and intensity. Simple and transparent, but struggles with sarcasm, context, and domain-specific slang.

Machine Learning Classifiers

Trains supervised models (Naive Bayes, SVM, BERT) on labeled datasets to learn complex patterns. Higher accuracy for specific domains but requires significant training data.

Aspect-Based Sentiment Analysis (ABSA)

Deconstructs feedback into specific attributes (e.g., "Food was **great**, but service was **slow**") to assign granular sentiment scores rather than a single document-level metric.

Business Value: Move beyond star ratings to pinpoint exactly *what* drives satisfaction. E.g., Use ABSA to detect that a product has high sentiment for features but low sentiment for battery life.

NER and Information Extraction

Converting Unstructured Text into Structured Business Facts

Standard Entity Classes

NER models automatically classify key tokens into predefined categories: **PERSON** (Executives, Customers), **ORG** (Companies, Agencies), **LOC** (Cities, Countries), **DATE** (Deadlines, Events), and **MONEY** (Prices, Revenue).

Compliance & Risk (KYC)

Use NER to scan millions of documents for names appearing on sanctions lists (LOC, PERSON) or adverse media reports involving specific companies (ORG) to automate Know Your Customer (KYC) workflows.

Financial & Legal Extraction

Parse unstructured contracts and invoices to extract payment terms (DATE), transaction amounts (MONEY), and counterparty names (ORG) for automated entry into ERP systems.

Example: Automated Parsing of News/Financial Text

"**`Apple Inc.`** announced on **`Tuesday`** that CEO **`Tim Cook`** visited **`Singapore`** to discuss a **`$250 million`** expansion."

Topic Modeling with LDA

Latent Dirichlet Allocation: Structure & Hyperparameters

The Generative Assumption

LDA posits that each document is a finite mixture of latent topics, and each topic is an infinite mixture over the vocabulary. Writing a document is modeled as rolling dice to pick a topic, then rolling again to pick a word from that topic.

Key Hyperparameters (K, α, β)

K (Topics): Number of topics to discover (must be fixed in advance).
α (Alpha): Controls topic density per document (Low α = few topics per doc).
β (Beta): Controls word density per topic (Low β = few words per topic).

Topic-Word Distributions

The algorithm learns which words co-occur to define a topic. Interpretation relies on examining the top probability words.

Conceptual Analogy: Think of topics as "colors" (e.g., Red, Blue) and documents as "paintings". LDA reverse-engineers the palette (topics) and the mixture ratios (how much Red vs. Blue is in each painting) just by observing the pixels (words).

Text Clustering & Similarity

Grouping Documents by Semantic Meaning

t-SNE Visualization of Embeddings

Tech Finance Healthcare

Cosine Similarity

$$\cos(\theta) = \frac{\mathbf{A} \cdot \mathbf{B}}{\| \mathbf{A} \| \| \mathbf{B} \|} = \frac{\sum A_i B_i}{\sqrt{\sum A_i^2} \sqrt{\sum B_i^2}}$$

Measures the cosine of the angle between two non-zero vectors. Value ranges from -1 to 1 (usually 0 to 1 for text).

Key Techniques

K-Means on Embeddings: Applies standard K-Means clustering to dense vector representations (e.g., Word2Vec, BERT) to group semantically similar documents.

t-SNE / UMAP: Dimensionality reduction techniques that project high-dimensional (768+) embeddings into 2D/3D space for visualization.

Why Cosine over Euclidean?

In high-dimensional text data, the magnitude (document length) often varies. Cosine similarity captures orientation (topic) regardless of length.

Embeddings: Word2Vec & Beyond

Vector Space Representations of Semantic Meaning

Skip-gram Objective Function

$$J(\theta) = \frac{1}{T}\sum_{t=1}\sum \log p\left(w_{t+j} \middle| w_t\right) \quad s.t. \; -c \le j \le c, \; j \neq 0$$

Maximizes the probability of predicting surrounding context words w_{t+j} given a central target word w_t.

Softmax Probability (Output)

$$p(w_O|w_I) = \frac{\exp\left(\mathbf{v}'_{w_O}\mathbf{v}_{w_I}\right)}{\sum_{w=1}^{W}\exp\left(\mathbf{v}'_{w}\mathbf{v}_{w_I}\right)}$$

Calculates likelihood using dot products of input vector v_{w1} and output vector $\mathbf{v}'_{wO}$, normalized over the vocabulary V.

Sentence Embeddings (Concept)

$$\mathbf{v}_{\text{sentence}} = \text{Pool}\left(\text{Transformer}(w_1, \cdots, w_n)\right)$$

Beyond words: Modern models (BERT, SBERT) generate dense vectors for full sequences, capturing context and syntax.

Semantic Vector Space (Analogies)

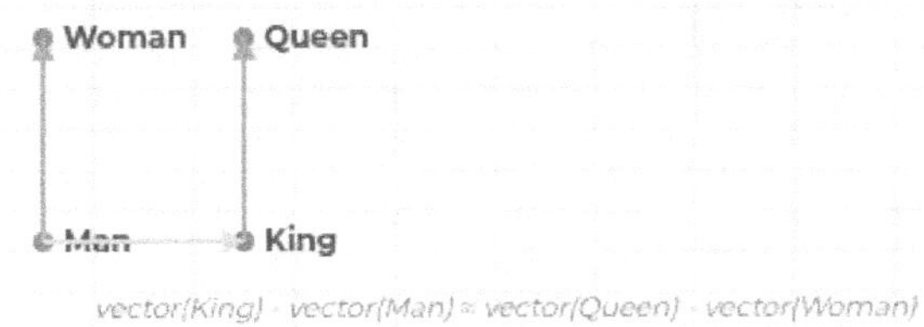

Skip-gram Architecture

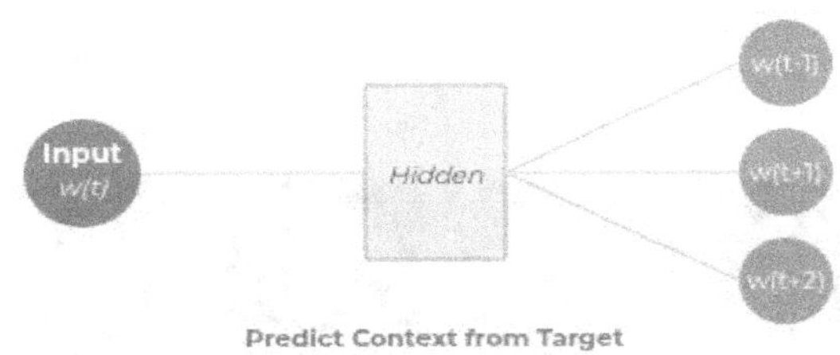

RAG & LLM-enabled NLP

Pipeline Architecture: From Retrieval to Zero-Shot Classification

Input & Prompting

Task Definition

User defines the task via natural language prompts. Includes **Zero-shot** or **Few-shot** examples to guide the model without training.

Zero-Shot Few-Shot Templates

Vector Database

Knowledge Store

Unstructured text is chunked and converted into **embeddings** (dense vectors) to capture semantic meaning numerically.

Pinecone Milvus Embeddings

Retriever

Semantic Search

System calculates **cosine similarity** between query and stored vectors to retrieve the top-k most relevant document chunks.

KNN Search Hybrid Search Reranking

Generator (LLM)

Context Integration

The **LLM** receives the original query + retrieved context to generate a grounded response, reducing hallucinations.

GPT-4 Llama 3 Claude

NLP Tasks

Business Value

Final output delivered as structured insight: Enterprise Q&A, Document Summarization, or **Classification**.

Q&A Summary Classification

→ Data Flow & Processing Pipeline →

Modeling with Text Features

Augmenting Predictive Models with Unstructured Data

Hybrid Feature Matrices

Enhance traditional tabular data by appending text-derived columns. Combine structured features (e.g., age, spend) with unstructured signals like sentiment scores, topic probabilities, and entity counts.

Managing High Dimensionality

Text features (e.g., TF-IDF or embeddings) often introduce thousands of new dimensions. Use regularized regression methods like **Lasso (L1)** or **Ridge (L2)** to select relevant features and prevent overfitting.

Interpretability & Explainability

Analyze regression coefficients to discover causal links between specific language and outcomes. Identify which words, phrases, or topics significantly drive the target variable (e.g., "expensive" negatively impacts conversion).

Business Application: Predicting quarterly stock returns by combining standard financial ratios (P/E, Debt/Equity) with **Earnings Call Sentiment Scores** and **Executive Confidence Metrics** extracted via NLP.

Text Analytics Business Applications

Real-World Case Studies in NLP & Unstructured Data

Voice of Customer (VoC)

Challenge

E-commerce giant faced 8% churn but surveys were inconclusive. 50k+ monthly support tickets were unanalyzed.

AI Approach

Deployed Aspect-Based Sentiment Analysis (ABSA) to tag tickets by topic (Shipping, UI, Price) and sentiment score.

15%

Reduction in churn after fixing specific UI pain points identified by NLP.

Financial Intelligence

Challenge

Hedge fund analysts couldn't process thousands of daily earnings calls and news reports fast enough to trade.

AI Approach

Used FinBERT embeddings to classify executive tone and extract forward-looking statements from transcripts.

< 50ms

Latency to generate trading signal from new earnings report release.

Legal & Compliance

Challenge

Bank legal team spent 2000+ hours/year manually reviewing vendor contracts for non-standard liability clauses.

AI Approach

Implemented Named Entity Recognition (NER) and semantic search to auto-flag risky clauses for human review.

80%

Reduction in manual review time, saving $1.2M annually in legal costs.

Pro Tip: Use ChatGPT to prototype these solutions. Upload a sample anonymized CSV of tickets or contracts and ask it to "perform aspect-based sentiment analysis" or "extract key liability clauses" to validate value before full engineering.

NLP with Julius AI and ChatGPT

From Unstructured Text to Structured Insight

Natural Language Prompt

Julius AI / ChatGPT

```
User:

Upload 'product_reviews.csv'.
1. Clean the 'review_text' column (remove stopwords,
   punctuation).
2. Perform Sentiment Analysis (VADER) to get a compound
   score.
3. Extract the top 5 Topics using LDA.
4. Visualize the Average Sentiment Score by Topic.
```

Summarization Request

GenAI Summarization

```
User:

Focus on the topic with the lowest sentiment score.
Summarize the top 3 specific complaints mentioned in those
negative reviews.
```

Analysis Output

Preprocessing: Processed 12,500 reviews.
Topic Modeling: 5 Topics identified via LDA.
Sentiment: Scores calculated (-1.0 to +1.0). Visualizing average sentiment per topic below.

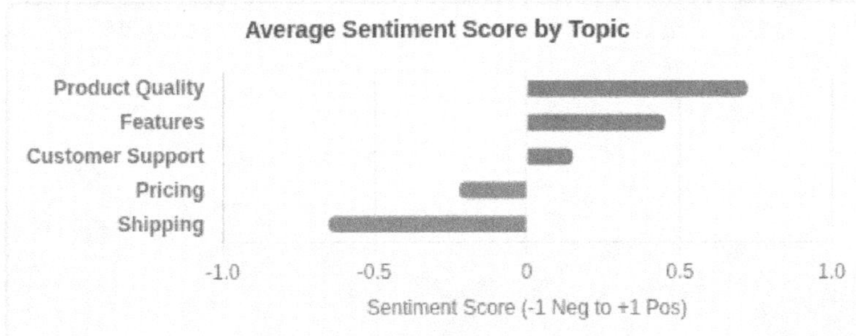

AI Summary:
"Shipping" has the lowest sentiment (-0.65). Key complaints: (1) Late deliveries exceeding 5 days, (2) Damaged packaging upon arrival, and (3) Lack of tracking updates. Conversely, "Product Quality" shows strong positive sentiment (+0.72).

AI Maturity & Strategy

From Ad Hoc Experiments to Transformative Capability

Stage 1: Ad Hoc Experimentation

Siloed teams conduct disconnected Proof of Concepts (POCs). Focus is on exploration rather than production. Infrastructure is manual and fragmented.

Stage 2: Systematic Deployment

Standardized MLOps platforms and governance models established. Focus shifts to repeatability, scalability, and integration with core business processes.

Stage 3: Transformative Capability

AI is democratized and embedded in the organization's DNA. Automated decision loops drive strategy. Focus on creating new business models and competitive differentiation.

Use Case Portfolio Prioritization

Prioritize initiatives by mapping them on a **Value vs. Feasibility** matrix. Sequence *Quick Wins* (High Value/High Feasibility) to build momentum before tackling *Strategic Bets* (High Value/Low Feasibility).

Build vs. Buy vs. Partner

Strategic Evaluation of AI Implementation Pathways

Option	Pros (Benefits)	Cons (Risks)	When to Choose
Build (Custom)	Full IP Ownership & Control Competitive Differentiation Tailored to exact needs	High Cost & Long Time-to-Market Maintenance Burden Talent Scarcity Risks	· Core competitive advantage creates value · Unique proprietary data exists · Strong internal AI engineering culture
Buy (SaaS/COTS)	Rapid Deployment Lower Upfront Costs Vendor Support & Best Practices	Vendor Lock-in Generic Features (No differentiation) Data Privacy/Security Concerns	· Standard business functions (CRM, HR) · Speed is critical; internal skills gaps · Commodity capability (e.g., OCR, basic NLP)
Partner (Hybrid)	Access to Specialized Expertise Scalability & Flexibility Knowledge Transfer	Dependency & Integration Costs Communication Overhead Potential IP Leakage	· One-off specialized projects · Need to bridge capabilities while hiring · Variable demand needing elastic capacity

ROI Analysis

Return on Investment calculation for AI projects:

```
ROI = (Net Benefits / Total Costs) × 100%
```

Metric: Hard savings (automation) + Soft value (decision quality).

TCO (Total Cost of Ownership)

Beyond initial build/license fees, consider:
- Data storage & compute (Cloud spend)
- Maintenance, retraining & MLOps
- Change management & training costs

Opportunity Cost

The cost of inaction or delay:
- Market share loss to AI-enabled competitors
- Efficiency drag vs. industry benchmarks
- "Buy" usually minimizes opportunity cost vs. "Build".

Align AI with Business Strategy

From Technological Potential to Competitive Reality

Competitive Advantage & Value Chain Fit

AI should reinforce unique value propositions rather than just optimizing commodity processes. Identify high-leverage points in your value chain where proprietary data and AI can create defensible moats.

Capability Sequencing

Plan the roadmap from "lighthouse" pilots to scalable platforms. Sequence initiatives to build foundational capabilities (data infra, talent) while delivering early wins to sustain executive momentum.

Operating Model Integration

Shift from ad-hoc experimentation to a systematic operating model. Align organizational structure, agile processes, and cross-functional teams to operationalize AI insights effectively.

Strategic Imperative: Don't ask "What can AI do?" Ask "What does our strategy need to succeed, and how can AI accelerate that differentiation?"

Organizational Readiness for AI

Foundations for Systematic Deployment & Scale

Data Infrastructure Quality

Robust data pipelines, modern cloud warehousing (e.g., Snowflake, BigQuery), and automated ETL processes are the technical bedrock. AI cannot function on fragmented or siloed legacy systems.

Governance & Master Data Management (MDM)

Establishing a "single source of truth" through MDM. Governance frameworks must define access controls, data lineage, security protocols, and compliance standards before models are deployed.

Talent & Cross-Functional Culture

Moving beyond isolated data science teams to integrated squads combining domain experts, engineers, and analysts. fostering a culture of data literacy and experimentation.

Executive Sponsorship

Active leadership commitment to fund initiatives, remove organizational roadblocks, and champion the strategic value of AI transformation to stakeholders.

Critical Insight: Technology is rarely the primary failure point. Most AI initiatives fail due to lack of cultural readiness, poor data governance, or misaligned executive expectations.

Integrated Analytical Decision-Making

From Problem Framing to Strategic Action via AI-Augmented Workflows

1. Frame

Define the Question

INPUT

Business Context & Stakeholder Needs

OBJECTIVE

Identify unit of analysis & success metrics.

Concept Map **KPI Tree**

2. Select Method

Analytical Routing

IF PREDICTING...

Use Regression, Time Series, or ML Classification.

IF EXPLAINING...

Use Causal Inference or Econometrics.

IF OPTIMIZING...

Use Linear Programming or Simulation.

3. Execute Chain

Julius + ChatGPT

STEP A: PLAN

ChatGPT: Draft code & cleaning strategy.

STEP B: COMPUTE

Julius: Run heavy stats, visuals, & models.

STEP C: REFINE

ChatGPT: Debug errors & format tables.

Tool Handoffs **Auto-Code**

4. Synthesize

Human-in-the-Loop

VALIDATION

Check assumptions & logic against domain expertise.

INTERPRETATION

Translate statistical outputs into business narrative.

Bias Check **Sensitivity**

5. Decide

Action & Monitor

OUTPUT

Strategic Recommendation with quantified risk.

GOVERNANCE

Deploy with monitoring for drift & fairness.

Implementation **Model Card**

Analytical Hierarchy & Judgment

Moving from Insight to Action with Human Expertise

The Value Chain Progression

Move systematically up the hierarchy: **Descriptive** (Hindsight: "What happened?") → **Diagnostic** (Insight: "Why?") → **Predictive** (Foresight: "What will happen?") → **Prescriptive** (Optimization: "How can we make it happen?").

Blending Models with Domain Expertise

Quantitative models excel at processing high-dimensional data, while human experts provide critical context, handle edge cases, and interpret "soft" factors (e.g., brand reputation, political risk) that data may miss.

Ethical & Strategic Constraints

Pure optimization can lead to ethical pitfalls or strategic misalignment. Use human judgment to impose constraints on model outputs, ensuring decisions align with organizational values and long-term goals.

Judgment Call: "A churn model might flag a high-value client as 'at-risk' due to low usage, but a relationship manager knows they are simply on vacation—overriding the algorithmic alert saves unnecessary intervention costs."

Ethics & Algorithmic Fairness

Bias Sources and Quantitative Fairness Metrics

Sources of Algorithmic Bias

Bias enters systems via historical data inequities, sampling selection bias, proxy variables (e.g., zip code acting as a proxy for race), and feedback loops in deployment.

Demographic Parity (Independence)

Requires that the positive outcome rate be equal across all protected groups $P(\hat{Y}| = 1A) = P(\hat{Y}| = 1B)$, ensuring representation regardless of ground truth.

Equalized Odds (Separation)

Requires equal True Positive Rates (Recall) and False Positive Rates across groups, ensuring that the model's error rates are distributed equally.

Calibration (Sufficiency)

Ensures that a predicted risk score carries the same meaning for all groups; a 70% score should imply a 70% probability of the outcome for any sub-population.

The Impossibility Theorem: Mathematically, you cannot simultaneously satisfy Calibration, Equalized Odds, and Demographic Parity if base rates differ between groups. You must prioritize.

Regulatory & Legal Landscape

Navigating Privacy, Risk Tiers, and Sector-Specific Rules

Data Privacy Obligations (GDPR & CCPA)

Mandates regarding data collection consent, the "right to be forgotten," and transparency requirements for automated decision-making processes.

The EU AI Act & Risk-Based Classification

A comprehensive framework categorizing AI systems into Unacceptable (banned), High-Risk (requiring strict conformity assessments), and Limited/Minimal risk.

Sector-Specific Regulation

Finance: SR 11-7 (Model Risk Management) & Fair Lending laws.
Healthcare: FDA frameworks for AI/ML-based medical devices.
Employment: Audits for bias in automated hiring tools (e.g., NYC Law 144).

Generative AI & IP Liability: Emerging legal challenges regarding copyright of training data, ownership of AI-generated code/art, and liability for hallucinations.

Responsible AI Governance

Frameworks for Transparency, Oversight, and Control

Model Cards & Datasheets

Implement standardized documentation detailing intended use, known limitations, training data provenance, and ethical considerations to ensure transparency across the model lifecycle.

Human-in-the-Loop (HITL) Thresholds

Define explicit confidence score cutoffs (e.g., probability < 0.85) where automated predictions are flagged for mandatory human review to mitigate risk in high-stakes decisions.

Audit Trails & Reproducibility

Maintain immutable logs of all model versions, input data snapshots, and decision outputs to ensure full reproducibility and regulatory compliance (e.g., for GDPR/CCPA).

Continuous Drift Monitoring

Deploy automated systems to track data drift (covariate shift), concept drift, and fairness degradation in production, triggering alerts or retraining pipelines when thresholds are breached.

Executive Communication Strategy

Translating Analytical Complexity into Business Value

Executives don't need to know *how* the model works (the math); they need to know *what* it means for the business (the impact). Structure your communication to drive decisions, not just inform.

Structured Narrative

- ✓**Problem First:** Start with the business question, not the data source.
- ✓**Bottom Line Up Front (BLUF):** State the recommendation immediately.
- ✓**Roadmap:** Clear timeline for implementation and value realization.

Visual Clarity

- ✓**Declutter:** Remove gridlines, excessive labels, and non-data ink.
- ✓**Annotate:** Use callouts to highlight the key insight directly on the chart.
- ✓**Risk Language:** Translate "95% CI" into "Best/Worst Case Scenarios".

Addressing Pushback

- ✓**Cost vs. ROI:** Frame AI investment against the cost of inaction.
- ✓**Feasibility:** Have a "Crawl, Walk, Run" pilot plan ready.
- ✓**Accountability:** Clearly define who owns the model output and governance.

AI Assistant Tip

Use ChatGPT to "Act as a skeptical CFO" and stress-test your presentation narrative before the meeting. Ask it to generate likely objection questions based on your summary.

Course Synthesis: Your Analytics Playbook

From Raw Data to Integrated Decision Intelligence

The End-to-End Workflow

1. Frame
Define unit of analysis, outcome variable, and success metrics.

2. Data
Assess sources, quality dimensions, and cleaning needs.

3. EDA
Univariate distributions, correlations, and anomaly detection.

4. Model
Regression, ML, or Forecasting based on problem type.

5. Evaluate
CV scores, confusion matrices, and error analysis.

6. Interpret
SHAP values, coefficients, and "why" explanation.

7. Decide
Optimization, experimentation, or policy rules.

8. Govern
Fairness checks, documentation, and monitoring.

Julius AI Role

Execution Engine

- Data ingestion & automated cleaning scripts
- Rigorous statistical tests (t-tests, ANOVA)
- Fitting complex regression & forecasting models
- Generating publication-ready data visualizations

ChatGPT Role

Strategic Partner

- Problem framing & hypothesis generation
- Drafting Python/R code for advanced custom pipelines
- Narrative interpretation of model outputs
- Stress-testing assumptions & executive comms

Capstone Project Brief

From Business Problem to Governed Solution

1. Problem & Data

Requirements

- Choose a real business decision problem (e.g., churn, pricing, inventory).
- Define unit of analysis & outcome variable.
- Source & clean dataset (min 1k rows).

Deliverable 1

Exploratory Data Analysis (EDA) report with data quality assessment and hypothesis generation.

2. Modeling & Causal

Requirements

- Build predictive model (Regression/ML).
- Evaluate performance (AUC/RMSE).
- Conduct causal inference or what-if scenario analysis.

Deliverable 2

Model notebook with interpretation (SHAP/Coefficients) and quantified business impact.

3. Action & Ethics

Requirements

- Propose specific business intervention.
- Assess fairness/bias risks.
- Design monitoring plan for deployment.

Deliverable 3

Executive presentation (10 slides) covering methodology, recommendations, and governance.

Use Your Toolkit: Use Julius AI for the initial EDA and modeling phases. Use ChatGPT to draft the narrative, stress-test your causal assumptions, and design the governance checklist.

Next Steps & Resources

Tools and Communities to Continue Your Journey

Practice Datasets & Repositories

Apply your skills on real data from **Kaggle**, **UCI Machine Learning Repository**, **Google Dataset Search**, and government open data portals.

Prompt Engineering Libraries

Refine your AI interactions using the **OpenAI Cookbook**, **Anthropic Prompt Library**, and community-curated system prompts for data analysis.

Metric & Method Cheat Sheets

Keep quick references handy for Scikit-learn algorithms, Pandas syntax, statistical test selection trees, and probability distribution maps.

Essential Reading List

Deepen knowledge with "Probabilistic Machine Learning" (Murphy), "Forecasting: Principles and Practice" (Hyndman), and "Causal Inference: The Mixtape".

Join the Community: Engage with peers on r/datascience, Stack Overflow, and tool-specific Discord servers to troubleshoot issues and stay updated on the latest trends.

References & Glossary

Key Texts, Documentation, and Essential Terminology

Category	Resource / Term	Description / Definition	Context
Key Texts	**The Elements of Statistical Learning** Hastie, Tibshirani, & Friedman	Foundational text covering the theoretical underpinnings of regression, classification, regularization, and unsupervised learning methods used throughout this course.	Modules 2, 3
Papers	**Attention Is All You Need (2017)** Vaswani et al.	The seminal paper introducing the Transformer architecture, explaining the mechanism of self-attention that powers modern LLMs like GPT-4.	Module 5
</> Docs	**Scikit-learn & Statsmodels** Official Documentation	Primary references for implementing machine learning algorithms (Random Forest, SVM) and statistical tests (OLS assumptions, ARIMA) in Python.	Toolkit
X^1 Notation	β Coefficients ε Error Term λ Regularization	β: Represents the change in Y for a 1-unit change in X. ε: The irreducible error or noise in a model. λ: Penalty parameter controlling shrinkage in Ridge/Lasso.	Math/Stats
Terms	**Endogeneity**	A condition where an explanatory variable is correlated with the error term, often causing bias. Addressed using Instrumental Variables (IV) or experiments.	Causal Inf.
AI Terms	**RAG (Retrieval-Augmented Gen.)**	A technique enhancing LLM output by retrieving relevant data from an external knowledge base before generating a response to reduce hallucinations.	GenAI / NLP

APPENDIX 1

RESEARCH LAYOUT

Dissertation and Research Article Publication

- Title of Research
  - Succinct but also descriptive
  - Highlights the main idea and purpose of your research topic
  - Contains relevant keywords for easier archiving and searching
- Abstract
  - The most important paragraph in the doctoral dissertation
  - Brief single-paragraph summary (100–300 words)
  - Identify the problem or research issue, purpose of the study, summary of the data collected, the main statistical results, and practical applications, as well as why this research is important
  - Concise, precise, readable, and simple
  - One of the first items to be written, the single paragraph that is edited the most, and one of the last things that you rewrite

1. INTRODUCTION CHAPTER/SECTION

1.1 Purpose Statement

- Clear, concise, informative, and specific
- Written in one or several sentences and encapsulates the intent of the entire study, making it probably the most important singular statement in the entire article or dissertation
- Don't include the research problem or hypothesis, or the circumstances that led you to perform the research as those appear elsewhere
- Use words such as *purpose, goal, objective,* or *intent*
- Examples: "The purpose of this study is to explore/investigate the effects of..." or "This research seeks to explain why..." or "This research describes a quantitative study of..." or "This study attempts to link [some variable] to the effects of [some variable] ..." or "The purpose of the current research is to examine and find the statistical relationship between..."

1.2 Research Question and Hypotheses

- Narrow down the purpose statement to a more defined and quantifiable set of criteria. Therefore, use specific variables whenever possible.
- Present either the research questions or a set of hypotheses to test.
- Hypotheses tend to be simpler to write in that they tend to follow a more formulaic sentence structure.
- There are usually multiple hypotheses to test. It is good practice always to include both a null and an alternative hypothesis for each item tested. The alternate hypotheses can be nondirectional or unidirectional.
- The null hypothesis means that there are no statistically significant effects of one or more independent variables on a dependent variable.
- The alternate hypothesis states that either there is some effect (nondirectional) or that the value of the dependent variable increases or decreases (unidirectional) based on the effects applied in the independent variables.
- Example of unidirectional null and alternate hypotheses: "There is no relationship between parents' wealth and their children's educational achievement" and "Children of wealthier parents tend to do better academically."

1.3 Contribution to Knowledge

- This section can either be simple to write or incredibly difficult.
- To write this section, you usually must first speculate as to what your theoretical contributions may be, continue with the research, and then come back and properly complete the section.

1.4 Report Layout

- The last section of the introduction should state the layout of the rest of the report and explain what to expect in the second and subsequent chapters, providing only cursory highlights and an outline of the content.

Dissertation and Research Article Publication

2. LITERATURE REVIEW CHAPTER

- Review of Literature
  - A search of the literature or a literature review is the next section.
  - A detailed search of the studies on the main topic related to your research, as well as reviewing and summarizing them.
  - Sources could come from academic journals, books, periodicals, articles, web blogs, and other research studies.
  - The focus should be on legitimate academically-based sources such as books and published academic articles, preferably from peer-reviewed and notable journals.
- Review of Relevant Theory and Deficiencies
  - You should also review existing theories that pertain both directly and indirectly to your current study. A literature review is not a book report, simply regurgitating all the information ingested. Rather, it requires distilling, culling, combining, and integrating various studies into a coherent story, setting the stage and supporting the need for your current research.

3. RESEARCH METHODOLOGY CHAPTER

- Details of the survey, experiment, and data collection mechanisms.
- Before deciding on the research instrument to collect your data and what type of data to collect, you need first to understand the types of data that exist and what you can do with said data. Then, you explain how your experiment works.
- How do you propose to obtain the data? A survey, a live audience experiment, a computer simulation, secondary data resources, and databases, etc.? What data would you require to model the hypotheses you have laid out? If you are performing an experiment, how are participants selected, that is, according to any specific criteria or background? How are these participants stratified or grouped? How would the data be collected?
- This section essentially tells the story of your approach such that any knowledgeable person would be able to follow along with the story and instructions provided and, in theory, be able to replicate the study.
- Detailed descriptions of surveys, questionnaires, and interview questions should all be collated and integrated into an appendix.
- Caution is required if there are ethical considerations or privacy laws and restrictions involved in your research. For example, HIPAA rules forbid releasing personal health records and information; information about the identity of individuals should not be released; programs classified by the government or military organizations need to be held in confidence; and so forth.

4. ANALYSIS CHAPTER

- Data Overview and Biases
  - Are there any data collection issues, such as survivorship bias, self-selection bias, and other types of sampling biases?
- Descriptive Statistics
  - Data collected should be subjected to some basic descriptive statistics and visualization.
  - Histograms or bar and line charts would go a long way in explaining the layout of the data and provide a high-level overview of the data structure.
  - Basic descriptive statistics, such as mean, median, standard deviation, coefficient of variation, and cross-correlations, should be done to help the researcher get a better sense and grasp of the data. Are there any outliers in the data? Are there significantly high or low correlations between certain variables, and why or why not? Are any variables wildly fluctuating about their means, and why? Descriptive statistics help validate data quality and lay the foundation for additional tests.
- Statistical Inferences and Hypothesis Tests
  - Lay out the hypotheses and show the tests used and the results obtained from these tests.
- Results and Interpretation
  - The results of the hypothesis tests are collated and grouped into tables. Hypotheses are rejected or accepted based on the researcher's predefined thresholds.
  - Interpret the results, look for interconnectivity and links.

Dissertation and Research Article Publication

5. CONCLUSION CHAPTER

- Conclusion and Recommendations
  - Draw additional conclusions and showcase how the work will benefit society or how the work can be made practical.
  - State your recommendations as a researcher.
- Research Limitations and Next Steps
  - Any research worth its weight should have a specific and narrow focus. Trying to take on the entire topic in a single research would be both foolish and intractable. Therefore, there will always be missing pieces in the research you performed.
  - List all deficiencies in this section. Note the limitations you faced in the current research, such as insufficient data, low response rate, too narrow a sample, limited resources, and so forth.
  - Expand upon how the research can be continued, or the next steps to be taken, should a fellow researcher who comes after you wish to take over the mantle and continue to pursue the research.
- Appendices
  - Appendices can include all the miscellaneous details that a reader would find too cumbersome to read in the main text of your research. For a doctoral dissertation or graduate thesis, they are where any details of the survey design, survey questions, experimental procedures and steps, raw data, analysis settings, method calculations, screenshots of software applications, and other items are provided. Appendices should be separated into different sections either based on the order in which they are referred to in the main body of the research or by relevant topics.
- References
  - Follow your academic institution's or journal's requirements when it comes to the style to use for references. The standard approach is to apply the APA (American Psychological Association) style and format. The rule of thumb is to have at least 30 references for any master's level thesis and at least 50 references for any doctoral dissertations. References should be listed alphabetically.

Dissertation and Research Article Publication

- Miscellaneous Items

  Front Matter

  - Cover Page
  - Signature Page (advisors' approval)
  - Declaration Page (declaring the work is original)
  - Acknowledgments and Tribute
  - Table of Contents
  - List of Figures
  - List of Tables
  - List of Acronyms Used

  End Material

  - Additional Appendices
  - Endnotes
  - Glossary of Terms
  - Index
  - Biography or Curriculum Vitae

APPENDIX 2

CAUSAL INFERENCE & PRESCRIPTIVE ANALYTICS

Module Objectives

Experimentation, Causal Inference, and Prescriptive Analytics

Design Robust Experiments

Master the design of Randomized Controlled Trials (RCTs) and A/B tests. Learn to define primary metrics, determine randomization units, and calculate sample sizes for statistical power.

Apply Causal Inference Methods

Utilize quasi-experimental techniques such as Difference-in-Differences (DiD), Regression Discontinuity Design (RDD), and Instrumental Variables (IV) to estimate causal effects from observational data.

Implement Prescriptive Optimization

Formulate and solve Linear Programming (LP) and Integer Programming (IP) models to optimize resource allocation, scheduling, and operational decisions under complex constraints.

Simulate Uncertainty & Risk

Quantify risk using Monte Carlo simulation and decision tree analysis. Stress-test business strategies against thousands of scenarios to ensure robust decision-making.

Correlation ≠ Causation

The Pitfalls of Observational Analysis & Interpretability

Spurious Correlations

Patterns driven by pure coincidence or shared temporal trends without any logical mechanism. *(e.g., The correlation between Nicolas Cage movie releases and swimming pool drownings is statistically high but meaningless.)*

Omitted Variable Bias (Confounders)

A third unobserved variable (Z) causes both X and Y, creating an illusion of a direct link. *(e.g., Ice cream sales correlate with shark attacks, but both are actually driven by the confounder "Temperature/Summer".)*

Reverse Causality (Simultaneity)

When Y actually causes X, or they reinforce each other in a loop, making it impossible to isolate a single directional effect. *(e.g., Do more police cause less crime, or does high crime attract more police?)*

Business Consequence: Acting on correlation alone leads to failed interventions—like banning ice cream to stop sharks, or firing high-performing teams due to metrics influenced by market conditions rather than skill.

Potential Outcomes Framework

Defining Causality through Counterfactuals & Assumptions

The Fundamental Problem

$$Y_i = T_i Y_i(1) + (1 - T_i) Y_i(0)$$

We only observe one outcome: Y_i if treated T_i=1 or Y_i if control T_i=0. The other is the missing counterfactual.

Average Treatment Effect (ATE)

$$\text{ATE} = \mathbb{E}[Y(1) - Y(0)]$$

The expected difference in outcomes between treated and control states across the entire population.

ATT & ATC (Subgroup Effects)

$$\text{ATT} = \mathbb{E}[Y|(1) - Y(0)T = 1]$$
$$\text{ATC} = \mathbb{E}[Y|(1) - Y(0)T = 0]$$

Effect on the Treated (ATT) measures impact on those who actually received the intervention.

Counterfactual Distributions (Hypothetical)

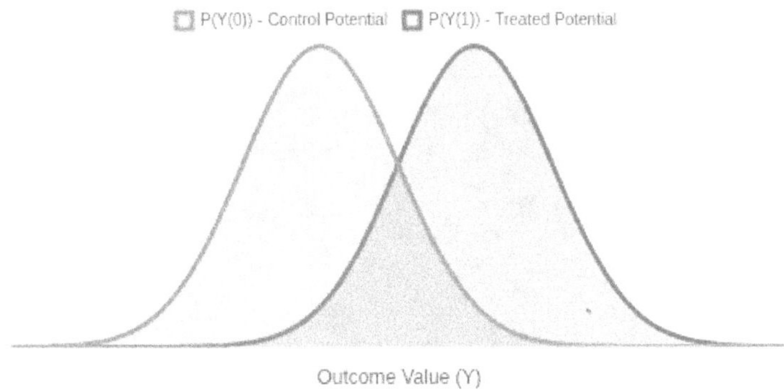

SUTVA Assumptions

No Interference

The treatment of one unit does not affect the outcome of another unit (no network effects).

Consistency

The potential outcome under treatment t is well-defined and equals the observed outcome if T=t.

Causal DAGs

Directed Acyclic Graphs: Mapping Relationships & Confounders

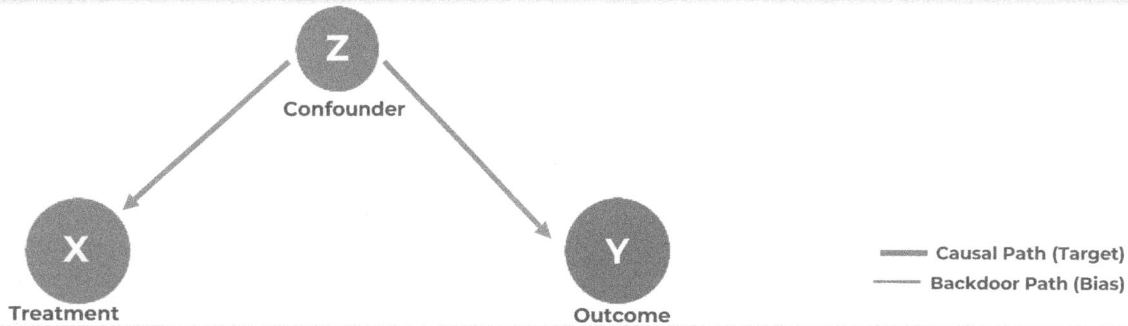

Nodes & Edges

Nodes represent variables. Edges represent causal direction. "Acyclic" means no feedback loops (X cannot cause itself).

The Confounder (Z)

A common cause of both Treatment (X) and Outcome (Y). It creates a spurious correlation if not controlled.

```
Z -> X and Z -> Y
```

Backdoor Path

A non-causal path from X to Y through Z ($X \leftarrow Z \rightarrow Y$). This "backdoor" allows non-causal association to flow.

Adjustment Set

To estimate the true causal effect, we must "block" the backdoor path by conditioning on Z (Adjustment).

$P(Y|do(X)) = \Sigma P(Y|X,Z)P(Z)$

Design of Experiments

Hypotheses, Metrics, and Randomization

Formulating Testable Hypotheses

Translate vague ideas into falsifiable statements. E.g., "Implementing feature X will increase metric Y by Z%." This defines the causal link being tested.

Metric Selection Framework

Primary: The main goal (e.g., Conversion Rate). **Secondary:** Related diagnostics (e.g., Add to Cart Rate). **Guardrail:** Constraints to protect business health (e.g., Latency, Unsubscribes).

Randomization Units & Bias

Define the unit of randomization (User, Session, Cookie) to ensure independence. Use stratification to balance groups and avoid selection bias where certain users are systematically excluded.

Metric Strategy: Optimize the Primary Metric while ensuring Guardrail Metrics do not degrade beyond a set threshold (e.g., < 1% increase in page load time).

Significance, Power, and Sample Size

Statistical Foundations for Experimental Design

Hypothesis Testing Errors

$$\alpha = P(\text{Reject}|H_0 H_0 \text{True}) \text{ (False Positive)}$$
$$\beta = P(\text{Fail to Reject}|H_0 H_1 \text{True}) \text{ (False Negative)}$$

Type I error (α) is typically set at 0.05. Type II error (β) is related to the power of the test.

Statistical Power

$$\text{Power} = 1 - \beta = P(\text{Reject}|H_0 H_1 \text{True})$$

The probability of correctly detecting an effect when it truly exists. A common target is 0.80 (80%).

Sample Size Formula

$$n \approx \frac{2\sigma^2\left(z_{1-\alpha/2} + z_{1-\beta}\right)^2}{\delta^2}$$

Required sample size (n) depends on variance (σ^2), significance (α), power (β), and minimum detectable effect size (δ).

Null vs. Alternative Distributions

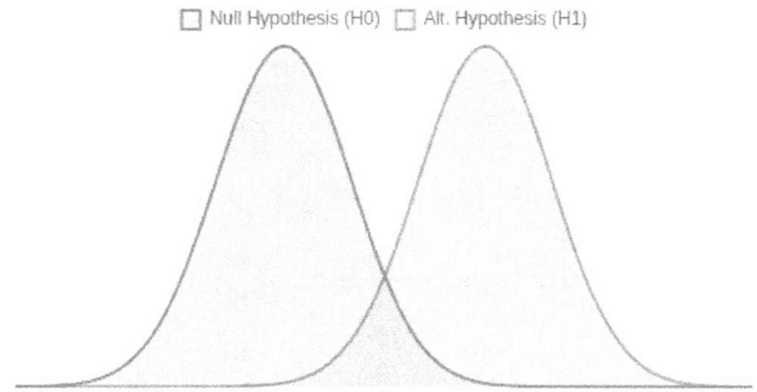

Power Curve

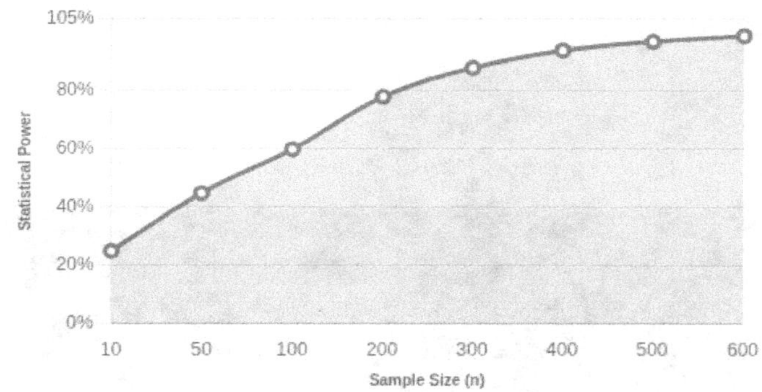

Heterogeneity & Feedback Loops

Moving Beyond Average Effects in Causal Inference

ATE vs. Heterogeneous Treatment Effects (HTE)

The Average Treatment Effect (ATE) often masks reality. HTE analysis reveals how effects vary across segments, preventing "average" strategies that help some but actively harm others.

Subgroup Analysis & Interaction Effects

Identifying subgroups (e.g., based on demographics or behavior) where interventions are most effective. Essential for personalization, uplift modeling, and efficient resource allocation.

Causality Loops & System Feedback

AI systems don't exist in a vacuum. Deployment changes user behavior, creating feedback loops (e.g., recommendation bubbles) and survivorship bias that can contaminate future training data.

Risk: A recommendation engine optimized for clicks (short-term metric) may narrow user interests over time, creating a feedback loop that eventually increases churn (long-term harm hidden by short-term gains).

Quasi-Experimental Methods

Inferring Causality from Observational Data

Difference-in-Differences (DiD)

$$\hat{\delta}_{DiD} = \left(\bar{Y}_{T,post} - \bar{Y}_{T,pre}\right) - \left(\bar{Y}_{C,post} - \bar{Y}_{C,pre}\right)$$

Estimates effect by comparing changes over time between treatment (T) and control (C) groups, assuming parallel trends.

Regression Discontinuity (RDD)

$$\tau_{SRD} = \lim_{x \downarrow c} E[\,Y \mid X = x\,] - \lim_{x \uparrow c} E[\,Y \mid X = x\,]$$

Exploits a cutoff c where assignment changes discontinuously. The jump at the cutoff is the casual effect.

Instrumental Variables (IV)

$$\beta_{IV} = \frac{\mathrm{Cov}(Y, Z)}{\mathrm{Cov}(X, Z)} \approx \frac{E[Y|Z=1] - E[Y|Z=0]}{E[X|Z=1] - E[X|Z=0]}$$

Uses instrument Z to isolate variation in X that is uncorrelated with the error term ε.

Matching & Synthetic Controls

$$e(X) = P(T = 1 \mid X)$$

PSM: Matches units on propensity score e(X).
Synthetic Control: Constructs a weighted combination of control units to mimic the pre-treatment trend of the treated unit.

Parallel Trends Assumption (DiD)

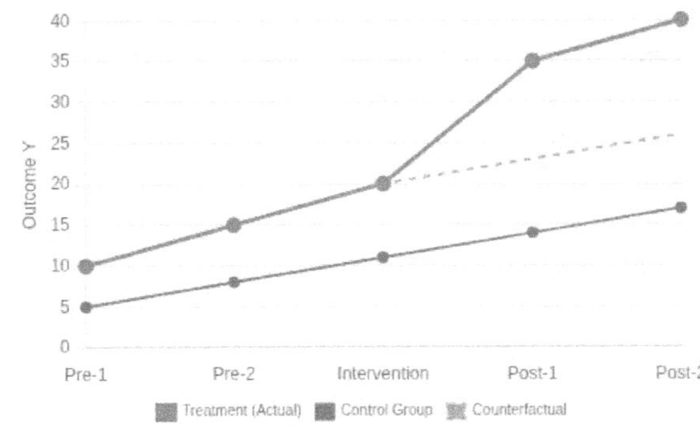

Discontinuity at Cutoff (RDD)

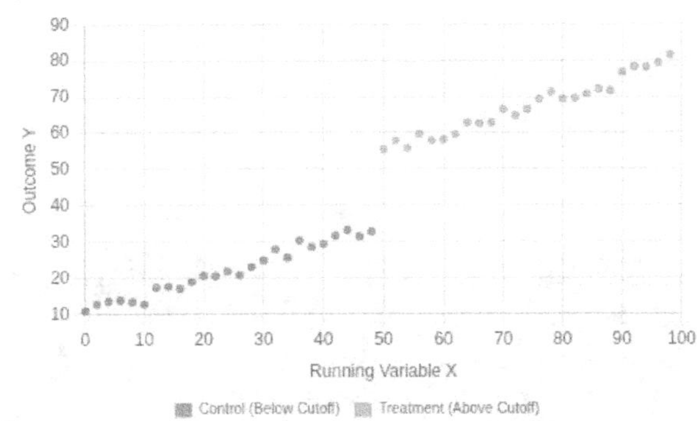

From Prediction to Prescription

Optimizing Decisions with Linear & Integer Programming

Linear Programming (LP) Formulation

$$\text{Maximize} \quad Z = c^T x$$
$$\text{Subject to} \quad Ax \le b$$
$$x \ge 0$$

Optimizing an objective function (e.g., profit) under linear constraints (e.g., budget, time).

Integer Programming (IP)

$$x_i \in \{0, 1\} \text{ or } x_i \in Z$$

Used for discrete decisions (e.g., Yes/No project selection, counting units).

Shadow Prices (Sensitivity)

$$\lambda_i = \frac{\partial Z}{\partial b_i}$$

The marginal value of relaxing a constraint by one unit. If $\lambda > 0$, the constraint is binding.

Feasible Region & Optimal Solution

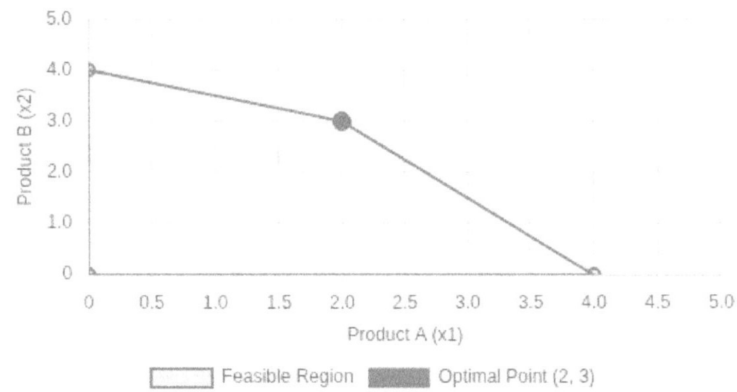

Binding vs. Slack Constraints

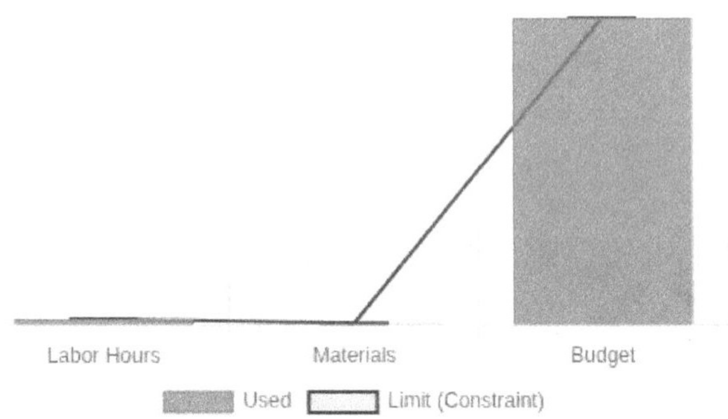

Uncertainty & Sequential Decisions

Strategies for Modeling Risk and Optimal Paths Over Time

Monte Carlo Simulation

Models' uncertainty by running thousands of scenarios with random inputs drawn from probability distributions. Used to quantify risk metrics like Value at Risk (VaR) or the distribution of Net Present Value (NPV).

Decision Trees for Sequential Decisions

Maps sequential choices (squares) and chance nodes (circles) to calculate Expected Value (EV) or Expected Utility. **Rollback analysis** (backward induction) identifies the optimal path from future outcomes to present decisions.

Reinforcement Learning (RL) Framework

A prescriptive framework where an agent learns a policy $\pi(s)$ to map states *(s)* to actions *(a)*. The goal is to maximize cumulative reward *(r)* through trial and error, suitable for dynamic pricing and supply chain optimization.

Core Distinction: Simulation helps you understand *what might happen* (quantifying risk), while Decision Trees and RL help you determine *what to do next* (prescribing strategy) given that uncertainty.

Causal Inference & Optimization

From Analysis to Action: Integrating DiD and Linear Programming

Causal Analysis

Julius AI

```
User:

Upload 'experiment_results.csv'.
1. Run a t-test comparing 'Spend' between Treatment B and
   Control.
2. Perform a Difference-in-Differences (DiD) analysis on
   the 'Conversion' metric using the 'intervention_date'
   column.
3. Plot the parallel trends.
```

Prescriptive Logic

ChatGPT: Optimization

```
User:

The DiD analysis shows a lift of $12 per user. Formulate a
Linear Programming problem to maximize ROI. Constraints:
- Budget: $50,000
- CAC: $15/user
- Max capacity: 5,000 new users
```

Analysis & Solution

Causal Result: DiD Estimator = **+4.2%** ($p < 0.01$). Parallel trends assumption holds pre-intervention.
Optimization Solution: Maximize $12x - $15x (Unprofitable). *Wait! Rerun with Lifetime Value (LTV).*
Update: Assuming LTV = $45. Objective: Max ($45 - $15)x.
Optimal Decision: Spend full budget ($50k) to acquire 3,333 users.

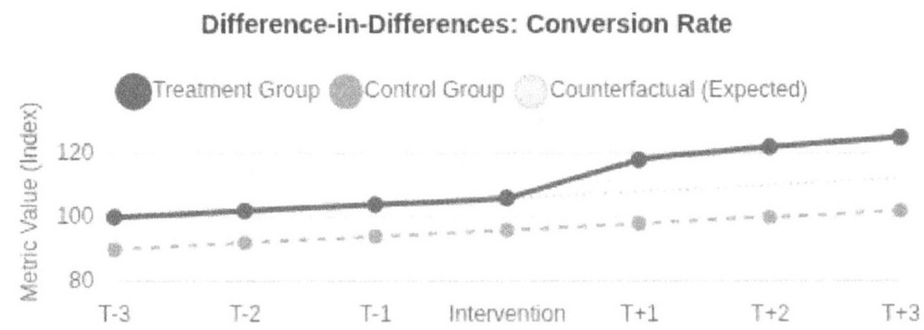

Strategic Recommendation:

The treatment causes a statistically significant lift. While immediate transactional ROI is negative, the LTV-based optimization suggests aggressive scaling. The chart confirms the causal impact diverges exactly at the intervention point.

www.ingramcontent.com/pod-product-compliance
Lightning Source LLC
LaVergne TN
LVHW080525210926
848481LV00022B/3080
* 9 7 9 8 9 9 9 2 6 7 4 1 2 *